1002885497

LEARNING RESOURCE
CENTRE
GRAN̲̲ N
EGE

S0-BTO-456

	DATE DUE	
FEB 1 6 2000		
1 1 NOV 2000		
0 5 MAR 2001		
0 8 DEC 2002		
2 3 JAN 2003		

THE STABLE MINORITY: CIVILIAN RULE IN AFRICA, 1960-1990

CHy Centre
SQ
1873.5
.C56
D43
1998

THE STABLE MINORITY: CIVILIAN
RULE IN AFRICA, 1960-1990

SAMUEL DECALO

LEARNING RESOURCE
CENTRE
GRANT MacEWAN
COMMUNITY COLLEGE

African Studies Series, Nº1

FAP Books
Florida Academic Press
Gainesville and London

Copyright 1998 by Florida Academic Press Inc.
All rights reserved.
This book may not be reproduced, in whole
or in part, in any form (beyond the copying
permitted by Sections 107 and 108 of the
U.S. Copyright Law and except by reviewers
for the public press), without the express
written permission from the publishers.

Designed by Rob Evans
and set in 10pt Calligraph
Printed in the United States of America

Publisher's Cataloging in Publication Data
Decalo, Samuel, 1938-
The Stable Minority: Civilian Rule
in Africa, 1960-1990
1. Africa: Civil-Military Stability
2. Malawi: Government and Politics
3. Gabon: Government and Politics
4. Kenya: Government and Politics
5. Africa: Democratization

ISBN 1-890357-00-6

LCCN 97-75050

10 9 8 7 6 5 4 3 2 1

To Roma, as always

CONTENTS

List of Maps

ACKNOWLEDGMENTS

Chapters One and Five have previously been published, in slightly different versions, as articles. The former under the title "Modalities of Civil-Military Stability in Africa," in *The Journal of Modern African Studies*, March 1990; and the latter as "The Process, Prospects and Constraints of Redemocratization in Africa," *African Affairs*, January 1992. Permission to reprint both is gratefully acknowledged.

CHAPTER ONE

MODALITIES OF STABLE CIVIL-MILITARY RELATIONS 1960-1990

"Democracy, prosperity and self-rule—this was the vision of African independence. But today, few Africans express satisfaction with the fruits of *uhuru*"—so begins one incisive post-mortem of the African political dream.[1] Over three decades after the continent's decolonization, scholars debate in ever-despairing terms the root causes of Africa's socio-economic and political decay. Though prescriptions and verdicts vary widely "the overwhelming majority view...is that 'Africa is a disaster.'"[2] *West Africa* summed it well: "the optimism that attended independence has in most cases been eroded by bad government, inefficient management of resources and political instability, while the much-hoped-for accountability in government, has remained a seemingly unattainable ideal."[3] As another observer put it, "few illusions [are] left about economic development as this was optimistically conceived in the 1960's... hopes for democracy seem to have faded completely; the very basis of effective government seems scarcely to obtain in Africa today."[4]

Objectively, the record was bleak. As the 1980's drew to a close, few social, economic or political success stories remained in Africa. Indeed those states that had attained some advances in the socio-economic front, had done so at the cost of crippling national debts, lopsided developmental thrusts, massive regional and income disparities, the entrenchment of personal and/or authoritarian rule, ossification of civil rights and political space, ongoing dependency relationships and political instability.

Little of consequence had changed in the countryside in most states during three decades of independence. In some negative rates of growth mocked simplistic developmental theories of yesteryear with their assumptions of unidirectional progress to the economic take-off stage. Telling was the fact that "tiny" Luxembourg's GNP dwarfed the combined GNP of ten of Africa's weaker states, while Brazil's was larger than Africa's ten richest countries combined.[5] That many African states were unable to pull themselves up by their own bootstraps had been clear for some time; increasingly, however, it was apparent many African states never had any boots to start with, while others had discovered more appealing uses for bootstraps.

Disillusionment with Africa's developmental prospects triggered fundamental re-examinations of core assumptions hitherto taken for granted, and re-conceptualisations of the nature of the African state. During Africa's first two decades of independence many had focused on the syncretic features of African states and problems of nation-building. Analysis soon shifted to issues relating to state-building when the "softness" of post-colonial states was seen as constraining policy-formulation and policy-implementation. Still later the "preda-tor" or "vampire" nature of the state came under attention as the prime developmental culprit.[6]

Parallel to the more critical scrutiny of the African state, came awareness of the non-aberrant nature of coups and military rule on the continent. Until the current spate of democratization on the continent, with the exception of Mauritius not one African leader had lost power via elections. Such an event was impossible anyhow since only six of fifty-five states allowed for the existence of any but the governing party. Less than three percent of Africa's population (16 of 493 million) ever exercised political choice.[7] African leaders clung to power for decades; petty monarchs for life, they set global records for longevity in office (see Table 1). Their monopolistic reigns seemed "inspired by the solar system...[where] all life proceeds from a single center. Everything turns around this pole."[8] Within this context coups were the sole manner of ousting incumbent leaders; the functional equivalent of elections.

If during the 1960's coups became the most recurrent feature of African political life, by the 1970's permanent military rule, of whatever ideological hue, had become the norm in much of the continent. At any moment over half the states in Africa, and up to 65% of its population, was governed by military juntas. In several countries civilian rule was for many people a distant memory. Few were the states that at some juncture had not been governed by military juntas; fewer had not been rocked by at least one attempted coup. According to one tabulation "only six states have *not* witnessed some form of extra-legal armed involvement in national politics since 1958."[9] While a small core of states remained immune to the Man on Horseback

TABLE 1: TENURE OF CIVILIAN LEADERS (1960-1990)

Habib Bourguiba	31 years
Houphouet-Boigny	29
Hassan II	28
William Tubman	28
Sekou Toure	28
Kamuzu Banda	25
Julius Nyerere	25
Kenneth Kaunda	25
David Jawara	24
Omar Bongo	22
Ahmadou Ahidjo	22
Leopold Senghor	21
Leabua Jonathan	20
Moktar Ould Daddah	18

Of the 15 longest-tenured leaders, seven remained in office 25 years or more, three died in office and three resigned voluntarily. Military leaders likewise held record terms of office: Sese Seko Mobutu (24 years); Gnasingbe Eyadema (22 years), Moussa Traore (21 years), and Siad Barre (19 years).

syndrome[10], their number slowly dwindled. By the 1980's civilian rule had become the statistical "deviation" as army cliques laid a permanent claim to the political throne in much of Africa.

Theories of Civil-Military Stability and Instability

Stability and instability are extremities of a continuum. Hence theories accounting for civil-military instability should have been be useful in assessments of conditions that have deterred coups in Africa. Unfortunately this is not the case.

Despite the abundance of case-studies on the continent, all theories purporting to explain why coups take in Africa have not been grounded in empirical reality. Riveted to universalistic (and ethnocentric) assumptions of the alleged destabilization caused by societal problems, they have paid little attention to personality dynamics, intra-military or civil-military tugs-of-war—all rich human textures at the bedrock of behavioral motivations. The mere absence of social and economic problems has not assured civil-military stability in Africa, nor has the existence of sharp polarizing issues necessarily triggered civil-military confrontations. Just as the study of civil-military *instability* impels us to analyze the internal dynamics of military hierarchies (where coup motives often reside), so the study of civil-military *stability* calls for an examination of the features and policies of civilian leaders, and the strategies they devise to bond military leaders to postures supportive of civilian rule.

There have been two main schools of thought attempting to account for the incidence of coups in Africa.[11] The first, rapidly eclipsed, was lodged in organization theory, and attributed to African armies cohesiveness, professionalism and patriotism, features allegedly impelling them into the political arena to save their nation from the rapacious grip of self-seeking political leaders. The second school of thought, that in modified version remained the dominant one, pinpointed structural flaws (social, economic and political) as factors creating legitimacy voids sucking in armed forces into the political center-stage, where they tried to "surrogate for absent or politically underdeveloped regulative instruments"[12] of the state. Such reasoning received some support from quantitative studies correlating structural stress with systemic instability.[13]

Yet, as I have argued elsewhere[14], such contentions possessed little explanatory value when tested against concrete motives of coup-leaders. Few officers have led their troops against the seat of power purely out of altruism or patriotism, though instances do exist. Socio-economic stress, conflict, and legitimacy voids are universal backdrops of political life in much of Africa, but their existence has more often than not been used as legitimating cloaks for much more mundane reasons for power-grabs often lodged in intra-military tugs-of-war or very personal motivations. Zolberg's early conclusion that "it is impossible to specify as a class countries where coups have occurred from others which have so far been spared,"[15] has been fully vindicated by empirical research, leading new generations of scholars to conclude that "both the successes and failures in political control over the military are scattered along the spectrum from the more orderly and socially homogeneous states to the more disorderly and socially fragmented."[16]

African armed forces never were cohesive structures, nor have they been particularly infused with patriotic zeal. Quite the reverse, neat hierarchical command-flow charts have glossed over abrasive internal divisions either mirroring society's own cleavages, or reflecting the non-representative ethnic/regional composition of armed forces. (In the 1960's only one third of Africa's armies were ethnically-balanced.) [17] Conceptually most armies could better be seen as "coteries of distinct armed camps owing primary clientelist allegiances to a handful of mutually antagonistic officers of diverse rank, seething with a variety of corporate, ethnic or personal grievances and only nominally beholden to military discipline and hierarchical command." [18]

Within such armies, the very smallness of the force blocks personal career advancement by capping both the top rank and the number of senior officers, "creating" grounds for a coup. (There has to be a correlation with the size of the force lest the "Argentine Generals" syndrome creep in!) Petty personal jealousies and rivalries, normal behavioral drives (fear and ambition), and corporate gripes against "the politicians," *within* the context of beleaguered civilian regimes can trigger personalist takeovers, *rationalized* (to camouflage motives) as aimed to correct any number of flaws which the regime clearly exhibits. Even the coups that ushered in Marxism in Africa had very mixed motivational pedigrees[19] and subsequent tugs-of-war over "Socialist rectitude" have really been little more than conflicts "between the ins and the outs, each interpreting the ideology to suit its needs."[20] In some instances military juntas may indeed be altruistically reacting to set the ship of state on an even keel. But in many more cases individual officers have used legitimacy voids for the attainment of personalist goals. We have always credited civilian leaders with a multiplicity of motives—some noble, others self-seeking—in their quest for political power: yet theories of coups have assumed their military cousins are saints, immune to identical behavioral temptations and drives!

Coups thus stem from an array of motivations. The role of fundamental sources of societal stress—implicit in structural explanations of coup-behaviour—cannot be ignored. To do so would imply absence of causality between societal conditions and military upheaval, a theoretical improbability if not impossibility. But conversely, to ignore the multitude of personalist motivations, perverts the empirical reality, resulting in intrinsically flawed insights and/or theories. Unless behavioral or intra-military variables are given their due (including for those statistically oriented, in data-sets used for regression analysis), all correlations that emerge will continue to have no congruence with the real world, though beguiling with their neo-scientific language. Witness Jackman's correlations of instability (with predictive powers!)[21] that claim to exclude no important variables—though ignoring *all* behavioral ones—that end up explaining little about the incidence of coup behavior in Africa. Or Johnson's regression analysis of ten structural variables, purporting to establish "highly significant" correlations accounting for 90% of the variance in coup-prone states, though again none of the variables codify political leadership traits, civil-military variables, or concrete motivations for coups.[22]

Civil-Military Stability

If there has been a great deal of literature (even if not theoretically incisive) on sources of civil-military strife, there remains to this day a near total lack of attention to the reverse condition—stable civil-military relations. Harbeson correctly notes that "much of the literature on the military in African politics has centered on army intervention as a departure from an implicit norm of civilian rule"[23]—though by the 1980's this "norm" obtained in only a minority of the states of Africa! On statistical grounds alone how these "deviant" states managed to avoid coups had become far more significant than why coups erupt. Since the current wave of democratization is very likely to ebb (if it has not already begun to), an understanding of how the military has been subordinated to civilian authority acquires additional urgency.

The high incidence of coups in Africa has deflected attention from the fact that a number of states have been immune to coups for over three decades of statehood. Until 1990 Africa contained both acutely unstable countries *and* a number of stable polities. The latter appear to have few things in common: they include countries that are among Africa's most undeveloped as well as some of the continent's most developed; arch-authoritarian as well as relatively open. Yet they have all clearly succeeded to bind their armed forces to the political supremacy of civilian rule, or at least to have deflected military ambitions elsewhere with the same end result.

It was always possible, of course, that some of these civilian regimes would stumble at their first political succession—one acid test of civil-military stability[24]—that a third had not faced by 1990. Conventional wisdom has often been found wanting when allegedly stable countries crumbled like houses of cards—at times within days after the passing of a founding father (e.g. Guinea)—suggesting whatever the glue that bound the military to civilian rule, it had a fixed, temporal, personalist and non-transferable dimension. Legum pinpointed a crucial fact when he noted "all African regimes are essentially temporary, or transitional, since with very few exceptions they do not operate within an established framework of viable and widely based institutions, even when they have been legitimized."[25] Yet Khama's Botswana; Nyerere's Tanzania; Senghor's Senegal *did* pass the succession threshold with hardly a ripple (See Tables 2 and 3), and universal doomsday prognoses about the Kenyatta succession were also proven wrong.[26]

TABLE 2: CONSTITUTIONAL SUCCESSION 1960-1990	
Angola	1979
Botswana	1980
Cameroun	1982
Congo	1977
Gabon	1967
Ghana	1969, 1979
Kenya	1978
Liberia	1971
Mauritania	1979
Mauritius	1982
Mozambique	1986
Nigeria	1976, 1979
Senegal	1981
Somalia	1967
Sierra Leone	1963, 1968, 1985
Swaziland	1982
Tanzania	1985

The academic literature is remarkably barren about conditions that bind the military to civilian authority in Africa. Decades ago Hodder-Williams lamented that "explanations for political survival in independent Africa are badly catered for in the literature of political science,"[27] a criticism no less true today. To this day not one book addresses the issue of the sources of stable civilian rule in Africa. And one of the few works to survey the phenomena in the Third World does not even include an African case study, arguing that "with a handful of exceptions...newly independent African countries have yet to establish means of civilian control that have withstood the test of time."[28]

TABLE 3: CONSTITUTIONAL SUCCESSION 1960-1990: STABLE CIVILIAN REGIMES

Country	Date	New Leader	Occasion
Botswana	July 13, 1980	Quett Masire	Death of Khama
Cameroun	Nov. 6, 1982	Paul Biya	Ahidjo retires
Cote d'Ivoire	n.a.	n.a.	n.a.
Gambia	n.a.	n.a.	n.a.
Gabon	Nov. 28, 1967	Omar Bongo	Death of Leon Mba
Kenya	Aug. 22, 1978	Daniel arap Moi	Death of Kenyatta
Malawi	n.a.	n.a.	n.a.
Mauritius	June 11, 1982	Aneerod Jugnauth	Elections
Senegal	Dec. 30, 1980	Abdou Diouf	Senghor retires
Swaziland	Aug. 21 1982	King Mswati III	Death of Sobhuza
Tanzania	Nov. 5, 1985	Ali Hassan Mwingi	Nyerere retires
Zambia	n.a.	n.a.	n.a.

Whatever analysis has focused on Africa was usually (a) extrapolations from universal theoretical frameworks, of little utility since African civil-military relations do not conform to Eurocentric models, (b) country-specific assessments of sources of *political* stability, something quite different, or (c) was anchored in assumptions that military quiescence stems from the absence of socio-economic conditions triggering military coups—a flawed correlation, as noted previously. Moreover, as will shortly be argued, factors that trigger coups are very different from factors that bond the army to civilian supremacy.

An alternate suggestion that coups mark "a period of Africanizing, nationalising, and integrating the army, a segment of the public service that has alien roots," and that civilian supremacy could be established through re-education under "a strong national party professing socialist ideology"[29] (as allegedly in Guinea, Tanzania and Mozambique) is also flawed. The hypothesis was negated even before it appeared in print (when General Conte seized power in Conakry), being rooted in a confusion of the *rhetoric* of a "powerful, dedicated, institutionalized, nationalist, and socialist Guinea" with the *reality* of corrupt personal dictatorship in a decaying backwater with two million economic refugees abroad. Only David Goldsworthy has tackled the question of the stable African civilian state, to leave a major imprint in what otherwise remains to this day an empirically unexplored area of research.[30]

Stable Civilian Regimes

Prior to assessing conditions and strategies that have stabilized civil-military relations, a few qualifications are in order. First, our analytical focus is solely on civil-military stability—i.e. the political subordination of military forces—and not on *systemic* stability that involves a host of socio-economic and political variables, that would be of relevance to the study of all kinds of regimes, including military ones. The study of the subordination of the military to civilian rule is therefore by definition in part an analysis of *mechanisms of control* and leadership styles.

Second, civil-military relations need be perceived as a *continuum* with no absolutes, since either extremity is only theoretically possible. Total "governmental control of the military"[31] suggests complete control over all organizational, operational, strategic and tactical deployment detail of armed forces—unlikely anywhere, least of all in weak African states, attempts towards which end would in itself be adequate justification for a military upheaval. At the other extremity of the continuum, even the harshest military tyranny includes some civilian participation in decision-making.[32]

The political subordination of the military does not imply total and unquestioning obedience by the military, or utter non-involvement in political matters. As Samuel Finer reminds us, the absence of coups does not mean the absence of military influence in civilian regimes, that can range from minimal to maximal levels.[33] The edict of the oft-quoted Clausewitz, "the subordination of the military point of view to the political is...the only thing that is possible,"[34] does not lead to Nkrumah's maxim that "it is not the duty of a soldier to criticise or endeavour to interfere in any way with the political affairs of the country; he must leave that to the politicians, whose business it is."[35]

Being an arm of the State, drawn from various strata of society, the armed forces cannot be isolated from the mood in the country, or the burning issues of the day, and obviously will have political input, clout, and influence. Such influence not only cannot be precluded, but may even be desirable, if restricted to operational details or military/security implications of political problems, within the clear context of the ultimate decision-making superiority of the political hierarchy. Even the most highly developed democracy will reveal a dynamic tug-of-war between the military and political establishments, with oscillations in the degree of *influence* the military wields depending upon a variety of circumstances. The subordination of the military to civilian rule thus allows for considerable latitude in the military's influence: at its core, however, is unequivocal acceptance by the military of civilian supremacy in decision-making *after* the antecedent give and take.

Thirdly, the factors that sustain stable civilian rule are fundamentally different from those that trigger military upheavals. Coups are clear-cut acts, with concrete, specific motivations; the subordination of a country's armed forces involves stabilizing dynamic relationships through an array of strategies and policies by civilian hierarchies, whose leadership skills are often an important ingredient in the matrix itself. Thus the analysis of the sources of civil-military stability lacks the sharpness of explanations about coup motivations. If in assessing generic causes of civil-military instability one can pinpoint specific factors, in assessing *stability* one is more likely to identify operational *modalities*—clusters of factors and strategies that assure "the officer corps has internalized the value of civilian supremacy as part of its ethical make-up."[36]

Finally, a *realistic* assessment of what constitutes civil-military stability is in order. Overly strict criteria to define civilian supremacy would exclude most African states! Only two (Botswana; Mauritius) have not had a single instance of serious civil-military friction, though fully a dozen would slip through a slightly looser net. Civil-military relations in Africa will here be seen as a dynamic continuum on which the threshold of instability is breached by the eruption of a successful coup d'etat that ushers in a military interregnum; while stability is marked by the absence of such a military intrusion/interregnum. Stable civilian rule is thus a civilian administration that despite a possible modicum of civil-military tension has managed to subordinate its military to the political center as attested by a non-interrupted civilian reign since independence (or at least for twenty-five years) until 1990.

Twelve countries (twenty percent of the continent) had met these criteria in 1990, when the "rules of the game" changed, as discussed in chapter five. These countries had not faced leadership-continuity disruptions, though half had at one time or another been rocked by attempted coups. The "stable minority" of 1960-1990 comprised of Botswana, Cameroun, Cote d'Ivoire, Gabon, Gambia, Kenya, Malawi, Mauritius, Senegal, Swaziland, Tanzania and Zambia. (Gabon's 1964 48-hour military interlude is ignored, for reasons discussed in chapter three.) Stable civil-military hybrids and military regimes are excluded from this study, though some of their sources of stability are no different from those of their civilian counterparts[37]. An examination of this data-set reveals few internal commonalities. (See Table 4.) The group includes Anglophone (Gambia, Botswana, Kenya, Malawi, Mauritius, Swaziland, Tanzania, Zambia) and Francophone states (Cameroun; Cote d'Ivoire; Gabon; Senegal)—though the percentage of Francophone states under civilian rule has declined over the years. This variation between the experience of the two former colonial zones is a factor of import in light of the unique modality whereby civilian rule has been stabilized in French Africa. It is not seen as significant to scholars utilizing factor analysis since their sifting devices zero in on *overall* high instability scores in both groups[38], and not on different stabilizing strategies.

Geographically the countries were in West (four), Equatorial (one), East (four) and Southern Africa (three)—the latter two regions over-represented. The group included both single-party states, the dominant modality in Africa until 1990 (Cameroun, Cote d'Ivoire, Gabon, Kenya, Malawi, Tanzania, Zambia), as well as virtually all of the

TABLE 4: STABLE CIVILIAN REGIMES—BASIC INDICATORS

Country	Pop in sq kms.	Area per cap.	GNP per an. Growth	GNP/c % 1960 1970	1970- 1982	Exp. 1982	Life Prod 1982	Index of Food
Botswana	0.9	600	900	6.8	2.4	11.5	60	73
Cameroun	9.3	475	890	2.6	4.2	10.7	53	102
Cote d'Iv.	8.9	322	950	2.1	2.8	12.4	47	107
Gabon	0.7	268	4000	4.4	5.4	19.5	49	93
Gambia	0.7	11	360	2.5	2.2	9.7	36	74
Kenya	18.1	583	390	2.8	1.6	10.1	57	88
Malawi	6.5	118	210	2.6	2.4	9.5	44	99
Mauritius	0.9	2	1240	2.1	2.2	15.0	66	110
Senegal	6.0	111	490	0.9	1.9	8.5	54	88
Swaziland	0.7	17	940	4.2	2.4	12.8	54	107
Tanzania	19.8	945	280	1.9	1.8	11.9	52	88
Zambia	6.0	753	640	-0.1	7.6	8.7	51	87
Africa	380	22,207	491	1.5	2.7	11.4	49	88

Source: The World Bank, *Towards Sustained Development in Sub-Saharan Africa*, Washington D.C., 1984, Appendix Table 1.

continent's pre-1990 multiparty systems (Botswana, Gambia, Mauritius, Senegal), also a factor of some significance.

Democratic (Botswana, Mauritius), as well as authoritarian regimes (Gabon, Malawi) were found in the group, with the majority median on this dimension. Only one (Tanzania) was committed to radical social and economic change. Rhetoric aside, all others had pursued capitalist developmental paths, and were staunchly pro-Western, some even ultra-conservative (Gabon, Malawi). This erstwhile distinction is not as significant as it may appear since the Marxist developmental path was always a military-adopted option in Africa[39].

Nor did the twelve states share similarities in military statistics (see Table 5) that might have granted them immunity from civil-military strife. Analyses of intra-military cleavages and role-aggrandizement aspirations within their officer corps also reveals little of value. Granted that idiosyncratic factors and personalist ambitions may be difficult to discover and isolate except *ex post facto* (a point well made by Liebenow)[40] what *can* be verified presents a mixed picture. The stable group of states included countries with armies that were paragons of professionalism (Senegal, Botswana)—a trait allegedly disinclining them from intervening in the civilian arena, as well as others seething with internal tensions (Gabon), with most (e.g. Kenya, Zambia) in median position.

TABLE 5: STABLE CIVILIAN RULE 1990: BASIC MILITARY DATA

COUNTRY	Armed Forces in 1,000's	A.F. per 1,000 pop.	A.F. per 100 sq.m.	Mil.Expd. as % of GNP	Mil.Expd as % Budget
Botswana	3	3.3	1.4	3.5	6.4
Cameroun	14	1.6	7.6	1.5	9.9
Cote d'Ivoire	11	1.4	8.6	1.2	3.6
Gabon	2	3.3	1.6	0.4	1.1
Gambia	1	1.7	25.0	0.0	0.0
Kenya	16	1.0	7.1	3.8	12.9
Malawi	6	1.0	16.2	1.8	6.0
Senegal	14	2.5	18.4	2.6	11.4
Swaziland	3	5.0	44.7	2.5	6.2
Tanzania	57	3.1	15.7	5.0	16.3
Zambia	15	2.6	5.2	3.8	8.6

Source: United States, Arms Control and Disarmament Agency, World Military Expenditures and Arms Transfers, 1971-1980, Washington, DC. 1983.

Nor did the group exhibit major socio-economic similarities that could have accounted for the marked continuity of civilian rule. Some had few ethnic problems (Botswana; Swaziland); others (Gambia, Malawi, Tanzania) had relatively calm inter-ethnic relations despite greater cultural heterogeneity including moderate regionalism as in Malawi. But the group also included states with as intense regional (Senegal) and social cleavages (Gabon, Kenya) as in countries where these tensions led to the collapse of civilian rule.

The group did not include any of the (least developed) Sahel belt states, and only a few were predominantly Muslim. Most states are those with high percentages of Christians, the significance of which cannot be assessed. Gabon, for example, is the continent's second-highest Christianized country; Kenya and Malawi rank seventh and eighth-highest in terms of percentage of Christians, Botswana is median (at 18th rank) and in Cote d'Ivoire the animist/Muslim majority lowers the country to 21st rank, of 35 states.[41]

In terms of economic indicators the twelve stable entities included a few of the world's 25 Least Developed Countries—Malawi, Gambia, Tanzania—*a major anomaly for structural explanations of stability*, as well as those with high per capita GNP (Gabon, with Africa's second-highest) and sophisticated economies (Cote d'Ivoire, Kenya.) Though "middle-income" countries are over-represented (see Table 6) the *range* of national economies found—agrarian/extractive; parochial/cosmopolitan; weak/developed; capital intensive/labour intensive—is a cross-section of the continent. However, when assessed not in absolute terms, but in *rate of economic development* and agrarian success, the group emerges unrepresentative of the continent, in that it included the continent's economic pace-setters, but only a few (Senegal, Tanzania and Zambia) of its laggards.

The economic transformation of Cote d'Ivoire, Kenya and Gabon—recent backsliding and income disparities notwithstanding[42]—is well-known. However, the rapid economic development of Botswana, Cameroun and Swaziland, are no less striking and atypical of the continent as a whole. Even Malawi—among the poorest of the 25 LDC's—was seen until recently as a major Third World success story. In short, while levels of economic development of the twelve case-studies vary widely, in terms of relative growth and development, the majority were successful.[43] Yet even here there was no uniformity, with the presence of several laggards, once again underscoring the

TABLE 6: STABLE CIVILIAN REGIMES—PER CAPITA INCOME

Low Income Semi-Arid	Low Income Other	Middle Income Oil-Importing	Middle Income Oil Exporting
Gambia	Malawi Tanzania	Botswana Cameroun Cote d'Ivoire Kenya Mauritius Senegal Swaziland Zambia	Gabon

Source: The World Bank, Accelerated Development in sub-Saharan Africa, Washington, D.C., 1981.

futility of the quest for structural causes of stability and instability—and suggesting that there may be different paths to civil-military stability in Africa.

Finally, the question of quality of political leadership in the twelve countries. That leadership style must be of great import in assessments of regime performance is obvious, though it has rarely been addressed in the literature. The longevity of civilian rule could well be, atleast in part, a function of astute leadership capable of binding fissiparous social and military cleavages, and of initiating praxiologically-correct policies that avert military grievances. Here too the record is mixed, suggesting the group's score on leadership traits cannot alone account for the record of civil-military stability.

Corruption, endemic in several states (Gabon, Kenya, Zambia), was quite low (at the time) in some (Botswana, Malawi) and modest in others (Swaziland, Tanzania). Botswana's exemplary record notwithstanding, grossly wasteful domestic policies abounded in most. These included Cote d'Ivoire's two decades of costly construction work in Yamoussoukro—especially on the the world's second-largest Basilica, built at the cost of several hundred million dollars of "Houphouet-Boigny's own money"[44]. Other extravaganzas include Bongo's massive urban renewal of Libreville, new jet Air Force, and the laying of the incredibly expensive and inherently uneconomic Transgabonais; one can also cite Banda's pretentious Kamuzu Academy that taught, *inter alia*, ancient Greek and Hebrew to small classes at the cost of one tenth of Malawi's entire primary education budget.

Yet, while a host of other "misdemeanours" and/or grand larcenies can be laid at the doors of Kenyatta/Moi, Kaunda, Ahidjo and even Nyerere, it is difficult to avoid the fact that notwithstanding this, the twelve states were led by a much higher *percentage* of relatively astute politicians. The integrative leadership of many statesmen in this group (including the paternalistic Banda) stands out when compared to the lackluster performance of others on the continent. Leadership is an important political variable that has to be inputted in all equations relating to stability and instability in Africa. Leadership traits and skills have little to do with issues of development, institutionalization, or structural "determinants" of stability or instability. Rather, they relate to behavioral and idiosyncratic traits of personality pure and simple: charisma, acumen, astuteness in juggling of personal ambitions, capability in balancing alliances and networks, awareness of invisible nuances. Some leaders have these traits, others do not. Those that possess them may surmount structural limitations and problems that destabilize other states with less capable leaders.

Neither the astuteness or incompetence of leaders has been given its due in African Studies. Yet, as Goldsworthy so clearly points out "Nyerere and Banda have managed [to keep the military subordinate] with low national incomes; the Liberian and Congolese (Brazzaville) leaders, with considerably higher national incomes to allocate, could not."[45] Goldsworthy, the sole scholar to place his finger on this crucial dimension, argues "outstandingly able, or dominating, or even in a few cases popular," are the traits of many of the stable civilian rulers, "whereas in the great majority of the coup-prone states, these sorts of things simply cannot be said about the civilian leaders who were overthrown."[46]

Toward a Theory of Stability

The previous comparative analysis underscored that while at first glance the group of twelve civilian systems appear disparate on a host of dimensions, they were not a representative cross-section of Africa. On at least two dimensions most differed from the wider universe from which they were drawn. These were (a) the astuteness of their leaders and (b) the strides most have made in the economic domain. Are these sufficient conditions to confer civilian stability?

Even a cursory examination reveals that if placed on a civil-military stability continuum, the twelve countries spread out across the spectrum. Though individually meeting the criteria of stability, the group includes states with little civil-military friction, as well as countries with a history of civil-military unrest. The spectrum runs from Botswana and Mauritius, where civil-military tension has been virtually non-existent, in ascending order through Swaziland[47], Cote d'Ivoire, Malawi, Senegal, and Tanzania, where occasional military plots have been nipped at the bud, through the other extremity of Gambia, Zambia, Cameroun, Gabon, and Kenya, where coups have erupted and the subordination of the military is none-too-secure, or was increasingly challenged (Zambia, Kenya). Table 7—with a slightly different rank ordering—illustrates the spread of "Total Military Involvement" scores (TMIS) and civil-military friction in the twelve countries concerned. All the stable civilian regimes in our sample were in the bottom twenty of the 45 African states in the data-base, though ranging from a "relatively stable" Zambia in 25th rank, to the "totally stable" Botswana, Mauritius and Swaziland, at the stable extremity.

The issues that aggravate civil-military relations in these polities have a variety of corporate, personalist and systemic roots. The twelve civilian polities illustrate that while some states have forged remarkably easy-going civil-military relations in which the security forces unequivocally accept subordination to political authority, in others, tensions are not absent, but are rather successfully constrained. Armed forces can be *neutralized*—the elusive "third" approach to stable civil-military relations. Tension between civilian rule and military forces was visible in Gabon, Kenya, Zambia and Cameroun, for example, long before pro-democracy movements gathered steam there in 1990. Serious back-sliding was visible in Kenya, where both Kenyatta's and Moi's ethnic favouritism and land-patronage were only partly successful in binding the army to civilian rule. Gabon's sharp ethnic divisions, mirrored in the army, were barely contained by a control vise of expatriate officers, virtual mercenaries. Cameroun's progressive disenchantment with Biya's rule exacerbated civil-military relations, but Biya retained power. And in Malawi, Banda's skipping over senior officers in search for ultra-loyal Southern commanding officers and retention of the detested Tembo as *de facto* successor heightened military gripes. But he *did* retain the loyalty of the army until the multiparty movement finally reached Malawi in 1992, despite questions about his senility!

TABLE 7: STABLE CIVILIAN REGIMES: MILITARY INVOLVEMENT

Rank	Country	TMIS	Coups	Att.Coups	Reported Plots
25	Zambia	7	-	2	1
28	Kenya	5	-	1	2
29	Tanzania	5	-	1	2
30	Cameroun	4	-	1	1
31	Gambia	4	-	1	1
34	Gabon	3	-	1	-
35	Cote d'Ivoire	3	-	-	3
37	Senegal	3	-	1	-
38	Malawi	1	-	-	1
40	Botswana	0	-	-	-
44	Mauritius	0	-	-	-
45	Swaziland	0	-	-	-

Source: Extracted from a complete listing in McGowan and Johnson, "African Military Coups d'Etat," *Journal of Modern African Studies*, vol. 24 no. 4, 1984, p. 638. Omitted intermediate-ranking countries omitted have either had coups or did not meet the longevity criteria.

Empirical analysis thus underscores that overall the armed forces in the twelve civilian regimes were not entirely free of the kinds of internal cleavages, competitions and personal grievances that have triggered coups in their less stable neighbours, though in most of them civil-military relations were more relaxed, and tensions did not translate into actual mutinies, and definitely not into coups. The fact that civil-military tension can co-exists with low TMIS scores suggests two things. First, that the quality of civilian leadership must be a crucial variable, in that astute leadership can mediate and soothe civil-military disputes, garnering army loyalty by praxiologically correct military-related policies and/or strategies. Second, the fact that the twelve countries had few commonalities, and even levels of civil-military stability varied across them, strongly argued that the search for systemic conditions that act as "causes" of stability definitely is a false trail. There are alternate "roads" to stability, that stabilize different sets of countries, thus accounting for the dissimilarities of the case-studies on a host of dimensions. The question therefore has to shift to the kinds of military-related control policies that have been pursued by civilian leaders in these twelve countries, that might account for decades of stable civilian rule.

The standard methods of political subordination of the military—through either subjective or objective control, to use Huntington's terms—have worked poorly in Africa, theory notwithstand-ing. The root of the failure of these, and other, Eurocentric theoretical constructs when applied to the African context, has been in their insistence on the universality of theory, and the latter's often patently utter irrelevance when applied to multi-fractured African polities that only semantically resemble the states and structures that formed the basis for the generalizations that became "theory." Theory that is not solidly grounded in reality can obviously have little explanatory value.

Neither politicization (or civilianization) of the armed forces—making them an integral part of the productive forces of society—nor their militarization—i.e. sealing them from society by instilling in them a sense of professionalism and *esprit du corps*—have succeeded in Africa. Inculcating into soldiers the value of servile obedience to civilian authority, and non-interference in the political domain so that "they become no more of a risk than say, the civil service"[48] has eluded most African leaders. The complexity of the intertwined civil-military nexus of power in Africa; the near-universal softness of African administrative and political hierarchies; and the legitimacy and support voids in much of the continent, all assure that few of the "constraints" listed by Welch, for example[49], are heuristically of value in African contexts. Yet the military *has* been bound to civilian authority in twelve cases. It is here argued this has transpired not by subjective or objective controls, but—as in some other parts of the Third World—by their neutralization.

Since independence African armies have been significantly up-graded in terms of quality of manpower and professionalization. Today's officers are better-educated, better-trained, and have more modern attitudes than at independence. Cadets attend metropolitan staff colleges where training programs stress infinitely more than in early years the paramountcy of the political order—all with little effect on the incidence of coups on the continent.

Nor does whatever allegedly went into creating a "People's Army" make the latter necessarily different from "bourgeois" armies, as argued by some scholars. Reference to the nationalism and dedication to sacramental values of such armies was always a fictitiouscontention. In Guinea/Bissau it was Africa's prime "People's" army that toppled the founding fathers of a much-acclaimed regime, in a coup that revealed no fewer ethnic, separatist and idiosyncratic motivations than those prevalent in coups in "bourgeois" countries. The superior quality, greater intellectual capabilities, and ideological dedication Bissau's leaders, and the indoctrination of the army did *not* prove an adequate bulwark against coups.

Nor was the Tanzanian army less restless *after* it was politicized and retrained following its 1964 mutiny.[50] Other plots were hatched in the purged and politically re-educated forces, Nyerere's status notwithstanding, and despite the correction of many of the complaints that had triggered the 1964 coup.[51] The neutralization of the army was not attained through Nyerere's populist policies, many of which were unpopular[52], but by policies enhancing their pay and conditions of living.

Mozambique also merits attention in this context, since the country was viewed by many as a paragon of Marxist sincerity with a nationalist military forged during the lengthy struggle for national liberation. In reality, of course, the country's always undisciplined forces retained their original regional cleavages, brutalized and demanded bribes from farmers, and were led by inept, corrupt and certainly non-Marxist officers, to become a major drag on the new state's attempt to establish effective mass-elite relationships. Political re-education did little to stem unrest in the army, that was rooted in non-ideological issues not addressed by a regime suffering from ideological blinkers: poor service conditions, military facilities and materiel, unpopular developmental tasks, little home leave, inept commanding officers and ethnic bias. Only the 1984 shuffle at head of the force, rewarding loyalty to the Presidency over ideological rectitude[53], and a return from retirement of officers loyal to Machel, as well as the erection of competing militias, restrained the unruliness of the Mozambican army—not efforts at political re-education.

Strategies of Control

We now move to several concrete control strategies that civilian hierarchies pursued in the twelve states in order to subordinate the military. The following were the most prevalent: some have been followed, with stabilizing effects, in military regimes as well.

1. A policy of preferential recruitment into the armed forces, its officer corps and specialized units of repression, of groups supportive of the regime. This "ethnic matching of regime and army,"[54] has at

times been destabilizing in Africa. But a concerted and consistent recruitment of elements (ethnic, regional, religious) supportive of the civilian hierarchy, keeping out others, leading to approximations of "ethnic armies" can powerfully stabilize civilian rule. A continuation of colonial preferential recruitment policies (though targeted groups may be different), such drives are pursued by many regimes in Africa, civilian and military, to this day.

A good example from our sample is Kenya. At independence Kenyatta inherited an army overwhelmingly officered by Kamba, and was faced, already in 1964, by a plot involving the Kamba Chief of Staff. Kenyatta subsequently moved rapidly to transform the ethnic balance in the armed forces in favour of the Kikuyu. Creating a largely Kikuyu army was impossible in a country where the group was in a minority (21 percent), and where other groups (the Kamba, Kalenjin) had historic "claims" to military careers. Some other African leaders did start similar policies, "parachuting" their ethnic preferences as Chiefs of Staff, and ended up ousted. Kenyatta was not so foolish: he began to pack the officer corps *at junior levels*—for the long run—while setting up other new control units with Kikuyu personnel, within a context of an expanding armed force from which other groups were not *a priori* excluded.

The thrust behind Kenyatta's policy was to attain a balance of power whereby "a move by the army as a whole would call for a degree of trust and cooperation between Kikuyu and non-Kikuyu officers beyond what now seems to exist. A move by Kikuyu officers alone would probably bring a reaction from non-Kikuyu in the lower ranks, while intervention by non-Kikuyu officers alone could be expected to bring a counter-move by the General Service Unit and other elements of the police under Kikuyu control."[55] The key balancer was the General Service Units—"a political force, the regime's coercive arm against its internal enemies"[56]—that were well-trained, mobile, heavily armed formations that rapidly became all-Kikuyu units. With their main base at Gatundu, near the Presidential estate, there was no doubt of their function, which was in any case clearly spelled out.

The Kikuyuization of the armed forces proceeded at such a rapid pace that at the time of the political succession Moi was faced with a security apparatus (army, police, Special Branch, CID and GSU) in which the majority of the key command posts were Kikuyu. To a Kalenjin President such an ethnic array was threatening. Hence from the moment he assumed power Moi pursued a policy of neutralizing the Kikuyu military stranglehold without appearing to do so. Kikuyu officers up for promotion received economic sinecures rather than senior operational commands; the GSU was partly disarmed at the first pretext that presented itself; recruitment drives were mounted at minority ethnic groups formerly in disfavor, in the name of equity, but in reality a prelude to the Kalenjinization of the top command—that was attained as rapidly as its previous Kikuyuization.

Another example comes from Malawi where Banda blocked entry into the army and promotions in the officer corps to individuals from the Northern Region, as well as to Yao Muslims (former slavers) from the Central Region. Yet Banda's own Chewa, (half the population in a country where regionalism rather than ethnicity is a problem) were not attracted by military careers, and were less upwardly-mobile. With an all-Chewa command impossible, the southern Army and Police that emerged reflected a greater percentage of Nguni (19th century invaders from Zululand) in the Police, and of Lomwe in the army, the latter seen as unlikely to pose a threat due to their non-indigenous origins. Such policies greatly stabilized civilian rule since Northerners in the army/police would most certainly have reflected the bitter gripes the North has harbored about its socio-economic neglect.

2. The erection of elite armed control structures—Presidential Guards, Republican Guards, General Service Units, paramilitary structures, intelligence gathering units, informal networks of political spies and the like—all aimed at creating a loyal armed counterweight against possible assaults from the regular armed forces, and to monitor any plotting within them. Such units are often set up even when the armed forces are suffused with ethnic intakes supportive of the civilian elite, and certainly when the ethnic or regional coloration of the army is not synchronous with the regime.

At times the nature of the intake of such support/control units make them virtual ethnic mercenaries. Such was the case of the all-Tuareg Republican Guard set up as a praetorian guard by the former Djerma-dominated regime of Hamani Diori in Niger, to guard against Djerma or Hausa plotting within the armed forces. After the 1974 coup—which the Guard resisted—it was reconstituted to include only Djerma, and placed under the command of a cousin of President Seyni Kountche. Kountche's successor, the army's Chief of Staff, also a Djerma, continued these policies and appointed one of his relatives in command of the unit. When civilian rule came to Niger in 1993, and with it the rise of a Hausa President, the force was dismantled, though the troops were not dismissed (that would have been destabilizing) but dispersed among other units of the army. At times even more specific drives have beenmounted to tap maximum loyalty not just from ethnic kinsmen, but from a clan or even home village. This was strikingly visible in General Eyadema's 1,000-man presidential body-guard in Togo, where origin from a specific *quarter* of Eyadema's home-village, Piya, was the recruitment criteria.

Large networks of ethnic informers and spies may be used to keep track of potential opposition. Eyadema employed three separate intelligence networks, two headed by relatives, and one controlled by his office to monitor the other two. In Sudan there were an estimated 30,000 plainclothes security men in Khartoum alone during Nimeiry's reign. And during Banda's lengthy presidency in Malawi the Young Pioneers served as a countryside control network for the regime, reporting on newcomers and on any unusual traffic in the country's villages, as well as on the mood of soldiers and police during their home-leave.

As with ethnically-skewed armed forces, so creating competitive armed structures can set loose destabilizing forces. The existence of better-equipped and (usually) better-paid praetorian guards has trig-gered inter-arm jealousies that became prime motivations for coups, as with those against Nkrumah and Keita in Ghana and Mali respec-tively. However, it is here that astute leadership can play a role. If executed on a grand enough scale to deter plots, while at the same time without overly diminishing the corporate status of the armed forces, the strategy has been proven to work well.

The General Service Units in Kenya immediately come to mind. Despite superior status, firepower and materiel, they were not regarded as corporate competitors by the regular army and police—whose interests were not ignored—since their prime task (protecting the Presidency) was seen as legitimate. And during the 1982 Air Force attempted putsch against Moi, while regular military units straddled the fence, it was the GSU—still largely Kikuyu—that promptly moved to crush the rebellion, ungluing other military units from their inertia to tilt the balance against the insurgency.

In like manner Bongo set up in Gabon an elite Presidential Guard of ethnic Bateke kinsmen, equipped with ultra-modern light weaponry, as a counter-weight to the restless, unreliable largely Fang army, that was kept at arms length. The Presidential Guard was larger than the military itself and was assessed as "considerably more capable than the army"[57]. Given the fact that the Bateke are a very small ethnic sliver in Gabon, virtually all able-bodied Bateke in the country served in the unit, that was headed by officers personally selected by Bongo. The heavy cost of maintaining parallel armed hierarchies was reflected in Gabon's defence budget that was as large as Cote d'Ivoire's and eighty percent higher than Senegal's, though Gabon's armed forces were one third the size of the latter's and half the size of Cote d'Ivoire's.[58]

3. Another prime control mechanism is the appointment of members of the Head of State's family to key command posts in the army, Military Intelligence and paramilitary. This strategy keeps presidential fingers on the pulse of the army, and presidential hands in operational control of the armed forces. In extreme form it may result in the *privatization of the security forces* parallelling the privatization of the State, that, conceptually, is what the personal rule modality of governance in much of Africa was all about.[59]

Ian Khama's entry and eventual promotion to ultimate command of the Botswana Defence Force is one illustration of this strategy. In this specific instance, Botswana's sources of civil-military stability were not rooted in the Seretse Khama's extension of a personal control network in the army via his son's military career—that actually reached its peak *after* Khama's death. But Ian Khama's *entry* into the army was certainly based on an awareness that having a Presidential hand on the reins of the military might avert problems.

In Gabon, several of Bongo's relatives—some through marriage—were appointed to key police/intelligence posts as surrogate controllers, though the break-up of the Bongo's marriage in the 1980's shattered these alliances and brought the purge of incumbents now seen as potentially antagonistic rather than loyal. In Zambia Kenneth Kaunda's concerted efforts to promote his son to senior rank in the army (thwarted by the latter's mediocrity) is another example. Other instances abound, including in Swaziland: there, however, the royal family being particularly large, ended up with inter-clan cleavages spilling into the officer corps. In Kenya Mbiyu Koinange, related to Kenyatta by marriage, performed a similar function, though due to his advanced age not through direct command of armed units. And reference has already been made to Kountche in Niger, where trusted presidential cousins were in charge of the Presidential Guard and other structures.

In Equatorial Guinea, after the overthrow of Nguema's reign of terror, his nephew Teodoro Mbasogo, the prime executioner of the regime assumed power. During much of the Nguema dictatorship the entire core of the officer corps and regional military command was composed of a familial network of some thirty cousins, nephews, uncles, mistresses and relatives that only moved against their benefactor when Nguema's demented swathe of destruction began to affect them personally.[60]

Many of Eyadema's relatives were in like manner appointed to key posts in the security forces that Eyadema did not wish to fall into "outside" hands, their youth or junior rank notwithstanding. At times, where Presidential relatives were unavailable, privatization of the forces has been attained through in-laws (Gabon) or by marrying off one's daughters to key military officers. Bienen has reported that in Kenya such family alliances between military and civilian elites had become common by the late 1970's.[61] Cox also recorded the communion of interests that developed between civil and military elites in Sierra Leone, and how subjective factors—family links, kinship, ethnicity—determined the outcome of such military issues as promotion and control of troops, with direct implications on the political subordination of the military.[62]

4. Another policy pursued by some regimes has been the retention, or recruitment, of expatriates to the officer corps. Such personnel have at times exercised actual operational control of troops, though more normally they have headed structures that monitor the loyalty of the armed forces or serve as buffers against them—i.e. Military Intelligence, the Presidential Guard, and the like. The best-known example comes from the Comoros, where mercenaries under Bob Denard for long assured President Abdallah's security. (When he later tried to "dismiss" them, they seized the country.) In a number of states entire Moroccan mercenary units have acted as buffers against possible internal armed assaults: in Malabo a 1,000-man force is in place today. In the former People's Republics contingents of East European or Cuban specialists manned Intelligence, at times (as in Congo) also stiffening the resolve of local troops in actual assaults. And in Angola, of course, Cuban troops acted in operational support positions to a fighting army.

Such recruitments have also rarely captured academic attention.

Though carrying with them the potential of antagonizing local forces, they are at times welcome by the officer corps itself. For in highly factionalized armies having disinterested "foreigners" in sensitive posts may at times be preferable to risking having such posts fall to antagonistic cliques that might use their status to discredit or purge other groups.[63] From the standpoint of civilian rulers, of course, non-nationals are loyal neutral technocrats (above factional manoeuvrings in the army) and personally at the service of the Presidency.

Such appointments, rationalized as enskilling African armies, are often a camouflage for attempts to monitor local forces. In Kenya, after Moi inherited from Kenyatta an army packed with Kikuyu in senior posts, a slow de-Kikuyuization of the force was accompanied by the emergence of several Europeans in "acting" senior roles, one of whom was given command of the GSU—still predominantly Kikuyu.

Expatriate officers have served, and continue to do so, in a host of sensitive posts in many African armies. For two decades the second most powerful person in the Central African Republic was the French Colonel Manson, the head of Intelligence who had wide executive powers as well. (Until civilian rule came to Bangui he was referred to as "General Kolingba's President.") In like manner a French officer "oversaw" Niger's army during Diori's civilian reign.

The best example from the case studies are the expatriate officers charged with monitoring the armed forces of Gabon. One mainstay of Bongo's control of his restless and unreliable army are mercenary appointments of this kind. Hired at extremely high salaries and very generous fringe benefits, as ultra-conservative as the President to whom they are accountable, these expatriate officers have neutralized potential coups, helped refine Bongo's campaign strategies in France, and assisted in occasional military sorties abroad.[64]

5. Another option—but available only to a select few states—is securing guarantees of military support from external powers against domestic power-grabs. The prime such external guarantor has been France. Other colonial powers have not extended blanket military guarantees, any military support extended being usually on an *ex-post-facto* and *ad hoc* basis, and usually, also, against external aggression.

Until the 1990 policy shift at the La Baule conference (but possibly to this day) France was the guarantor of the stability of a number of civilian regimes in Francophone Africa, through treaties of military cooperation signed at independence. These guarantees had credence since French troops were dispatched to rescue some flailing allies[65], and because French troops and jet aircraft were stationed in strategic bases in some countries. These *in situ* units are part of a rapid-deployment force based in Southern France that is capable of arriving in sufficient strength at any trouble-spot within fortyeight hours. Though France at times failed to deliver on its pledges (e.g. *Operation Cheval Noire* was not activated to rescue Hamani Diori in Niamey), few indigenous officers have been willing to hazard their careers (or lives) to discover the depth of France's strength of resolve to honor its commitments.

Among the regimes under analysis Cameroun, Cote d'Ivoire, Gabon and Senegal had mutual defence treaties with France. As one scholar put it, in these "core neo-colonies...things are not permitted to degenerate to the point where...intervention was needed."[66]

6. Moving from external guarantees, that will be elaborated on shortly, one notes that a number of regimes have attained sufficient internal legitimacy to insulate civilian rule from power-grabs. A societally legitimated regime—seen as ruling in the best interests of society—is likely to be similarly regarded by the armed forces, that are, after all, drawn from society. And if this feeling is not pervasive in some quarters, awareness of the regime's social bases of support is likely to deter power-grabs. Moreover, if corporate or individual grievances do develop in the army, these are more likely to be presented for mediation, rather than leading to plotting. Seizure of power is also averted by trepidation about the loyalty of other, loyalist units, that might block the power-bid and lead to internescine bloodshed.

It has always been difficult to assess the legitimacy of political hierarchies in countries without competitive elections. The cleavage between rhetoric and reality that characterizes many political phenomena in Africa has resulted in gross misjudgements about regimes viewed as legitimated that suddenly reveal their feet of clay. Even levels of institutionalization have not been accurate gauges of legitimacy, despite reminders that "legitimacy is only durable if linked to a solid institutional base at the center"[67] or if coupled with "a strong complex of organizational and institutional controls."[68] African regimes have confounded scholars by being both institutional voids *and* immune to coup for prolonged periods as was the case with Hamani Diori's 1960-1974 reign[69] and Ngarta Tombalbaye's 1960-1975 rule[70]. And, while after a certain point it may appear the longer the duration of civilian rule the higher its chances of subsequent survival, this has not proven of universal validity either.

Civilian rulers may stabilize their administrations by legitimating traditional, modern and/or anti-colonial credentials; by judiciously balancing regional/ethnic pulls and demands; by piling up solid economic attainments, satisfying societal needs, providing political space, and in general providing good governance, though not necessarily by Western standards. Dunn has noted "good government may exist *outside* democracy, because it refers to the consequences of [the rule of leaders] for those over whom they rule"[71]; and the framework within which these stabilizing actions may take place can be relatively oppressive (e.g. Malawi). Astute leadership may be the factor that secures a measure of legitimacy for regimes neither particularly democratic nor very institutionalized.

A number of stable civilian regimes have secured varying amounts of societal legitimation. They include Cote d'Ivoire, Malawi, Mauritius, Senegal, Tanzania, and to some extent Kenya. Legitimacy in Africa, however, has to be viewed as something that must constantly be nurtured against myriads of socio-economic counter-forces that daily act to erode it. Few regimes have succeeded to so thoroughly legitimate themselves that the threat of military intervention is averted *solely* because of this. Consequently the study of stable civilian rule in Africa cannot be just the study of legitimated civilian hierarchies.[72] Other control strategies, such as those enumerated here, are, individually or in unique combinations, pursued by relatively legitimated civilian leaders to restrain praetorian tendencies on the part of military forces.

7. Finally, civil-military relations may be stabilized by conscious "pay-offs" by the civilian hierarchy to the army as a corporate group and/or to key individual officers. Providing officers with relatively high salaries (Botswana, Malawi, Swaziland), or objectively high ones (Gabon, Cote d'Ivoire, Cameroun, Zambia, Senegal), as well as fringe benefits, supernumerary posts etc., are well-known strategies for buying the loyalty of armed hierarchies. It unites the corporate and individual pecuniary self-interests of the military to those of civilian leaders; it deflects emergence of political ambitions among officers, and bonds military support to civilian rule through self-interest.

Buying the instrumental allegiance of officers through pecuniary rewards may also be seen as merely an extension of the normal grant of patronage to societal influentials by political power-brokers. Within the context of acute scarcity that prevails in African societies, the army inevitably is an actor that cannot be assumed to be disinterested in the political tug-of-war, and whose loyalty must be secured on a *quid pro quo* basis. As Goldsworthy stresses "soldiers are among the players—actual and potential—of the political game...civilian rule may generally be seen as a function of military loyalty to the person of the ruler rather than to the abstraction of the state."[73] Civil-military stability may well rest on a clear-cut understanding that "reciprocity....could be called into play whereby army officers might agree not to intervene so long as certain "rewards" were forthcoming from the civilian sector."[74]

Thus conceptualized, purchasing the loyalty of the military with material rewards is one of the rules of the game in systems of personal rule; a card that if astutely played may swing into supportive stances the main force that can topple African leaders. It is also a cost-effective strategy, since the pay-off—retaining power—is immense in comparison to the cost involved. The number of officers that need to be "bought" in African armies is objectively small. Indeed, the total number of a society's influentials—civil and military—in many states numbers a few hundred; in relatively large Cameroun, one calculation had the political and military hierarchy of "the ruling class" numbering only 950 people.[75]

Botswana and Mauritius notably apart, military officers in every one of the stable civilian states have to varying degrees either been allocated economic sinecures (the prime modality in Zambia), or were allowed to develop personal economic enterprises (the epitome reached in Kenya.) During the Kenyatta era any officer above the rank of Major could secure large farms and estates at rock bottom prices, and many also developed trading enterprises. After the succession that brought Moi to power, such fringe benefits were extended to more junior officers, as Moi "made a point of keeping officer ranks well cared for."[76]

In most African states military personnel acquire economic interests, and at times play a major role in sectors such as commerce, urban transport and long-distance trucking. Such personal enterprises, however, are usually developed in contravention of existing legislation, though the regime may turn a blind eye to them. As a control-mechanism one is here referring to legally-sanctioned economic activities of officers who in effect either draw two State salaries (when they hold supernumerary posts), or are occupied with their private economic concerns while drawing full military salaries.

In assessing the particular "mix" of the seven policies that have stabilized civilian rule in the twelve case-studies, it becomes clear there are several sources of civil-military stability in Africa. The twelve states shared few structural commonalities because they had none, this not being what set them off from their unstable neighbors. The twelve were an artificial grouping of states differentially stabilized by different factors or combinations of factors. Their points of similarity were not in their socio-economic features—the focus of aggregate data analysis—but in the kinds of control mechanisms adopted by civilian leaders.

It is because of this that efforts to isolate structural variables accounting for absence of coups in certain states yielded little of value. Absence of causality in such a central issue is a statistical abomination. It suggests the analytical focus is fundamentally wrong, and that the dataset employed is incomplete. But if the universe being observed comprises of distinct subsets of states each stabilized by different variables, then the dilemma vanishes and the roots of stable civilian rule in Africa falls into sharp perspective.

Of equal theoretical import, these conditions (modalities) that produced stable civilian rule in Africa during 1960-1990, are *mutatis mutandi* the same that sustained relatively stable military rule as well. There have been major variations in longevity and/or stability between military regimes on the continent. Mobutu's lengthy reign in Zaire, despite all odds and predictions over three decades of its imminent demise, may, for example, fall into better perspective if one assesses it in terms of control strategies employed, compared to other less adept manipulators of force the continent has seen. Since military rule is extra-constitutional and inherently (i.e. on the long-run) unstable, few scholars have explored "deviant" stable military regimes in a comparative fashion. If attempted it might fit in with Goldsworthy's early observation that "long-lived military rulers survive not because they dispose of armed force (for they may well be, and often are, the targets of counter-coups by other armed men), but because of the same sorts of political factors—acumen, skills, fortune—which sustain long-lived civilian rule."[77]

Returning to our main thrust, a re-examination of the dynamics of civilian control of armed forces in pre-1990 civilian ruled Africa suggests that three generic modalities of rule have been at work. (See Table 8.) Each modality stemmed from specific stabilizing conditions, and was found in a number of civilian regimes. Common policy threads bound states within each grouping. Some were shared across groups, but each modality rested on one central technique of neutralizing the military. The three modalities can be now defined as (a) The External Guarantor Modality; (b) The Trade-off Modality; and (c) The Legitimized Modality. The African "stable minority" of pre-1990 can now be regrouped where they properly belong.

TABLE 8: MODALITIES OF STABLE CIVIL-MILITARY RELATIONS 1960-1990

External Guarantor Modality	Legitimized Modality	Trade-Off Modality
Cameroun	Botswana	Kenya
Cote d'Ivoire	Gambia	Zambia
Gabon	Malawi	
Senegal	Mauritius	
Swaziland		
Tanzania		

Modalities of civil-military stability

The External Guarantor Modality

The first profile of civil-military stability may be referred to as the external guarantor modality. Over and beyond other strategies adopted to neutralize the threat of coups, it is the existence of external guarantees of military assistance in case of domestic upheavals that inhibits civil-military turbulence. (In the case studies that follow, Gabon has been selected to illustrate this modality.) France is the sole power with *a priori* military commitments, and a credible in situ deterrent military presence in Africa. And despite the fact that France renounced in 1990 future interventions in African domestic affairs (see Chapter Five), this "diminished" French military role on the continent has already been violated twice. While blanket protection of key civilian regimes is no longer automatic, the external guarantor modality is clearly not yet dead.

In the past such a modality of stability was very efficacious. So long as the external prop was assured (or was given credence locally) military gambits were extremely foolhardy since they would axiomatically be reversed by external force of arms, even if (as in 1964 in Gabon) initially successful. As one despondent Gabonese officer put it, "what is the point of speculating about change in Libreville if the very next day the RIAOM will land at Mba airport?"[78] As Clayton concluded "there is no doubt that the garrisons of Senegal...and Ivory Coast...have by their presence contributed to the political stability of these two states."[79] The powerful psychological deterrent of France's military guarantees has blocked much military adventurism in Francophone Africa, while at the same time allowing for a phenomenal reduction of French forces in the continent since decolonization.

France's guarantees were in the form of bilateral defence agreements appended to twelve of the treaties of military cooperation signed at independence with the twenty-three countries of Francophone Africa. Some contained secret (or not so secret) provisions for operational eventualities, including evacuation of civilian leaders and their personal households. Apart from an *ad hoc* presence of French military personnel, small complements of troops on technical assistance missions, and free provision of war materiel[80], eight African states retained full-fledged mutual defence treaties with France: Cameroun (signed in February 1974), the Central African Republic (August 1960), the Comoros (October 1978), Cote d'Ivoire (April 1961), Djibouti (June 1977), Gabon (August 1974, 1985), Senegal (March 1974) and Togo (July 1963). Thus fully one third of the continent's stable civilian regimes and the totality of Francophone Africa's presence in this grouping—Cameroun, Cote d'Ivoire, Gabon, Senegal, referred to as "France's core neo-colonies"[81]—have benefited from ongoing French commitment to their internal civil-military stability. Or, put more dramatically, no Francophone country on the continent has ever attained stable civilian rule except through French force of arms!

France's commitment was tangibly visible, and acquired operational credibility, via bases France maintained in three of these countries (adjacent to their international airports), though the number of French troops and jets in Cote d'Ivoire and Gabon were always modest.[82] Overt intelligence gathering—through well-staffed French Embassies—on domestic (civil and military) moods, neighbouring states, and foreign activities (e.g. American economic initiatives; Libyan initiatives) was openly conducted by French SDECE and SAC agents in close symbiosis with their domestic counterparts.

Depending upon the level of conflict in Chad, France maintained some 8-10,000 troops (down from 21,300 in 1964) in six bases in Africa (down from 100 in 1960), with the capability of airlifting 4,000 more from France within 48 hours. (In reserve was France's rapid deployment force of 40,000 troops in Provence that could reach any hot spot on the globe—e.g. New Caledonia—in two weeks by sea, or, with US air transport, within one week). Such small forces have been more than enough to quell upheavals or deter power-gambits. In 1988 the dispatch for three days of 250 troops and a few jets from Libreville to Lome was an adequate show of force to remind restless elements in the Togolese army of the still-binding nature of the Franco-Togolese military treaty.

The largest concentration of French troops in Africa were in strategic Djibouti (4,000), Dakar (1,250, down from 4,000 till 1974), and Bouar, the Central African Republic (1,000)—the latter force both propping up a virtually re-colonized country and serving as a rear base for French troops in Chad. French units in Gabon have numbered as few as 400 (increasing to 900 when Gabon served as a reservoir for the effort in Chad), with Libreville also Equatorial Africa's regional center for the activities of the French secret service. In Cote d'Ivoire (at the Port Boet air base) the French presence gravitated between 400 (the norm) and 900 when (as in 1980), social unrest called for a stepped-up French presence.[83]

These prepositioned French forces were supplemented by a varying number of military advisers in tactical, technical and intelligence posts, ranging in number from 34 in the professional Senegalese army, 74 in Cote d'Ivoire, 84 in Cameroun and 122 in Gabon.[84] The 1984 Presidential Guard plot in Cameroun—triggered by ex-President Ahidjo's desire for a comeback via ethnic kinsmen—had been thoroughly penetrated by French Intelligence from inception, to be crushed by President Biya with the help of his Cameroun armed forces.

There has been widespread awareness in all quarters, civil and military, that Paris would not allow the fall of the civilian thrones in Abidjan, Dakar, Libreville and Yaounde. Whether theoretically binding pledges of military aid would actually be honored was obviously an open question. For there have been instances of civilian leaders (Youlou, Diori, Dacko) who despite such "guarantees" were jettisoned by France. Consequently civilian regimes with treaties of military cooperation with France have regarded them as invokable only as a last resort, and have not acted with arrogance self-assurance might have endowed. And those countries that felt their value to Paris declining, or their credentials were becoming tarnished in French eyes (e.g. Gabon, Cameroun), cultivated alternate sources of civil-military stability so as not to put to test France's resolve.

In the case of Cote d'Ivoire this was secured through considerable mass legitimacy the regime had garnered, attested in the multiparty elections when they were held in 1990. But Houphouet- Boigny was much too astute to assume legitimacy alone could guard his regime against a praetorian assault, and other policies were pursued, including economic largess to the officer corps and the secondment of French expatriates to sensitive posts in the police and security apparatus. All of these bound the military to the persona of Houphouet-Boigny. The latter's death, the political succession, and the wobbly regime that emerged in Abidjan may have tilted the sources of that country's current civil-military stability squarely back to France's formal military guarantees. These, France has stated, are no longer binding, but to date few in the Ivorien army have opted to verify this[85].

In Senegal alternate supports for the supremacy of the civilian order has roots in legitimating historical factors, further anchored in the perpetuation of stabilizing alliances forged (by Senghor) with the country's powerful mourides, though these are eroding. Diouf's multiparty democracy and (post-1990) opening up of a wall-to-wall coalition has allowed for systemic safety valves, further cementing a sense of legitimacy, though political strife is not far beneath the surface. These factors have, however, subordinated to civilian authority a historically disciplined and professional army—despite escalating socio-economic problems, the country's increased political volatility, and separatist sentiments in Casamance and elsewhere.

Gabon also developed supplemental sources of civil-military stability during the 1960-1990 era, utilizing the whole gamut of strategies outlined previously, from a parallel paramilitary to lush trade-offs with key officers. The prime means utilized to neutralize the army has been by superimposing over it a veritable expatriate mercenary, monitoring/controlling vise with both operational capability, and an array of political spies. The regime has acted harshly when mutiny and plotting came to light, being criticized for its human rights record by Amnesty International, and generously when groups have been willing to accept subservience. And finally, Biya's Cameroun, in many ways the least stable of the four countries, even before the 1990's, was stabilized during 1960-1990 by the adoption of many of the traits of the "Trade-off" modality where the military's support was bought off through economic perks and advantages.

French former (and possible ongoing) military commitment to a stable civil-military balance in these four states had diverse motivations, but can be seen against the background of a large ongoing French presence and economic interest in the continent, and France's conception of her "own national destiny...being intimately tied to that of Africa."[86] Until 1988 Africa constituted for France her second most important export market after the European Common Market, and a guaranteed one at that.[87] The continent was the sole global region with which France consistently recorded a trade surplus, and was France's main supplier of a range of mineral ores from uranium through phosphates to iron. Moreover, one third of France's energy imports (18 million tons of oil) came from Africa. This helps explain France's resolve to "maintain its influence in Africa while preserving its ultimate freedom of action...to keep bases and facilities...ensure its supply of raw materials."[88] Francophone Africa also include states with which France has semi-emotional ties and/or constitute for her (as in the case of Djibouti) a major strategic anchor.

In 1988, despite several years of economic slowdown that saw a major erosion in the French presence, there were still 100 French industrial, commercial and service multinationals in Africa with over 1,500 local affiliates, 800 small or medium-scale enterprises and some 5,000 single family or individual entrepreneurs. There remained some 300,000 French nationals throughout French Africa, an important presence whose interests needed to be sustained. The continent's economic importance to France since then has declined enormously: in some countries (Niger, Gabon, Congo, even Cote d'Ivoire) the vacuum left by departing French entrepreneurs and investment is visible to the naked eye, and there is little evidence of a reverse in this outflow. Yet, notwithstanding periodic restatements that civilian regimes would have to fend for themselves, ambiguities remain to this day (including of actual military support) to throw doubt whether or not France has really "normalized" its relationships in the continent.

In the case of Senegal, moreover, emotional sentiment continues to play an important role in binding France to Africa. Senegal has pride of place in French history as France's "first colony" in Africa, a fact that has garnered Dakar support, more than compensating for the country's objective absence of economic importance beyond serving as a conveniently-near tourist playground for the French middle class and a productive outlet for French petty business entrepreneurs. The fact that Senegal was headed for two decades by Leopold Sedar Senghor—a living testimonial of the alleged cross- cultural transferability of French values—further sealed a "historic bond" between the two countries, strengthening the metropole's resolve to preserve the political tranquillity of its first colonial footprint in Africa.

In somewhat similar manner powerful personal bonds of amity were forged between President de Gaulle and Cote d'Ivoire's Felix Houphouet-Boigny, that *mutatis mutandi* were converted into durable bonds between all subsequent French Presidents and the Ivoirien leader. France's commitment to the stability of the civilian throne in Abidjan was possibly the firmest and most unequivocal of all its residual obligations in Africa. In the words of one senior French diplomat, France's commitment to the integrity of the political order in Abidjan "is immutable."[89] Chipman has also noted "so long as Houphouet-Boigny remains in power in the Ivory Coast, he can be sure of the protection afforded by French troops."[90] The fact that Abidjan unequivocally opened its doors to French petty entrepreneurs and usually saw eye to eye with France on most regional and global issues, added further dimensions to this alliance. And despite Cote d'Ivoire's economic downdrift in the mid-1980's the country's stunning development made her a valuable trading partner to France, something to a lesser extent also true with respect to Cameroun, that retained a French plantation presence in the country.

Such was not the case with Gabon. Despite military treaties and Gabon's much weightier economic role, Libreville's civilian regime was militarily sustained by an occasionally reluctant Paris ill at ease with Bongo's arch-conservative metropolitan political allies, heavy-handed domestic authoritarian style, and his family's various economic peccadillos. These included Bongo's personal idiosyncrasies; the embarrassing indiscretions and outright larcenies of his former wayward and profligate wife; the corruption of some of his most trusted lieuten-ants/relatives; Gabonese contributions to radio stations and electoral campaign chests of arch-conservative political contenders in France—even against Mitterand's candidacy—and the recruitment to key posts in Gabon's security services of Bongo's mercenary "Corsican Mafia" who at times mounted external sorties, as with the 1977 mercenary assault on Cotonou. However, the benefits of continued access and indirect control of the immensely important mineral riches beneath Gabon's topsoil more than compensated for embarrassments stemming from France's support of Bongo[91], and the country's being cited for violations of human rights[92].

The Trade-Off Modality

The second modality of civil-military stability rests on what may be called the Trade-off strategy, a dynamic modality in the sense that civil-military relations are intermittently in a state of flux, and long-term stability is not automatically assured but needs to be constantly tended to. A number of African states that in the past could be seen belonging in this grouping, have fallen by the wayside as the balance was upset.

The modality rests on a tacit but visible trade-off of material benefits (to the military as a corporate body, and to officers as indi-viduals) in exchange for political fealty. The quest for an alliance with the military is not unlike the patron-client networks political leaders establish with civilian influentials in both the traditional and modern sectors. Stability thus becomes a direct function of the satisfaction of group and individual needs of the armed forces. The military becomes yet another constituency that has to be "taken care of" through the spoils of office.

Insofar as the military is concerned, corporate trade-offs may include provision of (often unnecessary) sophisticated materiel and firepower that enhances the prestige of the force. It also includes increasing the size of the army—that raises the requisite rank of the Chief of Staff (increasing his status and remuneration), the number of officers needed (allowing for patronage), while assuaging officers in the pipeline with promotion where otherwise prolonged rank-freezes might have been in order. Individual perks include not just pay-hikes but provision of duty-free cars and luxury imports, rotated appointments overseas (as military attaches, Ambassadors) and "refresher" training courses in foreign staff colleges, a euphemism for foreign travel. Other inducements include the allocation of sinecures (through secondment to parastatal sectors), integration into the political hierarchy, or allowing officers to engage in private commercial activity while on active service. As with the previous modality, other stabilizing strategies may be adopted, but ultimately the glue binding military elites to civilian authority is at its core the pecuniary self-interest of the officer corps.

Two civilian regimes during 1960-1990 forged a measure of control over their armed forces in such a manner: Kenya and Zambia. Two others, Cameroun and Swaziland, showed powerful affinities to this operational modality, but are more properly seen belonging in the first grouping (Cameroun) or the third (Swaziland).

In both Kenya and Zambia military officers (especially as one moved to the senior ranks) have developed into economic potentates. They have have engaged in large-scale cash-crop farming on lands secured at give-away prices and at low interest rates (especially in Kenya); in lucrative smuggling activities (in both), trucking enterprises (especially in Kenya), trade and commerce (in both), and they have oftentimes also occupied remunerative posts on parastatal boards (especially Zambia).

In Zambia, Kaunda gave officers a privileged position in society, and they reciprocated by protecting their personal/corporate interests and their patron against the conspiracies from below. Officers wereextremely well-paid, received superior housing and fringe benefits. Moreover, many middle-ranking and most senior officers at one stage or another were either integrated into Kaunda's cabinet, or received parastatal appointments. The military as a whole had a corporate role in running certain divisions of the administration (the Mechanical Services Branch) that conferred both an enhanced developmental "role" in society, and sources of petty pilferage. The Zambian "approach" also meshed well with Kaunda's mercantilist philosophy to politics. As one observer put it, Kaunda "neutralises his opponents by finding them government or party jobs, rather than by facing grievances and problems face on...never rely[ing] on massive repression. One result is that the party is now bloated with full-time functionaries drawing salaries from government coffers, many of them without clear job descriptions."[93]

Kenya, with a more developed economy permitting greater sources of patronage, allowed an even fuller amplification of this strategy. Kenya officially encourages civil servants in general to set up private enterprises (despite conflicts of duty and other well-documented negative repercussions), with the result that many military officers have amassed an array of lucrative enterprises. It is no mere chance that every retired Chief of Staff, and many senior officers as well, are comfortably ensconced in large (5,000+ acre) farms. And this includes General Ndolo, the former Kamba Chief of Staff implicated in the 1971 plot, who is in retirement on a 9,416 acre Machakos farm, partly the government's "gratuity" and partly purchased at fire-sale prices in land-hungry Kenya.

Kenyatta utilized such policies quite liberally during his reign. On his accession to the political throne Moi, who needed to root his Presidency in an ethnically-hostile army, expanded the custom of buying military support through the grant of farming land, encouraged even more commercial activities, and turned a blind eye to other activities, some actually illegal. Many more grants of land were given to military officers under Moi—to Kikuyu officers to assure them of the continuation under his aegis of state munificence; to the Kalenjin, his core ethnic support; and to traditionally anti-Kikuyu elements in the officer corps previously bypassed in the allocation of benefits, in an effort to build a broader ethnic alliance. And shaken by the first Rawlings takeover in Ghana, and the wave of executions of public figures in Accra (that traumatized many other complacent African leaders as well), soon "land grants in Kenya went to junior officers as well. Large areas around Nakuru and Ngong were handed out to keep the armed forces behind the government."[94]

Through such policies military officers were deflected from attempts at economic aggrandizement via coupmanship with all the latter's hazards and uncertainties. They were personally bound to the regime by their *legal* integration into the allocation of patronage and largess, as opposed to their counterparts in other armies who have had to develop their private economic interests surreptitiously. Their personal loyalty and the full weight they exercised over units they commanded was assured by the threat to their own personal economic status, that would suffer in any political upheaval from any quarter.

The Legitimized Modality

The third modality of civilian supremacy is visible in a few polities that have been able to develop a measure of systemic legitimacy that in and of itself can serve to discourage praetorian assaults from armed forces. Alternate sources of stability are often pursued simultaneously, but ultimately civilian supremacy is secured consequent to acknowledgement of the systemic legitimacy of the ruling hierarchy. The legitimized modality of civilian rule is the ideal source of civil-military stability in that it attests to the *internalization* in the armed forces of the concept of civilian supremacy, and is the only one that links up with broader theories of civil-military stability outlined earlier on. But it too cannot be assumed to be a stable modality.

Systemic legitimacy—unlike civil-military pecuniary alliances, or military treaties with ex-colonial powers—has few constraining features or negative side-effects, is cost-effective and in theory transferable following a political succession. But this cannot be taken for granted. Systemic strain may affect popular attitudes, and a successor regime need not be necessarily viewed by the armed forces as popularly legitimated (even if it has been so, via the polls). In Africa systemic legitimacy still competes with, or is none too securely superimposed upon, group allegiances stemming from cultural subnationalism and/or regionalism, all linked to ambitious personalities. Power and legitimacy still have to be assumed as *a priori* linked to the persona of a specific leader, and not necessarily the heritage of a successor. As Banda's rapid loss of support in the pro-democracy environment of Malawi in the 1990's, and as Gambia's first successful coup further illustrate "legitimacy" in Africa is itself a temporally fluid and variable concept. Legum aptly noted that "all African regimes are essentially temporary or transitional, since with very few exceptions they do not operate within an established framework of viable and widely based institutions, even when they have been legitimated."[95] Degrees of legitimation exist, as well as levels of democratization, and the two do not necessarily go together. Of the twelve countries in this study several have forged a measure of civil-military stability based on systemic legitimacy. These include Botswana, Gambia, Malawi, Mauritius, Swaziland and Tanzania.

The legitimacy that underlies this modality may be lodged in a variety of cumulative factors. It may stem, for example, from the absence of competing subnationalisms in fundamentally compact single-ethnic polities (or approximations thereof), coupled with astute leadership buttressed by traditional and/or modern credentials (Botswana, Swaziland). Alternately, consequent to the dynamism, dedication or charisma of leaders who despite their society's more fractured nature and/or other socio-economic strains, have succeeded to glue potentially destabilizing cleavages (Gambia, Malawi, Tanzania). Or, from the permeation in society of cultural values steeped in the give and take of democratic life that by definition shift politics from the status of a zero-sum game, defusing tensions and competitions (Mauritius, Botswana).

Three of the civilian regimes in our sample (Botswana, Gambia, Mauritius), were further sustained by their competitive multi-party democratic political life, while the other three (plus Botswana) have had their political order legitimated by the force of the personality of their founding fathers (King Sobhuza II; Kamuzu Banda; Seretse Khama, Julius Nyerere). All these variables insulated the civilian order (in four instances, second-generation) against usurpationist tendencies of their armed forces. Military personnel with corporate or personal gripes and ambitions no doubt exist in the armies of such states. But manifestation of such inclinations will be repressed in light of the legitimacy of political leaders that possess a multiplicity of loyalist sources of retaliation against praetorian assaults.

As with the previous two modalities of stability, the legitimacy of civilian rule has been buttressed by an array of policies aimed at assuring civil-military peace. Even in Botswana, where civilian supremacy is strongly ingrained, presidential restraints over the Botswana Defence Force were exerted through the presence in the officer corps of Seretse Khama's son, Ian. In Swaziland, the spread of economic patronage to societal influentials (especially of the royal family) kept their kin in the army in line. In Tanzania a concerted drive was mounted to eradicate elitist tendencies from the army after the 1964 military mutiny. Despite re-education efforts, much of the military's relative quiescence since that event (for there have been several plots), has been secured by tactics not unlike those adopted by Zambia: through the integration of key officers into the parastatal sector, increases in military pay-scales, granting the army greater social status, and monitoring it through paramilitary hierarchies. And in Malawi Banda has used a network of spies and ancillary structures (including the Young Pioneers) to keep military unrest controlled. [96]

Conclusions

A survey of the political, socio-economic and military characteristics of twelve stable civilian systems during the 1960-1990 period revealed that as a group they were heterogeneous. Only on two dimensions—quality of civilian leadership and patterns of economic growth—were most, but still not all, different from neighboring states with chronic histories of coups and military rule. Moreover, Botswana and Mauritius notably apart, none were completely free from intra-military tensions and/or civil-military confrontations. Stable civilian states thus surmounted obstacles tripping their neighbors, at least in part through the quality of their leadership, and specific strategies they adopted to deflect military aggrandizement tendencies. Neither the stabilizing role of astute leadership nor the concrete policies they have pursued have been given their due in the past.

On closer analysis seven specific control-mechanisms can be seen as having played a role in assuring the civilian subordination of the military in the twelve case-studies. No single one of these, or any combination, accounts for the stabilization of civil-military relations in all twelve countries. Rather, three profiles of stable civil-military relations suggest themselves. One of states primarily stabilized by the deterrent implicit in treaties of military cooperation with a credible external power; another, of regimes that symbiotically integrate their armed forces, and especially members of the officer corps, in the distribution of the spoils of political office; and finally, another group stabilized primarily through the legitimating aura of the civilian leadership that both attracts loyalty as well as deters power grabs. Only by separating out the twelve countries along these three modalities—rather than through attempts to detect and isolate statistically-meaningful structural and socio-economic determinants of stability—do the sources of stability and instability in Africa clearly stand out. Since the strategies outlined above have the capacity to confer stability to any power-wielder, civilian or military, and indeed have been used to secure internal stability in military regimes in Africa, they have relevance for the development of a general theory of stability and instability in Africa that is not as Eurocentric as past efforts.

The chapters that follow examine in depth one specific country from each of the three modalities. They present comprehensive overviews of the historical, political and socio-economic evolution of each country, the stabilizing role of leadership and the policies pursued, and outline the main sources of civil-military stability. The concluding chapter examines the new post-1989 pressures for political and economic liberalization, and prospects for continued civil-military peace in the three case studies and on the broader political map of Africa.

NOTES

1. Richard Sandbrook, *The Politics of Africa's Economic Stagnation*, Cambridge, Cambridge University Press, 1985, p. 1.

2. Colin Legum, "Africa's Search for nationhood and Stability," *Journal of Contemporary African Studies*, October 1985, p. 21.

3. "As 1984 slips into 1985," *West Africa*, January 7, 1985, p. 3.

4. Patrick Chabal (ed.), *Political Domination in Africa. Reflections on the Limits of Power*, Cambridge, Cambridge University Press, 1986, p. 2.

5. See also Adebayo Adedeji, "Foreign Debt and Prospects for Growth in Africa during the 1980's," *Journal of Modern African Studies*, vol. 23 no. 1, 1985.

6. Robert Jackson and Carl Rosberg, "Why Africa's Weak States Persist," in A. Kohli (ed) *The State and Development in the Third World*, Princeton, Princeton University Press, 1986 and "The Marginality of African States," in G. M. Carter and P. O'Meara, *African Independence; The First 25 Years*, Bloomington, Indiana University Press, 1986.

7. See Dov Ronen (ed.), *Democracy and Pluralism in Africa*, Boulder, Co., Lynne Rienner, 1986.

8. Gerard Conac," Le Presidentialisme en Afrique Noire. Unité et Diversité. Essai de Typologie," in *L'Evolution Recente de Pouvoir en Afrique Noire*, Bordeaux, Centre d'Etudes d'Afrique Noire, 1977, p. 25.

9. Patrick McGowan and Johnson, "African Military Coups d'Etat," *Journal of Modern African Studies*, vol. 22 no. 4, 1984, p. 634. The six were Botswana, Cape Verde, Djibouti, Lesotho, Mauritius and Swaziland. Since the article was published Lesotho was taken over by the military, and Swaziland has had civil-military rumblings.

10. Samuel Finer, *The Man on Horseback: The Role of the Military in African Politics*, London, Pall Mall, 1962.

11. The literature on coups is too voluminous to even selectively cite. One particularly useful guide to the literature and approaches is Staffan Wilking, *Military Coups in sub-Saharan Africa*, Uppsala, Scandinavian Institute of African Studies, 1983.

12. Amos Perlmutter, "Civil-Military in Socialist Authoritarian and Praetorian States: Prospects and Retrospects," in Roman Kolkowicz and Andrzej Korbonski (eds.), *Soldiers, Peasants and Bureaucrats, London*, George Allen & Unwin, 1982 p. 313. See also T. O. Odetola, Military Regimes and Development, London, George Allen & Unwin, 1982.

13. Thomas H. Johnson, Robert O. Slater and Pat McGowan, "Explaining African Military Coups d'Etat, 1960-1982," *American Political Science Review*, vol. 78 no. 3, September 1984, pp. 622-40; Robert Jackman, "The Predictability of Coups d'Etat. A Model with African Data," *American Political Science Review*, vol. 72 no. 4, 1978, September 1978, pp. 1262-75.

14. Samuel Decalo, *Coups and Military Rule in Africa: Motivations and Constraints*, New Haven, Yale University Press, 1990.

15. Aristide Zolberg, " Military Intervention in the New States of Africa," in Henry S. Bienen (ed.), *The Military Intervenes*, p. 71.

16. David Goldsworthy, "Armies and Politics in Civilian Regimes," in Simon Baynham, *Military Power and Politics in Black Africa*, London, Croom Helm, 1986, p. 117.

17. Decalo, *Coups and Military Rule in Africa*, p. 5.

18. Eric A. Nordlinger, *Soldiers in Politics: Military Coups and Government*, Englewood Cliffs, Prentice Hall, 1977, p. 39.

19. Samuel Decalo, "The Morphology of Radical Military Rule in Africa," *Journal of Communist Studies*, January 1987.

20. David and Marina Ottaway, *Afrocommunism*, New York, Africana Publishing House, 1981, p. 201.

21. Jackman, "The Predictability of Coups d'Etat."

22. Johnson, Slater and McGowan, "Explaining African Military Coups d'Etat, 1960-1982." See the insightful criticism of the latter research and its oversights by David Goldsworthy, "On the Structural Explanation of African Military Interventions," *Journal of Modern African Studies*, vol. 24 no. 1, 1986, pp. 179-185. For another critical review of aggragate data analysis see John Ravenhill, "Comparing Regime Performance in Africa: The Limitations of Cross-National Aggregate Analysis," *Journal of Modern African Studies*, vol. 18 no. 1, March 1980, pp. 99-126.

23. John Harbeson (ed.), *The Military in African Politics*, New York, Praeger, 1987, p. 2.

24. See Arnold Hughes and Roy May, "The Politics of Succession in Black Africa," *Third World Quarterly*, January 1988, pp. 1-22.

25. Colin Legum et. al., *Africa in the 1980's*, New York, McGraw Hill, 1984, p. 25.

26. Though see Joseph Karimi and Philip Ochieng, *The Kenyatta Succession*, Nairobi, Transafrica, 1980.

27. Richard Hodder-Williams, "Dr. Banda's Malawi," *Journal of Commonwealth and Comparative Politics*, March 1974, p. 110.

28. Claude E. Welch Jr. (ed.), *Civilian Control of the Military: Theory and Cases from Developing Countries*, Albany, State University of New York Press, 1976. p. xi. See also Henry S. Bienen and Nicolas van de Walle, "Time and Power in Africa," *American Political Science Review*, March 1989, who conclude that "the risk of losing power is a decreasing function of time that is little affected by country or leadership qualifications." (p. 19).

29. Elise Forbes Pachter, "Contra-Coup: Civilian Control of the Military in Guinea, Tanzania and Mozambique," *Journal of Modern African Studies*, vol. 20 no. 4, 1982, p.596. Others offering various asides include William Gutteridge, "Undoing Coups in Africa," *Third World Quarterly*, January 1985, pp. 78-89; William Tordoff, *Government and Politics in Africa*, London, Macmillan, 1984, especially pp. 149-50.

30. See David Goldsworthy, "Civilian Control of the Military in Black Africa," *African Affairs*, January 1981, pp. 49-74 and his "Armies and Politics in Civilian Regimes," in Simon Baynham (ed.), *Military Power and Politics in Black Africa*.

31. Samuel Huntington, "Civilian Control of the Military: A Theoretical Statement," in Heinz Eulau, Samuel J. Eldersveld and Morris Janowitz (eds.), *Political Behavior: A Reader in Theory and Research*, Glecoe, The Free Press, 1956, p. 380.

32. See Samuel Decalo, *Psychoses of Power: African Personalist Dictatorships*, Boulder, Co., Westview Press, 1989.

33. See Finer's classic, *The Man on Horseback*, pp. 77-8, as well as his equally path-breaking "The Morphology of Military Regimes," in Roman Kolkowicz and Andrzej Korbonski (eds.), *Soldiers, Peasants and Bureaucrats*.

34. Carl von Clausewitz, *On War*, London, Routledge and Kegan Paul, 1966, vol. 3, p. 125.

35. Kwamah Nkrumah, "Politics is not for Soldiers," Accra, Government Publishing Company, 1962, p. 6.

36. Claude E. Welch Jr. and Arthur K. Smith, *Military Role and Rule*, Duxbury Press, 1974, p. 6.

37. On the other hand, Chief of Staff Momoh's rather unusual constitutional rise to political office, creating a remarkable civil hybrid, argued for caution.

38. McGowan and Johnson, "African Military Coups d'Etat."

39. For details see Samuel Decalo, "The Morphology of Radical

Military Rule in Africa," *Journal of Communist Studies*.

40. Gus Liebenow, "The Military Factor in African Politics: A Twenty-five Years perspective," in G. Carter and P. O'Meara, *African Independence*, pp. 126-159.

41. Donald G. Morrison et al, *Black Africa: A Comparative Handbook*, New York, The Free Press, 1972.

42. The distorted income distributions seem to be more a matter of *degree*. Muller and Seligson have noted that the income share of the top 20% of the population was highest for Zimbabwe (69.1%), followed indeed by Gabon (67.5%), one of the case-studies. Lower down the list came Kenya (60.4%) and Cote d'Ivoire (57.2%), but *the lowest such percentage for Africa was 47.8%* (in Ghana), so that while the much criticized income disparities in Gabon, Cote d'Ivoire and Kenya are high, the "norm" in Africa as a whole is also relatively high. See Edward N. Muller & Mitchell A. Seligson, "Inequality and Insurgency, *American Political Science Review*, June 1987, vol. 81 no. 2, p. 446.

43. A somewhat similar observation was noted by McGowan and Johnson who concluded that African states whose economies grew faster experienced less coups. See McGowan and Johnson, "African Coups d'Etat," p. 658.

44. See for example "The gravy train," *West Africa*, May 1, 1989.

45. Goldsworthy in Baynham, (ed.), *Military Power and Politics in Black Africa*, pp. 117-119.

46. *Ibid*, p. 117.

47. The unrest in Swaziland was primarily linked with the royal tug-of-war related to the succession. See "The Post-Sobhuza Power Struggle," *Africa Report*, January-February 1984, pp. 51-54.

48. As cited in Colin Legum, "Why Tanganyika accepted a Chinese Mission," *Africa Report*, vol. 9 no. 9, October 1964, p. 16.

49. Welch (ed.), *Civilian Control of the Military*, p. 5-6.

50. For one mutiny in Tanzania see *The New York Times*, January 23, 1983 and *The Christian Science Monitor*, January 14, 1983. Between 6-700 troops, including several senior officers, and 1,000 civilians were allegedly arrested for their involvement, or for not reporting the plot to the authorities.

51. Nyerere's decision, for example, to have every military unit grow its foodstuff needs on plots adjacent to military bases, and undertaking developmental tasks (for the Department of Public Works)—suggested by Chinese advisers—was extremely unpopular, and caused considerable grumbling.

52. See "Mozambique: Politicising the Ranks," *Africa Confidential*, 15 February 1984, p. 5.

53. Goldsworthy in Baynham, (ed.), *Military Power and Politics in Black Africa*, p. 98.

54. Cynthia H. Enloe, "The Military Uses of Ethnicity," *Millenium*, vol. 4 no. 3, 1975, pp. 220-233.

55. J. Murray, "Succession Prospects in Kenya," *Africa Report*, November 1968, p. 47.

56. Mordechai Tamarkin, "The Roots of Political Stability in Kenya," *African Affairs*, vol. 77 no. 308, July 1978, p. 310.

57.Walter L. Barrows, "Changing Military Capabilities in Black Africa," in William J. Foltz and Henry S. Bienen, *Arms for the African*, New Haven, Yale University Press, 1985, p. 106.

58. *The Military Balance 1983/4*, London, Institute for Strategic Studies. Part of the increased costs were, however, due to heavier expenditures on sophisticated war materiel.

59. For the main thrust on the concept of personal rule see Jackson and Rosberg, *Personal Rule in Africa*.

60. See "Francisco Macias Nguema: Tyrant of Equatorial Guinea," in Samuel Decalo, *Psychoses of Power*.

61. See Henry S. Bienen, *Armies and Parties in Africa*, New York, Africana, 1978, p. 185.

62. T. S. Cox, *Civil-Military Relations in Sierra Leone*, Cambridge, Harvard University Press, 1976.

63. During three years (1966-69) in Dahomey, for example, the Directorship of the Security Services (Intelligence) changed hands *six* times, as each incumbent (later demoted) utilized the post to promote personal interests, and to discredit other officers and competitive officer cliques. See Decalo, *Coups and Army Rule in Africa*, p. 62.

64. The best example being the 1977 unsuccessful mercenary assault on Cotonou airport. Political strategyincluded large contributions to election coffers of French presidential candidates deemed pro-Gabonese, and to radio-stations, commentators, and legislators that could sway public opinion or National Assembly votes.

65. See Anthony Clayton's "Foreign Intervention in Africa," in S. Baynham (ed.), *Military Power and Politics in Black Africa*, pp. 203-258.

66. Robin Luckham, "French Militarism in Africa," *Review of African Political Economy*, vol. 24, May-August 1982, p. 70.

67. Robin Luckham, "A Comparative Typology of Civil-Military Relations," *Government and Opposition*, vol. 6 no. 1, 1971, p. 11.

68. Jacques van Doorn, "Political Change and the Control of the

Military," in J. van Doorn (ed.), *Military Profession and Military Regimes*, The Hague, Mouton, 1969, pp. 27-8.

69. Finn Fuglestad, "The 1974 Coup d'etat in Niger: Towards an Explanation," *Journal of Modern African Studies*, vol. 13 no. 3, 1975; Samuel Decalo, "Niger," in *Coups and Military Rule in Africa: Motivations and Constraints*.

70. Samuel Decalo, "Regionalism, Political Decay and Civil Strife in Chad," *Journal of Modern African Studies*, July 1980, pp. 23-56.

71. John Dunn, "The Politics of Representation and Good Government in post-colonial Africa," in Chabal (ed.), *Political Domination in Africa*, p. 161.

72. Here we somewhat part ways from Goldsworthy, "Civilian Control of the Military in Black Africa," *African Affairs*, who asserts that they "must in the first instance be grounded on questions about the legitimacy and effectiveness of civilian institutions" (p. 56).

73. Goldsworthy in Baynham, (ed.), *Military Power and Politics in Black Africa*, p. 106.

74. Cox, *Civil-Military Relations in Sierra Leone*, p. 19.

75. See F.P. Ngayap, *Cameroun: Qui Governe?*, Paris, Harmattan, 1983, p. 14.

76. *Africa Confidential*, October 15, 1981, p. 3.

77. Goldsworthy in Baynham (ed.),*Military Power and Politics in Black Africa*, p. 112.

78. Interview in Libreville, August 12, 1988.

79. Clayton, "Foreign Intervention in Africa," in Baynham, (ed.), *Military Power and Politics in Black Africa*, p. 212.

80. For additional detail on Francophone African armies see Pierre Viaud and Jacques de Lestapis, *Afrique: Les souverainetés en Armes*, Paris, Fondation pour les études de defense nationale, 1987. For background on the early French military presence in Africa see "La Force d'Intervention et le Remaniément du Dispositif Français en Afrique Noire et á Madagascar," *Fréres d'Armes*, April 1963.

81. Luckham, "French Militarism in Africa," *Review of African Political Economy*. See also the scathing analysis of Guy Martin, "The Historical, Economic, and Political Bases of France's African Policy," *Journal of Modern African Studies*, vol. 23 no. 2, 1985, pp. 189-208.

82. See Jacques Guillemin, "L'Importance des bases dans la politique militaire de la France en Afrique Noire francophone et á Madagascar," *Revue Française d'Etudes Politiques Africaines*, August-September 1981, pp. 32-44. See also John Chipman, "French Military Policy and African Security," Adelphi Papers no. 201, The International Institute for Strategic Studies, London,

1985; and Pascal Chaigneau, *La Politique Militaire de la France en Afrique*, Paris, 1984.

83. "France: Intervention Capability," *Africa Confidential*, January 1, 1981.

84. The latter has the third-highest French military presence of the 26 countries in which France maintains such missions, below only Morocco with 183, and Chad with 125. For some important data on the structural reorganization of the Gabonese military see Moshe Ammi-Oz, "L'Evolution de la place et du role des forces publiques Africaines," *Le Mois en Afrique*, March 1977, pp. 59-78.

85. For an analysis of France's military interventions in Africa see Daniel Bon and Karen Mingst, "French Intervention in Africa: Dependency or Decolonization," *Africa Today*, vol. 27 no. 2, 1980, pp. 5-20, and Jacques Guillemin, "L'Intervention exterieure dans la politique militaire de la France en Afrique Noire francophone et á Madagascar," *Revue Francaise d'Etudes Politiques Africaines*, June-July 1981, pp. 43-58.

86. George E. Moose, "French Military Policy," in William J. Foltz and Henry S. Bienen, (eds.), *Arms for the African*, p. 60. See also Tamar Golan, "A Certain Mystery: How Can France do Everything that it does in Africa—and get away with it?" *African Affairs*, January 1981, pp. 3-11; Louis de Guiringaud, "La Politique africaine de la France," *Politique Etrangere*, June 1982.

87. "La Cooperation avec l'Afrique: perspectives pour les enterprises françaises," *Afrique Contemporaine*, no. 1, 1989, p. 45.

88. Chipman, "French Military Policy and African Security," p. 6. See also Chester Crocker, "France's Changing Military Interests," *Africa Report*, June 1968.

89. Interview in Abidjan, July 12, 1988.

90. Chipman, "French Military Policy and African Security," p. 30.

91. For some details see Pierre Peane, *Affaires Africaines*, Paris, Fayard, 1982.

92. See *inter alia* "Unfair Trial and other Amnesty International concerns in the Republic of Gabon," London, Amnesty International, 1984.

93. "Zambia: Party problems," *Africa Confidential*, 21 January 1987.

94. Tamarkin, "The Roots of Political Stability in Kenya," *African Affairs*, July 1978, p. 301. See also "Kenya: The End of an Illusion," *Race and Class*, Winter 1983, p. 238.

95. Colin Legum, "Fission and Fusion in Evolving Nation-States," in his *Africa in the 1980's*, p. 25.

96. See Robert B. Boeder, "Prospects for Political Stability in Malawi," in Calvin Woodward (ed.), *On the Razor's Edge: Prospects for Political Stability in Southern Africa*, Pretoria, Africa Institute of South Africa, 1986.

CHAPTER TWO

MALAWI: DICTATORSHIP BY CONSENT?

Partly as a result of its awkward insular location, but also due to lengthy self-imposed isolation, Malawi has attracted only "sporadic"[1] academic attention. Former President Banda's intense aversion to journalists (who tended to latch onto the more oppressive features of his regime) for two decades virtually barred them from the country, while his strict domestic laws (on spreading "rumours") likewise inhibited an outflow of information about the country. Even today only a handful of countries have resident embassies in Lilongwe, and few flights link Malawi with the outside world, bringing in barely 55,000 visitors a year, mostly from neighboring states. Indeed, as recently as 1992 the sweep of democratization in Africa seemed to have bypassed Malawi altogether.

Notwithstanding this, Banda's paternalistic leadership style and conservative policies attracted considerable, and often ideologically-motivated, diatribes. Yet Malawi—at independence with the second-lowest GNP per capita in Africa ($50), and today still among the world's 25 least developed countries—until the mid-1980's was widely viewed in global donor circles as Africa's economic Cinderella, a rare Third World success story! Malawi's civil-military relations were also among the most peaceful in the continent, reflecting a through subordination of the military to civilian authority, resting on considerable systemic legitimacy.

Despite a multitude of personal idiosyncrasies, and the oppressiveness of his rule, much of the credit for this subordination of the armed forces to the political center belongs to Banda, Malawi's founding-father, whose lengthy administration left an indelible stamp on all aspects of Malawi public and private life. Virtually until a few years before his political demise, Banda dominated every aspect of policy-making in Malawi, which he treated as his own household. As he put it in a famous early speech, "nothing is not my business in this country"[2]. Propelled to power by a massive groundswell of popular support, the physician-turned-politician Elder of the Church of Scotland "telescoped Malawi's development from parliamentary rule to personal autocracy into a few short years,"[3] though giving the new state a sense of identity, and outliving most of political opponents.

Acomplex urbane individual, who for twenty years resided in England and America, Banda nevertheless reflected the social and cultural ethos from which he had sprung, and in which he retained roots. Invariably dressed in severe black three-piece suits and a homburg hat, he also sported the chiefly fly-whisk of Africa. An arch-elitist, he relished populist mass meetings, speaking in English (poorly understood by the masses), which had to be translated into the lingua franca, Chichewa. He often concluded his public appearances by joining in traditional dancing, accompanied by troupes of women that were part of his retinue. His policies in office strove to catapult Malawi into the twentieth century, while entrenching traditional values and authority. His power base was at all times in the country's rural areas, where the majority of the people lived. Not surprisingly, even when defeated politically in the 1994 multiparty elections, he and his party secured a respectable vote in many rural areas, though condemned, *a priori*, by most observers to the dustbin of history.

Though many of his oppressive policies riled urban-based civil servants and drove into self-exile many intellectuals, Banda nevertheless retained, right to the end of his reign, significant sources of mass popular support in the countryside, where the regime's repressive features were not necessarily seen in so a harsh a light. "Dictatorship by consent" was how Banda defined his rule[4], and consent, including from the armed forces, was more or less forthcoming. Paradoxically, today, in the new democratic, constitutional, multi-party Malawi, and under a new President, many social ills the *ancien regime* kept at bay (rampant crime, inflation, rural-urban drifts, political squabbling, military unrest, etc.) have seeped in, triggering increasing grumbles about "the good old days!"

Malawi's social and economic background

Malawi is an elongated country 525 miles long and 50-100 miles wide that includes the bulk of the waters of the 350 mile-long Lake Malawi. Out of the Lake's southern extremity flows the Shire River that spills beyond the country's borders into the Zambezi, and that is flanked by

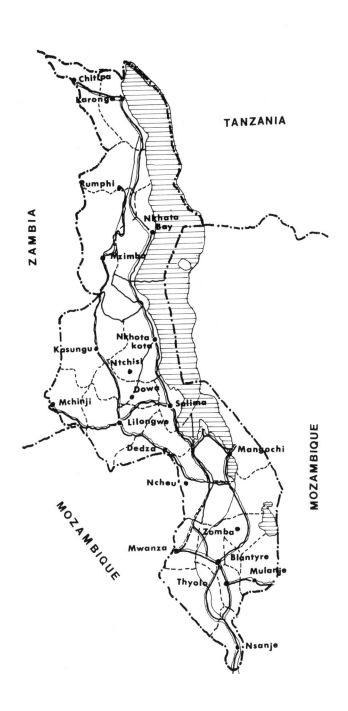

fertile highlands and estates beneath Mount Mulanje, Central Africa's highest peak. Despite infertile plateaux and rugged ridges reaching 8,500 feet in the north, good rainfall and some of the most fertile soils in Central Africa make over 50 percent of Malawi's land suitable for cultivation, thus assuring a stable subsistence agriculture.

Over eight million people live in Malawi, that is Africa's third most densely populated country. Though eight major ethnic groups reside in Malawi, the country is marked by significant ethno-linguistic uniformity. The national language, Chichewa, is understood by 75% of the population, and is the first language of over half of it. The population is unevenly distributed, however, with half—including part of the numerically dominant Chewa—found in the Southern Region. The latter is the most developed, and contains the country's former capital (Zomba), and its main economic nerve-center and largest town (Blantyre). The 1975 relocation of Malawi's capital to Lilongwe resulted in a demographic and economic shift to the fertile Central Region (Malawi's granary), where some 40% of the population resides, including the other segment of the Chewa. By contrast the Northern Region has rather poor soils and a lengthy history of economic neglect. Undeveloped, it contains 12% of the country's population and has been mostly a reservoir of manpower for the plantations in the south, and the mines of neighbouring states.

The country is named after the Maravi from whom Malawi's Chewa clans trace their descent. Oral tradition refers to the Maravi originating from Katanga (in Zaire), with the first clans arriving at the southwest shores of the lake possibly as early as the 13th century. Internal splits and migrations saw several chiefdoms founded in the region. A group that branched westward in the 18th century became the Chewa; those remaining by the lake became the Nyanja (lakeside people). The latter's dialect, Chinyanja (later renamed Chichewa) became Malawi's official language in the mid-1970's. As Pachai has noted, "what started off as Maravi ended as Chewa, Manganja, Nyanja, Chipeta, Nsenga..."[5] Peaceful farmers, the Chewa lived in decentralized federations of chiefdoms that in the 19th century fell to aggressive new arrivals—the Ngoni from the southwest, and Yao and Swahili slavers from the east.

Among ethnic groups north of the Chewa are the Tumbuka, Ngonde and the Tonga. The Ngonde, found in the extreme north, are the southernmost extension of East Africa's inter-lacustrine ethnic

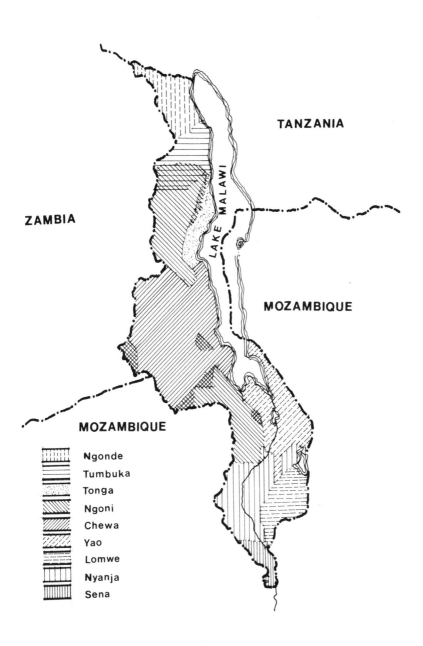

group. The Tumbuka, comprising 10% of Malawi's population and the dominant group in the North, are among the oldest indigenous people in the country, also originating in Zaire. Further south, in the Nkhata Bay district, reside the lakeside Tonga. Egalitarian, individualistic, and part-Chewa, the Tonga were deeply affected by the 19th century arrival in their midst of the Livingstonia Mission of the Free Church of Scotland. While assessments of the side-effects of missionary activity in the region are still debated[6], one result was a general upliftment of educational standards, modern skills, and personal aspirations among Northerners. Due to the superior education provided at Livingstonia, to this day Northerners are better educated than the more indolent Chewa. But the geographical isolation and poor soils of the north assured the region's neglect during the colonial era. And after independence, its weaker demographic clout, maverick political orientations, and Banda's anti-northern biases, shut it out of the power nexus in Lilongwe.

Throughout the colonial era large numbers of Northerners, especially Tonga, deserted their unproductive lands to seek employment further south, where they were in great demand because of their skills and literacy. This outflux was aggravated by the imposition of a hut tax that in the north could only be satisfied by salaried work, and that was actually aimed at garnering manpower for European estates in the south. (Most Chewa were able to avoid such work since their land was fertile.) In the process the north was grossly depopulated. A 1909 report noted that in Tonga districts "hardly an able-bodied man can be found...all the men having left for South Africa,"[7] many undertaking the 1,000 km trek south on foot. Migration in search of employment had become "a kind of initiation marking the passage of a boy into adulthood."[8]

Most of the other peoples of Malawi are newcomers that arrived in the 19th century. The Nguni, currently 10% of the population, and found especially in the Central Region, are kinsmen of South Africa's Zulu[9], who arrived in several waves starting in the 1850's, to occupy the cooler highlands that were suitable to cattle-herding. Aggressive conquerors, they erected hierarchically centralized states. Most Chewa chiefdoms succumbed peacefully to Nguni overlordship, and then progressively "Chewaianized" the minority Nguni—a fact that on the long run assured that lasting inter-ethnic animosities were not to develop.

The Muslim Yao are also newcomers, who had been expelled from their original lands in Mozambique. Starting in the 1860's they arrived in Nyasaland as refugees, later—having discovered the weakness of the Chewa—as overlords. The "greatest long-distance traders in East Central Africa,"[10] and in contact with the major entrepots on the Indian Ocean, their possession of firearms enabled the Yao to branch off into the slave trade, to devastate many southern districts. Currently comprising 15% of the population, the Yao reside in the districts of Mangochi, Ncheu, Blantyre, Zomba and Chiradzulu. They shunned Christianity—paradoxically first introduced in their midst—and resisted the British entry into Nyasaland. Still disliked by the Chewa for their role in the slave trade, the Yao have not played a major political role in contemporary Malawi.

Of several slave centers in the region, a Swahili Arab Sultanate emerged at Nkhota Kota in the 1840's, becoming the largest slave entrepot in Central Africa with 10,000 slaves annually "processed" in the 1870's. It was such predatory devastations of slavers in "one of the dark places of the earth, full of abominations and cruelty"[11] that prompted David Livingstone's plea for a British protectorate, that combined with Anglo-Portuguese competition for the interior of East Africa, led Britain to assume sovereignty over Nyasaland in 1891.

Finally one must note the turn-of-the century migration in the south part of the country of large numbers of Lomwe[12], and the more recent arrival of the Sena. Today the Lomwe make up fully 20% of Malawi's population, being the second-largest group in the country. Refugees from brutal Portuguese rule in Mozambique, the Lomwe at outset were subservient to the Chewa. Landless, many settled on European estates, trapped in the exploitative *thangata* (labour-rent) system then prevailing. Willing to undertake gruelling labor for low wages, they were the backbone of the plantation sector. It was largely Lomwe labor that developed, and to this day sustains, the country's tobacco and tea estates—the underpinning of Malawi's post-independence economic spurt. By the 1970's many Lomwe had moved into the modern work-force, staffing also senior positions in the security forces, where because of their "immigrant" status they were utilized by Banda as a neutral bulwark vis-a-vis his opposition.

Despite its heterogeneity Malawi has not been afflicted by interethnic strife, nor has ethnicity played a serious disruptive role in political life. This provided another pillar for the emergence of a legitimated political center. Ethnicity is not a problem in Malawi because of (a) the stabilizing role of the dominant Chewa, whose political role and interests cannot be shunted aside by any other group, (b) the easy-going inter-Chewa clan relations, and the non-emergence of supremacist bids by any clique that might have split the Chewa camp, (c) the fact that the Yao and Jumbe Swahili apart, all the groups in the country had been to some extent culturally "Chewaianized" over time, and (d) because political leaders have realized it was futile to try to play the ethnic card in the absence of any deep, historic ethnic animosities.

The country's economic disparities have, however, given rise to regionalist sentiments in the north, that were tightly suppressed during the Banda era, though many of his discriminatory policies actually exacerbated them. Resentments riveted onto the paucity of employment and services in the region; the preferential treatment accorded development projects in the south, and the fact that (in the mid-1970's) Blantyre, with 3.7% of the population, accounted for 66% of gross domestic product, 59% of all jobs in the manufacturing sector, and 26.3% of paid employment in the country.[13] Though such resentments were kept in hand under Banda, increasingly they have emerged into the open. When in 1994 the country voted in its first democratic elections since independence, the results clearly revealed the degree to which the regional split was now total and in the open, with some in the North even guardedly muttering about separate statehood.

Aspects of the Malawi economy

Malawi emerged independent as one of the most underdeveloped countries in the world, and little more than a manpower reserve for the mines of southern Africa. The new state even "lacked the resources with which to maintain its present level of poverty, let alone to embark on development."[14] Industrial activity was nearly non-existent, and what little commerce existed was dominated by expatriates (Asian or European) who also staffed every senior administrative and technical post in the country. A very narrow range of agricultural products brought in over 95% of the country's meagre export-earnings, that appeared resilient to expansion. With monumental infrastructural and developmental tasks facing it, no resources, a large debt, and a minuscule tax-base incapable of covering more than half of the government's recurrent expenses, most observers doubted Malawi's economic viability. Such considerations lay behind the colony's forced 1953 merger into the ill-fated Central African Federation.

For little infrastructure was laid in Nyasaland during its seventy years of colonial rule. Even the country's railroad, the sole tangible colonial heritage, was financed from the colony's resources, and not as elsewhere through colonial grants. Social services were "lifeless and inadequate"[15]. Life expectancy was low, and infant mortality was high. Indeed, despite major post-independence ameliorations, the 1:40,000 doctor/patient ratio of 1986 only brought Malawi up to par with African laggards such as Burundi and Niger. Schools were few and far apart as Britain until the 1950's delegated education to missionary groups. At independence there were only 400 matriculation candidates and 3,000 secondary school pupils in the entire country, with Nyasaland being the only colony to record a declining primary school enrollment in the years prior to independence!

Internal communications were very primitive, with only 300 miles of the country's 6,000 miles of tracks either paved or usable during the rainy season, when urban centers were completely cut off from the countryside. This fact inhibited the emergence of marketing networks, and discouraged the raising of agricultural surpluses since they could not be assured speedy evacuation to processing centers. With access to the outside world (through Mozambique) also cumbersome and costly, prospects of exports were stultified.

Much of Malawi's economic neglect during the colonial era, and current poverty, are a function of the country's costs of conducting trade with the outside world. The principal commercial routes are the railroads to Beira and Ncala in Mozambique (still in disrepair), and the very expensive truck route via Zambia and Zimbabwe to South Africa. Until 1990 Pretoria's support for Renamo, against the regime in Maputo, resulted in repeated minings of the railbeds in Mozambique, causing traffic disruptions, major domestic shortages of fuels and imports, and the stockpiling of local products awaiting evacuation. In 1988, when conditions were so bad that Malawi was forced to use the truck route via South Africa for its more precious exports, shipping costs consumed over 43% of the country's foreign exchange earnings[16], clearly constituting a monumental drag on the economy.

Malawi's major exploitable resources have been its fertile soils and energetic people. Fully 90% of the population is engaged in agriculture, the majority in the smallholder sector that cultivates 80% of the arable land, with maize being the main subsistence crop. Given adequate rainfall, under normal conditions Malawi can be self-sufficient in foodstuffs, and when offered decent producer prices Malawi's farmers can produce bumper harvests and hefty surpluses for export. However, though such exports have been important sources of revenue for farmers, the bulk of Malawi's export earnings (82% in 1986) have come from three cash crops grown primarily on large commercial plantations: tobacco, tea, and sugar. Tobacco production experienced phenomenal growth rates since independence, transforming the crop into Malawi's prime (50%) export. Tea comes second, with Malawi's 35,000 tons a year making it Africa's second largest tea exporter. And sugar, a relatively new crop in the country, by the mid-1970's had displaced cotton and peanuts to become the Malawi's third-largest export, and at times has even nudging tea from its second rank.

The rise of Banda

Banda rose to power by developing a powerful tide of mass nationalism in Nyasaland, that made him the continent's most popularly legitimated leader ever. His political vehicle, the Malawi Congress Party, was the outgrowth of the Nyasaland African Congress, that first convened in Blantyre in 1944 as a grouping of 17 Native Associations many staffed by mission-educated Northerners. This link supports the oft-made observation, that indirectly Livingstonia was the seed-bed of the Malawi Congress Party.[17]

    The NAC had a very checkered history, was plagued by personal rivalries and mismanagement of funds, and was always at the brink of insolvency. Lack of attention to administrative detail kept it an "unorganized collection of branches and affiliated societies" with "an atmosphere of disillusionment and despair pervading it consequent upon its ineffectiveness to achieve significant change."[18] When its campaign of civil disobedience failed to bloc the widely-detested federation with the Rhodesias, the NAC went into a major decline: in 1954 only fifteen of its 300-odd branches were operational, and only one (that in Blantyre) was actually active.

    The NAC was given a new lease on life with the return from

abroad of several young Malawians, including the charismatic 25 year-old Henry Chipembere, son of a Yao Anglican archdeacon, who emerged as their leader. Latching onto mass grievances, and pressing for universal suffrage and self-government, within a few years the group laid the basis for a viable mass movement. But they were unable to fully transform the party into a powerful political vehicle. What was needed, according to Chipembere, was more credible leadership than they themselves could provide. Specifically, an *older* individual was needed if possible, one who would be capable of mobilizing the still age-oriented countryside where the Young Turks were viewed primarily as youthful political upstarts: "a kind of saviour, a prestigious father figure who would provide the dynamic leadership necessary for success."[19]

In the Nyasaland of the 1950's, there were no such candidate for the mantle of leadership. But in London there resided Dr. Hastings Banda, who despite his prolonged absence abroad, had been an active NAC member, supporting the party, both financially and through the important contacts he possessed with British M.P.'s, the Labour Party and the Church of Scotland—all invaluable pressure points above the colonial administration in Zomba. To the young clique Banda seemed also to be the most ideal possible interim leader: as an middle-aged, established professional, they assumed that he could not conceivably harbor any long-term political ambitions that might stand in the way of a succession of the younger clique after his "task" was concluded.

The story of Banda's early personal odyssey is well known[20] and need not be recounted. Born between 1898 and 1902 to a Chewa chief near Kasungu, he entered Livingstonia to be trained as a teacher. Expelled from an examination due to (apparently) a procedural misunderstanding, he then embarked on the well-trodden path to the mines of South Africa. Studying at night, he was eventually sponsored by a missionary group, and proceeded to the United States where he obtaining a BA (in History and Politics), and an MD. Later he attended Edinburgh University, sponsored by the Nyasaland government and the Church of Scotland, of which he was to become an Elder.

Banda set up practice in London to become a respected doctor. There he maintained contact with the NAC, and did his utmost to sway London not to merge Nyasaland with the Rhodesias. However in the mid-1950's Banda was cited in divorce proceedings (allegedly due to a liaison with a married woman), and—as an intensely private and proud individual—unable to tolerate the indignity involved, he uprooted himself to embark on what turned out to be an immensely frustrating medical practice in the Gold Coast. It was during this difficult period in his life, that Chipembere's offer reached him to return after forty years abroad to head the NAC. Far from being the fulfilled individual the Young Turks thought they were inviting home as an interim "front-man", Banda was professionally at a dead end, their offer suddenly providing him with an alternate career, status and prestige.

Banda arrived in Blantyre on July 6, 1958 "cloak[ed] with a certain religious sanction" as a modern-day messiah. His motorcade was welcomed "by groups of ululating women symbolically sweeping the ground with brushwood in front of its path. Because of these histrionics he was immediately recognized as the de facto paramount chief and he rapidly assumed such a position within the minds of the people."[21] Also, despite his long stay overseas he remained "imbued with Chewa social precepts, with their stress on courtesy and respect for elders,"[22] and a world-view "based upon cultural nostalgia and...a rejection of many aspects of the modern world."[23] These traits struck a responsive chord among rural Malawians—also bewildered in a rapidly changing world, which explains Banda's instant legitimation as Malawi's leader when he returned home. A British Commission later noted that "the reverence and adulation with which he was treated everywhere he went was enough to turn the head of even the modest man, and Dr Banda is not that; it would not have crossed his mind that even his unexpressed wish was not law."[24]

However that may be, Banda immediately completely revitalized the political struggle against Britain, and gave it the momentum it had lacked. By 1961 the MCP was by far the most viable militant party in Africa, with a (real) membership of 250,000, and Banda was one of the most popularly legitimated leaders on the continent. Since he had specifically agreed (this had been his condition, to Chipembere, and the MCP) to assume the party's leadership "on his own terms, which were those of a virtual dictator"[25], and it was solely his drive, personality, and charisma in the country that had ultimately forced Britain to disengage Malawi from the Central African Federation, and set it on the road to independence, it would never have crossed Banda's mind that he was not indeed a "dictator by consent."

Reflecting his personal strict insistence on discipline, lack of which that he regarded was the main reason why Africa was backward, intimidating rules were promptly entrenched in the party. "Unity,

Loyalty, Obedience and Discipline" became the sacred tenets of the MCP, that further openly warned "people who discredit Congress would have their names written down"[26]—no idle threat, since there was much talk of compiling a register of punishments to be meted "to traitors" after independence. Later the MCP was to decree that "disloyalty, rumour-mongering, deliberate manufacture of destructive stories, invidious whisper campaigns, loose talk and character assassination against any member of the Party or the Party itself, shall be dealt with in such a manner as the President in his absolute discretion may see fit."[27] Nor was there any hesitation to use intimidation in the quest for political unity—something that was to become a nasty characteristic of public life from this point onwards.[28]

Ultimately the Devlin Report (on the State of Emergency that was imposed by the colonial administration during which Banda and 1,500 others were imprisoned) vindicated Banda's claim that Malawians were unanimously opposed to federation. This set the country's course toward separate statehood, by far "more united, more mobilized, more active than any other in Eastern Africa."[29] The MCP swept the polls in August 1961, gaining an awesome (and real) 99% of the vote in an unheard-off 95% turnout of lower-roll voters. Among opposition candidates, many did not even get one vote, as they feared to appear at the polls to cast their own ballot. The MCP repeated its sweep in the 1964 elections that preceded independence, with opposition groups intimidated from nominating their candidates. Banda's "victory" against Britain on the federation issue, and his leading Malawi to independence, were at the core of his popular legitimation. For thirty years these triumphs were to continue to figure centrally in all his public speeches.

Consolidation of Personal Rule

Despite its image of unity at the polls, the MCP leadership was actually deeply divided. A truly impossible situation had been created by the elevation to absolute power of an idiosyncratic, arch-conservative, domineering elder individual, by a youthful radical clique that saw itself as the country's pacesetters, and the power behind the throne. Three generations separated Banda from his ministers, who were not even born when he began building his own career. To Banda this

age-gap was yet further ground for the need for unquestioning obedience to his policies. Moreover, fundamental policy divisions, papered
over during the struggle for statehood, came to the fore with the
country's independence. It was thus not so much the strong presidency that Banda was to institute in Zomba that was at the heart of
the problem, but rather the policies he espoused. Indeed, four months
before being ousted from office, one of the Young Turks (the radical
Chiume) had argued "there is nothing wrong with dictatorship"[30]; later
he was to lament *Banda's* elevation to the political throne: "We called
him in to solve a problem; we had created one instead by doing so."[31]

Banda developed a habit of acting "with bluster and arrogance...[being] contemptuous, abrasive or intimidating with people
whom he controls or regards inconsequential"[32] thus undermining
the status of his young cabinet ministers. ("I talk to them as children
and they shut up.")[33] He even appealed to "his" masses: "You, the
common people, are the real Congress Party. Watch everybody. Even
Ministers ...Watch them everybody. If they do what you do not think
is good for Malawi, whether they are Ministers or not, come and tell
me...One Party, One Leader, One Government, and no nonsense about
it."[34] When his cabinet revolted at being so completely marginalized,
their "disunity, disloyalty, indiscipline and disobedience"[35] was viewed
by Banda not solely as "a political threat, but also as a personal betrayal...
analogous to the feelings of a father towards a wayward son."[36]

The issues that brought the 1964 crisis were ideological differences over Malawi's international posture vis-a-vis South Africa, Portugal and China (the latter had offered a loan subject to diplomatic
recognition), the retention of Britons in the administration, Banda's
rejection of salary increases for the civil service, and his decision to levy
a token sum (3d) for outpatient treatment in state hospitals. Staunchly
and unabashedly pro-Western ("99% of the time the West is right")[37],
Banda disdained the pan-Africanist and socialist pretentions of his
younger cabinet ministers. The Chinese fiscal overture (that was increased to counter his resistance), was to him *literally* synonymous to
the biblical offer of an apple by the snake—and hence axiomatically
unacceptable. Steeped in the values of thrift, hard work and self-sufficiency, free medical care was to Banda anathema, hence the token
levy he insisted on. And, seeking not to jeopardize the wage remit-
tances of Malawi's 250,000 mine-workers in South Africa, access to the
Portuguese-controlled Indian Ocean port of Beira, and possible invest-

ments from the two world pariahs, more moderate international postures seemed wiser to him. (South African credits later indeed flowed into the country, both for the construction of the country's new capital, and for Malawi's second railway to Ncala.)

Banda was also opposed to rapid Africanization, a very popular issue in urban areas where many Malawians waited to savor the "full" fruits of independence. Though Malawians occupied only 13.5% of the country's 1,271 administrative posts and five of the top 122 professional posts—with Europeans even holding 62% of the lowly clerical/technical posts and those below them[38]—there were less than 1,000 Malawians with a school certificate in the entire country at the time. So "the total number of Malawians in the upper grades of the civil service represented nearly the whole stock of available Malawians with the basic educational requirements,"[39] and Banda was adamant about maintaining quality at all costs. As he put it, much to the ire of youth and urban-dwellers, "I do not want to dismiss any European just because he has a white skin...our African civil servants...must be patient, they must be trained, they must become efficient before they can expect me to promote them into jobs now occupied by Europeans."[40]

Though Banda's policies were unpopular, he felt no need to cater to the interests of urban elements. The majority of those anxious to displace expatriates, moreover, were Northerners, and these were ideologically more attuned to the views of his cabinet colleagues, many of whom also hailed from the north. Banda's power base was (as it continued to be) in the countryside (where 93% of the population resided), and not in the small urban pockets that at the time encompassed barely 360,000 people. Localization did proceed in Malawi, even dramatically (trebling between 1964 and 1972) but at Banda's terms, and with *each* appointee personally screened by him.

The cabinet crisis of 1964 was thus totally unavoidable. Four Ministers were dismissed—including Chirwa (co-founder of the MCP and Malawi's first barrister) and Chiume—and two others resigned. (Chipembere was at the time overseas, but after his return he was to lead a disastrous armed incursion against Banda, as did another early aide of Banda two years later.) The Legislative Assembly for the only time in its history grappled with a real issue, but, personally hand-picked by Banda, confirmed the presidential decision. A dangerous strike in Zomba and Blantyre by what Banda referred to as "yelping intellectuals" and "ambitious parasitic clerks,"[41] enflamed by the ex-

ministers, was subdued by the still expatriate-officered security services and Banda's loyal Malawi Young Pioneers.

Personal Rule under Banda

The 1964 crisis was the only time Banda was ever challenged until the
1990's. His clear-cut victory in 1964 led to purges that cleared the way
for unfettered personal rule, setting the pattern for the remainder of
his reign. Malawi's political and economic policies came to completely
reflect Banda's personal predispositions and his personal interpreta-
tions of Malawi's traditions and goals. The country was strongly
suffused by a conservative and authoritarian ethos aimed at imposing
political unity, national discipline and stability, and in the economic
domain the stress was squarely on large-scale estate agriculture, that
aimed to boost exports and State revenues.

"Unity" for Banda meant a personal monopoly of political
power, thus averting "irrelevant" political and/or policy-disputes. In
privatizing political power, the State became his personal fief, and its
organs were transformed functionally into personal administrative
instrumentalities. For long personally holding at least four portfolios
(those of External Affairs, Justice, Works and Supplies, and Agriculture),
whatever limitations on executive power the country's constitution
originally possessed were whittled away by new legislation. Open
political debate, competitive politics, parliamentary opposition, freedom of association and of the press—features never overly developed
in colonial Malawi—disappeared, to be squarely equated with treason
against Banda's *persona* and by extension against the Malawi nation.

In 1965, with no dissent, Malawi officially became a one party
state, something oratorically justified by one fawning secretary of state
on quasi-theological grounds: "there is no opposition in Heaven. God
himself does not want opposition—that is why he chased Satan away.
Why should Kamuzu have opposition?"[42] Free debate in the Assembly
disappeared in 1965. The Assembly became a rubber stamp that "never
dissents from the President's reports of past and future action but
endorsed both overwhelmingly."[43] Banda unequivocally warned
deputies that "the minute you vote against the Government here, you
yourself are out,"[44] and one MP, to the roaring applause of the
Assembly summed up the ornamental role of the House by noting that

"the coming of members to parliament to pass laws is just a formality, otherwise Ngwazi [Banda] himself is enough to make laws for us. We happen to be here, Mr. Speaker, just to fulfil the procedure of making laws."[45] And in 1970, as a mere formality, the MCP amended the Constitution to make Banda President for Life.

As permanent head of the Malawi Congress Party Banda could now expel any member at will, and personally screened all applications for party membership that, though formally not obligatory, was virtually a pre-condition for any senior post in the country. As he also prepared the MCP lists for all elections, expulsion from the party for elected officials meant not only loss of a parliamentary seat, but also a likely loss of economic livelihood since Banda controlled all business licenses in the country as well. Hence the extreme deference of all freshmen members of parliament in their traditional maiden speech that without fail profoundly eulogized Banda, and thanked him for selecting them to "run" for office. The sycophancy in this ritual can be gauged from an extract from one such speech: "Allow me to name only a few of the things that make our Leader, the Lion of Malawi, the greatest man: (l) He is an upright Christian gentleman; (2) He is a most courageous man; (3) He is the greatest humanitarian; (4) He is the greatest scholar and historian; (5) He is the greatest nation-builder Malawi has ever had; (6) he is the greatest orator in Malawi if not in the World [applause]; (7) He is the greatest teacher. If I have to elaborate this, Mr. Speaker, allow me to do so."[46]

Extreme deference to Banda permeated even working sessions with age-old political allies. When the inner circle of the MCP used to meet in Banda's drawing room, for instance, all members always avoided assuming positions of physical prominence, and never showed zeal in any policy discussion, lest that be misinterpreted as lack of respect for Banda, or possibly even political ambition. It was noted once that Chirwa, the then-Secretary General of the MCP (and in theory the country's second most-important politician after Banda, but hence also the most vulnerable to such accusations), invariably tended to assume a position at such meetings by sitting on the floor at Banda's feet, the ultimate symbol of submission and humility.

Despite Banda's clear paramountcy in Malawi, considerable effort was expended to project the *appearance* of popular consultation of party leaders on both policy issues and in the compilation of MCP election lists, and Banda usually followed proper administrative pro-

cedures. This blend of formal democratic procedure and actual autocratic decision-making was for long a basic feature of Malawi public
life. It was best visible in the manner in which MCP electoral lists were
compiled for national election. Up to 5,000 MCP militants (members
of the League of Malawi Women, League of Malawi Youth, MCP district
committees, mayors, chiefs and subchiefs) used to participate in a
lengthy process of nominating and screening delegates, with constituency screening panels called upon to submit up to five rank-ordered
nominees for Banda's ultimate selection. Notwithstanding the cumbersome and lengthy process, in several instances Banda rejected *all* of
the names tendered to him, and in *half* the cases he refused to nominate
either the first or second-ranked delegate.

Later, stung by foreign criticism that Malawi elections were
meaningless, a multiplicity of party-approved candidates were allowed
to compete against each other in each constituency, starting with the
elections of 1978. Yet, despite the greater freedoms granted to districts
in compiling electoral lists, Banda still retained veto power, that he
exercised extensively. Moreover, English literacy tests were reintro-
duced. Stiffer than the ones dropped in 1964, these tests whittled
down delegate lists, in many instances to zero. In 1978 there were only
47 electoral contests in the country, and some districts were not
represented at all since no candidate could pass the tests. With serious
politicking not allowed—"people know whether a candidate is a good
man or not from personal experience. No candidate can be allowed to
try and persuade the electorate that he is a good person"—[47], not
surprisingly foreign assessments about Malawi's elections have always
been harsh.

On top of this a strict censorship code banned sending reports
overseas of events embarrassing to the regime, and insulated the
country from "dangerous" influences. In 1970 the Prohibited Publications Act allowed Banda to ban publications deemed objectionable for
whatever reason. The press had all along been tightly controlled. Local
reporters periodically were reprimanded or arrested for publishing
offensive material, and foreign journalists, screened by Banda himself
since 1973, were only tolerated subject to their submitting favorable
reports.

Yet though there was neither a viable legislature nor a free press
in Malawi until the liberalizations of the 1990's, a certain latitude for
"responsible" debate did exist, that defied categorization of the country

as nothing more than a run-of-the-mill dictatorship that it certainly was not. By African standards Malawi's political system was relatively institutionalized, and proper procedures played a significant role. The MCP was active in many domains, and in many districts, and surprisingly open debate was possible on most *local* issues during party branch meetings. Indeed, a very great degree of debate actually took place at these venues, and considerable criticism openly and freely spilled out against haughty ministers, corrupt party chairmen, and the paucity of state services in the countryside. And even when discussion at times latched onto ultra-sensitive issues normally totally taboo (at the pain of imprisonment) in Lilongwe (e.g. the succession issue), it was tolerated at rural levels, since it did not challenge Banda, was couched as an attempt to convey to him the concerns of his loyal people, and was manifested in the "proper" venue, and in a "responsible" manner!

On the other hand, Banda freely flouted judicial processes when these offended his perceptions of justice. Examples abound, but the classic case occurred after the judicial acquittals (for lack of evidence) in the politically charged Chilobwe murder cases that involved a spate of grisly Mfiti ritual killings in Blantyre and Lilongwe with significant destabilizing overtones.[48] Banda refused to free the accused, arguing justice had not been served due to what he regarded as "Western" technicalities: "No matter what the Judges are saying [I am] in charge here, not the Judges."[49] Legislation was subsequently promulgated that enhanced the jurisdiction and powers of traditional courts (something that led to the resignation of all the High Court judges, who were mostly expatriate), so that in the future "the Malawian sense of justice will...prevail."[50] It was to these traditional courts that many of Banda's political foes were subsequently sent for trial. And when even some of these courts acquitted individuals with local grassroot support, Banda did not hesitate to override and purge the "disloyal" judges since "lack of evidence is not proof of innocence...in this country, among the Africans, the court is not above the law, it is not above public opinion."[51]

Nor were expatriates immune from Banda's wrath. Already in September 1969 Peace Corps activities were terminated allegedly because of complaints about their "slovenliness," and in 1971 an American instructor at the local University who protested harassment of Jehovah Witnesses was without ceremony expelled from the country. So was an English woman who publicly referred to a Banda speech as "rubbish," and others were expelled for derogatory remarks made about the MCP or the Malawi Young Pioneers. Expatriates were hauled into court and fined for violations of the Malawi dress code—often being reported to the police by their own domestic help or normal Malawians—and one woman who defied the ban on miniskirts was even deported. A more draconian instance in 1976 saw 250 Asians of Goan descent expelled for gross "disrespect" of local sensitivities—they had switched off a broadcast of Banda's speech during a wedding reception.

Manoeuvring for political primacy

Greater dangers existed for Malawians near the pinnacle of power, as the constant expulsions (and occasional liquidations) of party members, district chairmen and Secretary Generals attested to. Most were ousted on the amorphous grounds of "gross breach of party discipline"—that really meant anything that Banda found objectionable. Every year between 1970 and 1980 an average of seven Malawi constituencies remained unrepresented in Parliament due to such expulsions; and of the 150 members expelled during 1964-81, forty ended up in prison. Only two of ten who voluntarily resigned from Parliament during this period remained at liberty.[52] Yet though the danger in seeking political office was high, competition—in a country with no alternate sources of power—remained fierce, with factions continuously manoeuvring for position.

One persistent feature of the Banda era was the fall from grace of every potential dauphine. The position of Secretary General of the MCP, in particular, was *not* the gateway to power, as most incumbents were to discover. Banda jealously guarded his power-base, aware "the danger to [his] rule comes not from any likely popular uprising, but from a 'palace coup' within his own ruling party."[53] And though his suspicions were always riveted to the North, all challenges that surfaced were actually from his own Central Region.

The mid-1970's were in particular tumultuous years. In 1975 an internal power-struggle camouflaged as a conspiracy erupted, bringing in its wake repression that engulfed the entire country. Over 300 Northerners, mostly Tongan, were imprisoned in Zomba, among them all sixteen members of the National Statistical Office and two Ministerial statisticians! In February 1976 the only remaining prominent northern Minister was purged as Attorney General and Minister of Justice. The University, always seen as inciting students against the regime, had its Principal, Registrar, and many lecturers and students arrested. Banda also appealed to the masses for ultra-vigilance since no one was inherently trustworthy: "not even ministers, clerks, students, pupils. Wives of soldiers should not trust their husbands, they can all be traitors even if they had party membership cards."[54] At the height of the repression over 2,000 political prisoners languished in detention camps.

The crisis abated with the arrest of MCP Secretary General Albert Muwalo Nqumayo, a political baron with a base in Karonga. He was tried (at the Southern Regional Traditional Court) for sedition and hanged in September 1977. Arrested with him, and also hanged, was Focus Gwede, the Special Branch police commander. Both were found guilty of being in league with opposition elements abroad, and of storing arms in preparation for a violent upheaval. Nqumayo (later linked to the Chilobwe murders) was blamed for fanning unrest via the repression of Northerners, and of tricking a trusting Banda to sign the detention orders of 1975/76, becoming the scapegoat for the repression. After the trials tension abated as most of the detainees were released, though few were ever rehabilitated.

In 1980 the three most influential people in Malawi after Banda lost their posts because "the power accumulated by these men was in itself enough to ensure their downfall."[55] One of these was the pillar of the regime, cabinet minister Gwanda Chakuamba, who was also Parliamentary Chief Whip, MCP chairman for the Southern Region and member of the Executive Committee, and Head of the Malawi Young Pioneers. Placed on trial for sedition, Chakuamba was charged with possessing two pistols, prohibited publications, a photo of Nqumayo, and of owning two fly-whisks—symbols of authority used only by Banda. He was sentenced to 22 years in prison: paradoxically in the 1994 free elections he (the jailee) and Banda (the jailor) were Presidential running mates on the MCP party ticket!

In 1980 another MCP Secretary General (currently President of Malawi) fell from grace, Bakili Muluzi. And in May 1983 his own successor, the very popular Dick Matenje (and several cabinet ministers suspected of disloyalty) were liquidated—the sole crimes for which Banda was actually charged in 1995. (It was originally alleged the group died in a "car accident," after Radio Malawi announced they were being sought by the police. Their bodies were not returned to their families, but hastily buried.) Indeed between 1976 and 1983 all four MCP Secretary Generals were killed or executed (Nqumayo; Matenje), or purged from their posts (Aleke Banda, and Muluzi), with similar eclipses of secondary MCP leaders.

At times these purges were due to Banda's ire over speculation about his successor, the most taboo subject ever in Malawi. Such was the case with Aleke Banda (currently Finance Minister) who was purged after being named in the *Times of Zambia* as Banda's heir-apparent, but also because he raised questions about misuse of funds by the regime. In other instances Banda moved to eliminate emerging power barons. And in yet other cases, rumours of disloyalty were spread by power aspirants, in order to torpedo the prospects of anyone who might be emerging in an overly strong political position.

For increasingly in the 1980's the succession issue, and, specifically, the question of John Tembo's presidential "prospects" dominated Malawi's rumour-mills. Tembo, a Ngoni from Dedza, had been Malawi's first Finance Minister, and between 1971 and 1984 Governor of the Reserve Bank. For reasons totally unclear (and, indeed, a major mystery) he had for long been a favorite of Banda, and though with powerful allies in the Police, was intensely disliked in Malawi. A curious Banda proposal to set up a Tembo Vice-Presidency (that would have given the latter a stepping-stone to power) was blocked by an MCP group headed by Matenje. Matenje's liquidation (no one believed the "accident" story) was thus at the time seen as a settling of scores, with or without the knowledge of Banda.[56] Later, in 1988-89 (as Banda's senility became visible) the successive rise and fall of four Heads of the Police was also symptomatic of the raging tug-of-war between pro- and anti- Tembo forces, underscoring the centrality of the succession issue in Malawi.

The Succession Issue

Because of the highly personalist nature of power in Malawi, as Banda aged the central issue facing the country became increasingly the succession issue. For whatever the ultimate verdict about the Banda era (and it maybe be too early to pass a balanced judgement), one of the harshest indictments against it may be that by totally freezing politics for thirty years, it kept Malawians political neophytes.

Not that speculation about the future was not rife, and political maneuverings were absent. But any overt talk about Banda's likely successor was *prima facia* evidence of treasonable intent. Short of actually aspiring to succeed Banda, the surest way to fall from grace was to *appear* to be in line for the succession. And the best way to deflect attention from one's political prominence was to adopt a supine demeanour, while conniving to assure that no one else moved closer to the Presidency.

In 1992 Banda was ninety-four years old and showing signs of senility. Yet he still believed himself utterly indispensable, endlessly remonstrating how without him Malawians would not have food and shelter, and would be gobbled up by more powerful neighbors. His ego had been constantly reinforced reinforced by external praise for Malawi's economic attainments. (Mrs. Thatcher, no less, had referred to Malawi as a "model to Africa"[57] during Banda's State Visit to London, a point he loved recounting.) And convinced of the correctness of his policies, both political (keeping divisive and wasteful "political activity" out of the country) and economic (bolstering the export sector) he continued to tolerate no strong personalities around him. Consequently, not only was no heir groomed ("Dr. Banda does not like heir-apparents")[58], but even interim procedures were eschewed. Potential successors were emasculated pre-emptively; and if any did appear to be emerging, fluid camps of MCP influentials ganged up to prevent any "unfair" advantage prior to the actual crisis.

The succession issue was actually broached once, in 1987, by Banda himself. At a meeting of senior MCP branch leaders Banda suddenly sought guidance—which he never did—asking, "What shall we do after I go, who shall we support?" Eyewitnesses note how immediately all those present looked down, afraid to be called upon to speak on the issue, certain the question was merely rhetorical, solely aimed at flushing out traitors.[59] Banda's attention was deftly deflected to other, less dangerous questions, but rumours promptly abounded that he was grooming a successor—Tembo.

For squarely within the Malawi political vacuum of the late 1980's stood a seemingly irreplaceable Tembo juggernaut family clique. An ambitious, rich opportunist, Tembo had no MCP power base or influence. His main support was in the budding business community (that he courted as head of the Reserve Bank), and among allies in the

Police where Ngoni were found in larger numbers, and where petty police-army intra-mural competitions also gave him an edge. Tembo's survival through all the shuffles in Malawi rankled many who had been purged for far lesser accumulation of influence.

The "Kadzamira-Tembo clique" included a brother heading the ADMARC economic giant. His (also wealthy) niece, Cecilia Kadzamira, was Banda's "Official Hostess" who controlled the portals of the Presidency, several women's groups, and was also the *eminent grise* in cultural matters. Her two brothers in turn were Vice Chancellor of the University, and Postmaster General of Malawi, and her uncle (Dr. Hetherwick Ntaba) was the Presidential physician. Several other secondary family members in the publishing, banking and diplomatic fields, further attested to the importance of this clique.

Notwithstanding his abrasiveness, his not being Chewa, his poor repute in foreign circles—where he was regarded incompetent, it being foreign pressure that caused him to lose his post in the Reserve Bank in 1983—and pressure from both Commanders of the Police and Army (Kamwana and Khanga) against Tembo's appointment to any high post[60], he was nevertheless appointed Banda's official Chichewa interpreter (a highly visible post), subsequently joining the MCP Executive as Acting Treasurer of the Party. And as Tembo's stature grew and Banda's health declined, the succession issue became the dominant issue in the 1990's.

Towards a Malawi Economic Miracle?

It will be recalled that at independence "outsiders did not rate Malawi's developmental chances highly."[61] The country was virtually insolvent, and with half of the recurrent budget met by British subventions, no one expected Malawi could attract much investment capital. Malawi confounded sceptics, however, to become one of a few states in Africa to attain sustained economic growth. Indeed, Malawi very early acquired the reputation of a country with "an efficient bureaucracy, stable political leadership, and confidence in the economy,"[62] with Banda being credited with having "concentrated on getting things done... administered the country and implemented its development program with considerable efficiency, and with a marked absence of corruption..."[63]

Budgetary balance was rapidly attained, with British subsidies being renounced two years ahead of schedule. State revenues tripled in the first decade with tight controls on expenditures. Between 1960 and 1976 Malawi chalked up Africa's third-highest GNP per capita growth rate (4.1% per year), with annual growth averaging 12% during the first decade, or 5.5% through 1980 that includes the 1977-79 recessionary years. Moreover, Malawi had one of the best *global* records of long-run growth in food production, despite a recession, the cost of evacuating produce through overland routes, a balance of payments crisis and other structural difficulties requiring debt restructuring.

That one of Africa's bleakest economies could attain such dramatic growth, fuelled by agrarian advances to boot, lent credence to donor views that other states could/should go the "Malawi route." When Malawi floated its first Euroloan ($25 million, for the construction of Lilongwe's International Airport) it was oversubscribed; later, the favorable terms at which Malawi's debt was rescheduled (debt servicing remained 44% of export earnings in the 1980's), was another manifestation of global confidence in the country.[64]

Consensus about Malawi's strong growth was increasingly tempered, however, by controversy about whether it represented meaningful development, and later, about whether the social costs involved were justifiable[65]—since the policies pursued were grossly discriminatory of small farmers. As one observer put it, "independence has broken the rigidity of the political economy that Malawi inherited from the colonial era, but it has not altered its essence,"[66] with the Malawi economic miracle being essentially "an efficient execution of the basic structures developed in the period from 1890 to 1910."[67]

Like all else in Malawi, the tenets of the country's economic policy have been set by Banda, reflecting his own orientations and concerns. Despite some experimentation in the first years of independence, Malawi's strategy until the mid-1980's (when IMF and World Bank pressures became more insistent) has been virtually unchanged. The main thrust was on increasing State revenues, the economy being run as a vast commercial enterprise with cost-benefit considerations dictating policy. State "activities" that were regarded as unproductive (e.g. social services), or unlikely to produce profits (the smallholder sector), were largely left alone in favor of others (cash-crop estates) that could generate exports and hence State revenues. A highly technocratic regime thus emerged in Lilongwe under the iron guidance of Banda, who supervised all execution of economic projects from the Presidential Office.

There were several components in Malawi's developmental strategy. Priority was given to disengage the country from demeaning external subventions. Secondly, large investments were made on a massive upgrading of the country's physical infrastructure (roads and railways), and to train indigenous technical cadres, the latter at the expense of expanding primary education. Third, import-substitution drives were mounted for which foreign capital was courted, and where not forthcoming, State funds were committed.[68] Commerce was also brought into African (as opposed to Asian) hands in the countryside. Several early (and not too successful) efforts to promote smallholder agriculture were aborted, since the keystone of Malawi's economic thrust was always on a "particularly impressive" emphasis on promotion of large-scale export-oriented plantation agriculture, aimed at generating funds for other developmental efforts.[69]

Eliminating Malawi's budgetary insolvency was Banda's first goal, since fiscal dependence on Britain was a personal affront to him. Increased taxation on an expanded tax base, fiscal restraint, cuts in expenditures, and a shift from free social services led to a balanced budget. Rigid wage restraint remained a basic feature in Malawi, and the union movement was neutralized by being absorbed into the MCP. Minimum wages remained frozen during 1966-1974 despite a 30% rise in the cost of living during this period. Though attracting foreign criticism, keeping urban salaries low discouraged rural-urban drifts, since cash-crop farmers could make more money than urban dwellers.

But Banda's clampdown on costs was not even-handed. Major price-tag projects close to his heart were exempt from fiscal stringency: the new capital, the elitist Kamuzu Academy, and Banda's "Hadrian-like obsession for building state-residences."[70] Spending on these was totally out of proportion with Malawi's resources. In 1983-4 the presidential mansions (in which he rarely resides) gobbled up 71-84% of public construction expenditures[71], and even during the height of the recession of 1978-80, while other projects were terminated in midstream, work on the Kamuzu Academy at Kasungu proceeded unabated.[72]

Though the strict regimen was alleviated in due course, Banda eschewed "distributionist" policies that he viewed as drains on Malawi's scarce resources. The low priority given to social services was visible to his last days in office. Health care and education lagged badly in Malawi: during 1964-1980 only 2.2% (and in some years barely 1%) of new development funds were spend on health infrastructure, much of it for Lilongwe's Hospital. The renunciation of the State's responsibility over expanding health care services assured the primacy of missionary health activities as in colonial days. A decade after independence Malawi only had 1.43 hospital beds per 1,000 people. Infant mortality, standing at 171 per 1,000 births, was one of the highest in Africa, and was the seventh-highest of the 25 LDC's with which Malawi is grouped. Life expectancy was 44 years, and malnutrition was rife despite a productive peasant sector. Hence the conclusion of some that "the great majority of the population cannot have experienced much improvement in welfare levels since independence."[73]

Advances in education were attained but only in accord with Banda's sense of priorities. Until the 1980's the emphasis was on expanding secondary and tertiary education. The latter alone consumed 40% of Malawi's education budget. These were deemed of priority since they could alleviate the shortage of skilled manpower that was a "most important constraint on Malawi's development potential."[74] Though this in due course raised the percentage of qualified teachers (to 85%), the spread of primary education remained roughly one third of school-age children—among the lowest ratios in Anglophone Africa. This dramatically changed in October 1994 when the successor Muluzi regime very reluctantly implemented an electoral promise of universal primary education—to face total chaos as pupils doubled to three million, with neither textbooks nor facilities available for them, and the awesome financial burden of having to recruit and train an additional 19,000 new teachers!

Growth without Development?

It is when one examines the stress on estate agriculture that one comes to the real heart of the controversy about Banda's economic policies. For the key ingredient in Malawi's economic transformation, currently also being somewhat reversed, was a "growth oriented, export-led strategy of development."[75]

The government did not completely ignore smallholder agriculture, as some have argued. Rather, disillusioned with the mixed results of efforts in 1966-74 to raise crops in the subsistence sector and shift cultivation patterns to the more lucrative cash crops, the regime de-prioritized the smallholder sector. Significantly, however (and part of the World Bank's current changed thrust), whenever peasants were offered *realistic* producer prices (as in the 1980's) bumper harvests of subsistence crops did ensue. However the pricing policy of ADMARC (the marketing board), was geared at generating State profits to be invested *not* in the peasant sector but in more cost-productive sectors of the economy—including new State plantations. Thus, despite some early experimentation and capital infusions Lilongwe "largely abandon[ed]...the peasantry as possible sources of real growth...in a way not done since the 1890's."[76] Banda himself has stressed that development would proceed much faster in Malawi if "responsible" elements entered agriculture, with direct State encouragement via ample loans: "Every Minister must have an estate...I am right up to my neck in debts, but I will pay the debt one day."[77]

Thus, estate agriculture was pampered by Banda *because* it was the only sector likely to generate profits that could sustain the transformation of the country. Under Banda's guidance, and harnessing all resources (including preferential allocations of land), Malawi recorded a 650% increase in exports between 1965-1978, and by 1982 the plantations' share of exports had risen to 80% from 32% in 1967. The plantation sector, "long an embarrassment to the colonial state, has blossomed at last; the peasant sector, long the hope of optimistic colonial administrators, is being throttled and the migrant labor sector remains what it always was: a way to escape from the grim situation in the country."[78]

State pricing, wage and loan policies were central to the flourishing of estate agriculture. ADMARC's pricing policies diverted profits from farmers in one of the poorest LDC, entrenching poverty and directly discouraging growth in subsistence crops. At the same time Lilongwe's policy of wage restraint kept costs of production on plantations low, with labor legislation virtually forcing migrant labour to seek employment on the estates. To provide ample finance for commercial agriculture Lilongwe also gained early control over most banks. By contrast peasants were forced to sell their produce to ADMARC at prices, as elsewhere in Africa,[79] substantially below global prices. Even the option of smuggling produce across national borders was not possible in Malawi in light of the even poorer prices and economic conditions in neighboring countries: indeed, ADMARC actually captured a significant portion of both Mozambique's and Zambia's agrarian produce.[80] In 1980 the output of estate crops was twice that of smallholders, the gap continuing to widen[81] with peasant incomes depressed, falling in real per-capita terms and relative to estate wages, with farmers even deserting their own land.[82] Estate employment on the other hand doubled during 1968-1976 and more since, notwithstanding low wages. In 1980 fully 50.8% of salaried employment was in estate agriculture producing novel patterns of rural-to-rural migrations since plantations are not equally distributed geographically in Malawi.[83]

Though the *thangata* system that coerced labour into the plantation economy during colonial days was long dead, the relative stagnation of employment opportunities and peasant incomes outside estates attained similar results after independence. Wage increases were few and far apart, during the Banda years, assuring plantations cheap labour "highly reminiscent of earlier British colonial policies, but carried out with a thoroughness that only an independent government without local political opposition could dare."[84] (Reports that Malawi plantations employed child labor at wages as low as $7 per month evoked major negative comment abroad in 1979.) The fact that agrarian employment was available in Malawi (and urban work non-existent, or less remunerative) kept destabilizing rural-urban drifts at bay. Though Malawi's urban population more than doubled, the country's urban component remained below ten percent of the entire population.

Thomas pinpoints the core dilemma in attempts to assess Banda's economic policies, the ultimate rationale for 'dictatorship by consent.' "If success...is to be judged by the achievement of the government's objectives, then Banda has, indeed, been very successful...[but] because of his inability to change traditional agriculture radically while preserving stability, Banda has sacrificed long term development for short run economic growth."[85] The criticism is clearly valid, but the issue could also be posed along the familiar question of whether growth without development is preferable to no growth as well as no development? Morton's early verdict was "given the constraints under which the government was operating, the apparent imbalance that has occurred with economic growth should not be too severely criticized. The test of government's good intentions will have to made in later years."[86] Banda remained steady in his emphasis on estate agriculture until forced to moderate his policies somewhat by the World Bank in 1987: Muluzi by contrast in May 1995 announced plans to redistribute estate lands to peasants.

Malawi's sources of civil-military stability

What were the sources of Malawi's civil-military stability during the lengthy Banda era? How can one explain the generally easy-going civil-military relations in the country, and the stability of the civilian political center for nearly three decades? What factors bound so tightly the country's armed forces to civilian rule in Malawi, especially to an aging, idiosyncratic, and autocratic leader, where elsewhere on the continent such subordination has eluded benign democrat and personal dictator alike?

The stability of the civilian order in Malawi always rested, as all political power indeed always rests, on a *blend* of moral authority (legitimacy) and coercive force. While one cannot ignore the powerful intimidatory features of the Banda regime, one cannot likewise not deny its significant legitimation in many strata of society. Since mere political quiescence can never be automatically equated with political support, in the absence of objective criteria about Banda's levels of support in the country, assessments of the regime in the past ran the gamut from "benign autocracy" through "the most efficient police state" in Africa.[87] In general, however, the oppressive features of the Banda reign have been stressed, while the regime's many sources of support and staying powers were ignored or deeply discounted. Yet repression alone cannot sustain a regime for three decades, especially since Banda's Malawi was not a brute dictatorship: indeed, to empiricists, within the African group of authoritarian regimes, Banda's Malawi was a very mild cousin! Both Banda, and the MCP itself, as Forster recently reminds us, were "characterized by a remarkably high degree of legitimacy."[88]

Banda's lengthy rule in Malawi was sustained by a number of factors, some unique to the country, and all of which conferred the regime systemic legitimacy. This was cogently visible in both the referendum (on multipartyism) and elections in the 1990's. Critics focus on the fact that Banda was ousted. What may be more significant, in a country where ethnicity is *not* a factor that can explain a leader's hold over his clientele, is that one third of the electorate freely voted for a ninety-five year-old leader who had been at the apex of power for over three decades!

Among these factors one can note (a) Banda's personal charisma, buttressed by his very real role as Malawi's founding father; (b) in the context of a population largely rural, conservative, religious, docile, respectful of age; (c) still swayed by traditional chiefs and local leaders fearful of urban influences, whose status and powers Banda augmented (and whom Muluzi, in 1994, consciously reassured, and to whom he pledged a state salary!); (d) within a society geographically isolated from external destabilizing influences and ideas; (e) characterized by a striking absence of (until recently) major rural-urban disparities, rural-urban drift, and with a low level of unemployment; (f) within which youth was integrated into supportive para-military units (regarded some as "mere thugs") with a psychologically satisfying societal role; (g) with all potential fissiparous tendencies quelled by Banda's total control over patronage and advancement; (h) with the ultimate sanction of arrest, detention, purges, and the occasional liquidation.

Within this context the sustaining pillars of the regime were (1) its security forces, leashed into supportive a-political roles by its largely Chewa/Lomwe commanding officer hierarchy, and (2) the country's political institutions: the pervasive, tightly organized MCP and ancillary organs, staffed by Banda loyalists, that reached into every hamlet to inspire a measure of popular participation, while assuring conformity.

In assessing the roots of civil-military stability in Lilongwe it is crucial not to lose sight of the stabilizing societal, or cultural, factors in Malawi. As Williams has stressed in a different context, "government policy in Malawi cannot be explained simply by reference to Dr. Banda's idiosyncratic personality, although there are few countries in which there is greater opportunity for a strong man to determine not only the answers that people will be given but the questions they ask."[89] The stability of the civilian order in Malawi was enhanced, even manipulated[90] by Banda, but has to be seen within the context of a society with powerful internal sources of stability.

Of major import, for example, is the fact that ethnicity plays only a minimal polarizing role in Malawi. Despite frictions attending the Ngoni invasions, and animosities set loose by the ravages of the slave raids in the 19th century, ethnic strife has historically been muted in the country. It has never been difficult to mix ethnicities in development schemes or new villages, something completely impossible in many other countries, especially in West Africa. Intermarriage is very common in Malawi, and even chiefly lineages are scrambled across ethnic lines. In the Southern Region, for example, there are Lomwe (newcomers!) chiefs ruling Nyanja subjects, as well as Nyanja ruling Lomwe. There are also Yao chiefs presiding over Lomwe, and in Mulanje the Sena have attached themselves wholescale to the existing Nyanja headmen in their district.

Marked similarities in cultural backgrounds and cosmologies of many of the ethnic groups, and their slow acculturation has resulted in a significant measure of ethno-linguistic uniformity that pulls the diverse strands of the population together. Note has been made of the process of Chewaianization in Malawi visible even before colonialism. This was given a formal impetus in 1968 when Chichewa was decreed the official language of the country alongside English, playing a cementing role in a country where the 1966 census revealed 75% of the population was conversant with Chichewa as either a first or second language. New immigrant communities (Lomwe and Sena) have been integrated into the national amalgam with remarkably little visible strain or friction.

Nor was ethnicity a major factor in the pre-independence period when competitive parties could emerge. And religious divisions have also not resulted, as elsewhere in Africa, in political friction. All this despite the fact that a large percentage of the early political/religious leaders in Nyasaland were Tonga/Tumbuka, and Presbyterian. These integrative features of Malawi stem in part from the absence of large or powerful kingdoms in the region that might have retained allegiances into the modern era. The pre-colonial scene was fragmented, with only the small Ngonde kingdom in the Far North having strong internal unity. The invading Ngoni were never united, and numerically few, they were susceptible to assimilation to the host culture. And even the Chewa's numerical superiority was diluted by their internal division into a multiplicity of clans and decentralized political systems. Moreover, every group except the Ngoni, had been defeated by one or another of their neighbors or by Arab slave-raiders, making the residual ethnic mosaic relatively weak and susceptible to centralization under a powerful national leader such as Banda.

Malawi chiefs have also been relatively weak. During the slave era many lost status and significant authority, and they were not subsequently given any particular standing in the administrative setup of colonial Nyasaland. Their relative weakness allowed the emergence of modern political leaders not beholden to traditional authority or seeking ethnic support. And common opposition to the colonial Central African Federation facilitated the emergence of a united national party.

Moreover, in the largely rural Malawi traditional norms and life-styles were never pulverized: "most Malawians still lived in an environment where rights and duties were defined by tradition, and where conformity and cohesion were emphasized...[and] honour accrued with age," providing a continued role for chiefs. After independence Banda augmented their powers "making them integral parts of party conferences, involving them in the selection of parliamentary candidates, and describing geographical areas by the senior chief's name." Later, traditional courts were given significant powers in adjudicating cases under the criteria of indigenous justice.

Much of the population had also experienced the culturally wrenching experience of working outside Malawi. Exposure to conditions outside parochial Malawi broadened the horizons of those who returned home, eroded feelings of ethnic exclusivity that some may have originally possessed, if only because they were collectively regarded abroad as "Nyassas," lived in the same quarters and spoke a common language, Chinyanja. A greater sense of commonality thus emerged, as many Tonga, Tumbuka, Yao, as well as Chewa, came to think of themselves primarily as Nyassas, abetting the process of nation-building on their return home, or at least preventing further national splinterization.

With a greater cosmopolitan veneer, with personal acquaintance of some of the harsher problems of a southern Africa afflicted by racism and discrimination, many came to be less critical of the slow evolution of Malawi, and more proud of that haven of peace under Banda.[91] As Hodder-Williams has argued, even northern migrant workers coming back from sojourns abroad supported the status-quo, and not change, in essence voluntarily "exchanging the frustrations of an urban and racially segregated habitat for the security of the rural and egalitarian home...[to] strengthen the traditional forces in Malawi and so support the status quo."[92] These cementing features of Malawi, Banda's con-

stant exhortations for unity, and his tight control over society, prevented the politicization of Northern gripes. His very strong anti-
Northern biases, however, inevitably heightened incipient regionalism
that burst out into the open once the central political vise was relaxed.

All of these factors are crucial in any assessment of Malawi's
sources of stability, and Banda's ability to establish a relatively legitimated system. His control over society could have easily slipped, and
rapidly too, had it relied solely, or even mostly, on means of coercion.
Moreover the armed forces themselves most certainly not have sustained the regime for three decades, were it devoid of popularly
ascribed legitimacy. Banda's natural constituency was the traditional
countryside that respected firmness and deeply suspected "city-boys."
From the very outset the groups that coalesced behind him—and
whose support he retained to the very end—were the less educated
and economically successful; older politicians jealous of young cabinet
ministers; and "chiefs and headmen whose authority nationalist politicians had done much to weaken."[93] As Ross noted about Banda's
power-base, "in seeking a personal base of power [Banda] turned not
to a tribe, but to the whole class of people left aside by the rise of the
new men...[creating] a social counter-revolution."[94] The roots of his
legitimacy was in the countryside. He acted "more like an old African
king than perhaps any other head of state, but without any traditional
limitations to his power. He cultivates supernatural connections. He
blesses the peasants' crops. He exploits traditional cults like the secret
Nyau society of the Chewa people."[95]

Malawi's Nyau traditional rites, widely ignored by academics,
yet "a central feature of Chewa culture for many centuries"[96] and still
widely practised in Malawi, were also used to powerfully solidify
Banda's legitimacy, since "to dance Nyau was to support traditional
society and to show respect for the elders."[97] During colonialism Nyau
secret societies had been hounded by the British since they reflected
opposition to alien control and missionaries. After independence Nyau
was given new respectability. Publicly praised by Banda, including in
speeches in the Legislative Assembly, all Independence Day celebrations contained abbreviated Nyau dances, in which Banda personally
participated.

Though the original need to stress one's "Chewaness" and ward
off alien contamination may have since objectively disappeared, Banda
helped revive Nyau in the countryside, creating a context whereby "in

many districts Nyau membership is far more meaningful to Chewa villagers than party membership."[98] During the Banda era MCP branches in Chewa districts directly associated themselves with Nyau societies, the police "notoriously reluctant to prosecute for offences associated with Nyau because of their fear of reprisals."[99] The popularity of Nyau, and its association with traditional authority, was widely used by Banda to consolidate his legitimacy in the countryside, and through it by definition throughout the polity. Traditional Chiwoda dances "once used to mobilize peasants against the colonial power, have been used to praise Banda and pour scorn on his opponents."[100] Nyau was harnessed to "frighten the average Malawian into obedience, and complements Dr. Banda's reputation of being not only a medical doctor but a witch doctor as well,"[101] keeping the countryside secure from the "negative influences" of modernizing missionary-educated elites.[102]

Nor did Banda ignore developing a power base among women, who were amongst his strongest supporters in rural areas. "Banda likes to portray himself as the male guardian of the Mbumba, the women's compounds of south and central Malawi, so that he is considered a women's president in particular."[103] Both directly and through the Official Hostess, Banda furthered (some) interests of Malawi's women (the dress code, the beer licensing monopoly of the League of Malawi Women, etc.), building up the LMW and the *Chitikako cha aMai m'Malawi* into important bulwarks of support. However, Cecilia Kadzamira's progressive unpopularity in the country, and the regime's lack of support for smallholder agriculture hit hard against the very large number of female-headed agrarian households in the country, preventing the fullest-possible manifestation of this support. Still, exit-poll surveys emphasize how well Banda did among women voters in 1994!

Also supportive of the stability of the Banda reign was the low level of unemployment in the country. Productive labor had viable outlets in the fertile countryside (though demographic growth progressively brought this to an end), as did the "tradition" of out-migration. Rapid urbanization and the emergence of an unemployed lumpenproletariat and class friction, were for long kept at bay in Malawi. Banda's economic policies triggered instead rural-rural demographic shifts with his stress on developing smaller rural centers, keeping rural-urban drifts at low levels. Economic strains periodically shattered the quiescent social picture. Unrest broke out when Malawi twice devalued the Kwacha in 1986 and 1987, and when atypical maize shortages cropped up in the late 1970's and again in the 1980's. These primarily affected urban workers, who could not cope with sharply increased food prices. And though the regime rapidly brought food prices and shortages under control (through large imports from South Africa), the potential for food-shortage related unrest was never far beneath the surface.

Also of import is Malawi's geographical isolation, its cultural insulation, the religiosity of the population, and the ouster (and self-exile) of opposition elements from the country. These kept Malawi insulated from divisive whirlwinds of novel political ideas, and the corrosive effects of modern lifestyles and material temptations. It prevented, well into the 1980's, the emergence of looser, free-wheeling habits, and/or socially iconoclastic trends, that tend to seep into less hermetically-sealed societies in the Third World. And though large class and income disparities developed, as elsewhere, the agrarian base of wealth in Malawi kept these within acceptable "norms."

Personal loyalty to Banda was the criteria for advancement in Malawi, and unless one erred from the straight path, or was at the summit of the political elite, there was little to fear. Only in the north, and among Northerners (especially in the 1980's) were resentments seriously festering. That the frozen social balance could not be maintained for decades; that the new international context called for liberalization; and that Banda's growing senility would become his prime enemy, were obvious only in the 1990's. It is within this context of a country relatively free of cleavages and/or social strife, that one can place in better perspective the structural pillars of Malawi's stability.

The Pillars of the Regime

The main pillars of Banda's regime were the Malawi Congress Party and the country's security services. The former, in its own manner politically legitimated the regime, assured it a measure of mass participation, and through local patronage and traditional authority bound the population to Banda. The latter, including the Armed Forces, Police (and the feared CID and Mobile Unit branches), and the paramilitary Malawi Young Pioneers, provided the necessary muscle to keep the non-conformists in line. Each in way safeguarded the regime from outside threats, enforced conformity, and through a network of spies and informers down to the village level assured that domestic sources of opposition were immediately located and neutralized. All, however, rested upon the tacit acceptance of the population of the political status quo.

The Malawi Young Pioneers

One of the bulwarks of the regime, particularly effective as a control mechanism, enforcing conformity, ferreting out opposition in rural areas, and "organizing society" behind the MCP were the Malawi Young Pioneers. The MYP's role in sustaining the regime, not often appreciated abroad, was monumental. The Pioneers were virtually the last structure in Malawi to accept Banda's eclipse in 1993, even fighting pitched battles with the army on the point, and for this loyalty to the *ancien regime* they were the first to be disbanded.

The MYP had two roles. First, in their developmental capacity the MYP were supposed to transform unemployed rural youth into cadres "of dedicated young people who will act as the 'spearhead of rural development' by practising improved agricultural techniques on their own land holdings."[104] MYP model farms were supposed to become catalysts for agrarian change, though later their developmental thrust was shifted to more technical and vocational activities, including construction, road building, well-boring and mechanical repairs. Secondly, the MYP were supposed to inculcate national values and civic-consciousness into society's youth, and through paramilitary training, assist Malawi's small standing army (750 men at independence) and Police in security work.[105]

As elsewhere in Africa where similar structures were set up, the MYP piled up a mixed record. Overall their economic impact was modest, despite the fact that as early as 1969 MYP farms were producing some 15-25 bags of maize per acre, compared to the average yield of 2-3 bags in the peasant sector, and World Bank evaluation teams assessing the farms termed them as "the most efficiently run in Africa."[106] It was, rather, in their internal security capacity, that the MYP proved invaluable to the regime—becoming its eyes and ears in the countryside, and providing also some of its muscle.

The Young Pioneers played an important supportive political

role from the outset. During the final stage of the struggle for independence from Britain, they had agitated in favor of Banda, "organizing" the rural countryside behind him, and intimidating opposition to the MCP. During the playing out of the dangerous 1964 cabinet crisis (when Banda was surrounded by jostling crowds of urban civil servants in Zomba) the MYP were literally Banda's stormtroopers, bodily protecting his car convoys, surrounding his podiums, and helping quell the urban unrest together with the armed forces and police. And during the several armed incursions from abroad (e.g. Chipembere's) it was MYP units that tracked down the armed rebels, and in one instance engaged them in battle.

Allocated a significant percentage of the defence budget, the MYP were autonomous, and directly accountable to the Office of the President. As ancillary paramilitary units, their powers were nearly equal to the police. MYP members were immune from arrest by either the army or police without the express permission of their own officers, and ultimately Banda himself, who in 1982 abolished the post of deputy Commander of the MYP, leaving the hierarchy under his sole personal command.

Starting modestly in 1963, by 1974 the MYP numbered 12,000. Their strength steadily continued to increase until by 1987 they numbered 60,000, being by then "a powerful force in exerting Banda's control over political life right down to village level."[107] Virtually the nerves of the regime, MYP members were found in even the smallest hamlet of Malawi, reporting to the President on the mood in the countryside, and on all significant individual new arrivals in every village in the country. Together with MCP and League of Malawi Women militants, the MYP also sought out violations of the dress code, banned publications (especially at the University), and disparaging remarks by expatriates. They were important in keeping order at MCP branch meetings, and assured, often with rough-armed tactics, that party membership dues in the countryside were paid-up. Their loyalty to Banda's regime was visible in 1993 when they were forcibly disarmed by the armed forces, with several thousand preferring self-exile in Mozambique.

The Security Forces

Banda's ability to rely on the total loyalty of all branches of Malawi's security forces has been a powerful factor stabilizing his rule, obviating, among other things, the need to utilize excess force against domestic foes. With the security forces intrinsically loyal to the civilian center in Lilongwe, and supported by the masses in the countryside and the MYP, external opposition groups have not been able to foment revolt in the country. Every penetration effort was disastrous, foiled either at the border or within days of its occurrence. And with the exception of pamphleteering, what local opposition existed in the country could easily be neutralized by the rather small CID and police. Though mass repression intermittently afflicted the country during several periods of paranoia about "the North" and political jockeying for position, in general brute force was usually utilized as an adjunct to legitimacy.

At independence Malawi inherited minute security forces, largely under expatriate command. The army—the Nyassa battalion of the King's African Rifles—had only 750 troops, and only nine of its 49 officers were African, the rest being Asian or European. In that year the police numbered 2,600, and were commanded by 96 officers, only 12 of whom were African.

The small size of the Malawi Rifles, and Police, were augmented as soon as possible in subsequent years, despite severe budgetary constraints. This was largely because of fear that de-stabilization efforts might be aimed at Malawi due to the unpopularity of Banda's foreign policies (his pro-Portugal and South Africa postures) in neighboring states. A second battalion (2,000 troops) was created in the army in 1975, with two more later. By 1984 the Malawi Army had expanded ninefold from its original size, to 6,000 men, including now a minute navy and a fledgling Air Force. The Police, whose duties in Malawi often had political overtones—i.e. monitoring and suppressing opposition and unrest—was likewise expanded, though more modestly, to over 3,500 in that year, with an additional 1,000-man Police Mobile Unit set up for riot control.

The army, with headquarters at Kamuzu barracks in Lilongwe, was always weak in logistics, firepower and materiel, and only pos-sessed armoured cars. Localization of the officer corps proceeded rapidly, despite Banda's initial preference for expatriates that so riled his young cabinet members in 1964. In 1971-1972 the command of both the Army and the Police passed into indigenous hands, though at all times a number of expatriate officers were retained, especially during the army's periodic re-training exercises, as in 1989.

The relations of the security forces with the population were significantly free of tension, if only because neither crime nor subversion afflicted Malawi. The army, played no real repressive role in any case, and was quite popular in the country, being viewed as "professional, uncorrupt and outside politics."[108] Nor was the police particularly disliked in the countryside, since it was the Special Branch and the Mobile Unit specifically that were charged with the more onerous political duties in Malawi. The police force, moreover, did not strut around in the countryside, and its demeanor vis-a-vis the citizenry was relatively even-handed. Even during the paranoid purges of the late-1970's, and the anti-northern crackdowns of the 1980's, discontent was not levelled at the police, but at the Special Branch. And like the civil service in general, though more surprisingly in light of its rarity in Africa, the force was not seriously tainted by corruption, something that further deflected the possible build-up of grievances against the regime.

The composition of the two forces reflected the different occupational preferences of the country's ethnic groups. Chewa and Lomwe were always over-represented in both, as were also Ngoni in the police. The number of Yao in the forces has been declining, a function of their greater interest in commerce, and government recruitment policy under Banda who neither liked them, nor Muslims in general. (He often referred to his own grandfather, who had been captured by Muslim slavers.) In regional terms, the sparsely populated North was over-represented, despite efforts to the contrary, as was also the western part of the Central Province. However, as in the civil service, few Northerners attained senior rank in either Police or Army. Chewa and "harmless" Lomwe staffed those levels, keeping operational command of troops and police solidly in "loyal" hands. While promotion through intermediate ranks was based on merit, the top ranks were always in effect "reserved" for individuals deemed reliable by Banda. Keeping the security forces under the tight rein of loyalist commanding officers no doubt contributed to Malawi's record of civil-military stability, but it also caused some grumbling (and defections, mostly to Zambia) among those officers aware that their prospects of further advancement were literally non-existent.

Banda's success in keeping Malawi's security forces on a tight leash, bound to him by commanders meticulously screened for loyalty, was no doubt assisted by the fact that as a whole few Malawi officers had either intellectual pretentions, or the kind of worldly exposure that might have given them political aspirations. But Banda also had the political acumen to directly tackle, and resolve, any military grievances when they arose, even when the solution was not ideal from his perspective. Petty internal frictions were closely monitored, and as with the Khanga-Kamwana competition and Matewere's demeanor, firmly and unequivocally resolved. Moreover, Banda accepted the armed forces' rejection of his proposal to establish an interim Tembo Vice-Presidency when similar opposition from political colleagues would have been perceived by him as treason. (As it was, indeed, if he was involved in the 1983 murders of senior MCP ministers.)

Signs of disloyalty, potential or real, were dealt with promptly, and at times harshly. The army was kept away from political duties and temptations, something that preserved its professional dignity. Military units, periodically rotated, were kept at the geographical periphery of the country where they were incapable of doing harm. Though this policy had obvious political motivations, the armed forces nevertheless were given cogent professional tasks—guarding the country against external enemies—something they could not grumble about. Without significant mobility, and under the ubiquitous observation of the Young Pioneers, possible unauthorized military movements were in any case effectively monitored, and hence neutralized. And the police—despite political, and at times repressive duties—was able to retain much of its probity in the countryside.

Notwithstanding their intrinsic loyalty to Banda, the security forces did not remain completely free of purges, nor were tensions absent in the officer corps. During the witchhunts against Northerners in the mid-1970's, as well as after Nqumayo's downfall, numerous officers, soldiers and constables were arrested. Gripes about conditions of service (or promotion bottlenecks) resulted in resignations, and some officers also resigned (or were dismissed) due to friction with the authoritarian Lomwe Chief of Staff, General Graciano Matewere. Indeed, the latter, whose loyalty to Banda was "too" absolute, had eventually to be shunted to non-military duties (in April 1980) when his relations with the officer corps deteriorated beyond repair.

Matewere's replacement was the Chewa General Melvin Mainda Khanga, who was promoted above the heads of more senior officers. Though Khanga soothed the internal rumblings in the army, his own promotion aggravated inter-arm bickering with the police, headed by the Chewa Inspector General Mac Kamwana. Persistent petty corporate jealousies, friction, and even brawls, had in the past erupted between police and army personnel, disquieting since this kind of conflict has often elsewhere brought in its wake military power-grabs. In 1987, with Khanga's star far brighter, Banda accepted Kamwana's "resignation" on the grounds of age—though Kamwana was only 51 years old. He was replaced by his deputy, also a Chewa.

But there has always been a political side to the mild friction between the military and the police, as has already been alluded to before. The police, with greater Ngoni personnel, was in general supportive of Tembo's possible designation as Banda's successor. Kamwana, though a Chewa, had moved to such a posture as well, but more out of antagonism to the army Chief of Staff, feeling his corporate primacy might be enhanced in a Tembo presidency. The Army, on the other hand, with its Chewa and Lomwe commanders, strongly resisted *any* role for Tembo, to the point of having blocked in 1983 the proposal for an interim Tembo Vice-Presidency, out of fear this would have granted him a stepping stone to power. Kamwana's eclipse was thus a blow to Tembo's prospects. Banda's constant shuffling the top command of the Police between 1988 and 1993 (and to a lesser extent of the army) cogently underscored the degree to which the succession issue was destabilizing Malawi in the last years of the Banda era, as nothing had done so in the past.[109]

None of these petty conflicts spilled out in the form of disloyalty against the center of political power. Indeed, right to the end the armed forces remained completely loyal to central political authority. Not even when "winds of change" began shaking nearby countries; when Banda's increasing senility was self-evident; or when power in the presidency slowly oozed into Tembo-Kadzamira hand, were the military leaders tempted to seize power. (And a possible opportunity indeed existed, in mid-1992, when the aging Khanga had finally to be replaced, by his deputy, widely known to be politically ambitious. As all observers acknowledged, despite the increasing strains on the civilian center, the military "could be expected to stay largely aloof from all but the most serious post-Banda infighting."[110] And, when the constitutional system changed, with the adoption of multipartyism, the army lashed out (with considerable zest!), in protection of the new system against the Malawi Young Pioneers (the paramilitary *now*, of *one* party) that were intent on manipulating events in favor of Banda. (The MYP were disarmed.) All this strongly underscores how, whatever its

shortcomings, Banda's reign was seen by the armed forces as fundamentally legitimate, and the officer corps remained suffused, as few
other regimes in Africa, with the ethos of non-intervention in the
political realm.

The Malawi Congress Party

If meticulous attention to the security services gave Banda the edge in
keeping the country's forces a-political, it was his awesome control and
manipulation of the country's single party, that gained him the aura
of legitimacy that sustained him in office. Awareness that the regime
possessed not inconsiderable sources of mass support was clear in the
1994 elections when the MCP, headed by Banda—though defeated—remained Malawi's second-largest party, despite indictments of Banda's
lengthy "dictatorship."

Banda ruled Malawi as his own personal fief, unilaterally imple-
menting in the country whatever policies he felt were necessary, and
brooking no opposition to his fiat. He arrogated to himself the totality
of decision-making powers at the national level, and used both the
MCP and the Legislative Assembly to rubber-stamp his policies, while
periodically appealing to the masses in the countryside for approval.

What needs to be underscored is that Banda's heavy-handed rule
in Malawi cannot obviate the fact (though causing classifatory and
epistemological problems) that *notwithstanding* it, he retained considerable support in the country. His support was especially strong among
the more traditional, elderly, less literate strata; in Nyau circles; among
religious leaders, chiefs, women, countryside youth, and the petty rural
bureaucracy. To all these Banda was the legitimated leader of Malawi.
His rulership style was of much lesser import *in these circles*. And since the
formalities of party consultation and national elections were very meticulously followed, the *image* of party-sanctioned governance accorded
Banda's regime the aura of legitimacy. That this was enough, for purposes of consolidating civil-military peace, has already been illustrated.

The Malawi Congress Party was a powerful centralizing tool in
Banda's hands, that he used to confer legitimacy to his regime, as well
as a societal control mechanism, patronage system, and as a channel
of communication between the center and periphery. A true mass
party before independence, unlike other political parties elsewhere, the
MCP neither atrophied nor fell prey to fissiparous cleavages. Though

after independence its flagging membership was fuelled by Young Pioneer intimidation and strong-arm tactics, the party continued to play a pervasive role in many villages in the country. Most party branches met on a constant basis, and popular participation at such meetings was surprisingly high.

MCP party meetings served as forums (and at times very lively ones) for discussion of local issues, as well as platforms to explain to the population important government policy. They bound the rural populace to the regime by conferring upon them rights and duties, and by spreading the idea of popular involvement in political life, legitimated Banda's leadership credentials as well. Hodder-Williams put it well when he noted: "the politically marginal are... harnessed to the system, symbols of a national unity and spokesmen for local interests and prejudices."[111] National values were inculcated at such meetings, anti-social behaviour was condemned, villagers were re-minded to watch for "enemies" from abroad, and the constant exhor-tations on the party slogans of Unity, Loyalty, Discipline and Obedience, indoctrinated into supportive roles large cross-sections of society.

Grass-roots participation, frequent competitive local elections, very high incumbent turnover, and periodic selection of delegates for higher levels of the party, all in turn conferred legitimacy to regional and national party conferences, the organs that "ratified" Banda's poli-cies. Such meetings were prime "not to be missed" events in Malawi, and their deliberations were very well publicized. The outside media may have derided them as "irrelevant," since they took place within the setting of a single party system. But in Malawi delegates regarded attending a branch or regional party meeting as a singular honor, as attested by their punctuality, preparation, attire, and demeanor there.

And it was at these conclaves that Banda's political style was particularly effective, and his popular approbation most visible. Uniquely capable as he was of bridging the gap between parochial and national concerns, as one observer strongly warned "it would be unwise to underestimate the impact of Banda's flamboyant style. His speeches at party conferences are remarkably adept for their purpose, sufficiently repetitive to ensure the comprehension of messages and to create a dramatic effect, sufficiently parochial to involve every region's delegates and to give an impression of personal involvement, and sufficiently homely and relevant to the delegates' immediate concerns to stir a sea of nodding heads."[112]

Though at such conclaves Banda's proposals were usually accepted by acclamation, often with no debate, this did not mean the conclaves were irrelevant or did not confer the regime legitimacy. A tacit division of power always existed between national and local elites, that was never challenged or disputed by local party influentials, whose prime interests were, in any case, narrow constituency concerns. MCP meetings provided a channel of communication between national and local leadership groups, and a forum for participatory politics. They conferred on Banda "a moderately free hand to delineate the major lines of foreign, economic and social policy," in exchange for attention to "local demands, usually conservative, traditional, and essentially 'petty capitalist,' that have been listened to."[113] For party conferences always served as the most important forums for thoroughly airing all local concerns, and bringing them directly to Banda's attention. Local complaints about unacceptable morals and/or social behaviour (immodest dress, nonconformist religious sects, disrespectful children, haughty expatriates) have been discussed at length at such venues. Plenary sessions have seen arrogant central administrators (including cabinet Ministers), authoritarian or corrupt district MCP chairmen, inattentive parastatal structures, and lax civil servants challenged, or called to account for their actions, directly in the presence of Banda.

Banda never denied local leaders scope for activity or patronage in their constituencies, which did not threaten his hegemony at the national level. Local elites had "standing authority and resources to redistribute, if only symbolic ones in some cases, so that an active political life can operate in a rural area with very little direct relationship with the national arena."[114] The end result, though not "Western democratic," by any means, was nevertheless a popularly sanctioned political system that survived, indeed thrived, "peaceably on a minimal amount of participation at the national level, provided that the local leaders...are themselves in the competition for office, enjoy the fruits of success, and receive support from the peasantry."[115]

Though local leaders were allowed a measure of autonomy and patronage, no political barons were allowed to emerge, for this threatened stability by inserting political competition. Periodic purges of overly ambitious party leaders, and constant cabinet shuffles were a regular part of the Banda era. At times these purges were due to abuses of power at lower levels, since the general absence of corruption in

Malawi did not mean financial irregularities did not afflict many MCP branches. (In April 1975, for example, the entire Southern Region MCP committee was replaced for embezzlement; two months later the same fate visited their Northern Region counterpart.) However, many purges, and especially the periodic cabinet shuffles (up to five per year) were an integral part of Banda's political "style," motivated by the desire to keep incumbents on their toes and aware of the true fount of power in the country.

Manifestations of ambition, or over-zeal, were nipped at the bud; populist power-bases were not allowed to develop into springboards to national influence. But Banda's hyper-sensitivity to the emergence of any potential political competitors—no doubt a function of his own personality—also reflected a very astute awareness of the personal roots of most political discord in Malawi. Namely, that every influential who jutted out too much from the rest of the pack would attract envy and rivalry, a fact that would inevitably lead to friction and conflict. Whether or not Banda had read his Machiavelli, his policy of "levelling off" society of its overly ambitious, powerful or popular personalities helped give Malawi its relatively even (and turgid) political tenor.

Control of patronage in resource-poor Malawi, employment prospects in the public sector, and business licensing in general, also bound society to the MCP and to Banda, by establishing a link between loyalty and sources of livelihood. Banda had ultimate control over licensing in Malawi, including the right to determine whether specific individuals could engage in certain occupations. These powers extended also to land ownership, giving the regime immense patronage to dispense to its supporters, as well as powerful sanctions to use against those whose loyalty is suspect. Banda also *pro forma* screened all civil service appointments in the country, ratified all promotions, and approved all appointments at the University. Few Malawians cared to jeopardize their prospects of public employment, especially since Banda (until senility caught up with him) kept a personal track of their progress and activities.

Notwithstanding two food-riots, that were very much *suis generis*, until the 1990's dawned demonstrations, strikes and labor unrest were unknown in Malawi. (Today they are, together with rampant crime, a basic staple of the "new order.") Trade unions had disappeared with independence, their functions "assumed" by the MCP that adjudicated wage or labor disputes. Nor was the University of Malawi ever shut down due to student unrest as in most other African countries (the first class boycotts only erupted in 1989 and 1992), as students put bread and butter considerations above ideology. Telling is the fact that not a single critical comment was ever published (at home or abroad) by any Malawi academic at the university, which, incidentally, had no department of political science, a discipline regarded as utterly unnecessary in Malawi!

Banda brooked no opposition because he sincerely saw himself entitled to rule, and in his own manner, fully legitimated by the masses, and sanctioned by the Malawi Congress Party! He never minced words: "Anything I say is law. Literally law. It is a fact in this country."[116] To enforce, what to him was fully legitimate political quiescence, he used the full range of coercive powers at his disposal (approved by the MCP and the country's Legislative Assembly), including detention laws and camps.

In 1965 (after the cabinet crisis) he had even warned the population that "if to maintain political stability and efficient administration, I have to detain 10,000, 100,000, I will do it...I will detain anyone who is interfering with the political stability of this country."[117] He did not have to utilize such draconian policies, except briefly in times of crisis, as during the Nqumayo unrest. Societal support, a monopoly over social, economic and political life, and only intermittent coercion were more than adequate. Telling is the fact that when the country's political prisons were "emptied" in 1994 after the succession, there were found to be only twenty-odd such prisoners! Political opponents found Banda's grip over the country so incontestable that "there are, in fact, no outlets, short of exile, for those opposed to the President's policies."[118] It was there, in self-exile, in Lusaka, Dar-es-Salaam and Harare, that most of Banda's opposition waited for him to stumble. And it was from there, once the changed international environment allowed it, that the challenge that unseated him, finally came.

Transition to Democracy

Until virtually the end Banda's main sources of political opposition included several groups set up in exile by his former lieutenants from the early 1960's: the Dar-es-Salaam based Congress for the Second Republic, led by the pretentious Kanyama Chiume; and the Lusaka-based Malawi Freedom Movement, set up by Orton Chirwa, the MCP's co-founder and former Minister of Justice—abducted in 1981, sentenced to death by a traditional court, and dying in prison in October 1992. Both groups were moribund, and attracted only a few supporters among intellectuals in Malawi and abroad. Two other of Banda's early lieutenants did not survive: Chipembere left Africa in 1969 for academia, to die shortly later; and Chisiza, another of the 1964 cabinet rebels, died during an ill-fated 1972 armed incursion into Malawi.

Several newer challenged included the Harare-based Socialist League of Malawi that grandiosely claimed a Cuban-trained People's Liberation Army. Riddled with personal and ethnic rivalries, the League had been set up in Mozambique in 1975 by Attati Mpakati, a former MCP Regional Secretary. The latter had been assassinated in Harare by the Malawi Secret Service in March 1983, after an earlier 1979 attempt, via letter-bomb, blew up his hands. The basic problem with all these opposition groups, as well as a few others that emerged, was that they were composed of exiled intellectuals, unknown in the countryside, with no grassroots support, and appealing primarily to urban dwellers.

The Transition

The only real challenge to Banda's political hegemony in Malawi, and the one that ultimately ousted him, was rooted in the changed international context of the 1990's (see chapter 5), that somewhat belatedly affected Lilongwe when global donors began to apply pressure for the democratization of their former "star pupil." Malawi, despite its considerable advances since independence, was still among the weaker states in Africa, and was, moreover, at the time in the midst of acute economic stress due to drought. The regime had no choice, therefore, but to cave in to external conditionalities. Indeed, the aid embargo, brief though it was, cost Malawi in 1992 fully $200 million in balance-of-payments support.[119]

The first spark for Malawi's transformation was a March pastoral letter of Malawi's Catholic Bishops on human rights abuses in the country. (Banda was under intense pressure from his advisors to crack down on the Bishops for their interference in temporal matters, but wisely desisted.) Another bout of anti-Northern witch-hunting in 1989, and tensions resulting from the clearly looming succession (since it was known Banda was sick with brain-cancer) had made Lilongwe a cauldron of rumors. Shortly after the pastoral letter, in April, in a brazen, calculated act of defiance, the Northern self-exiled trade unionist Chakufwa Chihana (whom Banda had imprisoned for eight years in the 1970's) flew into Lilongwe. He was arrested for sedition in December but released after only six months.

Malawi's first-ever pro-multiparty demonstrations immediately broke out in urban areas[120], resulting in 40 deaths and 125 people being injured. These demonstrations were unprecedented for Malawi, underscoring the country had turned the corner and had joined the democratization bandwagon that was sweeping Africa. As one observer put it, "Malawians are docile people, but once they lose control it is very serious,"[121] because "once you shatter the idea that no one can talk about issues, it is very profound."

Though the demonstrations were quelled by the police, the challenge had been thrown at Banda, publicly and within the borders of the country. An alternate leader had presented himself, and the picture could never be the same, as Chihana well knew it when he first decided to play his gambit. The regime could argue no more that there was no desire in the country for competitive elections, and short of actually legalizing a multi-party system, a referendum on the issue was the only action that could satisfy the outside world. There is no doubt Banda was certain at the time that the bulk of the population was still behind him. His inner counsel, including Tembo, also urged rapid action to catch the opposition unprepared. Banda agreed to a referendum on multipartyism on June 14, 1993; the latter saw the electorate approve multipartyism by two-thirds of the vote.

The formal opening of political space in Malawi, and the subsequent scheduling of presidential and parliamentary elections for 1994, led to an array of changes and tensions in Malawi, apart from the emergence of a number of political parties, and the return to the country of self-exiled politicians. The armed forces, for example, flexed their muscles, as for the first time their role and duty was not fully defined. Months before a constitutional revision (February 1994) spelled out the dimensions of the new order, the army unilaterally moved to ban and disarm the MYP, whose status had changed from a state-sanctioned organ (in a single party system) to an illegally armed party-affiliate in a multi-party system! The 1993 crackdown by the army on the Young Pioneers, the assault on their national headquarters, and later the army's illegal home-searches for weapons in

Lilongwe and Blantyre in April-May 1994 were all extra-constitutional.

Despite significant politicking there were only three presidential candidates. Four other "candidates" withdrew from the race in exchange for "promised" cabinet portfolios. Banda headed the MCP despite some early doubts—he was scheduled for brain surgery in Johannesburg on October 2, 1993. His remarkably-speedy recovery brought Banda to head a ticket which he shared with the Sena Chakuamba-Phiri, a former MCP Secretary-General whom he had thrown into jail in 1981, and only released in 1993 for this express purpose!

Facing the MCP in the May 17, 1994 elections were two formations. The Alliance for Democracy (AFORD) of Chihana, who, released in mid-1993, was politically-naive to act as if he could win the elections single-handedly. And the United Democratic Front (UDF) of Baliki Muluzi, a former MCP Secretary-General during 1977-1982, and an ex-convict (for the theft of six million pounds, etc.) in the 1960's.[122] The UDF was so "dominated by medium-scale industrialists and merchants"[123] formerly excluded from the MCP, and by MCP defectors smelling political victory, that many in society referred to it as the MCP-B team.

The elections were remarkably peaceful for a country facing competitive elections for the first time. Most foreign observers latched onto the loss of power by both Banda and the MCP, ignoring the disturbing signs of acute regionalism the vote actually reflected. *Africa Confidential* noted from the field that most voters saw the political race as one between regions, and not between individuals or parties, and hence the outcome could be foretold in advance since the Southern Region was more populous.[124] And Banda himself scored a very impressive 33 percent of the vote, with the MCP gaining 31 percent of the parliamentary seats. Clearly for many in Malawi, despite thirty years in power neither Banda nor the MCP were irrelevant political actors.

Table 1: Presidential	Table 2: Parliamentary
Elections, 1994	Elections, 1994
Muluzi 1,404,754 (47%) Banda 996,363 (33%) Chihana 552,852 (19%)	UDF 86 seats MCP 56 seats AFORD 35 seats
Three million (or 81 percent) of the 3.7 million electorate voted	None of the other five parties won a single of the 177 seats

Both the presidential and parliamentary election results illustrated how each party and leader was perceived in regional terms. (See Table 1 and 2 below.) AFORD, for example, won nearly all of its seats (31 of 35) in the Northern Region, 85 percent of whose electorate voted for that party. The MCP secured 56 seats, and was powerful in the Central Region, where it garnered 65 percent of the Region's popular vote; while the UDF won 86 seats (three short of an absolute majority), with a heavy (76 percent) vote in the most populous Southern Region. After his defeat Banda congratulated Muluzi, formally retired from public life, leaving behind Chakuamba as President of the MCP, and a few former allies (Tembo, Cecilia Kadzimira) to defend themselves against assorted charges of misconduct.

The New Democracy

Banda left behind him a heritage of sustained economic growth, fiscal responsibility, civil-military peace, and stability. But Banda's personal policy idiosyncrasies left, created, or enhanced huge social inequities, and ignored great social needs that no successor regime can afford any longer. Huge budgetary allocations for education and health are called for before the turn of the century just to maintain current low levels of services for the projected larger population. Food production, jobs in the urban and rural sectors, even firewood for the countryside population, will have to be dramatically augmented if shortages, with their destabilizing consequences, are to be averted.[125]

Banda's lengthy personalist rule also left Malawi very much a novice in the art of self-government, devoid of viable (i.e. untainted) alternate leadership, and acutely unprepared for the divisive rough and tumble of normal political competition that the country completely bypassed during the colonial era and Banda's authoritarian interregnum.

As the new era dawned in 1994 nearly every policy associated with Banda was dismantled. Land-hunger, looming as Malawi's greatest problem in a country projected to reach a population of 12 million by the year 2000, was decreed to be alleviated by a redistribution of the holdings of estates. The latter—that had generated the revenues with which the country's infrastructure was built, and represented "a continuation of basic ideas promulgated by the early Scottish missionaries, continued by the colonial government, and shared by many Malawians"[126]—were to be greatly downsized in a new emphasis on peasant food self-sufficiency, recommended by the World Bank.

An election pledge by Muluzi to bring about universal primary education was honored in 1994, despite the chaos that ensued as the number of pupils nearly doubled to three million with neither facilities, chairs, textbooks or teachers available to cope with the influx. Indeed 19,000 additional teachers had to be hired and trained to supplement Malawi's existing 29,000, at a cost the regime could not cover. And AFORD continued to remind Muluzi of similar "solemn" pledges he made "to build new roads, hospitals and a university in the North."[127] The UDF's not honoring pledges it made to develop the North may be understandable since AFORD won only 5 percent of the region's vote. (Every one of the UDF's four Northerners in the cabinet was trounced in the parliamentary elections there.) rather than being viewed as an "anti-Banda" party, the UDF was viewed instead as "another Southern" party: not surprisingly there has even been some talk of a secession of the North.

Another solemn UDF pledge, of establishing a "truth commission" on the Banda era, was also soft-pedalled, and to date has not been implemented. On the grounds of "national reconciliation" all crimes except the four killings of 1983 (notably of Dick Matenje) are not being pursued. (And even there, the courts have exonerated Banda, and later, in 1995 Tembo and Cecilia Kadzimira, opening a real hornet's nest as to who was actually responsible for the order to liquidate the group.) The reason may indeed be national reconciliation, but more likely that nearly everybody associated with the UDF has a dirty past that could come out into the open if examined more carefully.

Malawi's budgetary situation is also in total shambles. The heavy costs of the run-up to "democracy" and competitive elections (including widescale use of patronage, pay-increases, including to the military in 1993, deferring unpopular economic policies etc.), when added to the budgetary squeeze that already existed due to the economic slowdown in the early 1990's, have completely tarnished Malawi's former reputation of fiscal orthodoxy. Strikes have become a common occurrence in Malawi, and the Muluzi regime has found itself unable to either derail demands for new pay-hikes, or to maintain freezes in civil service establishments. And governmental extravaganzas are now necessary to help make democracy "stick". Parliament is now composed of 177 deputies, and Muluzi's cabinet included thirty-five ministers (up from the 10-15 under Banda), that triggered a (June 1995) World Bank suggestion that he streamline it. And though a coalition government was set up between the UDF and AFORD in 1994, the constant petty party sniping undermined much of the image of disunity. At the constitutional conference of 1994, for example, the UDF proposed dismantling the post of the country's second vice-president (to dislodge Chihana from the office), while AFORD suggested a clause preventing convicts from seeking office, that would have disqualified Muluzi.

With both a devaluation of the kwacha (allowed to float), and rampant inflation (34 percent in 1994; 80 percent a month in 1995), a rural-urban exodus commenced, where for decades it was kept in check. Crime, especially violent crime, had never been a serious problem before; but under such economic conditions, and given encouragement by the dismantlement of Banda's ancillary forces of repression (the MYP), it had by 1995 reached endemic proportions. "This is not the Malawi most Malawians know,"[128] and some have already grumbled about "the good old days."

Even military unrest is no longer in the province of the unlikely in Malawi. The armed forces have rapidly been politicized *because* there is no real center of political power under Muluzi. As one observer put it "democratisation is politicising an army which was apolitical."[129] And Muluzi's personal credentials (his conviction for theft in the 1960's, shady business deals, record of womanizing, and bouncing checks) do not inspire unmitigated loyalty, as did Banda's despite the latter's idiosyncrasies, with which one could disagree but not fault with lack of sincerity or commitment. Moreover, while Muluzi's several anti-Northern discriminatory command appointments can be understood, his promoting of officers predominantly from the South has caused grumbling. (Banda sought personal loyalty, but did not discriminate against the Southern Region.) Rumours of unrest in the army were given cogent credence by the mysterious April 19, 1995 killing of Chief of Staff General Chigawa. His death was originally linked to Malawi's crime wave, but was later connected to an alleged coup attempt for which five officers were arrested.

There is no doubt that transitions from authoritarian rule are difficult and replete with pitfalls. In Malawi, however, "Malawians are discovering that democracy alone is not enough."[130]

NOTES

1. For an annotated bibliography on Malawi see Samuel Decalo, *Malawi*. Santa Barbara, Clio Press, 1995.

2. Cited in Colin Legum (ed., *African Contemporary Record 1973-4*, New York, Africana Publishing Co., p. B 210.

3. L. H. Gann, "Malawi, Zambia and Zimbabwe," in Peter Duigan and Robert H.Jackson (eds), *Politics and Government in African States 1960-1985*, Stanford, Hoover Institution Press, 1986, p. l91.

4. As defined by President Banda himself. *Malawi News*, February 22, 1963.

5. Bridglal Pachai, *Malawi: The History of the Nation*, London, Longman, 1973, p.6. For Malawi's ethnic groups see John G. Pike, *Malawi: A Political and Economic History*, London, Pall Mall Press, 1968.

6. John McCracken, "Underdevelopment in Malawi: The Missionary Contribution," *African Affairs*, April 1977. See also that author's seminal *Politics and Christianity in Malawi 1875-190: The Impact of the Livingstonia Mission in the Northern Province*, Cambridge, Cambridge University Press, 1977.

7. Cited in McCracken, *Politics and Christianity in Malawi*, p. 115.

8. Harold D. Nelson, *Area Handbook for Malawi*, Washington, Government Printing Office, 1976, p. 99.

9. See D. D. Phiri, *From Nguni to Ngoni*, Limbe, Popular Publications, 1982, and J. D. Omer-Cooper, *The Zulu Aftermath*, Longman, 1966.

10. Pachai, *Malawi: The History of the Nation*, p. 53.

11. J. W. Jack, *Daybreak in Livingstonia*, Edinburgh, 1901, p.18. See also George Shepperson, "The Jumbe of Kota Kota and some aspects of the history of Islam in British Central Africa," in I. M. Lewis (ed), *Islam in Tropical Africa*, London, 1966.

12. Robert B.Boeder, *Silent Majority: A History of the Lomwe in Malawi*. Pretoria, Africa Institute of South Africa, 1984.

13. Ngoleka Mlia, "The Role of Capital Cities in regional and national Development in Malawi," Zomba, National Archives of Malawi, 1983, p. 138.

14. Kathryn Morton, *Aid and Dependence. British Aid to Malawi*. London, Croom Helm, 1975, p. 12.

15. George Schuster, *Private Work and Public Causes: A Personal Record*, Cambridge, 1979. p. 77.

16. *Africa Confidential*, May 21, 1988.

17. See George Shepperson and Thomas Price, *The Independent African*, Edinburgh, 1958, p.414.

18. Tangri in Roderick J. Macdonald (ed), *From Nyasaland to Malawi*, p. 261.

19. Report of the Nyasaland Commission of Enquiry (Devlin Report), HMSO, London, July 1959, p. 13.

20. See for example Philip Short, *Banda*, London, Routledge and Kegan Paul, 1974; David Williams, *Malawi: The Politics of Despair*, Ithaca, Cornell University Press, 1978; and Pike, *Malawi: A Political and Economic History*.

21. Pike, pp. 170-1. A discordant and somewhat petulant note is introduced by Kanyama Chiume, who was to claim after his 1964 ouster that on arrival Dr Banda was "to all intents and purposes a white man" (p.91) because he insisted on European housing in Blantyre. M. W. Kanyama Chiume, *Kwacha. An Autobiography*, Nairobi, East African Publishing House, 1975, p. 89.

22. Short, p. 23.

23. Martin L. Chanock, "Ambiguities in the Malawian Political Tradition," *African Affairs*, vol. 74, 1975, p. 345.

24. Report of the Nyasaland Commission of Enquiry (Devlin Report), London, HMSO, Command 814, July 1959, par. 96.

25. Pike, p. 143.

26. K. Nyamayara Mafuka, *Missions and Politics in Malawi*, Kingston (Ont.), The Limestone Press, 1977. p. 181.

27. Cited in Short, p. 169-70. See also Malawi Congress Party, "The Constitution of the MCP," Limbe, Malawi Press, 1965.

28. Of import is also Malawi's authoritarian tradition, stemming from pre-colonial culture as well as from the model of British rule in the colony. See for example Martin Chanock, *Law, Custom and Social Order: The Colonial Experience in Malawi and Zambia*, Cambridge, Cambridge University Press, 1985.

29. Richard Hodder-Williams, "'Support' in Eastern Africa: Some Observations from Malawi," in Timothy M. Shaw and Kenneth A. Heard, *The Politics of Africa: and Development*, London, Longman's, 1979, p.161.

30. Malawi, *Legislative Assembly*, 26 May 1964, pp. 124-5.

31. Chiume, p. 91.

32. Williams, p. 207.

33. Malawi, *Legislative Assembly*, 29 November 1961, p. 101.

34. Cited in Short, pp. 203-4.

35. Malawi, Ministry of Information, "Address to the National Assembly," September 8, 1964.

36. Chanock, "Ambiguities in the Malawian Political Tradition," p. 346.

37. Cited by Short, p. 240.

38. Morton, p. 147. It was not until 1968 that the first African attained the rank of Permanent Secretary, while the security services only came under indigenous command in 1971 (Police) and 1972 (Army).

39. *Ibid*, p. 148.

40. Malawi, *Proceedings of the Legislative Council*, 76th Session, 8th Meeting, July 1963, p.756.

41. Morton, p.144

42. *Malawi News*, December 20, 1964.

43. Henry J. Richardson III, "Administration in the Malawi Government and its relationship to Social Change," in E.P. Morgan (ed) *The Administration of Change in Africa*, New York, Dunellen, 1974, p. 345. See also Richard Hodder-Williams, "Malawi's Decade Under Banda," *Round Table*, No. 249-52, 1973, pp .463-70.

44. Malawi, *Legislative Assembly*, 17 May 1966, p. 550.

45. Malawi, *Legislative Assembly*, 21 April 1965, p. 642.

46. As recorded in Malawi, *Legislative Assembly*, 30 January 1968, p. 248.

47. The chairman of the Electoral Committee prior to the 1983 elections. See *Africa Research Bulletin*, Political Series, August 1983.

48. The true culprits were never caught. There was a rash of ritual killings in Blantyre and Lilongwe in 1966-70, and recurrences in 1973 in Kasupe district. In 1969 Banda had to deny over the radio dangerous rumours that the killings were government-sponsored to provide the "blood" demanded by South Africa in exchange for the Lilongwe Project grants. (The rumours may have been sparked off by the concurrent drive of the Malawi Red Cross for stocks of fresh blood.)

49. Malawi, *Legislative Assembly*, 28 July 1970, p. 501.

50. Malawi, *Legislative Assembly*, 24 March, 1970. p. 482.

51. Malawi, *Legislative Assembly*, 7 December 1971, pp. 223-5

52. Mekki Mtewa, *Malawi Democratic Theory and Public Policy*, Cambridge, Mass., Schenkman Books, 1986, p. 67.

53. Colin Legum (ed.), *Africa Contemporary Record 1975-6*, p. B268.

54. *Africa Research Bulletin*, Political Series, January 1976.

55. Colin Legum (ed.), *Africa Contemporary Record 1980/81*, p.B689.

56. Le Monde, May 24, 1983. See also Legum (ed.), *Africa Contemporary Record 1983-4*, pp. B650-1 for the entire affair, and *Africa Research Bulletin*, Political Series, July 1983.

57. See *West Africa*, May 30, 1994.

58. Legum (ed.), *Africa Contemporary Record 1972-3*, p. B.193.

59. Interview with a senior Western diplomat in Lilongwe, April, 1987.

60. Colin Legum (ed.), *Africa Contemporary Record 1984-5*, p. B664. See also "Malawi: Sucked into War", *Africa Confidential*, November 18, 1987, that suggests that in October 1986 there was an attempted assassination on Tembo when his vehicle was ambushed by military personnel.

61. Morton, p. 17.

62. Robert E. Christiansen, "Financing Malawi's Development Strategy," in *Malawi: An Alternate Pattern of Development*, Edinburgh, Edinburgh University Press, Centre for African Studies, 1985, p. 409.

63. Morton, p. 36. One observer has noted Banda's loathing of incompetence and corruption and "frightening intolerance of mistakes." See Henry Richardson III, "Malawi between Black and White," *Africa Report*, February 1970, p.l9. Clapham notes that "effective control over corruption is difficult to maintain" but that someone like Banda, "an autocrat with the rigid morality of an elder of the Kirk of Scotland, is able to enforce his own standards on his subordinates." Christopher Clapham, *Third World Politics*, p.52.

64. See Simon Thomas, "Economic Developments in Malawi since Independence", *Journal of Southern African Studies*, vol. 2, 1974, pp. 30-51. and N. N. Miller, *Malawi: Central African Paradox*, Hanover, 1978.

65. For an excellent analysis of these competing views see Leroy Vail, "The State and the Creation of Colonial Malawi's Agricultural Economy" in Robert I. Rotberg (ed.), *Imperialism, Colonialism and Hunger: East and Central Africa*, Lexington, Mass., Lexington Books, 1983.

66. Vail, *Ibid*, pp. 77-8.

67. Kydd, "Malawi: Making Effective Use of Aid Resources," *Aid Bulletin*, vol. 17, No. 2, 1986, p. 77.

68. "If private enterprise is afraid and hesitant to invest in Malawi, I will be forced to introduce in this country state socialism, or its alternative. I am not going to wait. We want development in this country, and we are going to develop this country by all means, by all ways open to us." Malawi, *Hansard*, 22 January 1965, p. 414.

69. Dharam Ghai and Samir Radwan, "Growth and Inequality: Rural Development in Malawi 1964-78",in their *Agrarian Policies and Rural Poverty in Malawi*, Geneva, ILO, 1983, p. 73. For an overview of several aspects of recent socio-economic policy in Malawi see the "Contemporary Malawi" section of contributions in *Malawi: An Alternate Pattern of Development.*

70. Legum (ed.), *Africa Contemporary Record 1972-3*, p. B192.

71. Kydd, "Malawi in the 1970's", p. 306. The Presidential mansion in Lilongwe was especially plush. Costing 30 million Kwacha, it included solid gold bathroom fixtures, and inside window covers painted with scenes of British country life.

72. A "lavishly equipped grammar school in his native village where 50 highly qualified teachers (all white) teach a very traditional curriculum, including Latin, to 350 selected boys who are to be Malawi's future elite," (*The Washington Times*, June 29, 1966) symbolizing Banda's "identification with the values of the British upper middle class and his desire to transmit these values to a future elite in Malawi." Kydd, "Malawi in the 1970's," pp. 306-7.

73. Kydd, "Malawi in the 1970's", p. 301.

74. Morton, p. 14.

75. Ghai and Radwan, p. 93. See also Simon Thomas, "Economic developments in Malawi since Independence," *Journal of Southern African Studies*, vol. 2 N.1, 1974.

76. Vail, "The State and the Creation of Colonial Malawi's Agricultural Economy," p. 74.

77. Malawi, *Legislative Assembly*, 9 March, 1971, p. 835. The fertile area around Mchinje is where Banda and some of his Ministers had their estates. Banda also has personal farming interests in Kasungu, Nkhota Kota and Nkhata Bay.

78. Vail, "The State and the Creation of Colonial Malawi's Economy," pp. 77-8.

79. See for example, Robert Bates, *Markets and States in Tropical Africa: The Political Basis of Agricultural Policies*. University of California Press, Berkeley, 1981 and R. Mulomboji Mkandawire, "Markets, Peasants and Agrarian Change in the Post-Independence Malawi," *Journal of Contemporary African Studies*, vol. 4 No. 1/2. April 1985, pp. 89-102.

80. Christiansen, "Financing Malawi's Development Strategy," p.447.

81. Robert Christiansen, "The Pattern of Internal Migration in Response to Structural Change in the Economy of Malawi 1966-1977," *Development and Change*, vol. 15, 1984, p. 127. See also Jonathan G. Kydd and Robert E. Christiansen, "Structural Change in Malawi since Independence. Consequences of a Development strategy based on large-scale agriculture,"

World Development, vol. 10, May 1982, pp. 355-375.

82. Christiansen, "The Pattern of Internal Migration in Response to Structural Change in the Economy of Malawi 1966-1977," p. 128.

83. Edwin S. Segal, "Projections of Internal Migration in Malawi: Implications for Development," *Journal of Modern African Studies*, vol. 23, No. 2, 1985, pp. 315-29. See also Christiansen's seminal "The Pattern of Internal Migration in Response to Structural Change in the Economy of Malawi."

84. Vail, "The State and the Creation of Colonial Malawi's Economy," p. 75.

85. Thomas, p. 51.

86. Morton, p. 48.

87. *The Washington Times*, June 29, 1983.

88. Peter G. Forster, "Culture, Nationalism and the Invention of Tradition in Malawi," *Journal of Modern African Studies*, vol. 32 no. 3, 1994, p. 477.

89. Williams, p.16.

90. Forster, p. 477.

91. See for example Pike, p. 102; see also Robert B. Boeder, "We won't die for Fourpence", *Journal of Modern African Studies*, January 1977, pp. 310-315.

92. Richard Hodder-Williams, "'Support' in East Africa," p. 116; see also Hodder-Williams, "Dr. Banda's Malawi," *Journal of Commonwealth and Comparative Studies*, vol. 12 no. 2, 1974, p. 98.

93. Richard Hodder-Williams, "'Support' in East Africa," p. 92.

94. A. Ross, "White Africa's Black Ally," *New Left Review*, No. 45, September/October 1967, p.92.

95. "Malawi: Playing with fire," *Africa Confidential*, September 3, 1988, p.3.

96. J. W. M. van Breugel, "The Religious Significance of the Nyao among the Chewa of Malawi," *Cultures et Developpement*, vol. 17, No.3, 1985, pp.487-517. See also Ian Linden, "Chewa Initiation Rites and Nyau Societies: The Use of Religious Institutions in Local Politics at Mua," in Terence O. Ranger and John Weller (eds), *Themes in the Christian History of Central Africa*, Berkeley, University of California Press, 1974, p.30.

97. See Linden, *Ibid*, p.31.

98. *Ibid*, p.38.

99. *Ibid*.

100. A. Chilivumbo, "Malawi's Lively Art Form," *Africa Report*, October 1971, p.17.

101. Robert B. Boeder, "Prospects for Political Stability in Malawi," in Calvin Woodward (ed.), *On the Razor's Edge: Prospects for Political Stability in Southern Africa*, Pretoria, Africa Institute of South Africa, 1986, p. 195.

102. See A. C. Ross, "The Political Role of the Witchfinder in Southern Malawi during the Crisis of October 1964-May 1965," in *Witchcraft and Healing*, Edinburgh, Centre for African Studies, 1969, p.63, 70.

103. "Malawi: Playing with fire," *Africa Confidential*, p.4.

104. A.W. Wood, "Training Malawi's Youth: the work of the Malawi Young Pioneers," *Community Development Journal*, No. 5, 1970, p. 132.

105. See Michael Curtis (ed.), *Israel and the Third World*, New Brunswick, N.J., Transaction Press, 1976.

106. Uma Lele, "African experiences with Rural Development," International Bank for Reconstruction and Development, Staff Working Paper No. 195, Washington, DC., 1975.

107. Colin Legum (ed.), *Africa Contemporary Record* 1982-3, p.B650.

108. "Malawi: Playing with Fire," p 4.

109. For the instability at the head of the security forces see especially *Africa Confidential*, March 14, 1979 and February 4, 1987.

110. "Malawi: The Waiting Game," *Africa Confidential*, June 9, 1982, p.6.

111. Hodder-Williams, "'Support' in Eastern Africa," p. 164.

112. Hodder-Williams, "Dr. Banda's Malawi," p.105.

113. Hodder-Williams, "'Support' in Eastern Africa," p. 168.

114. *Ibid*, p. 171; see also "Malawi: The Waiting Game."

115. Hodder-Williams, "'Support' in Eastern Africa," p. 171.

116. Cited in Short, p. 254.

117. Cited in Short, p. 256.

118. Colin Legum (ed.), *Africa Contemporary Record 1982-3*, p.650.

119. Economist Intelligence Unit. "Mozambique and Malawi, Country Report," 1994, p. 37.

120. "Malawi: Never the same again," *Africa Confidential*, May 22, 1992.

121. As cited in *Africa Research Bulletin*, Political Series, May 1992.

122. *Africa Research Bulletin*, Political Series, June 1994.

123. *Africa Confidential*, May 6, 1994, p. 6.

124. *Ibid*, p. 7.

125. *Africa Research Bulletin*, Political Series, June 1994.

126. Andrew Pryor, *Malawi and Madagascar*, Washington DC., The World Bank, p. 38.

127. *Africa Confidential*, August 12, 1994, p. 3.

128. *Africa Confidential*, May 6, 1994, p. 7.

129. *Africa Confidential*, 9 June 1995, p. 7.

130. *Ibid*.

CHAPTER THREE

GABON UNDER THE SHADOW
OF BIG BROTHER

Like Malawi, but for quite different reasons, Gabon is one of Africa's lesser-studied countries[1], surprisingly so since it boasts the continent's second-highest GDP per capita. Also like Malawi, Gabon is one of the few countries on the continent to have been continuously (except for two hectic days in 1964) under civilian rule. And this despite the presence of a host of potentially destabilizing factors, that elsewhere in Africa have triggered coup after coup. In contradistinction to Malawi, however, the source of civil-military stability is quite different. At least until the 1990 multiparty reforms—and, some might well argue to this very day—the stability of civilian rule in Libreville is solidly based on French military guarantees. This was the main underpinning of a Gabonese civilian order, possibly no less authoritarian than the one in Lilongwe. For despite supplementary strategies employed by President Omar Bongo, ultimately French force of arms directly or indirectly sustains the regime in Libreville.

Basic Socio-Economic parameters

Gabon is a small country astride the equator stretching 550 kms. from north to south in rain-soaked equatorial Africa. The country's relatively small size and minuscule population belie, however, its diversity and socio-economic problems, some of which are unique. Gabon's 267,667 sq. kms. are mostly heavily vegetated plateaus dissected by rivers, estuaries and swamps that greatly complicate surface travel, with rapids and waterfalls constraining riverain traffic as well. The country's waterways comprise the drainage basin of the 1,200 km-long Ogooue River that rises near Franceville, forms a large delta below Lamberene (of Dr. Schweitzer fame) and then flows into the Atlantic Ocean. Only in the late 1980's was the costly and still problem-ridden Transgabonais railway inaugurated, to constitute the first reliable land-link between the capital and the country's distant, mineral-rich, southern regions.

Unlike much of the rest of Africa, Gabon is a sparsely populated country, though one marked by very uneven densities and small settlements isolated from each other by totally unpopulated terrain. A virtually empty strip of land, for example, runs across the country from the coast south of Port Gentil. The Moyen Ogooue, Mayombe and Crystal Mountain areas, and much of the northeast are also nearly empty of people. Only in the Fang-populated Woleu Ntem region (abutting Equatorial Guinea's Rio Muni province) does the population density reach a high level (for Gabon) of 4 people per sq. km.

The actual size of Gabon's population is in dispute, overestimated by Libreville (after the discovery of its mineral wealth) by over 130% from United Nations figures. (By thus lowering per capita indicators, the new data entitle Gabon to preferential loans and aid as a developing country.) In 1960 the country's population, Africa's smallest after Gambia, was estimated at 485,000. Despite an influx of expatriates and non-nationals, World Bank figures—based on a growth of 0.9% per annum—placed the 1995 population at 680,000. Gabon's official estimates, by contrast posit a population of 1.7 million.

The country's small population and stagnant growth rate are a function of high infant mortality rates—over 30 per 1,000 births—and very high (30%) rates of infertility and sterility[2], the latter an outcome of the corrosive effect of the country's unhealthy climate, and the high amounts of toxic minerals in Gabon's topsoil. Such a small population acts as a major constraint on development. This is dramatically underscored by the fact that the male component of the country's productive population amounts to barely 113,800 people, of whom 70,600 are salaried workers (42,000 laborers and 3,740 petty traders) and 39,500 subsistence farmers. In the 1970's major manpower shortages forced the regime to import (by air) contract labor from other parts of Africa for the country's booming extractive industries. At the same time, only one half of one per cent of Gabon comprises arable land—less than one half an acre per capita—limiting potentials for agrarian self-sufficiency.

Given poor soils that rapidly leech when tilled, no rural all-weather roads, and poor marketing facilities, Gabon's farmers have in any case never had much motivation to fully exploit the land. Commercial agriculture has actually been in decline for decades, the prime

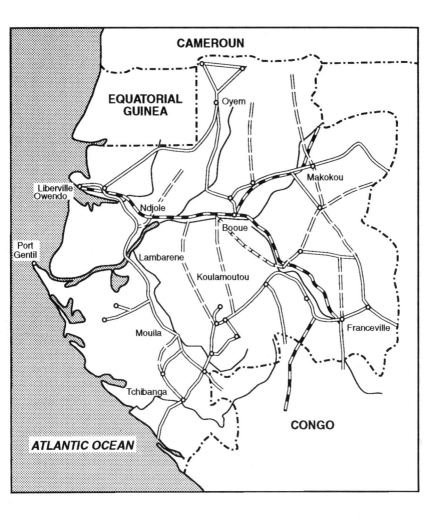

crops produced (apart from cane sugar introduced in the 1970's) being small amounts of coffee and cocoa in the north, and rice in the south. Malaria has kept cattle herds in the country at 5-7,000 head. But in contrast to its rural and agrarian stagnation, Gabon is one of Africa's most well-endowed countries in mineral wealth, and new exciting discoveries are made every year. Originally "merely" a source of valuable tropical timber, by the 1970's Gabon had become a globally-ranked major producer of petroleum, manganese and uranium.

Like other African states, Gabon is an artificial creation of the colonial era. With few exceptions archeological evidence suggests that most of Gabon's current ethnic groups are recent arrivals in their habitat. Virtually all of them had no prior political unity in the form of kingdoms. And, moreover, fully 85% of the population is artificially dissected by international borders, with their true center of gravity lying outside Gabon. This is especially true of the Fang, Gabon's largest and most dynamic ethnic group, of whom large numbers live in Equatorial Guinea and Cameroun. (Weinstein has noted that in the 1960's there was much more contact and better traffic between Gabon's Woleu Ntem region and Rio Muni, then part of Spanish Guinea, than with Libreville.)[3] Other boundaries in the east and south also separate groups strongly pulled to their "heartlands" in the Congo. Until the Transgabonais railroad reached Franceville in 1986, Gabon's Haut Ogooue province and population had much tighter social, cultural and economic links with Congo, with which country the region had indeed been attached during 1925-46, despite the latter's "Marxist" orientation.

Despite its modest population, Gabon has 49 ethnic groups, though some number only several hundred people. At the time colonial rule was imposed all groups were at a similar level of development, though some (notably the Fang) were in a major surge of expansion, while others (in particular the Myene) were in a state of decline. The groups fall into ten ethnic clusters. The figures for 1960 (the only reliable ones) list Gabon's largest ethnic groups as the Fang (141,000, or 31% of the total population), the Bandjabi (48,500) and the Bapounou (25,000), followed by 7 ethnic groups with at least 10,000 people. Two other, smaller, ethnic groups need to be mentioned. First, the numerically few Myene, who had historically been the "masters" of the country's lacustral regions from Rio Muni to Fernan Vaz (north of the Loango Kingdom in Angola/Congo), who, together with the Fang, are the political heavyweights in Gabon. And the Bateke ethnic sliver

GABON : ETHNIC DISTRIBUTION

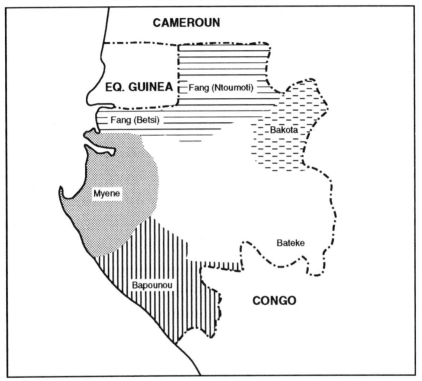

near Franceville (and in slightly larger numbers in Congo), who would not merit attention were they not President Bongo's ethnic group[4]—and hence, by definition, the group that has benefited most under his reign.

The Fang are found in Woleu Ntem, and along the Estuary, that had traditionally been Myene country, which they reached in the mid-19th century during an expansion toward the sea. They are divided into three major clans, but a more useful distinction is the geographical one, between the Fang of Woleu Ntem—which is their political core—and the Myene-assimilated "Estuary Fang." It is this internal division of the Fang that has, to this day, prevented the group from exerting the full political weight of their superior numbers.[5]

Among the more recent arrivals to Gabon, the Fang arrived in Woleu Ntem under indirect pressure from the Adamawa emirates in Cameroun in the middle of the 18th century. Fanning south, the much-feared Fang expelled, subjugated, or assimilated the groups that they encountered. Their advance to the Ocean was, however, blocked by France, and consequently their sense of cultural identity was shattered, with revivalist movements springing among them, aimed at national self-assertion. Though largely Christian (as is Gabon, second in Africa in percentage of Christian population), the Fang are dispro-portionately associated with the *Bieri* ancestor worship cult, the *Bwiti* secret society, and other occult practices[6]—in a part of Africa that has traditionally been, and remains, a fertile ground for syncretic move-ments and complex death rites.

Individualistic and upwardly mobile, the Fang neither created states nor engaged in the slave trade. A segment continued moving southeast from Woleu Ntem, to become acculturated with the Myene they there met, to become the Estuary Fang. The out-migration was due to multiple factors: soil-exhaustion; depletion of elephant herds hunted for their tusks; and a desire to establish direct contact with European ivory buyers on the coast who paid ten times the price the Fang received from middlemen. But there was also, in Fang cosmology, a "drive" to be re-united with an elder "brother" to their south, with whom they were destined to prosper.[7] Paradoxically Fang relations with the Myene Mpongwe, the only indigenous group to their south, were always antagonistic.

Being Gabon's most dynamic group, the Fang rapidly overtook the coastal Myene in every sphere of endeavor despite the Myene trade monopoly and prolonged contact with the French. Though Gabon's

first schools were established in the coastal Myene areas, by independence two-thirds of all teachers in private (Catholic) schools, and
half of those in public schools were Fang[8]. To this day it is easy to evoke
the Fang bogeyman in Gabon (as Bongo did in an effort to stave off
multipartyism in 1990), because the Fang are feared by the more
indolent groups of the south. The Fang in turn look down in disdain
at the "decadence" of the easy-going Myene, and at the stagnant
southern groups, until recently in control of the country. Such rivalries
have triggered intermittent ethnic violence, as the 1945 Fang-Myene
riots in Libreville.

The Eshira are Gabon's second largest ethnic group, with the
Eshira proper and the more numerous Bapounou jointly comprising
20% of Gabon's population, or 94,000 people. The Eshira live south of
the Ogooue, in inland regions of southwest Gabon, some having
arrived from Congo. Former slave middlemen, like most of Gabon's
groups their numbers are static, while their isolated location has seen
development bypass them. The more numerous Bapounou (63,000),
reside mostly in Nyanga, with others in Ngounie, Gabon's second
most-populated region after Woleu Ntem.

The M'Bete include the Bandjabi (their largest group), Badouma,
Ambamba, Banbana and other ethnic slivers, and number 15% of the
population, or 71,000 people. They are found in the upper Ogooue
basin in a broad arc between Lastourville and Franceville. The Kota
cluster includes the Bakota, Mahongwe, Shake and Dambomo, counting 61,000 people or 13% of the population. In the pre-colonial era
harassed on all sides, three-quarters of them are found in the Ogooue
Ivindo Province in northeastern Gabon, along the eastern tributaries
of the upper Ivindo River, cut in half by the Gabon-Congo border.

Finally, the six Myene clans—the Mpongwe, Orungu, Nkomi,
Adyumba, Enenga and Galoa—are small lacustral and coastal groups
(except the Adyumba, driven inland) found for 300 kms. along the
Atlantic Ocean and Gabon's inland lagoons south of Libreville, linked
by language though historically fractured into tiny entities.[9] The
Mpongwe were the main slave/trade middlemen of the region, and
their location made them the first to come into contact with the
French. They make up 5% of the population or 23,000 people. Though
very few, their early contact with the French, middleman role in the
slave-trade, and control of the Ogooue Estuary—that was the first
region in Gabon to be economically exploited—made the Myene

important far beyond proportion to their numbers. Economically devastated by the abolition of the slave-trade, decimated by a spate of epidemics accompanying colonialism (as well as by alcoholism), the Myene further splintered and fell into decay.[10] Still, Gabon's first priests, high school graduates and teachers were all Myene, and Myene were at the forefront of the nationalist phase and early political activity.

The Mpongwe (estimated at 5,000) are the Myene "aristocracy", and are found around the superb sixty-mile natural harbor Estuary. Divided into sixteen clans, during the 19th century they had four "kingdoms" in control of little territory and few people—in essence mutual-protection slave-trading extended families and their cohorts. Yet these entities were referred to by the French by the name of their reigning "monarch," and it was with them that France signed treaties and secured rights over what was to become the colony of Gabon. Among them was the pro-French "King" Denis (or King William to the English/Americans of the day, though actually Antchouwe Kowe Rapontchombo), whose grandson was to be Gabon's first high school graduate. Praised as a cultured man (who served his guests wine!), several hotels and restaurants, in both Gabon and France,are named after him today. Yet Rapontchombo was actually the leading Mpongwe slaver, whose "kingdom" encompassed barely 150 houses and 800 people (including fifty wives, relatives, and 400 slaves). It was he who signed the famous 1839 treaty with France, encouraged other Mpongwe chiefs to do likewise, and opened the door to French control of the Estuary.[11]

Of the other Mpongwe groups only the Orungu need be mentioned, if only because of their critical location. Also numbering *circa* 5,000, and divided into 24 clans, they are found along the Ogooue River, and at Port Gentil. The latter is Gabon's economic capital and the center of the modern oil industry. It is a modern town built on Mandji, the Ogouee delta sand-island, that happens to be the Orungu capital.

Nearly three decades of petrol-fuelled development has indelibly altered many Gabonese socio-economic statistics, while creating major anomalies and disparities in society. A massive rural-urban drift has transformed Libreville, Port Gentil and Franceville, creating a large urban-based, functionally-redundant civil service. At the same time one-third of the country's population continues living in decrepit small villages, isolated from each other by large distances, perpetually dependent upon State doles for sustenance, being incapable of attaining self-sufficiency in foodstuffs, and unwilling to experiment growing other crops.

Even as Gabon leads Africa on a variety of "development" indicators—including literacy, doctors, telephones, and radios per capita, the daily *Gabon-Matin* has a press-run of only 2,000; malaria periodically ravages society; and death and possession rites regularly take place throughout the country. With "Gabon...among the countries... with the richest customs, beliefs and secret rites," [12] belief in ancestral spirits, and the practice of fetishism and ritual murder co-exist—in urban as well as in rural areas—with universal primary education[13] and a 75% affiliation to Christianity.

Reports of ritual cannibalism surface with regularity in Gabon. On April 2, 1986, *L'Union* revealed that ritual murder and the consumption of human organs was practised regularly by *Bwiti* members at Owendo (the railway terminus across the Estuary from Libreville), who form a large percentage of dock workers, and six people were put on trial in December 1989 for ritual murder and cannibalism in Libreville[14], and again in 1994. Port Gentil, Gabon's center of "modernity" experienced in the 1980's several manifestations of "ancestral rage" at the progressive "decadence" of the town's Orungu population. And in the distant (Bateke) Franceville, another major center of industrial modernity, several efforts to rename the town (back to its original Masuku) have been "blocked" by ancestral spirits, that have indicated deep opposition.

Basic Features of the Economy

Despite some recent backsliding, Gabon boasts Africa's second highest per capita income ($4,500 in 1984—using IMF figures), a budget usually in surplus, a favorable balance of trade (but not of payments), huge mineral reserves, and until the late 1980's such investor confidence that Gabon was the only African state to float a Eurobond issue that was oversubscribed.

However, in contrast to its booming extractive economy, and global ranking as an exporter of petroleum, manganese, uranium and timber, Gabon's agrarian sector is in total decay, completely unable to feed itself let alone the growing urban populations. Foodstuffs have to be imported at great cost from abroad (mostly from France), and they constitute 18% of Gabon's total imports, a major drain on the country's resources. Moreover, despite a concerted effort in the 1980's to "Gabonize" domestic economic activity, apart from petty trade (and half of that as well!) most economic activity stubbornly remains outside national hands.

With only 0.5% of its superficity under cultivation, domestic agrarian produce has always been meagre, and locally-grown foodstuffs in short supply. While there is no starvation in rural areas, malnutrition among farmers is common, especially as youth have drifted in large numbers into urban centers. Currently up to 85% of Gabon's foodstuff needs have to be imported, including many luxury items (cheeses, wines, mineral water and champagne) for its large (up to 40,000) expatriate community. But many basic staples, that could easily be grown domestically but for apathy, lack of motivation, and a non-productive "tradition," also have to be imported. "This is how it is *chez nous*. It is easier, and cheaper on the long run, to import" explained a rural animator (of all people!) to the author in Franceville in 1991.

Two examples are cassava, that is indigenous to the country, and of which there is always an annual shortage of some 6,000 tons—though up to 100,000 tons of the crop is produced locally. And rice, 5-6,000 tons of which have to be imported every year—though rice is grown, and with ease, around Franceville, but only for local consumption. Fishing is also very undeveloped in a country with huge potentials due to its 800 km. coastline, large protein-needs, and the paucity of malaria-prone livestock.

The country's dependency on imported foodstuffs was given a major boost during the 1970's when agrarian activity recorded negative growth rates. Despite high prices for staple crops, farmers fled rural areas for jobs in the labor-starved extractive sector and the civil service. By 1978 the average income of urban workers was 22 times higher than those in the subsistence sector. As rural areas emptied out, Gabon's food imports quadrupled, and during 1970-1984 went up a further tenfold. Alcohol imports scored higher increases, as Gabon attained global leadership in champagne consumption per capita![15] Despite current heavy imports periodic food shortages are common: "villages have actually been receiving direct food aid from government and private charities, so serious is the economic stagnation" in the countryside.[16]

Bias against developing Woleu Ntem—the sole region with rosy agrarian prospects in the 1960's—also had major adverse repercussions. Most of Gabon's cash crops (coffee, cocoa) have traditionally been grown by the Fang of Woleu Ntem. As they abandoned their coffee plantations, Gabon's coffee exports plummeted to a paltry 100 tons from 1,280 in 1970. Cocoa exports also fell from an annual 5,000 tons to as low as 1,000 in 1984. A 1977 study estimated that every year 250 hectares of cocoa trees were being abandoned by farmers, with even Gabon's meagre cocoa and coffee exports increasingly actually of smuggled Equatorial Guinea origin.

Gabon's rapid recent economic transformation camouflages the fact that only a few areas—the Estuary, Haut-Ogooue, Ogooue-Maritime—experienced massive change, with others little, if at any. Excluding oil, those three regions gained 78.6% of all industrialization in the country (or 88.4% of industrial investment inclusive of oil), with the figure in 1979 as high as 91%.[17] A second set of figures suggests that percentage-wise only the Estuary and (Bongo's) Haut Ogooue saw *any* increase in salaried labor and gross net income during 1974-1981![18] Income distribution became so highly skewed in Gabon that "a little over 1 per cent of the population account[ed] for one third of total consumption," with, in 1985, fully 75% of Gabon's GNP going to only two percent of the population.[19] When in 1984 for the first time a modest income tax (1.5-2.5 percent) was introduced, only 2,000 people were affected by it!

At independence Gabon's sole towns were the decrepit tiny Libreville (44,600), founded in 1849 as the off-loading port for liberated slaves (mostly Vili from the Congo) intercepted by French naval patrols; and logging center (later oil-hub) Port-Gentil, with a population of 20,732. Every other "town" was a bushpost of less than 5,000 people. The economic boom of the 1970's saw Libreville mushrooming into a modern (if characterless) city of 300,000 people; Port-Gentil, with half of the country's expatriates, grew to 80,000. Because of its relative isolation and expatriate buying-power, the latter developed scores of boutiques, nightspots and restaurants, many fancier than Libreville's.

Gabon's economy reflects a phaseout of the colonial role of timber exports, by mineral exports, especially oil. Forestry, historically Gabon's source of wealth, as late as 1960 accounted for 73 percent of exports, with income from timber making up fully 50 percent of the national budget. By 1970 mineral exports (oil, manganese, uranium) had made such deep gains that forestry products brought only 40 percent of export revenue, declining to 7.3 percent in 1983. The timber industry still employed, however, twice as many workers as the extractive sector, and Gabon remained Africa's fourth largest producer of hardwoods, and the global producer of the valuable okoume, used in the manufacture of plywood.

Gabon's forests, Africa's most valuable after Zaire's, cover 85% of the country with logging having commenced at the outset of the century. By the early 1960's the 36 European timber companies had depleted timber stands along the Ogooue Estuary and its tributaries, the prime means of evacuation of logs. The high cost of logging in inaccessible virgin forests brought powerful industry pressures for the construction of the Transgabonais, that—by linking Haut Ogooue with Libreville—opened up new forest zones. The World Bank, disturbed by the clout of the timber lobby that it felt was behind Gabon's decision to build the costly railway, assessed the project uneconomical unless higher contributions were exacted from the timber industry since the first segment of the line benefited only them.

Oil, much of it in off-shore deposits, was first located in 1948, when manganese and uranium were also discovered. Sharply higher global prices in the 1970's triggered a frenzy of exploration that tripled production, increasing the role of oil to 83% of export earnings. While relieving Gabon of the stigmata of being a French timber concession, the country was transformed into a no less dependent rentier state.[20] And though Africa's fourth largest producer, oil exploration continues frenetically today, as do efforts to locate other minerals. For the fear is that the developmental role played by State royalties may be short-lived since actual reserves (10 years production) are modest. Even the major 1985 Rabi Kounga oil-strike (among Africa's largest), has only 60 million tons—barely changing estimates of Gabon's oil-production life-span.

Huge 250,000 ton tankers berth at the two refineries (annual output 2.2 million tons) in Port Gentil, the Orungu capital, loading crude for Latin America and the US. Oil exports rose nearly ten-fold a decade, from 178,200 tons in 1957 to 1.4 million in 1966 and 11.2 million in 1976, when they plummeted to 7-8 million tons a year before rising in 1990 to an all-time peak of 13.8 million tons. Located in swampy malarial areas, and costing ten times more to bring on stream than Middle East oil, Gabon's entire coast is divided into concessions leased to 25 French, British and American companies. Nine hold title to most permits (60% are held by ELF-Gabon), and three produce the bulk of exports. The American companies claim they are discriminated against, and that French national interests dictate *under-exploiting* Gabonese deposits, keeping them as a reserve against shortfalls elsewhere.

The paramount role of oil has indelibly transformed the country, and especially Port Gentil with its ostentatious life-style, luxury night-clubs and boutiques. The oil-port is serviced by more flights than any other African non-capital city. Fresh meat and produce, and luxury commodities arrive daily by air from Paris, and prior to 1989, in unmarked cargo planes from South Africa. Literally a few miles from the bustling oil-hub is the swampy Estuary where life still revolves around dugout canoes, imports are unknown, and infant mortality stands at 70%.

Oil is at the base of Gabon's transformation, since the 1970's saw the dashing of high hopes for two other minerals that were supposed to stoke industrialization: uranium and manganese. Located in large concentrations in the 1940's in the Haut Ogooue, both were being exploited at independence. Uranium (with 20 years reserves) is mined at Mounana by a company with 25% State equity, and exported via Congo. Despite a ceiling on how much can be marketed due to a global uranium glut and French quotas (at a 50% subsidy above market prices), Gabon is still the world's eighth largest producer.

The country's manganese at Moanda are the largest such con-centrations in the world.[21] Found in a unique five meter band near the surface over a 26 sq. km area with a high mineral content, reserves are estimated at 200 million tons, or 25% of global reserves, assuring current levels of exploitation for 150 years. Gabon is the world's third largest producer of manganese and with a 22% market-share, the largest exporter. But demand has been erratic ranging from 1.4 million (1982) to 2.3 million tons (1979). Until the Transgabonais was completed manganese was evacuated south by the longest (76 km) overhead cablecar in the world to M'Binda in Congo, and then by the Congo-Ocean railroad to Point Noire. Part of the rationale for the Transgabon-ais was that high freight levies of manganese—assumed to increase by another million tons, and that the cablecar could not accommo-date—together with timber evacuation levies would make the railway self-sufficient, even while opening up to exploitation other mineral reserves.

For though Gabon's full range of resources has not been mapped, many confirmed deposits await in inaccessible localities, with new ones being discovered all the time. These include 800,000 tons of barytes; huge amounts of talc; large deposits of Colombium that could make Gabon the world's second producer, found virtually on the surface 40 kms. east of Lamberene; and nearby, with a waterway making evacuation economical, at least 50 million tons of phosphate deposits. Other valuable deposits were discovered during the laying of the railbed of the Transgabonais, that had to be rerouted on two instances. But the *cause celebre* has always been Belinga's massive iron deposits in the isolated Northeast. These are the world's third-largest such deposits, with a very high ore content, but they cannot be tapped unless linked to the railroad via a spur. Despite little global interest in Gabon's iron, Bongo has been committed to the spur. For Gabon's limited oil reserves, coupled with low earnings from timber, uranium and manganese (that account for 7.4%, 3.3% and 4.2% respectively of export revenues) drives the regime into a never-ending quest to tap all riches beneath the country's topsoil.

The Colonial Era

The first people encountered by the French in what became Gabon were the Myene, who were middlemen in the slave-trade, and provisioners to European vessels. In 1839 a treaty of friendship was signed by "King" Denis (head of a clan to disappear in the 20th century) and naval Captain Bouet-Willaumez (who had no authority to do so) who was ecstatic about the naval potentials of the Estuary. This minor treaty gave birth to the myth of a benevolent French entry in the region.[22] Leon Mba, Gabon's first (Estuary Fang) President repeated the myth in a 1965 speech: "the Gabonese people were never conquered because the tutorship exercised by the French was the result of agreements freely entered into with her beginning in 1839."[23] And linking this to Fang cosmology about a historic quest for an elder brother, Mba urged to "love the foreigner; he makes people rich. Be diplomatic with him and eloquent; be hospitable"[24] for France and Gabon had a common destiny.

The reality was different. Neither King Denis (possibly unusual, but still just a rich slave-dealer) who ceded the left bank of the Como

(Ogooue) Estuary, nor other Myene "kings" who signed away their independence (e.g. Re-Dowe, "King Louis," in March 1842), controlled much territory or held sway over more than a thousand people, including slaves. As early as 1862 opposition to French presence was manifest in Como, with revolts in 1873; some clans (e.g. the Orungu) ceded land for French settlements under duress; others ("King" Glass, or R'Ogouarowe) after bombardment.

The same was true of the interior, that was penetrated under Savorgnan de Brazza (who founded Franceville in 1880) and occupied between 1874 and 1914. The Fang in particular resisted the "pacification" of Woleu-Ntem. Some groups freely entered into treaties of dependency (at times not realizing physical domination was involved) while others resisted, some even after WWI.[25] Yet the myth of a special relationship between Gabon and France endured, anchored in the 1839 treaty with Antchuwe Kowe Rapontombo. This is remarkable since the occupation of the interior was accompanied by forced labour for porterage and construction of tracks, while the *indigenat* code in French Africa between 1910 and 1946 exacted similar levies from the populations. And the forced cultivation of cash crops (e.g. coffee and cocoa in Woleu Ntem) that France demanded from various groups, produced mediocre harvests on Gabon's poor soils, at the cost of famine and disease, as staple crops suffered.

Worse abuses occurred under the concessionary system that was imposed on French Equatorial Africa during 1899-1930. To minimize State outlays, private companies were granted virtual monopolies of plunder within delineated zones, with power of life and death in their fiefdoms, and the right to ignore traditional land rights (especially in coastal areas.) While the brutality of exploitation differed from company to company, it was onerous and was enforced by private militias and summary punishment, with news of the atrocities very tardy in reaching France. Forty companies were granted concessions in Equatorial Africa[26], and Gabon was carved up by eleven. The largest concession was over the bulk of the neither fully occupied nor accessible interior; the others were smaller parcels of land along the Estuary that allowed access and exploitation of Gabon's coastal and lacustral resources. (A 1905 reorganization saw some of the interior concessions ceded in exchange for grants of small but prime timberland along the Estuary.)

France had hoped that a viable infrastructure would as a consequence be laid out in the interior, but most companies, undercapitalized and understaffed, sought immediate profits at minimal expenditures. Their agents were often venal adventurers, rarely salaried, and living off the land, stole goods and commodities for their own account. Revolts erupted, especially against the avaricious (SHO), that had a monopoly over half of Gabon. This was capped by a Mbete uprising during 1928-29, when after decades of SHO brutalization they faced demands from Libreville for forced labor (1923), head tax (1926) and in 1928 a compulsory crop production (at low producer prices) for the local garrison.

The brutalities of the concessionary era saw an out-migration of tens of thousands of people who fled the Ngounie and Ogooue valleys. Population levels subsequently remained static for 30 years: traditional migration patterns were disrupted, and historic commercial networks collapsed as traders fled trade prohibitions by European competitors, taxes or confiscatory policies. Food production plummeted with starvation and epidemics resulting as entire villages relocated to avoid company agents and their demands for forced labor, foodstuffs (in lieu of taxes), or the compulsory cultivation of cash-crops.

Though in 1930 the concessionary system was terminated after public outcries in France spearheaded by Andre Gide's visit to the region[27], abuses continued as administrative appointments to the unglamorous colonies of Equatorial Africa were reserved for novices entering the service, or those demoted and given a "last chance" after atrocities committed elsewhere.[28] Remote Gabon was also the ideal place to banish rebels from other parts of Africa. It was on an Ogooue island off Ndjole, that Samory Toure (Sekou Toure's grandfather) was exiled after a decade of armed resistance to France, and it was to Gabon that the last king of Dahomey was exiled to in 1900, as was also Morocco's Allal el Fasi.

During 1921-1934 some of Gabon's population was also forced-drafted to construct the Congo-Ocean railroad in neighboring Congo. Little has been written about this sad episode that saw further population dislocations and armed expeditions hunting for labor quotas. But missionary reports from throughout the region documented these ravages. One report on Woleu Ntem noted that "the whole sector is in disorder...all available men are in the brush...while others with ropes around their necks are taken towards Congo."[29] Thousands died in assembly camps, on the trek to Congo, in camps there, or under harsh construction conditions.

Colonialism affected Gabon's groups in a different manner. The Myene had been pauperized before colonial rule by the abolition of the slave-trade, and their commercial monopoly was also eroded by the arrival of French settlers and concessionary companies. They were transformed "from powerful middlemen dominating the trade of the Estuary into a group of wandering peddlers."[30] Soon also ravaged by epidemics, the Myene were also dispossessed of prime land by settlers, timber companies along the Estuary, and the administration that built its urban centers in Libreville and Mandji Island. (In 1950 France belatedly offered modest financial compensation for these confiscations.) As their numbers shrank some clans disappeared completely; others abandoned their remaining lands, relocating *en masse* to the new urban centers, as did "King" Glass's followers who established a Libreville quarter where his lineage remains.

Being the first in contact with the French, and residing at the nerve-centers of the new cash economy and civil administration, the Myene were, however, the first to Westernize, producing Gabon's first graduates, priests, academics and politicians. (Close behind them were the Fang, among whom British and American missionaries found avid converts.) By the 1930's a small minority in their ancestral lands, the Myene formed pressure groups to reclaims lands lost to the French and to regain regional primacy they had lost to the Fang, by now the dominant group in Libreville and throughout the Estuary. Thus was born in 1936 the *Comite Mpongwe*, created by educated Mpongwe nobility. They elected a Mpongwe-assimilated Benga *evolue* of chiefly descent, Francois-de-Paul Vane[31], to the Governor-General's administrative council, where his campaigns led to France's 1950 compensation of some long-standing claims. The early rise of a Myene elite did little, however, to stem growing Fang power especially with the expansion of suffrage after the Second World War.

Insular groups reacted differently to colonial rule. As was noted some fled the abuses of the concessionary system, others rebelled against it, but all resisted France's policy of forcibly merging their small villages into larger centers for purposes of easier colonial control, taxation, and provision of services. Often the French razed entire villages, their farmland and crops to secure the relocation they desired to new centers that are today recognized on the map by their suffix of "ville." The Fang, for the first time humbled militarily by French force of arms, and drafted into timber concessions and the construction of the Congo-Ocean railroad, as well as required to undertake demeaning "female" agrarian work, withdrew inwards, seeking spiritual strength through syncretic cults (*bieri, bwiti*), and cultural reassertion through *elar ayong*, a movement that alarmed France. Later, with renewed confidence, the Fang were to dominate most spheres of modern activity.

Bwiti, which remains a powerful political force in Gabon today, was initially a Mitsogo male secret society (most groups had similar spirit cults) that spread via the slave trade to become ingrained among the Fang who shed less elaborate secret societies (e.g. *Bieri*) to adopt *Bwiti*. Strengthening group solidarity and Fang cultural homogeneity against socio-cultural threats in times of stress, *Bwiti* utilizes secret rites and consumption of vital human organs to link members with powerful ancestors and spirits. Being Gabon's most Christianized group, the Fang integrated elements of Christianity into the cult that today includes at least one-tenth of the Fang in over 100 chapels. The ten percent figure suggests a minority are affiliated with *Bwiti*; in reality many more participate *intermittently* in its rites, so that leadership in *Bwiti* confers considerable political influence, as was evident with Leon Mba, Gabon's first president. At the same time the *Mademoiselle* cult, arriving from Congo in the 1950's, and providing antidotes and protection against witchcraft, struck roots among those Fang resisting *Bwiti*, also conferring power to its leaders.

The *elar ayong* (meaning "unite the clans") movement in 1920-1930 by contrast aimed at spatially reorganizing the 150-odd Fang clans via voluntary regroupment of villages to secure better services, and culturally, by breaking inter-clan divisions.[32] Though initially viewed favorably by the French, soon *elar ayong* was seen as an early form of nationalism. One French official sent specifically to investigate it reported, "it is certain that once their regroupment is entirely finished...they will form a kind of government presided over by an elected official...capable of governing itself...organized democratically and...arriving at the stage foreseen by article 75 of the charter of the U.N...which gives them the right to demand independence."[33] However a united political force did not emerge among the individualistic Fang with their intrinsic divisions, something that worked against them as France scrapped the indigenat and corvee systems after WWII, legalized political activity, and set Gabon on the road to independence.

The Early Political Scene

Two early political parties emerged in Gabon: the first was the *Bloc Démocratique Gabonais* of the coastal Myene and Estuary Fang under Estuary Fang Leon Mba and Orongu Myene Paul Gondjout, that was linked to the inter-territorial *Rassemblement Démocratique Africaine*, and France's SFIO. The second was the *Union Démocratique et Socialiste Gabonais* of the Woleu Ntem Fang, headed by Jean-Hilaire Aubame, linked with the UDSR in France, and with the inter-territorial *Parti du Regroupement Africaine*. Early political life was dominated by these three leaders, in essence reflecting a tug-of-war between the two branches of the Fang.

Mba's presidency set Gabon's isolationist course for the new Republic, that has not changed much since. Born in 1902 in Libreville, a son of one of the first evolues, Mba was educated by missionaries, finishing his education via correspondence courses. Employed as a customs clerk he also became the ethnic *chef de canton*, and served as traditional judge until 1931, mediating intra-Fang disputes. Through his mother's family (that came from Lamberene) he was befriended by Paul Gondjout[34] an important Myene political ally.

Though one of Mba's brothers was the country's first Fang Catholic priest, Mba specialized in occult practices, and was a *Bwiti* leader. In 1931 he was arrested allegedly for militance on behalf of the League for the Rights of Man, but in reality for his involvement in ritual murder and sale of human flesh in Libreville's market. All details were censured since it was a major embarrassment to the French that an Estuary evolue leader, who had been at Government functions and dinners had been practising "cannibalism." Sentenced to exile in 1933, Mba remained under house-arrest for 13 years in Bambari in Oubangui-Chari (today's Central African Republic.)[35]

The reforms of the French Fourth Republic, and Mba's rallying to Free France during WWII saw his rehabilitation in 1946 through the good offices of Paul Gondjout who was now on the French Senate. Not particularly charismatic, Mba was defeated in his political bids several times, including by Aubame for a seat in the French National Assembly. However, with Myene support (who were too few to elect one of their own) Mba won the Libreville seat on the local Territorial Assembly, and in 1954 forged an alliance with Paul Gondjout to merge his Estuary Fang party with Gondjout's Myene *Bloc Démocratique Gabonais*, to become the party's Secretary under Gondjout's overall leadership. The alliance was successful and in 1956 Mba was elected Mayor of Libreville, to become a credible national leader.

Leadership of the Woleu Ntem Fang was captured by the "outsider" Jean-Hilaire Aubame, who after a career in the AEF federation capital (Brazzaville) blitzed to win the 1946 election for a seat in the French National Assembly in Paris. His victory electrified Woleu Ntem whose notables and *evolues* rallied behind him to form the *Union Démocratique et Socialiste Gabonais* (UDSG) in support for his re-election bids in 1951 and 1956. Overwhelmingly Fang, the UDSG enjoyed solid support among Catholic missions and in French colonial circles, in part due to Mba's *Bwiti* and radical (RDA) inter-territorial links.

Born in 1912 near Libreville, Aubame obtained a seminary education under Leon Mba's brother, entering the customs service with Mba's aid. Moving to Brazzaville in 1936, he became Governor-General Felix Eboue's protege, pursuing a distinguished career until his return to Gabon and election to the French National Assembly (1946-1958.) But as independence loomed near Aubame began to be viewed with unease, while Mba's stock began to soar, in local French timber circles, nervous about the future. Mba was a "safe" Francophile conservative (despite his RDA link) compared to Aubame, who had begun to voice populist goals. Indeed Mba's general political lusterlessness was seen as an asset, since if aided in his drive for power, he would be beholden to his benefactors. (Mba's true colours were visible when he suggested, to be rebuffed by De Gaulle, a third option for Gabon in the 1958 referendum—becoming an overseas *departement* of France.[36] The small but extremely powerful expatriate French community openly organized to support Mba, and he also acquired important aid from the Freemasons (a major force in Gabon) of which he was a member, alongside the French Governor-General.

Neither the BDG nor the UDSG were mass movements, both relying for support from societal influentials and chiefs who—in extremely underdeveloped Gabon—could be bought off. Intimidation and corruption were the means by which Mba defeated his more popular Fang protagonist. Though in the elections of 1957 the UDSG won 60% of the vote, it secured only 18 of 40 seats; the BDG and independents joined to form a majority (21:19) that resulted in a government with Mba as Vice President under the French Governor, and Gondjout as President of the Assembly. Deputies were literally bought for cash that had been liberally donated by what one observer called the French Expatriate Clan of Gabon, in a drive to install Mba as puppet leader in Libreville.[37] In 1958 a devolution of executive power made Mba Premier.

The Mba-Gondjout alliance rapidly fell apart, with the BDG splitting into its ethnic components when Mba drafted a Presidential constitution, while Gondjout supported a parliamentary system. Timber interests alerted Mba of Gondjout's determination to bloc parliamentarily the new Constitution, and on November 16, 1960 Mba imposed a state of emergency on Libreville, and arrested several PDG leaders including his former ally, Gondjout. The action derailed the planned motion of no-confidence in the Assembly, and ushered in a Presidential system. In 1961 Mba and Aubame joined to form a National Union alliance that lasted until 1963. Mba won an alleged 99.6% of the votes cast for the Presidency, with Aubame serving under him as Foreign Minister.[38]

The Mba Interregnum

The Mba Presidency was very much a transitional regime. Already ailing with incurable cancer in 1964, and incapable of performing his duties since 1966, during half of Mba's reign expatriate interests (the "Gabonese Clan") exerted prime influence in Gabon.[39] Some scholars see no difference between the neo-colonialist regime of Mba and that of his successor, Bongo. Yet, whatever their common denominator[40], it was greatly overshadowed by Bongo's dynamism, and the much greater sophistication of his reign.

Unlike many African "founding fathers," Mba was very insular, poorly educated, had not served in any of France's post-1946 political structures or colonial armies, nor worked in any capacity in France herself. Indeed Mba's sole foreign "exposure" was his lengthy incarceration in the Oubangui Chari backwaters! Emerging on the coattails of expatriate interests, heading a coalition of Myene and Estuary Fang notables, and sustained by conservative *Bwiti* leaders, Mba's reign was Francophile, isolationist, traditionalist and authoritarian. He rarely delivered speeches, and few on foreign policy. He rather offered codicils on personal values, reflecting a self-conception of a never-erring *pater familias* dispensing discipline and justice to his children. His homilies stressed the need for hard work, honesty, morality, and cooperation with France.[41] A "Gabon-firster," he wished no association with neighboring states, fearing a dilution of Gabon's economic prospects. And with lengthy ties in *Bwiti*, Mba protected its rituals and promoted its leaders, receiving in turn support from the powerful and feared cult, one center of which was Mikolongo near Libreville.[42] Right to his death Mba acted as if he possessed magic powers[43], even alluding to this on a number of occasions.

A temperamental leader content with *laissez-faire* policies, Mba catered mainly to the expatriate community. Though only 4,000 in 1960, their role was critical in timber, that was then Gabon's sole economic mainstay. Not particularly astute, Mba was not very capable of formulating or initiating new policies, exercising political leadership or controlling the unruly National Assembly, and he tolerated growing corruption in society. His appeals for honesty were rejected by deputies smarting over an edict lopping off 10% of their salaries *in lieu* of the State benefits they were receiving. And as his efforts at becoming Gabon's unchallenged political leader were thwarted, Mba's fits of temper and pledges of retribution (including via occult powers) became violent, triggering plotting within and without parliament.[44]

Mba started off with an ethnically-balanced cabinet but by 1967 the Fang were over-represented by 200%. Until 1966 a docile but irrelevant Bapounou trader (Paul-Marie Yembit) was his deputy (and heir apparent), solely in order to offer a balanced ethnic ticket. Aubame and the three UDSG ministers in Mba's government were largely powerless, with Aubame exercising his duties mostly from abroad. The alliance in any case lasted only until 1963, with Aubame constantly clashing with Mba on most programatic issues, becoming Mba's *bete noire* due to his great popularity among Fang deputies and Libreville's youth. Demoted in 1962, in 1963 Aubame was dropped from the cabinet altogether and appointed President of the Supreme Court. The ploy to neutralize him failed; faced with legislation making Supreme Court tenure (at twice the remuneration) incompatible with Assembly membership, Aubame resigned from the Court, opting to remain a deputy.

Exactly as in neighboring Congo, a coup erupted in Gabon when Mba tried to impose by force what eluded him through persuasion—single-party supremacy. Renouncing the UDDS alliance, Mba changed the electoral laws, rebuilt his bridges with the Myene by releasing Gondjout and appointing him President of the Social and

Economic Council, dissolved the Assembly, and announced new elections for February 1964. Aubame refused to contest the elections under rules that assured a BDG victory, and pledged to resist Mba's single party rule. Shortly later Gabon's military coup erupted.

The 1964 Coup

A week before the scheduled elections, two junior Lieutenants and 150 troops (of the mostly Fang 400-man army) seized Mba and his aides and forced him to broadcast his resignation. Both the army and the ethnically balanced gendarmerie at the time had few Gabonese officers, and were under French command. A military committee next annulled the scheduled elections, and named a ten-member ethnically representative Provisional Government headed by Aubame, and including Gondjout and a number of celebrities—a movie actor and the country's only MD. Bongo, who had just been appointed as Mba's cabinet director, was the first to alert the French commander of the gendarmerie of the coup, scoring his first good mark with the French.

The coup had a variety of motivations. Mba had played off the army against the gendarmerie, favoring the latter with its Estuary Fang and Myene, over the Army's heavy Woleu Ntem Fang composition, and inter-arm jealousies were voiced in rationalizations for the coup. (The gendarmerie did not join in the coup, but neither did they come to protect the regime.) Also, there was "dissatisfaction among the troops with Gabonese society under Leon Mba," and "resentment of the luxury in which the ministers lived in the capital compared to their own poor pay and the miserable existence of their families in their squalid villages,"[45] a point searingly made by Dumont who noted that Gabonese deputies had higher incomes than British Lords![46] There was also discontent over the retention of French officers in the army, and the status of the French in Gabon in general. And all the local lieutenants were "reported to have a personal grievance related to assignments or promotions," claiming ethnic discrimination and that their advancement had been blocked by the French command in the army. Aubame was very popular with the force, having earlier criticized Mba for not proceeding with localization.[47]

Despite Mba's ouster and the absence of support for him in society, the coup was reversed the next evening by six hundred French troops that were flown in, allegedly at the invitation of Vice President

Yembit who had invoked the Franco-Gabonese Defence Treaty.[48] This was an ex-post-facto legitimation of France's action since Yembit—who was barely literate and totally unversed in affairs of state—was incapable of invoking the Treaty since at the time he did not even know of the coup, being incommunicado with Libreville during a tour of Ngounie! Reversal of the coup was rather the express order of De Gaulle, who heeded the counsel of French Ambassador Cousseran (derided in Gabon as "Mba's President") who sided with French expatriates who were alarmed by an alleged American role in Aubame's rise to power, and feared the loss (to America) of Gabon's uranium, needed for France's independent *force de frappe*.

Morrison has commented how "under the presidency of De Gaulle, France maintained especially close relations with Gabon, and the threat of French intervention undoubtedly contributed to regime stability in Gabon."[49] As Chipman notes "it would be wrong to presume...that France would inevitably intervene militarily in Niger or Gabon merely to assure uranium supply."[50] Indeed, De Gaulle's *personal* sympathy for Mba is documentable in De Gaulle's memoirs, published long after the events.[51] "Complicity" of the US in the coup (in support of which was cited the American Ambassador's fraternization with known enemies of Mba) may have further triggered De Gaulle's anti-American biases.

Some 25 Gabonese and 2 Frenchmen died in the intervention. Mba, who had been detained in Lamberene, was reinstalled in office, a fact that provoked "popular outbursts and daily protests against the regime in the following three weeks."[52] All those named to the new government and 140 more were arrested. Gondjout, who had been negotiating with the putschists at the time, was tried for treason but acquitted under pressure from France, that was by now worried about the depth of societal resentment against France's restoration of Mba. Aubame and his key lieutenants were not so lucky, and were incacerated for the remainder of Mba's reign. A wave of repression afflicted Woleu Ntem, Aubame's district, as Mba sought revenge for his humiliation. The French Ambassador tried to blunt Mba's more fitful acts, counselling power-sharing, to no avail. Mba was prevailed upon, however, to hold the elections under an electoral system allowing participation of the UDSG. (For his troubles Cousseran was recalled from Libreville, at Mba's request.)

All those influentials who had jumped on the bandwagon of the putschists were purged from Mba's new cabinet. The latter was expanded as the era of austerity was beginning to disappear; lucrative appointments became a tactic of binding political support to the regime. But due to the coup both government and administration became more unrepresentative of Gabon's cultural pluralism, with the Estuary Fang the main gainers, their Woleu Ntem cousins the prime losers. For long peace did not return to Libreville. Schools closed down as pupils gathered in the streets to call "down with dictatorship"; workers struck for higher salaries; tract warfare continued, especially prior to the elections in which the political clout of expatriates and Mba's illness and his *Bwiti* leadership were openly discussed. So fearless had society become after the catharsis of Mba's temporary eclipse that even *Bwiti* members stepped forward to reveal Mba's secret *Bwiti* name, something unheard of since in the world of the occult this stripped him of his powers, making him vulnerable to attacks by other practitioners.[53]

The April elections were rigged in some districts, while in others meaningless since many opposition leaders were in detention. The BDG won 31 seats (to Aubame's 16), narrowly winning Ngounie and the Estuary despite falsifications of results. The interior voted for Mba more out of historic fears of the Woleu Ntem Fang, while in Libreville the BDG obtained only 20,556 votes versus 19,503 for the opposition. After the election *every single opposition deputy* was either enticed, or hounded, to cross the aisle until a *de facto* one party system ensued. With no opposition party presenting itself in the next elections in 1967, the BDG took all the Assembly seats, paving the way for Bongo's *de jure* legitimation of one party rule after the succession in 1968.

Mba's remaining few years in office saw the coming of age of the Gabonese economy. Huge new investments poured in, new mineral deposits were discovered, and tens of thousands of Frenchmen arrived to help in their exploitation (their number tripled between 1960-1970.) The "new" Gabon clearly needed a smooth succession, lest civil-military peace be punctured again. As Mba's medical condition worsened, French expatriate interests cast their eye around to find a reliable replacement. The key traits needed were (a) strong pro-French sympathies, and (b) non-Fang origins, since most Fang were simmering with resentments at their truncated leadership, and their leaders were in any case far too militant for comfort. Yembit was too incompetent to retain in power in a no longer sleepy Gabon. He was prevented from

developing any such aspirations when he was demoted for involvement in November 1966 plot, though he was kept from bolting by
being appointed Minister of State! The "Gabonese Clan" then prevailed
upon Mba to do what he detested most of all—face his imminent death
and appoint a successor in advance—the choice being Albert-Bernard
Bongo.

From the distant South and totally without a power base (his
Bateke ethnic sliver being politically irrelevant) Bongo was both ethnically safe and above both inter-Fang and the Fang-Myene conflict. He
was also young, a hard worker, pro-French and sufficiently (but not
too) vain and avaricious. As one source put it, "Bongo's chief virtues
[were]...a clear awareness of the bases of power, and his amenability
to the wishes of the French."[54] In short an ideal combination of
competence and malleability that could assure dynamic leadership in
the new era, while fully safeguarding French interests.

Little known in Libreville until tapped for higher office, Bongo
was indirectly beholden to Aubame for his meteoric rise, having been
recruited into Aubame's Ministry from an earlier minor civil service
post. On Aubame's demotion Mba appointed the 27-year old Bateke
as deputy director of his cabinet. Bongo's loyalty and abilities brought
his promotion a few weeks later when he replaced his French superior,
becoming Mba's main administrative aide and trouble-shooter. In that
capacity Bongo came in daily contact with Mba's French advisers, and
attracted the attention of the Clan as a competent Francophile ally. He
became the protege of the then-French Ambassador, Maurice Delauney, an influential advisor of De Gaulle's African kingmaker Jacques
Foccart. Bongo's hard work also suited the ailing Mba who passed on
to him much decision-making; by 1966 most of Mba's meetings were
presided by Bongo who learned from his master the keys to power in
Gabon, including the importance of Freemasons, magic and occult
practice. It was also during this apprenticeship that the penniless
Bongo bought his first overseas residence, in Paris; for while Mba loved
only power, as has been observed, Bongo "loved power but did not
detest luxury."[55]

Bongo became Mba's successor after first being elected Vice
President of Gabon, a post expressly created for him by Constitutional
amendment, and as promptly eliminated after he assumed the presidency. When he became President he was 32 years old, one of the
youngest Heads of State in the entire world. Bongo remembered well

all his benefactors. Delauney, shifted by Paris to Madagascar after his lengthy tour of duty in Gabon (1965-1972), was reassigned back to Libreville at Bongo's request, showing how by the mid-1970's the tail was capable of wagging the dog. Neither did Bongo forget his prime ally, Jacques Foccart. When the latter was finally removed from his 14 year stranglehold over Franco-African affairs by President Giscard D'Estaign, he was invited to Gabon's independence celebrations, and accorded much better treatment than that given the Minister France officially sent to Libreville for the occasion.

The Bongo Presidency

Bongo—who in 1973 converted to Islam and changed his first name to Omar—was born near Franceville in the Haut Ogooue on December 30, 1935, the youngest of nine children of a peasant Bateke family. (He was by 1990 by far the richest person in Gabon, a multi-millionaire.) He completed his education in Brazzaville, the Haut Ogooue at the time being part of Congo. There he met and married his first wife, Marie-Josephine Kama, also a Bateke of Haut Ogooue. After studying communications in France Bongo worked with the French Air Force until late 1960, and then joined the Gabonese Foreign Ministry as a minor functionary, following which his meteoric rise to power took place.

Within months of Mba's death it was clear that while in style and thrust the regime was very different, little of substance had changed in Gabon. "Political realism" still required economic development in association with French private capital, that demanded political quietism. Everything remained, as in Mba's days, subordinate to the goal of development, though Bongo pledged his regime would be free of the petty political harassments of the past.

To allay doubts about his southern origins, Bongo also pledged continuity of policies, and especially of Mba's "Big Three" projects—the Transgabonais, the Owendo port, and Kinguela dam, 120 kms. from Libreville. But though he did deliver "continuity," with a vengeance, Bongo's presidency nevertheless marked two breaks with the past: first, a dynamic, modern leader succeeded the vindictive, parochial Mba; and second, a major ethnic re-array of power had taken place as both the Myene and the Fang were sidelined. Indeed, Bongo, according to some observers, was catapulted to power by the Clan both because of ability and due to his non-Myene ("decadent") and non-Fang ("aggressive") origins.[56]

Mba's power-base had been the Estuary, resting on a Myene-Estuary Fang alliance. Bongo, while at outset also forging an Estuary Fang-Myene alliance, rapidly ushered in a monopoly of the Bateke (who at 10,000 barely constituted 2 percent of Gabon's population) and other hitherto ignored southern and central groups. Though Myene were integrated into Bongo's regime (e.g. Gondjout as President of the Supreme Court 1968-1975, later of the National Assembly), the inner circle was always a clique of Bongo's ethnic kinsmen and family members.

Despite his minority origins, and being foisted on Gabon by foreign interests, Bongo attained a degree of political stability that Mba was never able to, and this for several reasons. First, in the stagnant Gabon of the 1960's and its slumbering capital of 70,000, the potential leadership strata was extremely limited. The few Fang from Woleu Ntem (notably Aubame) who could possibly offer a viable political challenge were in prison after the 1964 coup d'etat. (Aubame was released in 1972, and lived in Paris until his death in 1989.) And what few other aspirants existed were (if Estuary Fang) tainted by the corruption and/or oppression of the Mba era, or (if Myene) of minority origin, and aware of Bongo's support among French expatriate circles. But of equal importance, despite his idiosyncratic penchants, Bongo was a genuinely able leader. He was, moreover, ethnically an acceptable compromise, coming from outside the historic Myene-Ntoumou Fang-Estuary Fang tricornered tug-of-war, and from a distant non-threatening ethnic sliver to boot. (Myene politicians in particular felt at outset they could manipulate him, since being far from his home-region Bongo had no allies in "their" Libreville!)

Thirdly, the reversal of the 1964 coup d'etat by French force of arms convincingly underscored that the Franco-Gabonese Treaty of Mutual Defence had real teeth in it, and the folly of resisting the inevitable—a Bongo Presidency, that as noted *was* a major improvement on the Mba *ancien regime*. In subsequent years Bongo adeptly strengthened the perception in Gabon of the futility of opposition to his rule, through highly visible Franco-Gabonese military manoeuvres, the secondment of French officers to his armed forces, and the erection of a virtual mercenary security force beholden to him personally.

And finally, it is crucial to remember that the Mba era was one of scarcity and stagnation, unemployment and minimal social services, with internal tensions accentuated by heightened expectations of a better future. The Bongo era coincided with a most phenomenal growth of the Gabonese economy, and the modernization of every aspect of life and society. Bongo literally led the nation into the Promised Land that turned out more bountiful than any had imagined. The Gabon of the 1990's—despite recent backsliding—bears no resemblance whatsoever to the Gabon of the 1960's. This phenomenal period of sustained economic boom, development and industrialization allowed full scope for the implementation of an extremely potent policy of the carrot concurrent with the French bogeyman stick.

Bongo easily secured political quietism via the massive societal upliftment that took place in Gabon in every domain, in the process *recruiting virtually every adult Gabonese already in the modern sector* into the State payroll or patronage trough! He also literally bought the instrumental allegiance of key Woleu-Ntem Fang notables by turning a blind eye to their private (smuggling) economic empires (with Rio Muni), even as playing upon fears of the Fang "menace" by forging a wall-to-wall anti-Fang political coalition. Simultaneously, both society and the armed forces were permeated by a system of political spies and a disciplined expanded all-Bateke *Garde Republicaine* that, larger and better armed than the army itself, became the main "rampart of the regime,"[57] sustained in Paris by the clout of Gabon's French expatriate interests' lobby.

In foreign policy Bongo broke with Mba's acute isolationism, but only marginally so and very slowly. Libreville's total preoccupation with developing the economy in symbiosis with French capital precluded much interest in "irrelevant" global affairs; still Bongo's greater vigor, and Gabon's heightened world stature, did translate into a more dynamic foreign policy, though often anchored in pro-French postures. Some initiatives, however, aimed at changing *metropolitan* postures. This was especially visible after the rise of the Mitterand presidency, and the latter's re-assessment of the moral imperative of sustaining African autocracies devoid of much internal legitimacy. Though in 1990 political liberalization came to Gabon due to the changed global context, Mitterand's quandary until then was easily neutralized by Bongo's periodic threat of a possible "tilt" towards American economic interests, producing predictable knee-jerk reactions and appeasement in Paris.

Bongo's regime was different in style, drive, regional bias and

personal idiosyncrasy, from Mba's. It was more developmentally dynamic, politically astute, *cost-effective*—a function of Bongo's youth,
modern outlook, greater administrative capabilities as well as Gabon's
greater economic options and strength. Bongo's regime rested less on
fear or harassment—to induce societal compliance and quietism—though repression and occasional liquidations did punctuate
Bongo's tenure, and more on patronage. As Decraene has noted
"Authoritarian [Bongo] is neither an autocrat nor a demagogue. His
most ferocious detractors grant him real political wisdom."[58] Still, both
Mba and Bongo were authoritarian, dominating all decision-making.
Mba in a fear-inspiring, vindictive, personalist way; Bongo in a more
sophisticated, calculated manner. Each favoured his own ethnic region, was vain, utilized "alternate" sources of societal support (*Bwiti*,
Njobe, Freemasons), and both were ultimately sustained by France and
resident French economic interests.

The Transgabonais

One of Bongo's major attainments was the controversial construction
of the Transgabonais and Owendo's mineral port across the Estuary
from Libreville. The rationale for the railroad[59] that connected Owendo
with Franceville was dual. First, the need for an all-weather communications network to link regions totally isolated from each other for
much of the year except by air—a network to bring not just greater
physical, but also social contact. Second, the need to create the conditions that would allow exploitation of the vast mineral deposits in the
interior, hitherto physically impossible in the absence of means of
bringing machinery and manpower to the sites, and evacuating ore to
the coast. (A road system was not a viable alternative, as Gabon's
climate made upkeep too costly.) Constructing the Transgabonais thus
became both a *sine qua non* for economic development and for nation-
building.

Both Mba and Bongo argued with France, the European Development Fund, and the World Bank that the railroad was inherently a
profitable proposition. Even before half the rail had been laid, the
railroad was to be generating revenues, having opened to logging virgin
timber zones, reviving a flagging sector that had exhausted the Estuary's forests. And on arrival at Franceville the railroad would again be
assured of immediate revenues from the hauling to Owendo of large

tonnages of uranium and (especially) manganese, hitherto evacuated south via Congo. Additional revenue would accrue, it was argued, as Belinga's iron—860 million tons—came on stream, as well as other valuable deposits along the track's route that could now be mined.

The World Bank had powerful reservations, arguing that the mere existence of untapped deposits did not justify huge capital outlays for a railway. There existed adequate means of evacuation of minerals—via Congo; and the railroad would only benefit French timber interests—who should be called upon to pick up a heavier price-tag. Moreover, the cost estimates provided for clearing virgin forests and laying a 650 km track-bed on Gabon's thin topsoil were viewed as far too low, and maintenance costs in particular were judged likely to undermine any possibility of the railroad's becoming profitable. The Bank also added insult to injury by arguing that a standard gauge railroad was in ordered, tendered globally, while Bongo had already decided upon a narrow gauge one, to be built by French contractors.

The Bank's reservations were rejected by Bongo who in 1968 commenced setting aside fiscal allocations for the railroad. Work on Owendo also commenced. Shortly later new oil discoveries and the 1973 Middle East War brought Gabon a 260% royalty bonanza, that allowed construction to commence, that was buttressed in 1975 by Gabon floating Africa's first Eurobond. Signifying his utter confidence in the project, Bongo had Franceville's train terminal built in 1975—ten full years before the track actually reached the city![60]

The reservations about the railroad's were justifiable. Even building the port of Owendo—that when completed proved unsuitable for its purpose—cost many times original estimates. Sloppy surveys by European contractors failed to detect a major silting in the Estuary, requiring periodic dredging, and the port was much too small and shallow to berth the mammoth Japanese ships, all bringing about the construction of another new port at Santa Clara, north of Libreville, and then extending the Transgabonais to it![61] The original cost-estimates, and the completion deadline—$155 million over six years, plus $30 million for rolling stock—also turned out wildly optimistic. Incredible and utterly unanticipated problems raised the railroad's cost twenty-fold to $3 billion. Even laying the "easy" Phase One track (Owendo-Booué) was slower than expected. Beyond Booué major technical difficulties were encountered that created cost over-runs and a delay of over four years. Access roads supplying the railroad site washed away, delaying the arrival of construction supplies and idling workers. And after the forest was cleared it was found that track simply could not be laid on the thin topsoil that washed away in the torrential rains. Huge amounts of gravel had to be imported at great cost from France—with construction crews again idled—before the track could be safely laid.[62]

The railroad, one of the largest construction jobs in the world, and a major feat of civil engineering, was inaugurated in Franceville on December 30, 1986 (Bongo's 50th birthday) in the presence of Congo's President Denis Sassou Nguesso (soon Bongo's father-in-law) and French Prime Minister Jacques Chirac. Even then the railroad was not operational. Trains could not travel beyond Lastourville, 165 kms. away, due to constant waterlogging of the track-bed that required extensive additional shoring up of the final stretch, and costly regular maintenance. The final price-tag pauperized even mineral-rich Gabon, that to this day covers large annual running deficits, as revenue on some segments of the railroad do not cover half of operating expenses.

Cost apart, however, the railway stunningly attained its goals. At one stroke the Transgabonais bound the country together. For the average citizen in the interior the former hazardous, often impossible, trip to the capital became a mere two-day comfortable journey. (Passenger traffic is, however, low: those who need to travel—bureaucrats—can fly!) And the interior's mineral riches were opened to exploitation in ways never originally anticipated. Even as laying the track, drillers exposed huge new mineral deposits at times virtually on the surface soil. In two instances this caused a zig-zag deviation of the original rail-bed, and train-stops were arbitrarily erected every 50 kms. in terrain utterly empty of people—lonely sentinels marking future centers of exploitation of new-found riches.

La Systeme Bongo

Though Bongo presided over one of Africa's greatest rags to riches economic transformation, his political tutelage of the Gabon, and his conservative pro-French policies were constantly challenged. At outset the challenges originated mostly from radical youth and intellectuals smarting at Gabon's neo-colonial status; later they came from Woleu

Ntem Fang at their political marginalization; but as society developed due to its transformation (universal education; Africa's highest literacy rates, etc.) wider opposition developed against the Bateke power monopoly, and "la systeme Bongo" of the carrot and the stick—patronage and mercenary force.

Patronage and Personal Rule

Until 1989 when the changed international context began affecting Africa, Gabon was one of the continent's stablest civilian-ruled countries. Notwithstanding his personal idiosyncrasies, strong rule, and lengthy tenure in office, Bongo, was *not* particularly unpopular among elites and their ethnic clienteles. A public poll in the 1980's (regarded as reliable) indicated 61.6% of Gabonese were satisfied with Bongo's PDG rule—no mean feat in Africa![63] Apart from satisfying society's material interests through an ample spread of Gabon's oil-royalties, Bongo was also seen as a protective bulwark against Fang control of the seat of power. It was an axiom of faith among many groups in Gabon that should the Woleu Ntem Fang come to power they would monopolize all positions in society. Bongo capitalized on this fear, developing important support from strata beyond his ethnic core by leading an anti-Fang alliance of southern and central ethnic groups.

Bongo also tapped societal support by latching onto anti-foreign xenophobia against Gabon's large (15-25%) non-national minority that dominates several sectors of the economy. He has intermittently lashed out (most recently in 1994), and ordered expulsions, of Fulani and Lebanese traders whose presence in the country allegedly blocks locals from roles in commerce (that few of them seek); against non-Gabonese Fang laborers (who monopolize manual jobs, that few locals deign to take); prostitutes (for spreading AIDS) from neighboring Equatorial Guinea; and against the large numbers of West Africans attracted to Gabon by the latter's rosy economic prospects.

Bongo's reign was most stabilized, however, by the huge patronage at his disposal, not least of which are the 50,000-odd civil service salaries he controls (up from 3,000 when he took office), overseas bursaries (2,000 in 1986; 39 when he assumed power), parastatal appointments, contracts, and concessions. (Many Gabonese fortunes were made from concessions and kickbacks related to the Transgabonais.) In spreading patronage he astutely did not bypass the Fang, who are too numerous and educated to be ignored: many were integrated into the civil service, and some in his PDG party hierarchy. But most patronage went to personally loyal Estuary Fang *clan leaders* such as Leon Mebiame (until 1990 his powerless Vice President) and Henri Minko (cabinet Minister), conveniently at loggerheads with each other, who spread it among their supporters binding a layer of Fang to the regime without any political concessions. Woleu Ntem Fang influentials were bought off by Bongo's turning a blind eye to their smuggling activities, that actually benefited Gabon by bringing into the country various agrarian goods from chaos-ridden Equatorial Guinea.[64]

Other important ethnic leaders, notably Bapounou (that Bongo feared might ally with the Fang), and Myene (concentrated at the strategic Port Gentil and Libreville nerve-centers), were integrated into the cabinet. There has also been a complementarity between the Politburo of the PDG (until 1990 the sole party in Gabon), that was a conclave of key ethnic leaders, and Bongo's cabinet. Duhamel has argued that it was proven *incompetence* at the PDG level that resulted in promotion to the cabinet, rather than the reverse![65] Such appointments have been seen clearly for what they were—political, rather than administrative, imperatives, explaining the inordinately large cabinets under Bongo. In the "good old days" (when money was no consideration) Bongo had cabinets of 57 members, or one minister per 12,000 population, a global record! These Ministers received salaries of up to $200,000 a year, plus fringe-benefits, scope for kickbacks and second salaries (as front-men for companies conforming to "Gabonization") and power to recruit into their ministries family, ethnic, and regional kinsmen thus entrenching their own status. The cabinet also included considerable Bongo family appointees: at one point one quarter of the cabinet (12 of 48 Ministers) were Bateke members, most of them Bongo relatives[66], another reflection of how Haut Ogooue and Franceville benefited under Bateke reign.

Frequent cabinet shuffles (up to four a year) have been a regular feature of Gabonese political life. They have been a stabilizing device in that they gave every possible influential access, a turn, at the public trough, assured loyalty until the next go, and at the same time served to weed out totally incompetent staff who made governance difficult. Still, since patronage was the major ingredient keeping the system stable, on the long run "few faces actually disappear from the [cabinet] lists; when they do, they seem content to wait a while, then make their come-back."[67] With appointment to the cabinet *not* based on merit, Bongo has found it difficult to locate both loyal *and* efficient aides. His never-ending cabinet shuffles have continued "with little seeming difference in efficacy,"[68] while enhancing Bongo's personal control over the country as he has been forced to hold as many as seven portfolios himself.

Less important local notables were integrated into a powerless legislature whose deputies received salaries of $36,000 per year with few duties, no right to criticize the government—or to interfere in the administration of their own provinces. The country was "run" by nine omnipotent, hand-picked provincial Prefects, accountable solely to Bongo. Inefficiency has been so prevalent in Gabon, however, and salaries so unrelated to performance of duties, that the Prefects themselves have complained about the lethargy and absenteeism of their own personnel, many of whom have been permanently resident in the capital irrespective of the locale of their post. Worse, there has been a total lack of interest in Libreville's various ministries of the Prefectural activities, resulting tardy decisions on fundamental issues, that when they arrive show evidence of having been given only perfunctory attention unless personally handled by Bongo himself.

Patronage has assured a civil service salary for any national seeking employment in a country where most non-manual jobs are in the public sector. This has minimized the development of grievances in urban areas. (Later, however, faced with a fiscal crunch and a swollen civil service, problems were to arise.) State funds were used to erect 50-odd deficitory parastatal enterprises that provided yet another layer of jobs. (Most are currently being privatized or closed down.)

Massive funds were spent on a variety of Bongo's pet projects, especially ones he considered as "befitting" a country with Gabon's mineral riches. This included hosting OPEC's first meeting to be held in Africa in 1975; the purchase of a $1.2 million Los Angeles residence for the use of his daughters while they attended college in the U.S. (later this was part of Marie-Josephine's divorce settlement); a $3 million 1988 refurbishment of the Presidential DC-8 (news on which was kept out of Gabon by refusing delivery of all French dailies reporting on it); an opulent new $200 million Presidential Palace completed in time for the 1977 OAU Summit in Libreville—the latter itself being the costliest OAU Meeting ever held, on which directly or indirectly another $600 million were spent!

The marble-floored Presidential Palace, on which construction commenced in 1974, is a fortified extravaganza of the first degree. Its floors are laid with carrara marble flown in from Italy; the complex includes sliding doors and walls, rotating rooms, areas that sink in the ground, doors customized electronically to open at the sound of Bongo's high-heeled shoes, a nightclub, saunas, gymnasiums, swimming pools, concrete bunkers and two underground tunnels leading to two separate helicopter pads. For the OAU meeting all livestock, that might wander into the streets, was ordered out of the city; European waiters were flown in to serve meals, unskilled Spaniards to clean the streets, and a Yugoslav construction crew razed all old quarters on the airport road, and built new buildings and expressways to impress arriving guests.

The cost of these polices, as well as extravaganzas, when coupled with declines in global market prices for minerals, helped bankrupt royalty-rich Gabon. On several occasions starting in 1978 Gabon had to declare an (IMF-imposed) "financial Ramadan" in order to bring debt-servicing and fiscal expenditures back to manageable levels. Worse, the carefree attitude about money created a total paralysis of administration, and a complete moral decay of public spirit in Gabon. Problems in the increasingly depopulated provinces, isolated and far away, have been utterly ignored, or postponed, by Ministers and "unremovable" civil servants much more interested in tending to their private affairs and building up their fortunes. And this in part because for just about everybody a civil service post is functionally regarded as a basic national "entitlement" and not a "real" working job.

Thus the vast majority of civil servants refuse to serve in the countryside, even in their home regions, including when they have developed there economic empires or enterprises. Most remain physically in Gabon's two main fleshpots—Port Gentil and Libreville—discharging their duties, including revitalizing rural agriculture, from afar via infrequent visits to their posts. One estimate had it that even after the construction of the Transgabonais outside of Bongo's own Haut Ogooue province up to 75% of the provincial civil service was at any particular time to be found in Libreville![69]

Bongo has chastized such attitudes, but it is far too late to do anything about the political culture of apathy that has developed. The civil service is acutely bloated, in 1989 encompassing 50,000 employees, or *17% of all adult Gabonese*, costing the State 221 billion CFAF, or half of the investment budget. And it also includes a large number of phantom (i.e non-existent) workers, whose salaries supplement those of their supervisors, and that cannot be weeded out the State's payroll without antagonizing those who for political reasons should not be offended. Inordinately high levels of perpetual absenteeism is also a problem, though the redundancy levels are so high in Gabon that "if everyone were to turn up for work many would have no office space to occupy."[70] Reed put it well when he observed that "their occupational dream—often caricatured by the Gabonese themselves—is to wear a suit and tie, carry a briefcase, and work in an air-conditioned city office."[71]

And this apart from pervasive routine corruption without which nothing in the public domain seems to work in Gabon. And since the system of kickbacks reaches right into the cabinet nothing can be done. Telling is the 1979 fraud investigation in the Customs Bureau where up to 60 billion CFAF of goods were found to have entered the country improperly, leading to the arrest of 23 customs officers, 8 Lebanese businessmen, 2 French importers, and many others flying out of Libreville without even packing a suitcase. The French officer who stumbled onto the racket was shortly later expelled from Gabon, and within weeks things were back to "normal" on the wharfs.

Major corruption has seeped into Gabon because huge profits can be made in a small country that lacks everything but is flush with cash and is controlled by a small ultra-rich elite leading ostentatious life-styles. The *Banque du Gabon et du Luxembourg*, referred to as the "President's Bank" since it handled the financial affairs of Bongo and his lieutenants, was milked dry before going bankrupt. Patently uneconomical projects have been authorized by ministers solely for the kickbacks and/or concessions they generate for their sponsors: five-star "tourist" hotels (that stand empty) in one of the world's costliest cities which tourists cannot afford to visit; hydroponic farms amidst fertile countryside receiving more than adequate rainfall and a huge coast-line; Franceville's sugar projects, that now meet Gabon's domestic need of 8,000 tons, but pose problems by producing an additional 22,000 tons of high-bulk, low-cost and not easily exportable surplus; One former Minister, Paul Moukambi, became a billionaire in a few years solely out of kickbacks.

Even the Foreign Ministry pays a high rental for the premises used by its Embassy in Paris—to the owners—Bongo and Minister

Rawiri. As one source pointed out "the desire to capture the riches of the country by a few high personages seems obsessional. Every activity, every contract is the object of an important kickback."[72]

Though Bongo distanced himself from the repression of Mba's presidency, and even released the 1964 putschists and all subsequent plotters in Gabon, he could not keep his early pledge to neither harass nor imprison opponents. Keenly aware of his narrow ethnic support in Libreville "subversion [became] something of an obsession with President Bongo, who had minimal political experience and who was taken out of an office and given honours by Leon Mba."[73] Bongo periodically reminded Gabonese that active opposition was punishable: "I am the only one to decide our country's future...I want to warn all those who think the President's function is a collective responsibility," for his restraint was voluntary and "[I could] be forced to go against my principles."[74]

Yet, though obsessive with security, Bongo has not been vindictive or ruthless: when competent ministers objected to policies they were called to implement, they were not purged, but assigned to other posts. And, to avoid using the capital punishment, Bongo assured the passage of legislation in 1977 allowing him to commute death sentences to "civil death sentences"—that cut off offenders from society by depriving them of civic rights, listing them dead in civil registers, and even transferring their property to heirs.

This has not prevented a series of liquidations of potential trouble-makers, at times engineered by the Clan with full Presidential knowledge. The first may have been the 1971 "disappearance" of Germain Mba, a distant relative and vocal critic of Leon Mba, who was kidnapped by a group of Frenchmen outside his Libreville home, never to be seen again. His wife, a witness to the incident, was imprisoned for spreading "rumours" about the kidnapping when she went to the police. The notorious mercenary, Bob Denard, who had a home in Libreville, was arrested on her testimony before being ordered released on direct Presidential orders. Whoever was culpable, the hand-in-glove cooperation of Bongo with right-wing and mercenary elements for two decades has been a basic cornerstone of his reign, and a major anchor of civilian rule in Gabon.

The second anchor, however, has been magic. Every political aspirant coopted into the cabinet had to undertake sacred *traditional* oaths of allegiance to Bongo, pledging to renounce separatist or opposition activities. The oaths were in the past (while Bongo was married to Marie-Josephine) administered in his distant home town, by his powerful fetishist father-in-law, in complex occult Bateke ceremonies.

In a country as reverent of occult traditions as Gabon, "opposition" meant not merely political plotting, but also denunciations, ridicule, defamations, threats, *bwiti* curses, both publicly uttered or mailed to the Presidency, and the spread via the occult media of disinformation, or predictions that a believer might view as true of self-fulfilling. Indeed, to deflect corrosive delegitimation of his rule by curses, Bongo in 1972 instructed that mail addressed to the Presidential Office would only be accepted by post offices if tendered by Registered Mail—which being more expensive, was supposed to discourage casual, or constant, dispatch of missives containing curses. Later, an annual "purification" of the Presidential office (of any curses) was decreed as necessary. And two years later, with the volume of occult hate mail still not having abated, the postal rules for such mail were further changed. Mail would now only be accepted from people whose names had been *a priori* verified by postal authorities, with specified punishments for the dispatch of curses to the Presidential Office, including a mandatory five years imprisonment for the gravest offence—sending a *bwiti* curse that included animal or human organs!

Though personally ultra-suave, and a Muslim by conversion, Bongo has been very conscious of his need—within a Gabon very fixated on occult practices—to enhance popular belief in his magic powers. While married to Marie-Josephine (who, like 40% of Bateke women was sterile) this was easy. Bongo's father-in-law was a powerful occult leader from whom Bongo, according to common belief, derived his own occult powers. This was the reason for the trek all new cabinet ministers (and other influential appointees) had to make for their oath-taking in the distant Franceville. The collapse of the Presidential marriage in 1988, therefore, was a potential source of *major* political instability. For years before Bongo's actual divorce (and the reason why the Presidential separation and divorce were so extended) rumours were rife throughout the country of Bongo's imminent political end due to the eclipse of his occult powers. These rumours were especially widespread in Woleu Ntem, where they were even voiced by Roman Catholic priests associated with the Fang opposition movement MORENA.

Like other African Heads of State (and several Gabonese politicians) Bongo was forced, for political reasons, to secure the services of a personal *marabout* and sorcerer (the Malian M'Baba Cissoko) to assist him to personally "augment" his magic powers, in order to counter occult spells spreading from his former in-laws, and widespread rumours of his ritual death. Bongo was indeed candid enough to admit that his remarriage (to neighboring Congo's then-Head of State Sassou Nguesso's daughter, Edith) was delayed by over a year in order to avoid harm befalling her from evil spells emanating from Haut Ogooué.

Bongo also personally participated in the *bwiti* and *ndjobi* ceremonies of both his political associates and cabinet members, in the process gaining important further occult credibility, prowess, and political allies. One individual constantly at Bongo's side in the 1980's, and a key cabinet lieutenant, was the ultra-rich, Georges Rawiri, a Myene from Lamberene. The latter's longevity in office was axiomatically ascribed in Libreville as solely stemming from his amassed fetishes, sorcery powers, Beninois witchcraft aides, frequent ritual sacrifices (about which few wish to talk), and the fact that Bongo needs his magic powers to himself survive.

Bongo has also been buttressed politically by his own membership in the Freemasons, regarded in Gabon as the "White Man's secret society," and in which much of Libreville's political strata, "high society," and French expatriates participate. Bongo is Grand Master of the *Dialogue* lodge (also the motto of the PDG party!) and he indirectly controls Gabon's second lodge as well.

Freemasons are a potent force in only a few African states, but very much so in Gabon where most of the Gabonese Clan are active members in its two lodges. The expatriate freemasons have links with metropolitan lodges, and through them with influential French politicians, and not only arch-conservative ones. Indeed, during his tenure some of former President Mitterand's own aides were masons, including Defence Minister Charles Hernu, Foreign Minister Roland Dumas, and Advisor on African Affairs Guy Penne. Just as it is difficult to overemphasize the role of traditional occult practices in Gabonese life, so it is difficult to overestimate the political power of the Freemasons in Libreville. As one observer has put it most powerfully, "these two occult pillars of the system, Africa's *Ndjobi* and Europe's Freemasonry, symbolize the basic duality of power in Gabon."[75]

To protect himself from ridicule (a potent political weapon) that could undermine his political authority, occult mystique, as well as personal vanity, Bongo has had censors scanning all publications arriving from abroad, banning those (usually French) that contain anything that could be remotely interpreted as derogatory or embarrassing. This has included references to his use of platform shoes (he is inordinately short), possible pygmy ancestry, and the various liaisons of his tempestuous first wife. Entire press-runs of offending newspaper issues simply "did not arrive" in Libreville; one famous incident, in 1988, saw all copies of several French dailies and weeklies (including Le Monde), denied entry into Gabon since they carried factual reports on the 16 million French franc loan for the refurbishment of Bongo's luxurious Presidential DC-8 jet.

Major efforts have been mounted to protect Bongo's image in Paris as well. This was possible during the Giscard d'Estaign Presidency when France at times invoked censorship laws (prohibiting defaming foreign allies) even before Gabon's Embassy lodged protests. But this cosy arrangement changed with Mitterand's election, as the ultra-sensational publication of Pean's Affaires Africaines book in 1983 made abundantly clear. The latter documented in vivid detail the Clan's immense power in Gabon, and in French domestic politics. It linked the Clan and Bongo in political liquidations (including Germain Mba's, and the 1973 "suicide" of a prominent lawyer, Bouquet), as well as in revenge murders of Marie-Josephine's lovers. It alleged that her ex-husband poet, Ndouna Depenaud, was killed in 1977, as was also cabinet Minister, Owono N'Guena; that Bob Denard had been contracted to kill the Haitian Rene A. Joseph, who also had been intimate with Marie-Josephine, and that Robert Luong, another favorite, was also murdered in October 1979 in France. The book also gave graphic details on the scope of corruption in Gabon, and on Bongo's family extravaganzas, alleging that Marie-Josephine's unlimited line of credit on the Banque du Gabon et du Luxembourg was the main reason for its ultimate bankruptcy.

Frantic pressures by Bongo and Clan allies to have the book banned in Paris were spurned, as were offers to purchase the book's entire press run and global reprint rights. Partly because of these highly-publicized efforts the book sold six times its originally envisaged press-run. In retaliation Bongo mounted a libel lawsuit against Pean in France. Pean lost on one count, and was symbolically fined one French franc in damages: his Parisian house, however, was later bombed with impunity by the Gabonese Secret Service. And to "punish" Mitterand who had not protected his "grand ami," Bongo imposed a total diplomatic freeze on Paris. For six weeks all French journals and newspapers were banned from Gabon, and any mention in the local media of *anything* French was also forbidden. Bongo's attempt to tilt to the US—the ultimate punishment!—was not successful, however, since a State Visit to Washington did not produce an American pledge to "support" Gabon's future security. Wiser counsel soon prevailed in both Paris and Libreville, but the rift was only healed after Mitterand (a) acquiesced to send to Libreville his Prime Minister to "assist" in planning Bongo's next State Visit to Paris (in which he was accompanied by a retinue of seventy!) and (b) tendered a gift calculated to appease—a promise to build Africa's second-only nuclear reactor in Gabon.

Internal Security and External Military Guarantees

All the above notwithstanding, by far the most important mainstay of civilian rule in Gabon, at least until 1990, has been a variety of internal security strategies, in conjunction with the guarantees implicit in the military treaties signed with France. The latter, as already noted, may or may not be still valid. Though President Mitterand in 1990 explicitly renounced a future French military role in propping up regimes threatened internally, in a number of instances subsequently France has done exactly that, or through powerful *political* pressures has attained the same end. It is also not really clear whether France would actually adopt a hands-off policy if a *key* client-state, such as Gabon were to totter under internal assault.

At independence Gabon's security forces were minuscule units under French command, with few local officers (newly commissioned), poorly trained, under-paid, with primitive facilities, little mobility or military capability. There were major inter-arm cleavages that assured that the two units—the gendarmerie and the army—would not find it easy to act jointly in any emergency, as indeed transpired during the 1964 coup. The army specifically was heavily staffed with Woleu Ntem Fang. (This did not change under Bongo, with the Army remaining over 50% Fang.) By contrast the gendarmerie was much more balanced because it was a provincially-based force, with the key Libreville units including mostly personnel from the Estuary ethnicities, with a sprinkling of other groups.

Even before the 1964 coup Mba had favored the gendarmerie, that included his Estuary Fang kinsmen and was hence a more reliable instrument of control. In 1964 the gendarmerie did not join in the army putsch, though it only rallied to Mba when French troops began arriving. After Mba was restored to power a Republican Guard was set up at the suggestion of the badly rattled expatriate oil-interests (and paid by them), as an elite military organ charged solely with protecting the Presidency.[76]

The fact that France had actually intervened militarily to save Mba from ouster made a profound impression on the Gabonese armed forces. The existence of the Franco-Gabonese Defence Treaty was known, but few civilian or military personnel had accepted at face value France's resolve to shore up Mba's feared and disliked regime. Moreover, in several prior upheavals in 1963 (in Togo and Congo) Paris had *not* rescued founding fathers who "possessed" similar military guarantees.

This French inconsistency, and later the fact that France's greatest *grand ami*—Niger's Hamani Diori—was overthrown, convinced Bongo, well aware of his very limited core ethnic support in "hostile" Libreville, not to place all his eggs in the French basket, and to develop ancillary sources of military support. The first line of defence—because it was the surest—remained the French guarantees of the civilian order in Libreville. All effort were geared at reminding France that Gabon was too important a strategic reserve of mineral riches to be allowed to go down the drain into uncertain domestic or external hands, especially since France suffered "from an almost excessive dependence on African sources for the supply of cheap minerals essential to her economy and national defence."[77] It was thus axiomatic that in case of a serious instance of unrest, subversion, or external threat, Bongo would "invoke the defence accord, an act which would allow France to claim that she were protecting her own interests in the name of the wider cause: namely the security of Gabon."[78]

But for these guarantees to be acted upon, Gabon had to be perceived in Paris as a political ally, and not a liability. Bongo played his cards well, and in his early years in office he supported all French regional and international positions (on Rhodesia, Biafra, Chad), as France's "historic ally," even resurrecting the King Denis myth. Only later, as the Gabonese economy greatly expanded, did he begin to display independence on a variety of African issues. And to secure his economic and political demands, he did not hesitate to threaten "normalization" of economic relations by opening the door to investments from the U.S. As has been noted, "in any controversy with the French, the Gabonese are prepared to use the threat of transferring their allegiances to the U.S."[79] America had always been France's nemesis—doubly so in the 1980's when American companies were already in Gabon, pumping oil from abandoned French fields to boot, and co-owners of COMILOG.

France's Embassy in Libreville has always been by far the largest, most imposing and influential in Gabon, with "its staff reputed to duplicate government departments ...[and with] no important decision taken without its consultation."[80] This has always led to categorizations of the Franco-Gabonese relationship as "an extreme case, verging on caricature, of neocolonialism."[81] One can accept such an assessment, but conditional on an awareness of the very heavy price Bongo has exacted in turn for Gabon's political and economic fealty—something that actually calls for a redefinition of the term neo-colonialism itself. Because as Rosberg and Jackman so cogently note "it would be a mistake to view Bongo merely as some kind of neo-colonial 'puppet.'"[82]

Gabon has conducted as independent a foreign posture as required by its national interests (when these have been in conflict with France's) given the constraints of its dependent status. Or put differently, if a client-state, by the 1980's Gabon had become an extremely expensive one to keep in line. France retained the bulk of its desired mineral-stakes in Gabon; but Bongo also secured the bulk of his goals from France. These included obtaining vast amounts of public and private capital (on per capita basis, far more than any other African state) to open up Gabon's resources to exploitation, despite the same geographical obstacles that kept France out of other Francophone African deposits (e.g. Burkina Faso's); securing French military backing for his civilian administration; extracting protocol status second to none in Africa and normally accorded by France only to major allies, including multiple State Visits to Libreville by every French President.[83]

Bongo's tactics worked well until the 1981 rise to power of President Mitterand who, personally and ideologically, was disinclined to honor "Gaullist" military guarantees to authoritarian African client-states of which Gabon was seen as among the worst.[84] Bongo (and the right-wing Gabonese Clan) had originally supported the electoral campaign of Mitterand's protagonist, with Bongo cooperating hand-in-glove with right-wing ex-SAC (*Service d'Action Civique*) personnel in Libreville. (SAC, formed by De Gaulle in the 1960's as a covert action and intelligence unit bypassing the existing French secret service, was implanted in French Africa by De Gaulle's Jacques Foccart.) The strength of the "Gabon lobby" was strikingly visible when Mitterand was forced to reorganize his own Secret Service when SAC elements within it tried to discredit him by disinformation *from Libreville* on Chadian developments. The key actors were Maurice Robert, the founder of SAC's Africa branch and then Ambassador to Gabon; Colonel Mario, Casimir's deputy in the Presidential Guard and colleague of the infamous mercenary Bob Denard (who had a house in Gabon and direct access to Bongo); and Colonel Daniel at Elf-Gabon.

This external "meddling" in French activities brought about a sharp demand from Mitterand for the dismantling of Bongo's "Corsican Gang," and the retirement of Ambassador Robert—originally appointed to placate Bongo over the objections of the French Foreign Minister[85]—who was seen more of Bongo's Ambassador than that of Paris. Despite an effort to project a surface appearance of continuity in Franco-Gabonese relations, the 1980's thus saw the relationship being redefined, with Bongo increasingly uncertain about the binding nature of French military guarantees.

With Mitterand's accession to power gone also were the good old days when any anti-Bongo diatribe, press-report, or speculation in the Parisian press would *a priori* be blocked by France before Gabonese remonstrations were even tendered. Now every Libreville kickback scandal, or amorous escapade of Bongo's estranged wife, became fodder for the French press. Nor was Bongo's request for a "free" Sorbonne Ph.D. degree for his son Alain (soon Ali Ben) sympathetically viewed in Paris, even though African Affairs advisor Guy Penn went out of his way to obtain the offer of a provincial degree. Yet Mitterand's desire to "normalize" Franco-Gabonese relations was only partly successful until. Relations with Gabon remained "strictly limited by 'historical' constraints, and by the weight of economic, political and strategic interest,"[86] until the end of the Cold War when a greater measure of disengagement was feasible.

Bongo exploited France's need for a private reserve of strategic minerals by encouraging French mining and timber groups in Gabon to exert pressure on Paris to continue maintaining an active French military presence in Gabon. For notwithstanding her military treaties, the majority of the French bases in Africa (originally 100) were closed down by the 1970's, with France preferring to use her airborne rapid deployment force in Provence in case of emergency. This did not suit Bongo, who desired (and obtained) a high visibility of his "unvulnerability" via the continued presence of France's 6th Marine Infantry Battalion, and the squadron of French Jaguar jets conspicuously parked in a corner of Leon Mba International Airport's tarmac.

These have been a constant reminder of Bongo's external military props. As one senior Gabonese officer despondently lamented to the author in 1988 "what's the point of speculating about change in Libreville if the very next day the RIAOM will be landing at Mba airport?"[87] There have never been more than 2,000 French troops at Camp De Gaulle (that also serves as a rear-base for Chad), and then only at the height of crises. But the French military presence is suffocatingly felt from the moment one boards an Air Gabon jet in Paris until one lands at Libreville's Leon Mba airport. Both are inordinately crowded with military personnel in uniform, departing or arriving from France, with Libreville's airport and its perimeter heavily guarded by armed French, and not Gabonese, gendarmerie officers, who also scrutinize carefully every visitor—before allowing their passports to be stamped by the local team!

Utilizing other treaty provisions, Bongo has encouraged periodic joint Franco-Gabonese military manoeuvres. These, however, have not been aimed at giving the (largely Fang) Gabonese army enhanced professional expertise, but rather to impress local troops of the deadly firepower of French forces that could be used against them in an uprising. Indeed the small (2,500) Gabonese army is kept at a generally low level of preparation and training—causing some grumbling on the part of officers returning from French staff-colleges. The army rarely uses live ammunition that is strictly rationed, with every bullet accountable for (allegedly for financial reasons!), and Gabonese troops are never allowed to leave their bases with live ammunition unless accompanied by French units.

Learning a lesson from 1964, Bongo has taken other precautionary measures. The unreliable 50% Fang army is dispersed at remote outposts on the country's periphery, and all their intra-garrison radio transmissions are electronically monitored from Libreville (by ex-SAC men). The army's command hierarchy was not fully Africanized until

20 years after independence, with the officer corps to this day including between 110 and 200 seconded French officers. Though promotion has been routinized, Bateke, or in their absence (since most Bateke are in the Presidential Guard) seconded French officers are in most key operational commands. A network of spies, including mercenaries, report directly to Bongo on any subversive loose talk in the army.

Corruption in the army is endemic and pervasive, and is ignored, since it diverts energy, and attention, from possible political ambitions. Junior officers are extensively engaged in smuggling; senior officers, having already amassed the requisite capital, are building up and tending small economic empires in their "zones" of operation—cinemas, nightclubs, boutiques. And most of the senior command have princely salaries: since mid-1977 all heads of the security services had salary parity with cabinet ministers—i.e. up to $200,000 a year.

The up to 200 French officers at all times seconded from France to Gabon's security forces, are mostly in technical or sensitive posts. Libreville is also the regional headquarters of the French Secret Service (SDECE)—it was from here that the Biafra airlift was mounted—a fact that further directly or indirectly sustains the regime. Gabon has received much war materiel under treaty provisions, including several Mystere and Mirage jets in the 1980's. Yet despite developing one of Africa's few jet Air Forces, of 800 men, including qualified pilots, Gabon's jets are *only* flown by French pilots, and most other aircraft, especially helicopters, are for the exclusive use of the all-Bateke Presidential Guard.

Similarly while some mechanized equipment—in 1990 including 77 armored cars, amphibious tanks, 22 other vehicles, and 81 pieces of artillery—is spread across several camps, most is concentrated in Libreville for the protection of the Presidential Palace, or is in Presidential Guard reserve arsenals. Gabon also developed a Navy of 360 headquartered in Port Gentil, including 19 craft of less than 100 tons and two over that tonnage, but this force was erected primarily to give teeth to Gabon's territorial claims on offshore oil deposits, some of which were originally contested by Equatorial Guinea. Though each of these forces is objectively very small, given Gabon's population, even in 1967 Gabon ranked 6th of 32 African states in terms of armed forces per capita, with the highest per capita ratio of internal security forces.[88]

In reality, once petrodollars started streaming in regularly, Gabon's defence expenditures have been the largest item in the national budget, a major anomaly, and covered mostly from domestic revenue. (French military aid, inclusive of the cost of the 100-200 French officers on secondment, by contrast has been at a modest FF 65 million level.) These high expenditures of "defence" have been a function of the (a) high salaries in Gabon in general, and especially the (b) inordinately high salaries of the upper echelon of the officer corps, aggravated by the (c) very large number of such senior officers (over 60 Generals for a combined force of 5,000!) and the (d) very high cost of securing first-rate expatriate mercenaries, and running a Secret Service both with external capabilities and willing to operate in its home (France) country.

Gabon's forces were thoroughly and personally revamped by Bongo in 1970 when a large number of ethnic, family and mercenary appointments were also made. With few ethnic kinsmen in Libreville's gendarmerie, Bongo concentrated on the Republican Guard, that he renamed the Presidential Guard in 1970 that became his domestic bulwark against opposition. (The name change was aimed at legitimating its transformation into an all-Bateke force to protect a Bateke president!) The Guard was originally headed by its French creator "Bob" Maloubier, and officered by ex-French Legion mercenaries (referred in Libreville as the "Corsican Mafia" though most are actually from Provence.) Their hefty salaries are covered by contributions from several expatriate companies, and especially Elf-Aquitaine, that have a direct and immense stake in the stability of the regime in Libreville.[89]

Later, when Maloubier moved to a much more lucrative post with Elf, the Guard came under the command of ex-French Army Colonel Le Braz who completed its transformation. The country's security services—army, police, gendarmerie—were instilled with fear as the Guard was meticulously transformed into an elite all-Bateke force with a military superiority. Progressively augmented until it reached nearly 2,000 men, the Guard then included the majority of all able-bodied young Bateke in Gabon! Though slightly smaller than the army itself, the Guard has always been more than a match for it. It is concentrated in Libreville, has superior weaponry (including armor and air-power), mobility, training and mercenary officers. In many ways the Guard is the *only* real force in Gabon; in a 1988 parade the Guard displayed weaponry that Agence France Presse maintained had only just then been introduced in the French army itself. The pride of the Clan, the Guard has been referred as "the key element of perpetuating the Bongo system."[90]

And never one to go to half-measures, Bongo's palace includes underground bunkers that can withstand direct bombing and artillery pounding, and tunnels leading to helicopter pads. It is also equipped with state-of-the art electronic gadgets that allow easy control of the complex's perimeter, and the monitoring of everything that transpires in all State rooms and corridors. Bongo's Cap Estarias residence, and his Franceville "retreat" are similarly equipped and guarded.

Bongo also spends large sums on Military Intelligence, the Secret Service, and other units some not even appearing in organograms, all of which, however, are permeated by mercenary officers, including ex-SAC personnel enticed by high salaries to work for Bongo, some as "double-agents" against France! A scandal in 1980 exposed the fact that the Marseilles' SAC section head had actually been on Bongo's payroll since 1968 as a security advisor at a salary of $2,500 per month. He had been recruited, *inter alia*, to build up for Bongo a second intelligence service network in Libreville, parallel to CEDOC, Gabon's Secret Service, that Bongo viewed penetrated, and under the control of France's SDECE. In creating this second hierarchy Moroccan and French ex-SAC officers were recruited in Paris under the cover of a commercial firm.

Moreover, SAC personnel were behind several of Gabon's external covert forays and the string of mysterious "disappearances" of opposition figures. Among their prime attainments not hitherto mentioned was the murder in 1979 in France of Robert Luong, the Guyanese interior decorator who had been intimate with Bongo's wife; the bombing of Pean's house in Paris itself; the bungled 1977 mercenary invasion of Cotonou aimed at toppling the Marxist regime in Benin; and undisclosed activities against Libya, for which 37 Libyans were in 1989 trained in Republican Guard camps.[91]

Ultimately Bongo retained the loyalty of his security forces by the same combination of the carrot (high rank and salaries, lucrative personal enterprises) and stick (expatriate mercenaries, French military guarantees) used on society at large. Controlling the top command of the army and gendarmerie was somewhat easier for Bongo because he inherited from Mba a loyal Myene Gendarmerie Head (Nkoma) whom he promoted in 1977 as Commander in Chief of the Armed Forces.

More conveniently, two of the senior officers in the army (Nazaire Boulingui and Ba Oumar, to become Chiefs of Staff) were Bateke, a fact that gave Bongo time to recruit and groom for future command other Bateke, including his own family members. In 1988 a Bongo's nephew, Major General Andre Oyini, became head of the Presidential Guard just in time to keep the force solidly behind Bongo who successfully weathered the multi-party crisis of 1989-90. The Guard's former commander for fifteen years, and ex-Dien Bien Phu veteran, General Louis Martin, was not retired, however. Military prowess is dearly valued in Libreville: he was appointed as yet another Presidential Security Advisor, at his old super-salary.

The command of the National Police (important because it includes the Secret Service and several spy networks) was very early on "privatized" by the appointment at its head of Boniface Assele, Bongo's brother-in-law. "Trusted relatives and other reliable figures in key positions in the armed forces alongside seconded French officers" [92] gave Bongo personal control over all the security forces, just as family ministerial appointments personalized politics.

Some of the presidential in-law appointments proved very problematic, however, when Bongo's marriage unravelled in the 1980's, and especially when in 1988 he contemplated remarriage.[93] Not only had first wife Marie-Josephine been from a rival Bateke clan with a father who possessed awesome occult power that had to be assuaged. (Bongo was forced to make a humbling special pilgrimage to his former father-in-law to secure a curse-free approval of his remarriage.) More importantly, the breakup of the marriage meant that appointees who were Marie-Josephine's relatives (referred to as *Le Clan de Madame*) had to be purged since they were now intrinsically unreliable! Some resisted being shunted from posts in which they had grown secure; others demanded and exacted an inordinately high price. Assele, despite the fact that he had been a long-time and trusted ally (to the degree that as Head of the Police he had kept Bongo posted on his sister's indiscretions!) simply had to go because he held one of the country's most sensitive command, and was now no longer "family." He was pried, with considerable difficulty, from his security post (after "a stormy meeting" with Gabon's ten other Police Generals who were corralled to show they fully sided with Bongo) and given Gabon's plum diplomatic post—Ambassador to France. The incumbent Ambassador to France, General Gaston Felicien Olouna, a Bongo nephew, replaced Assele as Commander in Chief of the National Police.)[94]

Despite loyal ethnic and/or "family" commanders, high salaries, scope for petty corruption or grand larceny, and policies aimed at keeping the armed forces subservient, Gabon's military has not been free of unrest. Much of it has been of ethnic origin, mostly on the part Fang angry over their political marginalization, and the abject economic neglect of Woleu Ntem. Other sources of unrest had to do with individual grievances about discrimination in command allocations or the posting of units to remote uninhabited outposts with no recreation facilities. Other gripes were political, relating to the "Bateke" government, its iron control over society and monopoly of economic power.

In 1978 there was also some speculation about a helicopter crash that killed Bongo's brother-in-law and Chief of Staff of the Land Army Colonel Djoue Dabane, and the disappearance of Colonel Fabien Ntoutoume. Both officers had criticized the prevalence of corruption in Gabon, ethnic favoritism, and the concentration of power in the hands of Bongo, Marie-Josephine, Assele and their cohorts. In May 1985 an Air Force Captain was arrested for plotting a coup. Condemned to death, his televised execution on the capital's beach conveyed Bongo's clear message that *armed* plots would face the capital punishment. Though the plotter acted alone (he was a member of an semi-secret evangelical order called by God to kill Bongo), his grievances were echoed by many officers returning from foreign training programs to powerless commands at home, based in peripheral areas, in an unprofessional army, headed by corrupt senior officers, where promotion to senior command was purely a function of ethno-political merit.

A much more serious all-Bapounou plot was nipped in the bud in September 1989. It involved trusted senior security officers including the Head of Franceville's Presidential Guard, a former Bongo aide-de-camp, and an array of external interests that financed mercenary recruitments for Bongo's assassination. The ultimate mastermind was Pierre Mamboundou, the Bapounou leader heading a multiparty movement in Paris. In unravelling the plot the French investigating officer came across a *second*, concurrent plot, with possibly active French participation, that, together within the rapidly changed global context, may have led to Bongo's turnaround views on multipartyism.

Privatization of democracy, or a lengthy transitional era?

The unrest, plots, and strikes of 1989, within the context of a strong French economic disinvestment from Africa in general (that *halved* the number of French expatriates), a major recession, acute fiscal austerity, and pressures from Paris for political reform as a precondition for continued aid, helped convince a reluctant Bongo that loosening his political monopoly was necessary. As late as 1989 he had argued against multipartyism, vilifying it as nothing more than elite ethnic politics. Speaking in his own province, and referring to Gabon's "unfortunate former experience" with multipartyism, he urged kinsmen that "if anyone speaks to you about multipartyism, catch them and hit them hard. I give you permission,"[94] for "while I am President of this country there will be no multiparty system."[95]

Bongo persisted in his stance until the significance of the erosion of his support among the—large, critical swing group—Bapounou, as manifest by the 1989 plots, sank in, against pressure from a Fang opposition in Paris, that had gained the ear of Mitterand. Expatriate security advisors and Clan leaders, many now gone due to age, recession or French pressure, were also arguing that the interests of all involved—Bongo, the Bateke and the expatriates—could still be controlled by the same mix of patronage and force as in years gone by, even within a more liberalized political system acceptable to Paris and Washington.

The view seemed to be vindicated when late in 1989 Bongo was able to entice to Libreville one of his main foes, Father Paul Mba Abessole. The Woleu Ntem priest had been in self-exile for thirteen years in Paris, where he headed a segment of the loosely organized MORENA movement. Talks with him about a return to a multi-party system revealed he was neither beholden to a more radical Fang wing, nor insistent *a priori* on Bongo's resigning as president. Suddenly the future was not too bleak after all.

Bongo turned out to be one of a handful of early Francophone African leaders to heed the writing on the wall, to take seriously Mitterand's new line that was soon made explicit at the La Baulle Francophonic summit, and to seize the initiative *vis-vis* the opposition rather than to wait for events to catch up with him. Like Houphouet-Boigny in Cote d'Ivoire, this early acquiescence to the inevitable allowed Bongo to dictate the nature and pace of the reforms in Gabon, thus outmanoeuvring and ultimately defeating an opposition both divided, disorganized and unprepared for the popular elections they had so adamantly been clamoring for.

In February 1990 a PDG committee—that did nothing without Bongo's approval—"concluded" multipartyism might, after all, be

beneficial for Gabon. The next day Bongo "ratified" this recommendation. He then convened a National Conference of 2,000 members from
over 70 social, economic, political, regional, ethnic, and occupational
groups, that met on March 27th and for three weeks, to deliberate the
future shape of Gabon. The conference agreed to respect Bongo's tenure
(expiring in 1994, amended to include only one possible re-election)
so long as Bongo remained above the political fray.[96] Among proposals
debated was one envisaging significant regional economic decentrali-
zation and autonomy. Couched to appeal to the Woleu Ntem Fang, it
was in reality a "doomsday" escape clause for the Bateke, aimed to keep
the mineral-rich but demographically-weak Haut Ogooué free from
any possible future ethnically-hostile central regime. (Nothing came
of the clause, that was ratified, since Bongo's political supremacy was
maintained.)

    Bongo then promptly resigned from the PDG party, calling for
double-phased multi-party elections in October 1990. When the opposition parties requested a delay (so they could get organized), Bongo
turned against them their own rhetoric and demands for immediate
elections. The result was that the PDG, the only organized national
party in the country, had a major electoral advantage. All the competing parties were little more than elitist regional or ethnic formations.
Pierre Mamboundou's UPG was a mostly Bapounou party; the Agondjo
Okawe's PGP was a mostly Port Gentil Myene party; and MORENA-
Bucherons ("the woodcutters"), led by Abessole, was one of the two
major Woleu Ntem parties, the individualistic Fang vote splitting
between several.

    Apart from ethnic divides, there are ideological, clan, and per-
sonality cleavages (as between the two Fang MORENA parties), that
made it impossible in 1990, and to a large extent to this day, for the
opposition to unite effectively against Bongo. The PGP leader Agondjo,
for example, is totally unacceptable as a political ally, on ethnic
grounds, by MORENA-Bucherons (later, renamed RNB)—due to the
Myene being Bongo's allies in the uniparty era—and, on ideological
grounds as well, since Agondjo's ultra-Left stances are anathema to the
Catholic priest Abessole. Bongo, historically mistrustful of the Fang in
general, and those of Woleu Ntem in particular, is totally alienated
from Abessole—who several times called him "mystically dead"[97], that
in to those in the occult world is akin to pronouncing a death-curse!

    The elections saw the PDG losing ground in the ethnic strongholds of the opposition, but remaining Gabon's strongest and only multi-ethnic formation. (Studies have suggested its activities in urban areas have significantly eroded members' primary ethnic allegiances.)[98] State campaign funds were allocated to all parties—some took the money and dropped from the contests—with additional funds and a vehicle going to any party electing at least one deputy in the first round.

In the first round of Gabon's first free elections in twenty-two years, 553 candidates from 40 parties contested the 120 seats, only seventeen being from Haut Ogooue. Only 58 were elected (36 from the PDG) with the absolute majority needed, after a violent campaign and charges of vote-rigging. After the second round was over the PDG commanded a majority of 64 delegates. The PDG's strongest challenge came not from the Fang vote, that typically divided among several parties concentrating on Fang areas, but from the Myene, including the ideological PGP that fielded 52 candidates and emerged as the second strongest party, ahead of MORENA-Bucherons of Abessole, despite the numerical preponderance of the Fang in Gabon. Partial elections in 1991 increased the PDG majority to 66, with the PGP next in strength with 19 deputies, and Morena-Bucherons with 17. All the other parties had seven or less seats.[99]

Casimir Oye Mba, a former "Bongo" Estuary Fang banker of impeccable integrity, who headed the 1990 transitional administration, was subsequently sworn in as Prime Minister. The new "national" government was a coalition with an "austerity" 29-man cabinet, that in short order increased to a "normal" for Gabon 36-member body. Fully 28 of these were from the PDG, the rest from other parties including two from MORENA-Bucherons and one from MORENA-Originel. The key portfolios were retained by incumbent PDG ministers, including Presidential family members. Foreign Affairs, for example, was retained by Bongo's son Ali Ben (ex-Alain); later, when a new minimum age law for cabinet members (35 years) took effect, Presidential daughter Pascaline took over for her under-aged brother! The Oil Ministry was similarly allotted to (well-regarded) Jean Ping, Bongo's son-in-law, who is in turn a cousin of the PGP Myene leader. Some detested old-guard politicians had to be sacrificed, including Georges Rawiri, though they got other rewards.

The 1990 liberalizations catapulted Gabon into the ranks of the "new democracies" in Africa, transforming Bongo into a sort of *pater familia* of the new wave of multiparty states—a role he relishes, advising all hold-out Heads of State that multipartyism is not all that bad. As a "national" President Bongo ruled with an executive Estuary Fang Premier, a Bapounou Prime Minister, an Estuary Fang Senate President and a Mpongwe Assembly President—and with significantly fewer Bateke kinsmen, thus soothing claims of ethnic favoritism. There were certainly more participants in the political game now, but all were elitist in orientation and concern, and easily "bought" by high office, salary, status, and a share at the patronage trough, with the net effect that *la systeme Bongo* seemed to have survived intact into the "democratic" era.

In May 1990 riots rocked Port Gentil when a Myene opposition leader dying of natural causes was suspected of being murdered. For ten days there was total anarchy, the town for all practical purposes in insurgent hands. Though France flew in troops to protect and evacuate its remaining (1,800) expatriates, Paris pointedly reminded Bongo that "he would receive no military help in maintaining law and order." Later the French Foreign Minister stated more emphatically that while France "would remain actively involved in the continent [it] wished to stay out of the continent's internal affairs,"[100] indirectly vindicating Bongo's mercenary force, and his moves to multipartyism.

Politically and economically Gabon remained in transition throughout the 1990's. The economy rebounded and then again plunged. The forestry industry, that employs 15% of the population, still is in crisis due to currency gyrations that favor Asian timber, leading to production cuts and layoffs. Oil, that subsidized Gabon's economic transformation, has lost its lustre, and is at depressed global prices and restrictive production quotas. All the other minerals that Gabon exports have also been under severe pressure. The sale of manganese, for example, remains mediocre, despite increased production. (Gabon was the world's third-ranking producer in 1995.) And the fate of uranium was even worse as the bottom fell off uranium market-prices in the late-1980's. The French mining company operating in Gabon lost $1.9 million in 1992 after cutting production by 40 percent, and by 1994 (when a recovery took place) had downsized its labor force to half its original size.

The austerity measures of 1987-90 were a stunning success, with the IMF impressed with Bongo's resolve. But Gabon was faced in the 1990's with a dreaded IMF suggestion of a 12% cut in all salaries and a freeze on civil service recruitment, both needed in order to shrink the wage bill by 20% in two years. In theory this might appear to be easy, since Gabonese salaries are 300% higher than those in neighboring states. But it was a part-enactment of these provisions in 1988 that triggered wildcat strikes, unrest and the forced shift to multipartyism. The regime was thus faced with increased demands for jobs and patronage due to "democracy," that it cannot easily satisfy because of its previous lavish commitments.

One measure adopted since the mid-1970's has been a periodic expulsion—or economically squeezing them via high residence permit fees—of illegal immigrants in the country: the massive expulsions of 1994/95 were the latest in this series. These expulsions have been motivated by the need to create sources of employment and commerce for nationals, but Gabonese have always shown little propensity for either teaching, trade or manual labor, the fields in which most African expatriates (up to 200,000 in 1995) were concentrated. Indeed, there are few Gabonese private enterprises, large or small, in Gabon even today. Most companies are affiliates of French firms, spruced up with the requisite indigenous front-men to conform with the "Gabonization" of managerial staff that Bongo pressed for in the 1980's. Only in the parastatal sector does one encounter local enterprises, erected with State funds, most of which are totally mismanaged, piling up annual deficits. These companies are the largest segment in the economy with a turnover of $1 billion, and accounting for 38% of the value of all economic activity in Gabon. But they suffer, according to the Minister for State Companies himself, from "lack of productivity, lack of management monitoring, and kickbacks"[101] and have become a serious budgetary drag.

The imperatives of living less lavishly has hit hard against "old habits." The ordering of champagne for all formal functions, even the most trivial administrative ones, had to be severely curtailed. Free civil service housing was abolished late in 1991, to a great deal of grumbling, followed later by some other cuts in fringe benefits. State department heads soon were no longer automatically provided with chauffeur-driven Mercedes Benz cars, and the unlimited privilege of national assembly deputies to fly by First Class at home or abroad was rescinded. Ten foreign Embassies were closed down in the early 1990's. And the privatization, liquidation, or restructuring, of the fifty deficitory State companies, started half-heartedly in the mid-1980's finally moved to the front burner in 1994-95 when the IMF made Gabon's "overhaul of public finances" a precondition for further aid.[102] But the CFA franc devaluation in 1994 caused monumental stress in Gabon, where to so many imports and/or travel abroad are a way of life. Violent student riots in mid-June closed down the local university, even as Gabonese in Paris also demonstrated against the de facto reduction of their bursaries.

More importantly, the fact that little of real substance had actually taken place since political space was created in 1990, and that in the December 1993 presidential elections Father Abessole was denied his victory by Bingo, brought the Gabonese system to a total standstill. A three week Paris meeting in September 1994, that included fifty Gabonese politicians, was necessary before a consensus was reached about how to resolve the political and economic deadlock that developed after the contentious elections. The Paris conference closed loopholes that the opposition had ignored at the time of the euphoric national conference of 1990. The Presidential Guard was slated to be transformed into a Republican Guard (with a national composition); the electoral code was revised; an independent electoral commission was set up; media guarantees were strengthened; new local and parliamentary election schedules were agreed on, though Bongo's re-election (for a final term of office) was again confirmed despite being the main original bone of contention.[103]

As in 1990 a new Prime Minister, also highly regarded, was charged with creating a broadly-based government with the main goal of preparing for parliamentary elections in 1996 and presidential ones in 1998. The government is hampered by the fact that Abessole's RNB categorically refuses to sit down in the cabinet, and is joined in its refusal by another fifteen-party opposition coalition. This has not affected the size of the cabinet, however, since apart from formal political party formations the need in Gabon to satisfy ethnic and regional interests makes "it...difficult in Gabon to form a government of less than 35 members"[104]

If only because of Bongo's youthful age, and a growing perception in society that he does *not* really intend to step down, the creation in November 1994 of a non-ethnic "apolitical" Movement of the Friends of Bongo, was viewed with great unease in opposition circles. Bongo's long-term intentions are difficult to ascertain, however. He clearly wishes to steer clear of controversy with France, while building up whatever credentials he can as a "national" leader, with possible broad appeal to non-Fang groups in the country. Whether he succeeds in this goal only the future will tell.

NOTES

1. "Gabon" comes from *gabao* (sleeve), the name given to the the the Como Estuary by the first Portuguese navigators, that came to refer to the entire territory. For some good overviews in French see Georges Balandier, *Sociologie actuelle de l'Afrique Noire*, Paris, Presses Universitaires de France, 1963; Nicolas Metegue N'nah, *Economies et societes au Gabon dans la premiere moitié du XIXe siécle*, Paris, Harmattan, 1979; Hubert Deschamps, *Traditions orales et archives au Gabon*, Paris, Berger-Levrault, 1962; François Gaulme, *Le Gabon et son ombre*, Paris, Karthala, 1988; Roland Pourtier, *Le Gabon*, 2 vol., Paris, Harmattan, 1989; and, in English, James F. Barnes, *Gabon beyond the colonial legacy*, Boulder, Co., Westview Press, 1992.

2. See also C. Jeannel, "La sterilité en Republique Gabonaise," *Offenberg Press Service Company*, Geneva, 1962.

3. Brian Weinstein, Gabon: *Nation-building on the Ogooue*, Camridge, Mass., MIT Press, 1966, p. 84.

4. Claude Cabrol and Raoul Lehaurd, *La Civilisation des peuples Bateke*, Lyon, Multipress, 1976.

5. See *inter alia* Pierre Alexandre and Jacques Binet, *Le Groupe dit Pahouin*, Paris, Presses Universitaires, 1958; Pierre Alexandre, "Proto-histoire Beti-Bulu-Fang," *Cahiers d'Etudes Africaines*, N.7, vol.2, 1962; and C. Chamberlain, "The Migration of the Fang into Central Gabon," *International Journal of African Studies*, vol. 11 No. 3, 1978.

6. An old cult, *Bwiti* was already danced by slaves on the way to the Americas. Though associated with the Fang, in older days it was a feature of Mitsogo, Bapindji and Myene ritual. The female counterpart rituals—*Ndjembe*—are more widely practiced. See O. Gollnhoffer *&* R. Sillans, "Phenomenologie de possession chez les Mitsogho," *Anthropos*, vol. 74 N. 5-6, 1979; Andre Mary, *La Naissance à lenvers: essai sur le rituel du Bwiti Fang au Gabon*, Paris, Harmattan, 1983, and James W. Fernandez's two articles "The Affirmation of Things Past: Alar Ayong and *Bwiti* as Movements of Protest in Central and Northern Gabon," in Rotberg and Mazrui (eds.), *Protest and Power in Black Africa*, New York, Oxford University Press, 1970, and "Christian Acculturation and Fang Witchcraft," *Cahiers d'Etudes Africaines*, vol. 2 N. 2, 1961.

7. See Pierre Alexandre, "Proto-histoire du groupe beti-bulu-fang," and M. Nguema, "Legende traditionnelle Fang," Libreville archives, mimeographed, cited by Weinstein, p.54.

8. Weinstein, p.42.

9. Among the considerable literature on the Myene see Jean M. Gautier, *Etude historique sur les Mpongoues et tribus avoisinantes*, Montpellier, Lafitte, 1950; Henry H. Bucher, "Mpongwe Origins: Historiographical Perspectives," *History in Africa*, vol. 2, 1975, pp. 59-90; Ambouroué-Avaro, Joseph, *Un Peuple Gabonaise à l'aube de la colonisation: le Bas Ogowe au xixe siécle*, Paris, Karthala, 1981; François Gaulme, *Le Pays de Cama: Un ancien état cotier du Gabon et ses origines*, Paris, Karthala, 1981; Elikia M'Bokolo, "Le Gabon precolonial," *Cahiers d'Etudes Africaines*, vol. 17, 1977.

10. See K. David Pattersen, "The Vanishing Mpongwe: European Contact and Demographic change in the Gabon River," *Journal of African History*, vol. 16 No.2, 1975.

11. K. D. Pattersen, *The Northern Gabon Coast to 1875*, Oxford, Clarendon Press, 1975, p. 49.

12. Pierre Pean, *Affaires Africaines*, Paris, Fayard, 1983, p.32.

13. Near-universal primary school attendance attained in 1983 was accompanied by high failure rates and many unqualified teachers.

14. *West Africa*, December 12, 1989.

15. Pourtier, p.279.

16. Legum (ed.), *Africa Contemporary Record 1976/7*, p.B 515.

17. Fidele Mengue Me Engouang, "Reflexions sur les regimes fiscaux priviligiés du code des investissements au Gabon," *Le Mois en Afrique*, June-July 1985, p. 58 citing data in Albert Ondo Ossa, "Le Paradoxe du Gabon: un pays riche, mais sous-developpé," Ph.D. thesis, University of Nancy, 1984.

18. Pourtier, vol.2, p. 238.

19. "Gabon," in International Monetary Fund, *Surveys of African Economies*, I.M.F., Washington, 1974, p. 278; and *Africa Research Bulletin*, Political Series, June 1990 respectively.

20. A state "renting" out its territory to foreign companies for exploitation.

21. S. Lerat, "Le manganese du Gabon," *Cahiers d'Outre Mer*, October-December 1966.

22. Elikia M'Bokolo, "Le Roi Denis," in Charles-Andre Julien (ed.), *Les Africains*, vol. 6, Paris, Jeune Afrique, 1977, pp. 69-95; *Le Roi Denis: La premiére tentative de modernisation du Gabon*, Dakar, Nouvelles Editions Africaines, 1976; and *Noirs et Blancs en Afrique Equatoriale: les sociétés cotiers et la penetration français 1820-1877*, Paris, Harmattan, 1977. Hubert Deschamps, *Quinze Ans de Gabon: Les debuts de l'etablissement français, 1839-1853*, Paris, Maisonneuve & Larose,

1965; Nicolas Metegue N'nah, *Economies et sociétés au Gabon dans la premiére moitie du XIXe siècle*, Paris, Harmattan, 1979. See also Phyllis M. Martin, *The External Trade of the Loango Coast*, Oxford, Oxford University Press, 1972.

23. *Gabon Aujourd'hui* (Libreville), 28 August 1965.

24. *Effort Gabonais* (Libreville), 3 January 1964.

25. H. Brunschwig, "Expeditions punitives au Gabon 1875-1877," *Cahiers d'Etudes Africaines*, vol. 2 No. 7, 1962; Nicolas Metegue N'nah, *L'Implantation Coloniale au Gabon. Resistance d'un Peuple*, Paris, Harmattan, 1981 and Elikia M'Bokolo, "La Resistance des Mpongwe du Gabon à la creation du comptoir français (1843-1845)," *Afrika Zamani*, December 1978, pp. 5-32.

26. See *inter alia* Catherine Coquery-Vidrovitch, *Le Congo au temps des grandes compagnies concessionaires 1898-1930*, Paris, Mouton, 1972; Pierre Phillipe Rey, *Colonialisme, neo-colonialisme, et transition au capitalisme. Exemple de la "Comilog" au Congo-Brazzaville*, Paris, Maspero, 1971. For the specific concessions and their zones of exploitation in Gabon see Pourtier, vol. 2, p. 138.

27. Andre Gide, *Voyage au Congo*, Paris, Gallimard, 1927.

28. William B. Cohen, *Rulers of Empire*, Hoover, Stanford University Press, 1971.

29. Cited in Weinstein, p. 50.

30. Patterson, p. 125.

31. For Gabonese biographies see David E. Gardinier, *Historical Dictionary of Gabon*, Metuchen, N.J., Scarecrow Press, 1981.

32. See James W. Fernandez, "Affirmation of Things Past: Alar Ayong and *Bwiti* as Movements of Protest"; and André Raponda-Walker and Roger Sillans, *Rites et Croyances des Peuples de Gabon*, Paris, Presence Africaine, 1962.

33. Cited in Weinsten, pp. 58-62.

34. Born in 1912 in Lamberene (to a politically active father), he was elected to the Territorial Assembly in 1946 as Port Gentil's deputy. The Assembly in turn elected him to the French Senate in 1949, where he served until 1957.

35. See Gaulme, *Le Gabon et son ombre*.

36. Pean, p.41

37. Ibid.

38. The approach of independence saw other parties being formed, the most important being the *Parti d'Union Nationale Gabonaise* (PUNGA)—its acronym meaning "tempest" in Eshira. Formed in August 1958 by Eshira and Bapounou dissatisfied by Fang/Myene leadership monopoly, PUNGA took a contrarian stand in the 1958 referendum but only carried Eshira-

Bapounou populated Nyanga. PUNGA was not invited into Mba's national government at independence and ceased to exist.

39. See Pean, *Affairs Africaines*.

40. Gabon's acute dependence upon France under both Mba and Bongo is dictated by the country's need for vastamounts of risk capital to develop its mineral deposits.

41. For some speeches see *Gabon d'Aujourd'hui*, (Libreville), 17 January and 28 February 1966. See also Brian Weinstein, "Leon Mba: The Ideology of Dependence," *Geneve-Afrique*, vol. 6 No.1, 1967.

42. Pean, p. 33.

43. In neighbouring Equatorial Guinea the also Fang President, Macias Nguema, had likewise a collection of skulls, and engaged in ritual *Bwiti* practices. See Samuel Decalo, "Equatorial Guinea," in *Psychoses of Power: African Personal Dictatorships*, Boulder, Co., Westview Press, 1989.

44. Alerted by French timber interests on growing unrest, Mba set up a State Security Court with jurisdiction over "rumor-mongering" and plots, and in 1962 passed a law against "idleness," that allowed the expulsion from urban centers to their rural origins of all those judged to be troublesome elements.

45. Charles F. and Alice B. Darlington, *African Betrayal*, New York, David McKay, 1968, p.139. See also "Gabon: Putsch or Coup d'etat," *Africa Report*, March 1964.

46. Rene Dumont, in his *Afrique Noire est mal Partie*, as cited in Pean, p.32.

47. Darlington, p. 139. See also pp. 126-55 for the coup as seen through the eyes of the US Ambassador.

48. Chipman, "French Foreign Policy," p. 9.

49. See Charles de Gaulle, *Memoires d'espoir; le renouveau, 1958-1962*, Paris, Plon, 1970, p. 73.

50. Chipman, "French Foreign Policy," p.31.

51. Morrison, p.245.

52. Gardinier, *Historical Dictionary of Gabon*, p. 59. See also Moshe Ammi-Oz, "L'evolution de la place et du role des forces publiques africaines," *Le Mois en Afrique*, March 1977 about the neutralization of the Gabonese army after 1964 putsch.

53. Cited in Pean, p. 55.

54. "Gabon: A Special Relationship," *Africa Confidential*, June 1975, p. 4.

55. Pean, p. 46.

56. Interview with a Western Ambassador, Libreville, August 1, 1989.

57. Pean, p. 66.

58. Philippe Decraene, "Gabon," in his *L'Afrique Centrale*, Paris, CHEAM, 1989, p. 85.

59. The first mention of a railway was made by Count Savorgnan de Brazza in the 1890's, when construction of railroads were in vogue, and it was assumed that the track would link up with Bangui (Central African Republic) and the interior of French Equatorial Africa.

60. Construction commenced in 1974 under Eurotrag—a European consortium with 4,113 employees: 1,714 Gabonese, 1,720 Africans, 327 Pakistanis, and 352 Europeans. The completed railroad had 50 bridges. See also "Gabon: Railways and Rivalries," *Africa Confidential*, May 25, 1973.

61. See "Gabon," in Legum (ed.), *Africa Contemporary Record 1970/71*.

62. For details see "Gabon: A Railway Saga," *Africa Confidential*, July 18, 1975.

63. Cited in Barnes, p. 57.

64. See Decalo, "Equatorial Guinea" in *Psychoses of Power*.

65. See the important article by Olivier Duhamel, "Le Parti Democratique Gabonais," *Le Mois en Afrique*, May 1976.

66. The development of Franceville and Haut Ogooue was, of course, a function of its economic potential, but it benefited immeasurably from the fact that Gabon's prime political elite originated from there. Franceville, founded as Masuku by explorer Brazza in 1880, has experienced a huge influx becoming an urban commune of 30,000 up from its tiny 1,200 population in 1961. See Mamadi Kamara, "Franceville: Activités et role dans l'organisation de de son arrière-pays," *Cahiers d'Outre-Mer*, vol. 36 N.143, 1983, pp. 267-292.

67. Legum (ed.), *Africa Contemporary Record 1976-77*, p. B511.

68. Gaulme, *Gabon et son Ombre*, p. 154.

69. Legum (ed.), *Africa Contemporary Record 1971-2*, p. B507.

70. Interview in Libreville, August 7, 1989.

71. Michael C. Reed, "Gabon: A Neo-colonial Enclave of Enduring French Interest," *Journal of Modern African Studies*, vol. 25 N. 2, June 1987, p. 302.

72. Pean, p. 105.

73. *Africa Confidential*, November 8, 1988.

74. *Africa Confidential* Aug 21, 1970, p. 4. After the appointment of Mebiame as Prime Minister in 1975 he reiterated, in case of confusion, "I remain Captain of the Gabonese ship." *Africa Research Bulletin*, Political Series, May 1975.

75. Pean, p. 35-6. According to Pean, those Gabonese that Bongo cannot seduce to collaborate with him due to his powerful alliance with France and resident French expatriate companies, he is able to scare off with his powers of sorcery. Pean, p. 36.

76. Legum (ed.), *Africa Contemporary Record 1976-77*, p. B 508. See also Moshe Ammi-Oz, "L'evolution de la place et du role des forces publiques africaines"; and Pierre Viaud and Jacques de Lestapis, *Afrique: Les Souverainetés en Armes*, Paris, Fondation pour les Etudes de Defense Nationale, 1987.

77. Guy Martin, "Uranium: A Case Study in Franco-African Relations," *Journal of Modern African Studies*, vol. 27 No.4, 1989, p. 625.

78. Chipman, "French Foreign Policy," p. 31. See also "Gabon: A Special Relationship," *Africa Confidential*, June 1975, pp. 5-6.

79. "In any controversy with the French, the Gabonese are prepared to use the threat of transferring their allegiances to the U.S." See Legum (ed.), *Africa Contemporary Record 1984-5*, p. B154.

80. Pean, p. 20.

81. See Reed, "Gabon: A Neo-colonial Enclave of Enduring French Interest."

82. Rosberg and Jackman, *Personal Rule in Africa*, p. 156.

83. In 1975 French President Giscard d'Estaign and a dozen African Heads of State had to cool their heels for 24 hours in Bangui when Bongo, attending an OPEC summit, requested the Francophone meeting about to take place not commence without him.

84. "Gabon: French disconnection?" *Africa Confidential*, March 17, 1982.

85. *Africa Confidential*, September 2 and December 9, 1981.

86. Martin, p. 625.

87. Interview in Libreville, August 12, 1989.

88. Morrison, p. 117.

89. "Gabon's Placid Veneer," *Washington Post*, January 3, 1983.

90. Pean, p. 150.

91. "Gabon: Police Power," *Africa Confidential*, January 6, 1989.

92. Legum (ed.), *Africa Contemorary Record 1977/8*, p. B572.

93. In 1989 Bongo married Edith, the daughter of neigboring Congo's President Sassou Nguesso, after paying the prescribed dowry for her. His name had been linked romantically with several eligible women including a niece of Morocco's King Hassan, and he had been under pressure to "seal political relations inside the country" by marrying a Myene. See *Africa Confidential*, December 1, 1989.

94. "Gabon: Bongo's security," *Africa Confidential*, 30 October 1985, pp. 6-8.

95. Legum (ed.), *Africa Contemporary Record, 1984-5*, p. B 149.

96. *Jeune Afrique*, April 23, 1990, p. 7. See also Gabon. *Conference nationale*. Libreville, Service documentation de l'Union, 2 vol., 1991.

97. Claude Wauthier, "Opposition in Disarray," *West Africa*, 31 August 1992.

98. See, for example, Duhamel, "Le Parti Democratique Gabonais."

99. See Maurice Ndoume Nze. *Elections legislatives gabonaises*. Paris, Harmattan, 1991.

100. "Gabon: Police Power," *Africa Confidential*, January 6, 1989 and "Gabon: Return of Morena," *Africa Confidential*, 20 January 1989.

101. *West Africa*, 31 July 1989.

102. *Africa Research Bulletin*, Economic Series, January 1995; February 1995.

103. See *Africa Research Bulletin*, Political Series, October 1994.

104. *Africa Research Bulletin*, Political Series, December 1994.

CHAPTER FOUR

KENYA: STABILITY THROUGH PORK-BARREL POLITICS

Unlike both Malawi and Gabon, Kenya is a key African country, receiving immense academic coverage.[1] Moreover, until the 1980's Kenya was considered one of the continent's success stories, exemplifying stability, free-enterprise, and relatively benign leadership; a rare example of a state with a vibrant legislature, free press, an independent judiciary, and institutionalized grass-roots political life—despite a cultural heterogeneity and socio-economic problems that had brought instability elsewhere in Africa.

Hardly all that was written about Kenya during this period was in a positive vein. Even the most laudatory assessments of Kenya's record—not to speak of the large corpus of arch-critical, often Marxist, critiques of Kenya's development—were gloomy in assessing the long-term impact of the country's socio-economic policies, that entrenched vast regional, class and income disparities, as attested by the wealth and ostentatious acquisitiveness of the country's elite compared to the poverty of the *wananchi* (common farmers). In gross economic terms Kenya may have been among Africa's better performers, but more critical observers focused, as in Malawi, on the *price* of this success. Even the World Bank tempered its strong commendation of the Kenyan "economic miracle" with urgings that more vigorous distributive policies be adopted to bridge social disparities with explosive potentials. Miller best summed up Kenya: "the 'Hong Kong' of Africa, a free-wheeling, materialistic place where the search for individual profit is the commanding ethic...simultaneously heralded as [a country] of achievement and economic success, and condemned as one of exploitation and elitism."[2]

Searching questions were also raised about Kenya's "inherent" civil-military stability. Until 1978 these were part of doomsday prognoses linked to the succession issue that loomed large. Though Kenya surmounted that crisis with surprising ease, the country's political and civil-military stability progressively became unhinged. The destabilizing effects of much-postponed problems came home to roost. Unemploy-ment, over-population, land-scarcity, mass-elite and regional economic disparities; corruption and inefficiency in the state sector; Moi's increas-ingly authoritarian rule—all created a cauldron of tensions seeking resolution. The country was rocked by a number of plots, reflecting ethnic grievances that need to be addressed, and political space that needs to be created. In 1991 Moi seemed to capitulate to domestic and external pressures for liberalization (see chapter 5), but thanks to a divided opposition seemingly more concerned about securing its day at the public trough, he has survived at the helm of the country.

The question about the Kenya of the mid-1990's is no longer whether Moi can sustain the "trade-off" approach to civil-military stability, though this is the main focus of this study. Rather, whether when Moi is finally ousted, the country can avoid bloody civil strife, the result of decades of ethnic politics exacerbated by the more brutal machinations of the regime in the past seven years. For, like Nigeria, Kenya is today the sick man of Africa.

Basic Kenyan Social Parameters

Kenya encompasses 569,137 sq.kms. (219,745 sq.m.) excluding the waters of Lake Turkana and Lake Victoria. The land slopes from a narrow coastal belt to the lush "White Highlands" where Nairobi is found at an altitude of 5,500 feet, and on to Lake Victoria, 450 miles from the coast. Three-quarters of the country to the North and East of the Highlands is a plateau of 2,000 feet, much of it hot and arid. The country is bisected by the equator (200 kms. north of Nairobi) and by the Great Rift Valley that in the Highlands measures 65 kms across and is bordered by escarpments 600-900 meters high.

Despite its cosmopolitan veneer, bustling modern capital, and heavy tourist traffic, Kenya is very much a rural country in which 87% of the people still reside in the countryside, engaged in agriculture. Large disparities are Kenya's hallmark, that is the only major African state with neither mineral resources nor adequate arable farming land. Only 15 percent of the country (the Highlands economic core and the immediate coastal area) can in normal years expect enough rainfall to sustain agriculture; two-thirds of the countryside, being sparsely vege-tated and semi-desert, is not suitable even for grazing purposes.

This affects demographic patterns. Some 60 percent of the people are found on 8 percent of the land, with high population densities along Lake Victoria and in the Highlands. Apart from a smaller cluster along the coast, the rest of the country is virtually empty. Put differently, despite an overall population density of 50.1 people per sq. km., densities of 500 per sq.km. exist in many rural districts, and in a few—e.g. in Kiambu, the heart of Kikuyuland—population density is higher than 1,500 per sq. km., which is among the world's highest. And these figures are rapidly increasing as the country's population expands.

For Kenya's annual population growth is 3.9 percent, the highest in the world. In some regions it reaches 4 percent, the biological maximum, leading to a doubling of the country's population every 18 years. The 1969 census fixed Kenya's population at 10.9 million, a figure that jumped to over 22 million in 1989, with projections of 35 million by the year 2000, and 60.5 million by 2020. Nairobi itself is expected to *quintuple* in size by the year 2000, reaching a population of eight million.

Kenya includes between 27 and 41 ethnicities, depending on one's typology. Many had few mutual contacts prior to the colonial era, being geographically apart, or through mode of life culturally distinct. Along the coast Persian, Arab, and Omani influences, as well as Islam became entrenched, with Swahili in due course becoming Kenya's lingua franca.

The Bantu groups are by far the largest (70%) of Kenya's population and include the Kikuyu, Embu, Meru, Kamba, Kisii, Baluhya, Taita, and Giriama. The Nilotics include primarily the Luo along Lake Victoria; the Nilo-Hamitics encompass the Maasai, Turkana and Kalenjin, while the Hamitic include the Galla and Somali in the Northeast. Kenya's largest ethnic groups are the Kikuyu (21%), Luhya (14%), Luo (13%), Kamba (11%) and Kalenjin (11%). Together with the smaller Kisii and Meru/Embu, these groups account for 75% of the population. Of the rest only the Mijikenda near the coast, numbering half a million, are of import.

Adistinctive feature of Kenya's peoples is the absence among most of strong chiefs, internal unity or historic kingdoms. Though in the late 19th century both the Luo and Luhya experienced centralizing drives, and strong leaders emerged among the chiefless Kikuyu and Kamba, "the idea of chiefs had no basis in the political institutions of

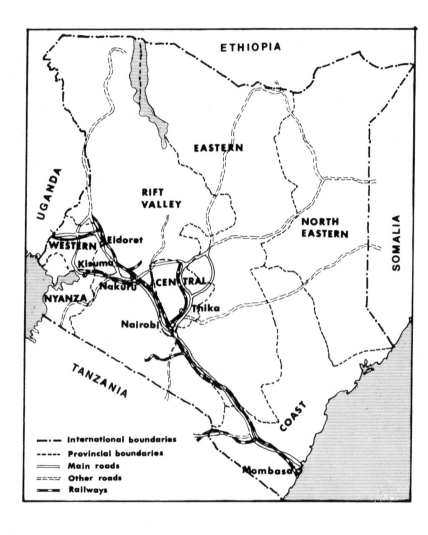

the Mt. Kenya peoples...[being] a creation of the British administration at the turn of the century."[3] Unlike neighboring Uganda, Kenya did not emerge at independence with kings and chiefs and primordial mass allegiances. This, however, did not lead to greater inter-ethnic affiliation, since the pull of ethnicity is strong in Kenya. But it did allow the emergence of modern leaders not beholden to traditional interests.

As elsewhere in Africa, Kenya's groups are concentrated in specific localities. British rule recognized each group as a separate entity within established borders, entrenching subnationalism, and transforming districts into ethnic constituencies. Nearly the entire population (96 percent) of the Central province is Kikuyu; and fully 73 percent of all Kikuyu reside in that province. The Northeast is nearly exclusively (96.4 percent) populated by Somalis—and 95 percent of Kenya's Somalis reside there. In Nyanza 63 percent of the people are Luo, and 31 percent Kisii—with 87 percent of the Luo, and 95 percent of the Kisii living in that province. The Western province is the home of the Luhya (88 percent); 98.4 percent of the cluster of "Coastal" peoples reside in the Coast province. The Eastern province is populated by the Kamba (54.5 percent) and Embu/Meru (39 percent) the majority of whom (87 percent and 97 percent respectively) are to be found only there. Only the large Rift Valley province is more heterogeneous, inhabited by the Kalenjin (95 percent of whom reside there, making up 51 percent of its population), Kikuyu (15 percent), Maasai (97 percent of Kenya's Maasai live here, though they make up only 7 percent of the province's population) and Luhya (7 percent). Nairobi, in colonial days inhabited largely by Kikuyu, is today still predominantly Kikuyu (47 percent) interspersed with smaller groups of Luhya (16 percent), Luo (15 percent), and Kamba (15 percent).

The largest group in Kenya are the Kikuyu, who are culturally close to the other Highlands groups, the Kamba, Embu and Meru to their east. Kikuyuland is a plateau at an altitude of 1,000-2,500 meters. Extremely densely populated and farmed, it has good soils, rainfall, climate, and no malaria. The Kikuyu live in scattered homesteads on top of ridges, grouped into autonomous communities governed by councils of elders. Attached to their lands (privately owned), the Kikuyu historically produced food in excess of their needs for trade with passing caravans. Currently over one-third of their land is planted with cash crops, the highest percentage for any group in Kenya. Individualistic and achievement oriented, "a man's status in society was measured by his wealth and capabilities rather than by his birth or social connections."[4]

Murang'a—under the British, Fort Hall—is the Kikuyu ancestral home, from which successive waves of land-hungry Kikuyu colonized in the 19th century areas to the north (Nyeri) and south (Kiambu). The latter (the Highlands)—today the core of Kikuyuland, and birthplace of their greatest leaders (Harry Thuku, Koinange wa Mbiyu, and Jomo Kenyatta)—was the last they settled prior to the arrival of the British. Hard-hit in the 1890's by epidemics, drought and famine, most Kikuyu temporarily retreated from Kiambu to family homesteads in Murang'a, giving the British the notion the Highlands were vacant and available for colonization.

The Kamba, the fourth largest group after the Kikuyu, Luhya and Luo, have a strong animist component (40 percent) in contrast to the largely Christian (73 percent) Kikuyu, but otherwise are close to them. Acephalous, "government operations are diffused in the life of the people so much that it is impossible to pinpoint the locus of political power."[5] In the 16th century the Kamba migrated north from the slopes of Kilimanjaro, to settle around Machakos, their current "capital." Only 13.5 percent of their land is arable due to inadequate rainfall, with the rest severely overgrazed and eroded. The Kamba consequently branched off into commerce in the 1780's, to dominate long-distance trade (ivory, foodstuffs, slaves) between the Maasai and the Coast, the root of Mombasa's prosperity.[6] Under colonial rule the Kamba flocked into the police and armed forces, and to this day are over-represented in these structures.

The Kalenjin are the principal group in Kenya's western Rift Valley province. (Before the 1950's the word "Kalenjin" did not exist, being coined to refer to the Nandi-speaking peoples.) They comprise of ten main groups with the Kipsigis numbering half their population, followed by the Nandi and the Tugen, Moi's group, 250,000-strong in the 1989 census. Southern Nilo-Hamitic, their origin is from the north (Lake Turkana, or Ethiopia), arriving in the Mt. Elgon region around 1500. They are found throughout the province that has immense contrasts in soil and climate. Some (e.g. the Tugen) inhabit the hot arid lowlands of the Valley, while others reside in the highlands. Kalenjin districts have a median population density (42 per sq. km.), and the lowest ethnic out-migration rates after the Maasai. Distant from the seat of colonial power, few Kalenjin were affected by modern education, something that explains the general backwardness of their districts. Though many are agriculturalists, the Kalenjin are pastoralists with the cattle-complex strong among them. The most "striking characteristic of many Kalenjin is the dignity and quietness of their demeanour and the restraint they show under all circumstances."[7] Egalitarian, they too never had centralized political unity. Opting for police and military careers, during the colonial era Nandi recruitment quotas were always oversubscribed, even though the Nandi were one of the few groups to resist the British entry into Kenya.

To their south live the Maasai (185,000 in Kenya, 95,000 in Tanzania), part of the Eastern Nilotic Maa group of peoples. Their demographic growth is low, and population density in Maasai areas (5 per sq.km.) is the lowest in Kenya. The origins of the Maasai origins are unknown. In precolonial days the Maasai were the much-feared "masters" of the Rift Valley from Lake Turkana to Tanzania, defeating all rivals under leaders with religio-magical powers. Just before the arrival of the British, however, internecine strife, devastating epidemics and droughts decimated their numbers, allowing the British to usurp their most fertile lands. The Maasai remain avidly pastoral, abjure agrarian pursuits, and nomadize hot arid lands with hardly a cash economy. Illiterate, only 20 percent Christianized, Maasai districts have seen little out-migration.[8]

In contrast to these groups, the Luo are Western Nilotics, their 30-odd clans residing in the Gulf of Nyanza province, with Kisumu as their capital. The Luo are Kenya's third largest group, and among the most Christianized (90 percent), though many syncretic cults exist among them, and they have retained polygeny and other traditional customs. Population density in Luo areas is second only to that of the Luhya. Originating in southern Sudan, the Luo arrived in Kenya in waves from Uganda. Originally pastoralists, they became agriculturalists out of necessity. Only one third of their crops is geared to the cash market, the lowest figure of Kenya's sedentary groups. Also in contrast to the Kikuyu predilection for private enterprise and trade, the Luo are drawn in large numbers into white collar jobs, the civil service and academia.[9]

Their neighbors, the heterogeneous Luhya, are Kenya's second-largest group, and the most Christianized (94 percent). Close to the Busoga and Baganda in Uganda[10], it is hard to reconstruct their past, but most migrated from East Uganda, with oral history referring to an origin in Sudan or Ethiopia. The Luhya inhabit areas along Lake Victoria to Mt. Elgon with high population densities (161-545 per sq.km.) and maximum growth (4 percent). Their land is fertile, but over-population has resulted in major land-shortages, Kenya's smallest homesteads, and the least acreage planted with cash-crops. There is "no uncultivated land in Luyia country"[11]—a fact making the Luhya prone to out-migration.

The coastal Mijikenda are nine peoples with common traditions and mutually comprehensible dialects.[12] Oral history has them settling nine fortified hilltop villages ("Mijikenda" means "the nine villages") arriving in the coastal hinterland in the 17th century from southern Somalia. They inhabit the plateau to the rear of the 4-7 mile wide coastal zone, up to the Taru desert. Numbering less than one million, the largest subgroup is the Giriama (350,000), with others as small as 18,000. Demographic growth is below the national mean, illiteracy is high, school attendance is low, and poverty rife. Religiously they are equally split between Islam and animism, with some 20 percent Christian. Despite fertile lands, their agrarian output is dependent upon the vagaries of rainfall patterns.

The coastal strip, mostly inhabited by Swahili Arabs (30,000), Asians (50,000) and other such groups, was until 1892 a dominion of the Sultan of Zanzibar.[13] Mentioned in 1st century Greek accounts, settled by Arab and Shirazi merchants as early as the 8th century, it was part of a belt of trade centers from Somalia to Mozambique, with contacts with Asia and the Indies. As the region prospered new arrivals came from southern Arabia. A distinctive Islamic culture emerged, giving the Coast a heterogeneous political history. By contrast 200 years of sporadic Portuguese rule left no residue, though the latter introduced new crops (potatoes, cassava, maize), and bequeathed contemporary Kenyan tourism the impressive Fort Jesus, that defends Mombasa harbor. After the tenuous Portuguese hegemony over the Coast was broken, the area and its several warring Arab city-states fell under nominal Omani suzerainty (exercised since 1840 from Zanzibar) until Britain secured a 50-year lease over the Coastal strip in 1892.

British Colonial Rule and Socio-Economic Change

The British arrival to *kere nyaga* ("mountain of white" the Kikuyu name for the 5,200 meter snow-covered Mt. Kenya) coincided with the collapse of Maasai power in the interior, civil war, and Nandi pressures; the consolidation of a Kamba monopoly over long-distance trade; a famine-induced Mijikenda thrust toward the coast where they clashed with the Arabs; and a temporary Kikuyu retreat from the Highlands. On July 1, 1895 Britain declared an "East Africa Protectorate" that included the ten mile wide coastal strip (for which an indemnity of 16,500 pounds a year was paid until 1963), and all land to the eastern edge of the Rift Valley. At the time Kenya was seen merely as the venue for a railroad to Uganda, much more attractive to missionaries, politicians (fixated on control of the Nile head-waters) and traders alike. Originally administered from Zanzibar with Omani staff, in 1907 Nairobi, a railway depot equidistant between Uganda and the Coast, was designated capital. It rapidly became Africa's most "European" city—though Europeans never made up more than a tenth of its population.

The Mombasa-Lake Victoria railroad was completed in 1901, and extended into Uganda (that in 1902 ceded territory to Kenya) in the 1920's. Indentured Indian labor was brought to assist in its construction, and many of these settled to join a growing number of fortune-seekers from Europe. In order to recoup the cost of the railroad, and to protect the growing non-African population, the territory was "pacified" and made self-paying. In the process military expeditions were mounted—some unauthorized by London—against the Nandi (in 1901, 1905, 1906)—who, having gained ascendance over the Maasai, offered the British stiff resistance[14]—against the Embu in 1904 and 1906, Gusii, in 1904 and 1908, Kipsigis (in 1905), and others in 1907.

From the outset it was clear self-sufficiency meant attracting European settlers; the inducement was millions acres of relatively vacant, well-watered, disease-free, high-altitude land the railroad had conveniently opened up, in the midst of which was Nairobi. Kikuyu claims to Kiambu were ignored by an administration for decades not even aware that private ownership of land was the norm in the region. Until this was accepted by Britain after World War II, Africans were kept away from the cash-crop economy, and were only seen as cheap labor for European planters. Kikuyu farmers, for example, were unable to grow coffee until 1948, under legislation aimed at quality control of export crops.

From the outset the Crown also demanded Kenya's administration be financed from domestic revenues. In the absence of mineral resources, self-sufficiency could only stem from advances in agriculture. Crop experimentation led to high quality coffee becoming as early as 1920 Kenya's prime export, and prime mainstay of the economy since. Large tea plantations, set up in the 1920's, became economically important in the 1930's. Pyrethrum flowers—the extract of which is used in insecticides—introduced in the 1930's, were within a few years pulling large profits. (Kenya now produces 65 percent of the global supply of pyrethrum.) Sisal also fared well in Kenya to become a staple export. Of the four, coffee and tea remain major exports today, with the role of sisal and pyrethrum declining after independence.

The number of European settlers increased to 4,000 in 1953, when they owned 7.3 million acres of farms of around 2,400 acres each. [15] As late as 1959 one-fifth of Kenya's arable land was reserved for colonists, for Kenya was seen as another settler colony along the lines of Canada, Australia, New Zealand and South Africa. Africans were force-drafted to work on European farms; later, the imposition of taxes they could not meet except through wage labor, and laws demanding from squatters at least 180 days of labor on European farms, attained the same end. And population pressures drove many Kikuyu to accept squatter rights on their alienated lands in the Highlands in exchange for work for European farmers who came to control an African workforce of over 250,000.

The squatters however, saw themselves as the legitimate owners forced to work for tenancy on land stolen from them. [16] As high birthrates created overpopulation, they were transformed from the richest Kikuyu (in the 1920's) to the poorest, most insecure and embittered. European settlers in turn were unhappy with high labor turnover on their estates, since Africans offered their services only for the 1-2 months necessary to earn their tax; and with the growing number of squatters on the lands. In 1934 there were 114,000 squatters, the number swelling to 610,000 in 1962. That year's census revealed that the Highlands, with a population of barely 100,000 in 1900, now sustained more than one million people.

The Kikuyu presence in Kiambu—astride the major lines of communication of the colony, and in proximity to the capital, its services, and employment opportunities—gave them enormous advantages. This despite the fact that social services were stingily rationed to Africans in general, and in the Highlands specifically. British policy rested on the premise that the Highlands were reserved for Europeans, with Africans there only as temporary residents with few rights to services. Despite such discriminatory policies, the upwardly-mobility of the Kikuyu rapidly made them the most educated in Kenya. And this despite the fact that until after the Second World War more funds were allocated for European and Asian education (3 percent of the population) than on Africans, and that the first secondary school opened in 1926, with only 18 in the entire colony as late as 1955.

With approaching independence education began to spread: from 2,167 students in secondary schools and 400,000 in primary ones in the mid-1950's, the figures jumped to 12,872 and 840,000 respectively in 1963. These advances camouflaged, however, wide disparities between educational levels of the various ethnic groups. In Nairobi, for example, 72% of school-age children attended school while in the Northeast Province only 4% were enrolled. Some 56% of Kikuyu school-age children attended primary schools compared to 33% among the next-largest ethnic group, the Luo. Literacy levels likewise ranged from over 51% in Kikuyu districts to below 22% among the Mijikenda, Kamba, segments of the Kalenjin, not to speak of the Maasai where it stood at 7.7%. Still, at independence Kenya had the 8th-highest literacy rate of 32 states in Africa, and the continent's second-highest daily newspaper circulation.[17]

The quest for education escalated after independence. The first decade of independence saw a doubling in primary school enrollment, as the regime made an effort to widen the spread of primary education. In 1974 school fees for the first four years of school were abolished and there was again a massive spurt in enrollment, to 2,700,000; and when fees for primary education were altogether scrapped in 1979, student numbers jumped to 4 million, or nearly 95% of all primary school-age children in the country.

Secondary school enrollment increased sixfold from its low base of 30,000 to 180,000, but much of this increase was in non-government schools. For the cost of expanding secondary education exceeded the government's willingness and ability to do so. Already in 1976 recurrent educational costs took up 40% of Kenya's budget, a percentage that increased after the abolition of primary school fees in 1979. Thus in secondary education a two-tiered system emerged. Parallel to 400 government schools, local communities maintained an additional 600, mostly *harambee* schools, that between 1967 and 1973 enrolled 43% of Kenya's secondary school pupils.[18] These schools, created through donations and funds raised by politicians, charged higher fees than government schools, offered inferior education, were over-crowded and poorly equipped. Nevertheless, parents were willing to undertake the necessary sacrifices for the sake of children locked out of government schools, and *harambee* schools continued to multiply in Kenya.

Wide disparities, from colonial days, also developed in health care. Though in 1968 Kenya had the third-highest doctor per capita ratio in Africa, over 70% of Kenya's practitioners were found in Nairobi and Mombasa, with the bulk of hospital beds likewise in these two cities. The prohibitive cost of spreading health facilities throughout the country restricted Kenya's efforts in this domain to one bout of development spending in the 1970's. The fact that missionaries had historically offered health care was a further inducement for the regime to abdicate its responsibilities.

Differential rates of acculturation of Kenya's ethnic groups consequent to varying degrees of integration in the European war effort also produced regional disparities. During the WWI over 195,000 porters and 10,000 soldiers were recruited from Kenya, mostly Kikuyu, Luo, Kamba and Nandi, who saw at first hand both the frailties of the European, and the importance of organization. Not surprisingly the earliest proto-nationalist and anti-colonial stirrings developed among the Luo and Kikuyu. The first pressure groups set up in defence of indigenous interests emerged simultaneously in Nyanza (the Young Kavirondo Association, founded in 1921 and appealing mostly to the Luo and Luhya) and the East African Association (after June 1921 the Young Kikuyu Association) in Nairobi. In both key early leaders (Jonathan Okwirri, Joseph Kange'the and Philip Karanja) served in the colonial army, though others (Harry Thuku; Jomo Kenyatta) rose to leadership via other means. By contrast the Nandi, who served in the colonial forces in larger numbers than any other ethnicity, remained "loyalist" during the Mau Mau Emergency due to their more conservative and isolated social setting, and the relative absence of land-alienation among them.[19]

The growing aspirations of the economically powerful Asian community, that demanded greater recognition, also played a role. Indentured Indian labor had been brought to build the railroad, and the idea of importing Asian farmers to develop the Highlands had been considered. Legally precluded from owning land, and by 1940 numbering 50,000 (double the number of Europeans, three times the indigenous Arab population), Kenya's Asians came to dominate wide sectors of the economy. A three-tiered system developed in Kenya as elsewhere in British East Africa. As Morris put it with reference to Uganda (that differed little from Kenya in this respect) in 1910 "administration and agricultural development were thought to be European occupations; trade and craftsmanship were relegated to Indians; and Africans were encouraged to work in the European agricultural system and to supply cheap labour in the towns...The picture did not substantially change in the next forty years."[20] In Kenya however, the pace of change did suddenly pick up, with the onset of the Mau Mau rebellion.

Mau Mau and the Rise of Kenyatta

Few subjects have received so much attention as the 1952 Mau Mau[21] rebellion. To Kenya's white community Mau Mau was a "return" to barbarianism by the always suspect Kikuyu. Jomo Kenyatta, who in 1947 became President of the Kenya African Union, and was imprisoned for his Mau Mau involvement (on evidence later discredited)—was viewed by the colonists as "a leader of darkness and death." British colonial authorities—whose inept and discriminatory policies finally came under critical review in London after the outbreak of Mau Mau—portrayed the rebellion as an atavistic phenomenon manipulated by power-hungry Kikuyu leaders. A few observers were riveted to the emphasis in Mau Mau on ritual (oathing ceremonies, animal sacrifices), and regarded the revolt as a syncretic religion. Only with the work of Rosberg and Nottingham was Mau Mau seen as the manifestation of a "nationalistic revolutionary movement... the evolutionary child of...the Kikuyu Association."[22] Because it expressed the assertiveness of the "House of Mumbi" (the Kikuyu), other groups in Kenya were frightened into collaboration with the British colonial authorities.

Whatever the ritual and symbolism in Mau Mau, its roots were squarely in the grievances of proud upwardly-mobile Kikuyu farmers of Kiambu (other districts were less affected by the disturbances), marginalized as squatters in what they regarded their own land. On a more general level Mau Mau was the result of the non-resolution by

the settler-influenced colonial authorities of three problems: the need
to modernize and reorganize peasant agriculture, through land redistribution; the need to create a stable, equitably-paid labor force in the
agrarian Highlands; and the need to grant direct political participation
to the Kenyan intelligentsia and middle class. Colonial officials sabo-
taged all initiatives to soothe points of friction in Kenya, even when
counselled by London to undertake conciliatory action.

African per capita income had not changed markedly in thirty
years. Standing at $9 it was *lower* than in less well-endowed Uganda
($32). Intent on building a settler society, the administration ignored
Africans, discouraged urbanization, and offered minimal social services. Nairobi's few amenities (to an increasingly large African population), for example, was part of a conscious policy to discourage
rural-urban drifts—but created instead slums and misery. As a member
of the Legislative Council lamented in December 1948, "there are very
few Africans in Nairobi at the moment who have more than one meal
per day, very few indeed."[23] And there were only *nine* Africans in the
civil service in 1947 drawing a salary of 300 shillings ($40) a month or
more.[24]

Notwithstanding efforts to insulate Kenya's population from
change, the Kikuyu "changed more than any other East African tribe,"[25]
and responded with alacrity to attempts to organize them into political
movements. Hence they were to play the dominant nationalist role in
colonial Kenya through their organizations, notably the Kikuyu Association and Kikuyu Central Association (KA, 1919; KCA, 1924), Kenya
African Union (KAU, 1944), and later the Kenyan African National
Union (KANU).

The outbreak of Mau Mau and the Declaration of a State of
Emergency signalled the failure of the policy of separate and unequal
development in Kenya. Though the authorities acted ruthlessly to
subdue the revolt, the shock of Mau Mau nudged London to assess the
triggering cause of the revolt, reach the appropriate conclusion, and
force the local administration onto the road to radical land reform and
ultimate independence. Though Mau Mau failed militarily, it succeeded politically in that it brought back to Kenya imperial supremacy,
that over-ruling settler influences, recognized Kenya as an *African*
colony.

For the political evolution of Kenya had lagged, with Africans
until 1944 "represented" by missionaries. Only in that year was the

first African (the Kikuyu Eliud Mathu) was *appointed* to the legislature by the Governor. (After independence he became Kenyatta's personal secretary.) Though the number of African appointees increased to four in 1947, the first African elections only took place in March 1957 *after* Mau Mau was contained, when seven Africans joined the Council. (Shortly later Africans were given parity with Europeans in that body.) It was only in 1954 that the first African cabinet Minister was appointed (B. A. Ohanga), though six years Africans were in a majority. The next Lancaster House Conference laid the framework for an independence never imagined seven years previously.

Party formation in Kenya

Political parties, prohibited in 1953, were again allowed, outside the Central Province where disturbances continued, in mid-1955. But *nation-wide* parties were proscribed until 1960; what developed in Kenya were personal machines, based on constituency/district lines, "often dominated by a single leader"[26]; these machines were ethnic ones, since each leader concentrated on organizing his ethnic vote—with major implications for the future. The edict against national forma-tions was challenged by Kenya's first African lawyer, C.M.G. Argwings-Kodhek—on the grounds that it encouraged tribalism—but the British refused to register his National Congress. The only early grouping with a national constituency was the Kenya Federation of Labour under the the young Nyanza Luo unionist, Tom Mboya. And it too was under constant threat of deregistration because of its political activities, protected from such a fate by the intervention of the British Trades Union Congress in England.

Mboya, one of Kenya's most non-ethnic spokesman, lamented this inability "to escape completely from the district consciousness which developed during this period. No other country under British rule started off with such difficulties in forming a national movement as we faced....because we could see district loyalties building up and reflecting tribal loyalties (since district and tribal boundaries were often the same)."[27] When nationwide parties were finally allowed, they came about through the merger of powerful existing district political ma-chines, to form either KANU or KADU "branches". The end result was "national" parties that lacked strong central cores. Since except in transitional areas ethnic and district lines closely parallelled, the "parties" were merely loose confederations of constituency ethnic machines under political barons possessing grass-roots power bases *independent* of the central party, prone to factionalism, and riveted to parochial issues.

National party-formation was further complicated by the fact that most ethnic groups had never been united, hence "cooperation on a tribal basis has been almost as difficult to achieve as on a multi-tribal basis."[28] What political unity did emerge was more an outcome of pragmatic cooperation of elected members of the Assembly. To this day, despite the coercive powers of the executive, the continued strength of ethnic leaders and constituency machines within the political system gives Kenya much of its uniqueness. Strong centralized Presidential autocracy, coupled with autonomous district political barons *and* varying measures of grass-roots democracy, are Kenya's political hallmark.

Two political formations emerged: the first, on March 27, 1960 when some thirty district political barons convened in Limuru (Kiambu) to form the Kenyan African National Union (KANU), under James Gichuru's interim presidency (Kenyatta, then in prison, was elected President), with Tom Mboya as Secretary General, Oginga Odinga (the latter's Luo archrival) as Vice President, Ronald Ngala (the coastal Giriama leader) as Treasurer, and the Tugen Daniel arap Moi as deputy Treasurer. The party was stillborn, however, since neither Ngala nor Moi would accept their relegation to minor posts, and KANU became in essence a tenuous alliance of the Kikuyu (and allied Embu, Meru) and Luo, represented by rival leaders—Mboya, Oginga Odinga, Kenyatta.

The second, the Kenya African Democratic Union (KADU) was formed at Ngong (near Nairobi) on June 25, 1960, as the party of those left out of the array of power in Limuru, and primarily representing the less developed groups (that had not participated in Mau Mau), and especially the Abaluhya (led by Masinde Muliro and his Kenya African People's Party), the Kalenjin (under Moi's Kalenjin Political Alliance), the Maasai (grouped in the Maasai United Front) and the Coastal associations, under Ronald Ngala—all fearful of domination by the "Big Two" alliance. Ngala and Muliro were elected as Head and deputy Head of the new formation that in essence pitched the periphery against the center, the more urban/modern against the rural and less developed, and minority ethnicities against the larger ones. Both were, however, little more than "cartels composed of district organizations over which the national leadership had little infleunce."[29]

KANU, was the outgrowth of the 1940-banned KCA (of which Kenyatta had been Secretary General prior to his going overseas to study) and KAU, set up by educated Africans after the Second World War to assist Eliud Mathu in the Legislative Council. In 1945 its guiding spirit, Harry Thuku, was replaced by James Gichuru who gave the party a militant stance by demanding land redistribution, and in 1947 Kenyatta—returning from his lengthy sojourn in England—assumed the presidency, and under his leadership (1947-52) the KAU attempted to become a mass party.[30] But KAU remained popular primarily in Kiambu. Despite strenuous efforts by Luo such as Achieng Oneko and Oginga Odinga, KAU did not appeal to many Kikuyu except those, like Mboya, willing to subsume ethnicity to nationalism. Despite the Luo leaders in KAU, there were no Luo land grievances around which they could mobilize the masses. Also, the party's moderate policies (except on Kiambu land) were outflanked by radicals calling for revolutionary militance and independence. (Led by Bildad Kaggia, a Kikuyu unionist from Murang'a, and Paul Ngei, the Kamba political boss, this clique in 1951 even captured the KAU Nairobi party branch.) During Kenyatta's lengthy imprisonment and the ban on politics in Kikuyuland, the Luo Odinga and Mboya became the *de facto* leaders of KAU, the latter winning the overwhelmingly Kikuyu-inhabited Nairobi constituency in the 1957 elections (to become leader of the African group in the legislature. "No other Kenyan politician before or since has so thoroughly divorced his politics from his own ethnic identity"[31]—with the result that most observers doubted Mboya could have won a seat in his Luo district in Nyanza.

Towards Unipartyism

Prior to his imprisonment Kenyatta had not been successful in expanding KAU's popularity much beyond the Kikuyu heartland. Yet by 1958 grass-roots nationalism transformed him into the symbol of protest, and no one could conceive of independence without him at the helm. Kenyatta's popularity in 1961, transcended ethnic allegiances, as reflected in Table 1. Another survey prior to independence underscored how deeply party preference was predicated by ethnic affiliation (See Table 2) while yet another revealed that most groups could not *conceive* of a non-ethnic candidate winning in their district, with only the Kikuyu and Kalenjin (by a slim majority) admitting the possibility.

Table 9: National Leader—Preference by Ethnicity

	Ngala	Muliro	Kenyatta	Mboya	Gichuru	Odinga
Kikuyu	2%	0%	35%	31%	11%	5%
Abaluhya:	10%	13%	25%	27%	2%	5%
Coastals:	28%	1%	34%	24%	5%	4%
Luo:	2%	0%	42%	27%	2%	18%
Kisii:	0%	1%	47%	33%	3%	12%
Kamba:	5%	1%	34%	31%	3%	8%
Kalenjin:	22%	8%	19%	19%	2%	3%
Others:	10%	4%	27%	32%	7%	6%

Source: "The Kenya Election: Public Opinion Poll N.3," Nairobi, The Market Research Co. of East Africa, 1961, p.7.

When Kenyatta was released from prison his main role was overseeing a land redistribution not compromising the viability of large-scale export-oriented agriculture—that gave rise to a wealthy Kikuyu plantocracy—and soothing animosities created by the rebellion. This involved assuring all groups of an assured role in independent Kenya. (British settlers reacted to the release from prison of the devil incarnate, with a capital outflow of one million pounds a month, and an exodus that threatened Kenya's viability.) Kenyatta also had to mend the intra-Kikuyu Mau Mau/loyalist rifts and mollify minority groups fearful of domination by the Kikuyu-Luo alliance. "Forgetting" Mau Mau became State policy since the rebellion had strongly polarized the country, and Kenyatta's ability to persuade all to join in *harambee* ("pull together" in Swahili), was his most important contribution to Kenya.

Despite his standing, Kenyatta came under attack for reneging on the goals of Mau Mau. His appointment of Charles Njonjo as Attorney General—whose father, Chief Josiah Njonjo, had been a Kiambu collaborator at the time of Mau Mau—was seen as a slur on those who died in the rebellion; so was his agreement to pay compensation for Highland farms that were to be expropriated from Europeans. And Oginga Odinga, Paul Ngei and Bildad Kaggia (the latter imprisoned alongside Kenyatta during the emergency) fought hard

Table 10: Party Preference by Ethnicity

91% of Kikuyu	supported	KANU	
84% of Luo	"	KANU	with 4% for KADU
82% of Kiisi	"	KANU	12% for KADU
77% of Kamba	"	KANU	5% for KADU
38% of Abuluhya	"	KADU	28% for KANU
49% of Coastals	"	KADU	38% for KANU
76% of Kalenjin	"	KADU	16% for KANU
61% of other groups	"	KANU	22% for KADU

Source: "The Kenya Election: Public Opinion Poll No.3," Nairobi, Market Research Co. of East Africa, 1961, p.6.

against setting minimum size criteria for the new farms, arguing for the allocation of smallholder plots to squatters. Though the other two soon muted their tone, bought off by high office—a tactic Kenyatta developed for securing compliance from influentials, Kaggia publicly questioned whether Kenyatta's policies did not mean he had been a traitor to the Mau Mau cause for forty years. Kaggia's obduracy on the land issue, Kenya's most sensitive one, led to his ostracism, ouster from KANU (May 1964) and imprisonment—the second tactic. (Kaggia later joined Odinga's KPU revolt, and only made his peace with the regime in 1970—being rewarded with the chairmanship of a State company.)[32]

The cost of Kenyatta's moderate appeasement policies "was the opening of an ideological breach between Kenyatta and his Luo ministers, Odinga and Achieng Oneko...[who were to resign] to combat what they believed had become a neo-colonialist Kenyatta administration."[33] The falling apart stemmed in Kenyatta's and Odinga's divergent views on how land should be redistributed, Kenya's relations with the West, and the role of multinational corporations in Kenya. (Odinga's radical credentials were always anomalous since he had large interests in farming, banking and transportation.) Their friction exacerbated by mismatched personalities, Odinga's political ambitions, the intra-Luo rivalry between Odinga and Mboya, all resulting in a cleavage between Kenya's most upwardly-mobile groups. Seemingly based on ideology, it really rested on fundamentally different group perceptions of what post-independence national priorities should be. An attitudinal survey revealed 56% of Kikuyu regarded *personal advancement* of *greater* import than *national political* advances (35%), in contrast to opinion among the Luo (also Kisii and Kamba) who favored political (66%) over economic advances (30%), including even personal wealth.[34]

In the 1963 elections KADU—that formed an interim government when KANU refused to do so until Kenyatta was released—obtained one third of the vote (as in 1961), 32 of the assembly seats and 16 of the Senate ones, to KANU's 70 and 18. (Paul Ngei, the Kamba leader, bolted KANU with "his" eight Ukambani Assembly and two Senate seats, when he was not given an important enough post.) Though KADU held on its core power base, even prior to independence it was falling apart. Two of its most important ethnic machines seceded: the Abaluhya Political Association, whose leader, Masinde Muliro, was enticed to KANU by an offer of a Ministership; and later Ngei, when he was recognized as the supreme Kamba political baron and appointed Chairman of the Maize Marketing Board, where he was later deeply implicated in fiscal irregularities.) Other defections took place as Kenyatta weaned away individual deputies in preparation for a parliamentary vote to eliminate the federal features of the constitution that KADU had extracted from Britain. Before a vote could be taken, however, Ronald Ngala announced KADU's voluntary dissolution, allowing the scrapping of the Majimbo constitution, the creation of a centralized state, and the emergence of a de facto single party system in Kenya.

Kenya's new cabinet grouped leaders of all ethnic groups and races (including European and Asian) with Odinga (Vice President and deputy President of KANU), Moi (Minister of Home Affairs), Achieng Oneko (Minister Information and Broadcasting), Masinde Muliro (Minister of Commerce), Ronald Ngala (Leader of Government Business and Minister of Education) etc., with Mboya as KANU's Secretary General. Such "wall-to-wall" ethnic cabinets (though reflecting a predominance of the Presidential group) was to become a Kenyan political hallmark. The result was not unity, however, but rather a deeply divided party over issues such as land policy, ideology and foreign policy, pitching Kenyatta against Odinga, with after-effects to this day.

The Little General Election

A new party constitution, drafted by Mboya in 1966 proposed the replacement of the party's deputy President (Odinga) with eight Vice

Presidents, one from each province. Technically a "populist" measure, the change aimed at undermining Odinga's power and the latter's prospects to succeed Kenyatta, while strengthening Mboya's. (Moi was to profit from Odinga's eclipse and Mboya's murder, but his promotion to the regime's No. 2 spot was viewed by all—until the day he acceded to the Presidency in 1978—as a sop to the ex-KADU ethnicities.)

By 1965 Odinga was claiming that "Communism is like food to me,"[35] and was resisting land-distribution to ex-Mau Mau freedom fighters in general, and, more importantly, to the wealthy who could buy large estates, as opposed to the landless who needed land most. The Million Acre Scheme, that saw the redistribution of the White Highlands, did little for squatters or the landless poor in Kiambu—on behalf of whom the Mau Mau rebellion had erupted.

In parliamentary manoeuvrings Odinga's clique lost on every point, and on April 14, 1966 he formally resigned Kenya's Vice Presidency claiming an "invisible government" controlled Kenya. Achieng Oneko, two assistant Ministers, and 26 MP's promptly pledged allegiance to Odinga and the new party he announced, the Kenya People's Union under himself and Bildad Kaggia, who had just been ousted as KANU chairman of Murang'a.) Kenyatta's retaliation was swift; a bill passed *retroactively*, calling all deputies resigning from KANU to seek re-election under their new party label. (No such re-election had been forced upon Ngei's APP or KADU deputies when they merged with KANU in 1963!) Immediately thirteen of the 26 turncoat MP's had second thoughts, though they were not readmitted into KANU. In control of the judicial system KANU was able to assure that most of the KPU nomination papers were declared irregular, *a priori* limiting the impact of the KPU electoral appeal.

In the by-elections (the "Little General Election") the KPU solidly won the six Central Nyanza (Luo) seats, with Odinga defeating in his contest Mboya's father-in-law, a Nyanza hero, with 16,695 votes to 1,942. But the KPU only won three additional seats, two in Ukambani thanks to Paul Ngei, who, suspended from the Maize Board, bolted KANU. (Later, absolved of gross misproprietry and integrated into the cabinet, the Kamba "crisis" was over.)

Kaggia lost in his home district; his populist campaign for "free land for the landless" was rebutted by Kenyatta who stressed the need for "hard work to avoid Communism in Kenya," something that appealed to the individualistic Kikuyu. Kenyatta also portrayed Kaggia as a political incompetent because he had failed to avail himself—un-like other politicians—of the more than ample opportunities for per-sonal self-enrichment that independence had presented (!)—a point again scoring heavily among the Kikuyu, to whom wealth, even ostentatious wealth, was a sign of success. Oneko, a Luo, lost in his mixed constituency of Nakuru (that had a large Kikuyu population), by 3,812 votes to 2,325. Generally, however, the vote was low, indicat-ing a lack of enthusiasm for the KANU ticket as well.[36] Harassment of KPU activities was capped by the party being banned as subversive, and its key leaders imprisoned in the aftermath of Mboya's assassination in downtown Nairobi by Kikuyu elements worried about his popularity.[37] Subsequent anti-Kenyatta demonstrations in Nyanza completed the Luo alienation, not reversed to this day, while Kenyatta—having been booed and jostled by the crowds at Mboya's funeral in Kisumu—never again revisited Nyanza.

The Political Economy of Kenya

Kenya is primarily an agrarian country, and the cultivation of subsis-tence and cash crops has always been the main occupation and source of income of the bulk of society. This despite Kenya's large and modern manufacturing and service sectors (that began sprouting in colonial days to cater to the needs of high-income European settlers and Asian merchants), that currently employ over 150,000 (or 14%) of the active labor force. The paucity of arable land, expanding population, and the fact that wealth is linked to farming has made land-related issues the center of politics and political strife in Kenya. On the one hand calls for more equitable land re-distribution have been riveting issues capitalized upon by political mavericks and populist leaders (such Odinga, Kaggia, Kariuki and others); and on the other hand, access to prime farmland has been the mortar binding the country's political barons, influentials and/or hopefuls to the political autocracy in Nairobi.

Though by the 1980's the harsher features of Kenya's political system, and the negative repercussions of the country's developmental approach had become more visible (with per capita barely $370, the World Bank's threshold of poverty), on purely economic criteria Kenya was still regarded as "an African success story, featuring perhaps the most advanced agricultural sector of any independent African country."[38] Despite over-population, acute land-shortage, virtually no mineral resources, an originally none too boisterous economy, and only modest assistance from the former colonial power, Kenya scored economic gains "better than most"[39] countries of the developing world, in what was widely assessed as a "clearly above-average performance."[40]

During the 1960's and 1970's average annual economic growth was between 6% and 6.5%, with the equivalent for the industrial sector over 10%. The national budget expanded dramatically, with some allocations up fourteen-fold (See Table 3.) Per capita income increased during the same period by an annual average of 2.7%—all figures well above the norm for the continent. By 1977 exports were up 650% over those at independence, and while imports also expanded, the ratio of imports to GDP declined from 43.2% to 30.8% during Kenya's first decade. Though the visible balance of trade was deficitory, until the crisis of the 1980's the balance of payments has more often been positive due to the strong role of invisible exports such as revenue from tourism, that quadrupled.

Table 11: Selected Budgetary Expenditures 1964 and 1977		
Agriculture	12.7m/-	to 37.5m/-
Transport	3.4m/-	to 47.4m/-
Education	6.8m/-	80.8m/-
Defence	3.0m/-	42.9m/-
Debt service	6.4m/-	36.3m/-

For other statistics see Hazlewood, *The Economy of Kenya*.

Unlike many other African states, Kenya produces an array of cash crops—coffee, tea, sugar, sisal, pyrethrum, and cotton for export—that somewhat insulate the economy from the vagaries of fluctuating global market prices. On the other hand, with a small percentage of land that is arable, little of it irrigated, droughts (like in 1984) can devastate the economy which even in the best of times requires imports of foodstuffs, mostly wheat.

Three commodities accounted for over 50% of export revenue in the 1970's and 1980's: coffee (that brings in 27-41% of export revenue) and tea (of which Kenya is the world's third-largest supplier); and petroleum products, a major export since the coming on stream of Mombasa's refinery in 1964. In 1980 tourism edged out tea as Kenya's second foreign exchange earner, and in 1989 it assumed first place as commodity prices slumped.

Agricultural production boomed at independence with a 5.4% annual growth in the 1970's. Gross agricultural production went up in value from 85 to 415 million Kenyan pounds between 1970 and 1977, with coffee, Kenya's prime export, zooming from 22.1 to 190 million pounds, and tea from 13.6 to 91.3 million pounds. Kenya is among only a handful of African states to boast such sustained growth.

Kenyatta's stated economic goals were (1) to attain rapid growth, (2) to Africanize an economy under European and Asian control, and (3) to re-distribute wealth across society, in accord with an ill-defined ideology of "Kenyan Socialism." The fact that Kenya's elite is "one of the most conspicuous in Africa for their rate of consumption and their 100 per cent sympathy for capitalism and its methods"[41] explains the rhetorical nature of the third goal. But, in assessing Kenya's attainments during its first decade the IBRD praised "the politically stable atmosphere necessary for a high level of private investment, and...consistent and generally sound management of the economy." The Bank also pointed out that "Kenya has not really reaped as many benefits as she should have from her impressive performance in resource mobilization and investment...[failing] to distribute the benefits of development as widely as the Government would like...[leading to] the twin problems of growing unemployment and continuing poverty of...the "working poor."[42]

Poverty had been one of Kenya's prime problems at independence when per capita income stood at $85. Despite tremendous development since then, and a tripling of per capita income, poverty remains Kenya's major scourge today. Though "the incidence of severe malnutrition is slight" and Kenya's poverty "only exceptionally... kills,"[43] still 32% of households are at poverty levels, unemployment is rife, jobs and land are scarce—a volatile mixture that in the late-1980's ushered in high levels of violent crime. Kenya's impressive advances were thus at the expense of deepening societal socio-economic disparities, creating major problems for the future.

The controversy in the 1970's and 1980's about Kenya's approach focused on its underlying philosophical tenets, the groups most benefiting from it, and the price-tag of (a) development based on export-oriented agriculture by large estates and (b) industrialization through import-substitution—criticisms not unlike those voiced, as we have seen, against Banda in Malawi, or Bongo in Gabon. The controversy did not latch upon the distinctive aspect of Kenyan "capitalism" (in part because the debate was often ideological, with all capitalism viewed as evil): that is was a means to an end—of profit and patronage for the ruling elite, and hence both wasteful and marked by excess corruption, points to be expanded upon shortly.

Since independence Kenya looked to the private sector and foreign capital to provide the major impetus for the development of its economy. Nairobi possessed numerous advantages over other African cities: a temperate climate, good communications, a sophisticated labor force, a large domestic market, political stability, a pro-West leadership. Large amounts of capital were attracted to the country, with Nairobi becoming the continental headquarters for many multinational companies accounting for 57-60% of gross domestic production.[44] Criticism of Kenya's *industrial* strategy attaches much importance to the fact that "the Kenyan 'economic miracle' is not indigenous to the economy,"[45] has not resulted in the growth of domestic capitalism, and remains controlled by non-nationals despite policies of Africanization that merely add layers of "front-men."

Most investment is concentrated in import-substitution manufacturing enterprises, 75% of which are protected from overseas price/quality competition by customs and import tariffs, and benefit from artificially low minimum wages, including, as late as 1985, 576 shillings ($36) a month for unskilled labor. The IBRD has noted "it would not be an exaggeration to suggest that several firms have a license to print money, being subject to no competition at home or abroad," while others have derided Kenya's "industry" noting "if Kenyan industry was not merely a 'finishing touch' affair, it was not very far off it."[46]

Rural Inequality in Kenya

The controversy about Kenya's *agrarian* advances is even more intense, focusing on the stranglehold of large farmers over prime farmland parallel to the emergence of a landless peasantry, and the growth in regional/societal income disparities. The process began as early as 1955, and in the Central Province was complete by independence when crop cultivation restrictions on Africans were removed. Men of substance and/or with political pull, many Kikuyu, benefited from Kenya's boom, producing export crops on large farms: small farmers, of necessity primarily growing subsistence crops, only marginally gained from Kenya's transformation.

Despite the fact that 500,000 farmers were resettled on 1.5 million acres of the White Highlands since 1964, a heavy predominance of large farms developed in the country. Over three-quarters of the land ended up in the hands of wealthy Kenyans with access to education, civil service salaries and political patronage. Leveraged by preferential loans from State financial institutions on whose Boards they serve or have relatives, these large holdings skew all socio-economic statistics in Kenya. And with political and economic elites deeply intertwined in Kenya, public policy has been geared to the interests of large cash crop exporters.

Table 12: Ownership of Large Farms, Nakuru	
MPs	6
Senior Administrators	5
Senior Police Officers	5
Land Board Members	2
County Council Officials	2
Ambassadors	1
Former Chiefs	2
Company Executives	1
Farmers, traders	14

Source: Crawford,E. and Thorbecke, E., *Employment, Income distribution, Poverty Alleviation and Basic Needs in Kenya*, Report of an ILO Consultancy Mission, Cornell, 1978. p.287.

Nakuru and Kiambu districts, where much of Kenya's prime farmland is located, provide excellent examples. There "91% of the owners held only 21% of the land and each had less than three acres, whereas 5% of the owners, those with over twenty acres, controlled 79% of the land,"[47] with an analysis of the ownership of farms of over 500 acres in Nakuru revealing the heavy predominance of politicians, police offices and administrators (see Table 4.) In the densely populated

Kiambu 50% of all land was owned by only 183 individuals, with the biggest 44 farmers holding two-thirds of this land. Moreover, eight of the large land-owners in Nakuru also possessed land in Kiambu, and an additional three owned land via holding companies. (For the occupational-distribution of the 44 large farmers of Kiambu see Table 5.)

Table 13: Ownership of Large Farms, Kiambu	
MPs	5
Ambassadors	3
Senior Civil Servants	4
Other Government Officials	4
Executives of parastatals	7
Church Officials	2
Farmers, traders, professionals	19

Source: Crawford,E. and E. Thorbecke, *Employment, Income distribution, PovertyAlleviation and Basic Needs in Kenya*, Report of an ILO Consultancy Mission, Cornell, 1978, p. 288.

Since by 1977 most of Kenya's arable land was privately registered—99.3% in the Central Province, 64.1% in the Rift Valley, 82.7% in Nyanza and 92.5% in the Western Province—an agrarian option for future generations is completely foreclosed, even as a dispossessed class of 500,000 landless peasants already exists. Overall one half of the population lives on 6% of the land area, and 80% of farmers, due to the small size of their plots, have to seek supplemental income from non-agrarian pursuits. In the late 1970's there were 3,273 farms averaging 775.5 hectares each, alongside 1.7 million farms, half under one hectare, and a third below 0.5 ha. Both of the latter figures are below the minimum size needed to sustain a family, and the majority of smallholder land still being planted with subsistence crops or used as pasture, underscoring that apart from the export sector "Kenyan agriculture developed very little in the two decades after the mid-1950's."[48]

All this has entrenched income disparities that the World Bank had already noted in 1969 (that the poorest 40% of society earned 10% of total income, the richest 10% earned 56%, while the top 5% cornered fully 34%) though some have argued the need "to temper a concern with inequality with proper attention to absolute levels of living" which *have* risen while bearing in mind that "the greatest regional inequalities are the work of nature."[49]

Pressure for land reform specifically, has been insistent since independence. As early as 1972 an ILO/UNDP team suggested *inter alia* the break-up of large farms, and other like recommendations have come from various other sources. Yet such policies go against all that KANU stands for, and in effect ask the regime to commit political suicide by moving against large landowners—its own political leaders, regional barons, and power brokers—and eliminating the mortar on which the highly decentralized party is imbedded, and the fundamentals of the trade-off modality of stability that Kenyatta built and Moi shored up.

It has always been Kenya's stated assumption that socio- economic inequality and regional disparities are a basic given of the human condition, and moreover, that large cash-crop estates are vital for the country's foreign revenues and public finances. Hence, it has been argued, Kenya's public policy cannot strike a balance between commitment to capitalism, and the distributionist policies urged on Nairobi by domestic critics and international agencies alike. But the reality has been, whatever the substantive merits of the above arguments, that given the acutely ethnic winner-take-all mentality in Nairobi—under both Kenyatta and Moi—and both leaders' instrumentalist views on public policy, land reform was never even a theoretical option to the ruling elites. Indeed, not only have the country's natural internal disparities not been reduced, but the policies emanating from Nairobi have consciously assured that they became greater.

The Parastatal Sector

Since independence Kenya has seen an expansion of the State's role in the economy, through the proliferation of marketing boards and parastatal enterprises. The State's stake in the economy, as a percentage of GDP, doubled between 1960 and 1980, from 11% to 20%. By 1982 there were 147 statutory boards, 47 companies wholly owned by the government, 36 others partly owned and 93 in which the government held a minority interest. The number of public employees also rose dramatically in absolute numbers (from 184,000 to 336,000 between 1972 and 1982, not counting the armed forces), as well as a percentage of wage employment (from 32% to 46% in the same period.) And economic planning proceeded in Kenya with the same state-centred approach as in other states not espousing Capitalism. What emerged in Kenya *structurally* was a mixed economy, in which private capital played a pivotal role, but where certain sectors (banking, insurance, real estate, water, electricity) were under the State's ambit, and others (agriculture) are under tutelage via marketing monopolies. In reality, however, the latter bodies—ostensibly aiming to assist and regulate marketing activities—are, like all the State sector, and indeed the State itself, nothing more than extentions of the Presidential patronage network, and lucrative siphons into the public purse, the essential mortar of the trade-off modality of rule. In 1990's, when Africa was pressured under external political conditionalities to privatize its State sector, Kenya resisted fiercely. But more recently Nairobi reluctantly acquiesced—discovering a new source of profit in the "auctioning" of State enterprises at low prices to members of the ruling elite and their cohorts.

The increased government role in the economy did not result in either a greater developmental thrust, or in greater State revenues, the rationale for such policies. The reverse was true. In 1983 only seven of Kenya's State companies were profitable, though many were established in inherently profitable areas. "State control" was merely the rhetoric under which the economy was systematically plundered by cliques surrounding the Presidency. Starting under Kenyatta, and increasing especially under Moi, the State has consistently acted against national interests, by providing minimal services (e.g. roads are in an acute state of disrepair; health care is still in missionary hands; secondary education facilities are not expanded, etc.) while establishing a large civil service and State sector bureaucracy concerned only with the benefits that can be extracted by virtue of their posts.

The International Coffee Organization several times drew attention to the fact that Kenyan farmers were receiving 30% less than global market prices for their crops from local cooperatives that "because they are able to set prices...can afford to be inefficient."[50] Efficiency would not have been possible in Kenya's public sector, if only because it has been the prime source for the creation of myriads of sinecure and patronage appointments—each with its sources and possibilities for graft, embezzlement, kickbacks, and other lucrative side-lines. Marketing boards, state and multinational enterprises, statutory boards, and the civil service in general, have been packed with political appointees and/or phantom workers, the higher echelons of which draw hefty multiple salaries and are totally immune from prosecution for their fiscal irregularities. All this apart from the fact that non-economic (political) considerations have determined the *location* of State projects, many of which "underwrite with government money risks which should be borne by private investors."[51]

Kenya initially proceeded pragmatically in Africanizing its economy, if only due to the low numbers of qualified Africans in high posts (22.7%), a consequence of low standards of education for Africans during the colonial era. The exodus of British personnel at independence produced a shortfall of 2,000 professionals for the remainder of the decade. Still, following the passage of the Immigration Act of April 1967, a Kenyanization of Personnel Bureau was set up charged with the control of work permits to non-nationals.

The brunt of Africanization was felt in particular by the 80,000-strong Asian community, whose number contracted to the current 40,000. In 1970 the Trade Licensing Act was passed, restricting goods and areas in which non-citizens could trade. Kenyanization led to an increased role of Africans in retail trade (from 55% to 89% within a decade of independence), and in the wholesale sector (up from 48% to 80%.) In due course other occupations were "nationalized," until in May/June 1988 legislation restricted the practice of medicine to nationals, with accountancy and law—all "Asian" vocations—next on the government's list.

The Crisis of the 1980's

In the 1980's the Kenyan economy faced a severe contraction; once very much the envy of Africa, the country was in the midst of a financial nightmare, with the 1984 drought adding insult to injury. Kenya's economic woes were the result of a number of cumulative factors: the fiscal burden of carrying the heavy deficits of the parasitical excesses of the State sector, and a public payroll grotesquely bloated by patronage appointments; revenue shortfalls consequent to drops in global commodity prices; and a fall in revenues from tourism, that contracted on reports of increased crime and the depletion of the country's National Parks after the slaughter of its wild game under Kenyatta.

At the same time imports remained high, reflecting habits developed during the 1970's boom years (oil bills alone absorbing *all* revenue from coffee exports.) Drought and other natural calamities reduced harvests of cash-crops and basic staples, causing shortages and necessitating imports of foodstuffs. There was a debt repayment burden of 35% in 1988, up from 4% in 1978 with a concomitant severe pressure on the Kenyan shilling. And there was also the corrosive effect of 22% inflation, that far outstripped growth in earnings, while demographic growth, land-hunger and unemployment fanned urban unrest. (In 1984 the regime even went so far to ban from Kenya labor-saving machines capable of doing the work of 400 workers in tea plantations.)

Pressure by the World Bank that Kenya set its house in order bore some fruit when Government overspending was temporarily brought under control (with the USA, Japan, France and West Germany waiving Kenya's outstanding debts to aid the recovery.) Though debt servicing remained high (over 40% in 1990), inflation declined to 9.1%. The parastatal sector (but not civil service) was slightly contracted, and some reforms were carried out in the marketing boards. When the drought ended the Kenyan economy showed its resilience as bumper harvests were recorded, including of grains. Indeed in 1988 some 200,000 tons of maize were available for export, whereas in 1980/1 people had to queue for their weekly supplies. Global market prices for tea and coffee rebounded; and tourists started flocking, though now mostly to Kenya's beaches, and in 1989 tourism became the country's prime foreign exchange earner. Despite the crisis of the mid-1980's, for the period 1961-1987 Kenya still recorded Africa's 8th highest sustained GDP growth.

Politically, however, Kenya's image suffered irreparable damage in the 1980's. The economic downturn was accompanied by severe political strains, with the 1982 attempted coup and Moi's subsequent increasingly repressive policies giving foreign investors a rude shock. In 1986, moreover, Kenya's banking system virtually collapsed, having been systematically plundered of huge sums of money. Though ultimately only six institutions closed down, mass panic created a run on all banks (three-quarters of all financial institutions were Kikuyu-owned), and revelations of details of the widespread embezzlement sent further shudders throughout the business community. All these triggered a basic re-evaluation of Kenya's "inherent stability," and a disengagement from the country by the large multinational companies. The disinvestments reached massive proportions when another economic slowdown developed in 1987. By 1990 fully 115 of the 140 American companies in Kenya had withdrawn from the country. Their British counterparts were also moving out as Kenya came to be viewed as a "high risk country" where investments were justified only if they could yield immediate hefty returns. The further bouts of presidential repression in the 1990's, the onset of state-sponsored ethnic cleansing in the Rift Valley Province, horrendously high crime rates, and further revelations of the monumental levels of corruption in the country, completely eroded the image of Kenya.

The Kenyan System: Presidential Autocracy and pork-barrel politics

In assessing the key features of Kenyan politics and the resilience of civilian rule, one is struck by the overwhelming centrality to it of Presidential networks of social and administrative control resting on a combination of coercion and pork-barrel politics, paralleled by the existence (until the mid-1980's) of a measure of local quasi-participatory politics with a degree of immunity from external interference. All have been at the root of the country's relative political stability, while strongly binding the military establishment to the political order in Nairobi.

An powerful oligarchy centered around the Presidency has always controlled Kenya. It's composition and ethnic coloration is different under Moi, but "presidential authoritarianism"[52] has been the hallmark of Kenya. At outset Moi's reign was only marginally different from Kenyatta's, standing out more sharply partly because of Moi's ethnic insecurity in a Kikuyu-dominated Kenya; but by the late 1980's this was to change substantially, as Moi emerged as a full-blown dictator, and in the 1990's as an ethnic cleanser to boot. Kenyatta's authoritarianism by contrast was somewhat more indirect, camouflaged by successive layers of cohorts, and cloaked by the patina of his legitimacy as Kenya's founding father. Both Presidents monopolized policy-making, regarded the Kenyan economy as their personal turf to plunder, and did not hesitate to utilize the full array of coercive measures, including liquidation, to crack down on their severest critics.

Participatory Grass-roots Democracy

Yet parallel to this monopoly of power at the center, Kenya developed (until Moi crushed them all starting in the late 1980's) a spirited and critical press, a boisterous National Assembly that intermittently locked horns with the executive, an independent judiciary, and a record of participatory grass-roots electoral activity unrivalled in other African states. The tug-of-war between what are in essence diametrically opposite vectors—Presidential authoritarianism and participatory politics—provides much of the tension in the country, and goes far to explain the political violence that periodically afflicts Kenya.

A good example is provided by Kenya's much-lauded freedom of the press (again until the mid-1980's). A remarkable degree of latitude was accorded to free speech in Kenya, "perhaps the most in almost any country in Africa,"[53] including via the country's newspapers, the two leading dailies which had a combined press run of 170,000, and a readership of half a million. At the same time all imported publications are screened for offensive material by Special Branch officers—which is why though they arrive in Nairobi on their day of issue, they are only on sale a day or two later. (Unacceptable issues are declared "sold-out" before they hit the stands, and destroyed.) And local editors and reporters toe the line on clear-cut taboos, grudgingly respecting the invisible transition line from permissible criticism to treasonable action. As one observer put it "surface politics in Kenya are a well regulated charade of what is permitted: the press, MP's and ministers know just how far they can go in criticising the government, and certain subjects are treated as taboo."[54]

Also, until the challenge of multipartyism in 1989, competitive elections *within* KANU became "an institutionalized and distinguishing feature of national political life."[55] Grass-roots politics were full of *local* political shenanigans, but relatively free of *central* strong-arm tactics or falsification of results so visible in other states. Kenya's record of eight elections is unrivalled on the continent. The cumulative effect of these electoral exercises, that polled large numbers of voters, created an image of a political system "accountable to the general public to a degree unmatched in most African polities...[evolving] despite the well-known authoritarian tendencies of the Kenyan regime and its periodic suppression of its most vocal critics."[56] The perception of the government's basic accountability garnered Nairobi a measure of legitimacy; it is precisely the "meltdown" of popular perceptions of the regime's basic accountability, that is destabilizing Moi's regime today.

Though by 1964 Kenya became a *de facto* single party state, this did not bring unity to KANU. The party remained a loose alliance of independent political bosses with grass-roots district ethnic power-bases. Unable to impose his authority on the multiplicity of ethnic leaders within it, and hence prevented from using KANU as a control mechanism, Kenyatta—never a party *organizer* (it was Mboya who excelled in organizational detail)—concentrated on developing alternate power bases, allowing the party to whither away at the national level. Indeed, during the Kenyatta era KANU was functionally dead—as pointed out in parliament by then-Assistant Minister Martin Shikuku (the Western Province Abaluhyia MP, originally of KADU), for which he incurred Kenyatta's wrath.

Yet, long before Shikuku's speech, KANU had its phone disconnected, and faced eviction from its headquarters because it could not pay its bills. "KANU headquarters in Nairobi remained empty except for the occasional minor official"; no Executive or Council meetings took place between 1963 and 1966, and the party elections of 1966 (to select office-holders after the KPU split) were the last ones until 1983. National activities were curtailed, and assistance for district branches was reduced to a minimum. The result was that "between elections...the party goes into a deep slumber, and literally dies."[57] Membership in 1969 amounted to 3,000, mostly of whom were incumbent MP's and power aspirants, required by law to be life-members. Functionally Kenya was not a one-party state but a no-party state presided over by the Mzee, ("wise old man"), father of the nation, a prince[58] above petty political squabblings.

Kenyatta's cabinets, just as Moi's, included an ethnic balance, though top portfolios were dominated by Kiambu Kikuyu (during Kenyatta's reign), and by Kalenjin (under Moi). All ethnic groups, regions, and local power-wielders willing to abide by the rules of the game, gained access to the National Assembly that became a "grand coalition of ethnoregional notables...resulting, to the extent that all main actors were included, in relatively stable rules of interaction."[59] In the absence of viable party machinery Kenyatta, heading a clientelist network stretching from State House to all corners of the country, arbitrated disputes, allocated patronage and high office, and dispensed *harambee* funds, in return for regime support.

Despite the disappearance of a meaningful party hierarchy, the ossification of party activity, and the disappearance of multi-partyism, elections—with many avid contenders in most districts (all under the KANU banner)—became exercises in grass-roots democracy, offering advantages to office-aspirers and voters alike. In Kenya elections served to recruit new district influentials into central-local patron-client networks, while binding the masses to the national hierarchy (thus legitimating the regime) through the spread of patronage to the periphery, mostly through funding for local *harambee* projects.

Patronage spread to the peasantry through funds for local projects (schools, clinics, cattle dips, boreholes, roads etc.) for which the President, cabinet ministers, incumbent deputies, local notables and political aspirants contribute funds. *Harambee*, starting quite haphazardly in 1963, rapidly became a national slogan, a motto on the national crest, and a staple of Kenyan political life, symbolizing the transfer of benefits from the rich to the poor. Securing *harambee* funds, even illicitly, is the prime "function" of an elected MP, Minister, President or Vice President. In 1983, for example, Moi was reportedly contributing 200,000 shillings a month for a variety of projects. The same year a parliamentary motion to set up a committee to ascertain where *harambee* funds were coming from, and to audit them, was squashed by Moi.

Electoral contests in many single-ethnic constituencies are thus functionally little more than tugs-of-war between different aspirants striving to convince villagers of their greater "ability" to secure funds for local projects. Ethnic considerations are, however, the building blocs of politics in Kenya, for as Ng'weno put it, "to get anywhere at all in Kenya...more often than not the easiest power base to set up, and the strongest, is one based on tribal, sectarian or clan affiliations."[60] The multiplicity of power-contenders at district level, and the minor role parliamentarians play in national policy-making, means that success in elections is more a function of personality, charisma, and one's ability to materially improve the lives of one's constituents. For this a deputy, or a contender for office, must be influential enough to be able to obtain *harambee* funds for local projects. One observer has even concluded that the *sole* motivation for involvement in *harambee* projects on the part of local notables is "personal political ambitions...to help maintain and perhaps even broaden their own political bases."[61]

Elections can thus be perceived as mass-elite compacts whereby voters sanction a successful candidate's future self-advancement in Nairobi in exchange for his securing pork-barrel benefits for his district. Replete with violence, huge sums are spent in electioneering, with victorious candidates sometimes spending 300,000 shillings to win an electoral contest. Ochieng has written that the electorate's sole concern was to "eat you up," giving a warm welcome to all candidates out of a desire to partake of the free beer and gifts routinely expected and provided,[62] since as the *Daily News* put it "rivers of free beer, mountains of free sugar, and wads of money" are doled out throughout the country at election time.[63]

Once elected MP's obviously need to recoup their election "investment" and enrich themselves (that is after all the whole point in the exercise!), as well as assemble a "kitty" for the next election, all explaining the reason for the extraordinarily high levels (even for Africa) of corruption and ostentatious living in Kenya. An example of the heights of wealth political office can provide, and the cultural sanction of ostentatious expenditure, is the one-million shilling ($65,000) wedding Stanley Oloitiptip (the Maasai political leader) provided in 1982 for his son. Rebutting criticism of its over-ostentatiousness, and that he had passed on the cost to the Nairobi City Council (!), Oloitiptip boasted that the sum was really quite petty, since he could have personally afforded even a 150 million shilling ($9.75 million) wedding—eliciting the *Weekly Review* comment that "the mind boggles at the figure and at Mr. Oloitiptip's acumen for gathering wealth in so short a time."[64]

At the same time MP's must work to assure their re-election prospects by meeting some constituency needs through periodic *harambee* contributions—that functionally resemble a tithe of their illicit gains in office. Barkan notes "political careers rise and fall on the performance records of incumbent and aspiring office-holders in respect to *harambee*."[65] *Harambee* funds amount to 30% of all local development investment, and between 1967 and 1973 made up 11.4% of overall national development expenditure. [66] *Harambee* projects are highly prized since they satisfy pressing local needs for which government priorities are low. *Harambee*-built schools, as noted previously, enroll over half of Kenya's secondary school pupils, and despite their poor quality, 50% higher tuition fees, and heavy (75%) attrition rates, often provide the only possibility for advancement for the children of *wananchi*.

Very important benefits accrue also to the regime from *harambee*. Deputies who need to meet *harambee* requests of constituencies in order to secure re-election are under intense compulsion to remain in the

Presidency's good graces in order to partake of the pork-barrel system, and have a blind eye turned on their sins of omission and commission. Falling out with the executive inevitably leads to criminal investigations into tax-arrears, routine (but suddenly "discovered") skimming practices, double or triple State salaries, or at the very least the drying up of government largess (both for deputies and their constituencies), and certain future electoral doom in a country with a high rate of defeat of incumbents. For like reasons, most deputies tend to act as (moderate) spokesmen for local interests, voluntarily relinquishing a role in national affairs, even if they were so inclined, which many are not.

The flow of resources from the center to the periphery through *harambee* also helps develop regions that might otherwise be neglected, and confers legitimacy to the political system itself, the resultant government corruption notwithstanding. At the same time, the spread of development projects through *harambee* camouflages the fact that Nairobi is stingy in its normal budgetary allocations for social services, and its stress (during the Kenyatta era) on export-oriented growth primarily in the Central Province.

For political contenders, who are after all local influentials with a measure of grass-roots support, election to the National Assembly is the beginning of a possible climb to greener patronage pastures. Important district leaders are routinely appointed as Assistant Ministers—that though irrelevant and powerless posts, are precious patronage plums. They are bonded with their ethnic/district networks to the central regime by their tangible integration into the nexus of power, their fealty secured by pork-barrel rights the post confers. Such appointments (that are numerous) result in longer electoral tenures (as Table 6 illustrates) if only because Assistant Ministers can secure and contribute more *harambee*, bearing in mind re-elections are "for all practical purposes, referendums on incumbents' assistance to self-help development projects in their constituencies. Those perceived by the electorate to have strong performance records are re-elected, while those with weak records or records surpassed by a challenger's go down to defeat."[67] The Presidency utilizes this patronage plum to its fullest advantage.

Over one third of all MP's are usually Assistant Ministers; when added to the additional 15-20% who are Ministers, half or more of parliamentarians are members of the government! In the 1990's under the severely beleaguered Moi fewer MP's were backbenchers than

Table 14: Electoral Success and Failure, 1969-83

	1969			1974			1979			1983		
	N.Won	Lost		N. Won	Lost		N. Won	Lost		N. Won	Lost	
Challengers	468	20	80	496	15	85	600	14	86	584	11	89
Backbenchers	86	37	63	78	35	65	90	47	53	75	57	43
Asst.Minist.	38	63	37	36	64	36	29	59	41	49	59	41
Ministers	19	74	26	19	79	21	20	75	25	26	81	19
Incumbents	143	46	54	133	49	51	139	53	47	150	62	38

Source: Joel D. Barkan, "The Electoral Processs and Peasant-State Relations in Kenya," p. 230.

frontbenchers—a vivid manifestation of the trade-off modality of governance in the civilian sphere.

The regime has additional immense patronage for its loyal MP's: highly remunerative appointments to boards of mixed economy companies, state enterprises, statutory boards, tribunals, school boards etc. Those not ending up Assistant Ministers can still be rewarded via administrative office that assures high salary, opportunity for graft and *harambee* funds. MP's are, moreover, entitled to engage in private business concurrent with legislative duties in line with the Ndegwa Commission recommendations that government workers enter private enterprise without prejudice. Most deputies exploit to the utmost contacts they establish in the capital, insider information, pressures they can exert on banks for preferential loans and interest rates, and become rich in short order. Not surprisingly elective office is hotly contested by contenders who resign very lucrative jobs in the private sector to enter even more lucrative political careers.

The ruthlessness of the Kenyan electorate has also seen large numbers of incumbents being defeated. In the October 1974 elections, for example, the only unopposed candidates were President Kenyatta, Vice President Moi, Mbiyu Koinange and Paul Ngei, the first two by tradition not contested, the latter two unbeatable in their fiefdoms, with a dynastic element reflecting itself in Alphonse Okuku Ndiege inheriting the seat of his slain brother (Tom Mboya), and Ngala's son elected to his father's former seat. On the other hand 88 of the 158 incumbents were turned out of office, including four cabinet Ministers and thirteen Assistant Ministers. Those not re-elected included Foreign Minister Dr. Njoroge Mungai (part of the Kenyatta Family), and the Kenyatta-backed Luo Minister of Natural Resources, who lost because

Odinga, not allowed to run himself, supported another Luo candidate. This high rate of attrition of incumbent MP's repeated itself in all subsequent elections in Kenya.

The center's "respect" for grass-root electoral outcomes has not been out of democratic benevolence. Rather, Kenyatta early on realized it would be impossible to establish central authority over the highly faction-ridden KANU, Kenya's myriad of ethnic loyalty pyramids and political barons, especially in the complex idiosyncratic Coastal Province, and over the Luo with their own charismatic leader. Intervention at the district level, to sway electoral outcomes and assure the success of favored candidates, carried too many risks, and even if feasible, was not necessarily desirable. (That it was not feasible is attested by the fact that gadfly MP's such as Shikuku, Rubia, Kariuki and others were constantly re-elected despite public knowledge of Kenyatta's displeasure with them.) Distancing the Presidency from local level personal and clan rivalries became a guiding principle of Kenyan-style "democracy" under Kenyatta. But conversely, since the executive was renouncing control over who ran for a seat in Parliament under the KANU label, the role of MP's in decision-making was greatly curtailed, and deputies were constrained from using the podium to air sensitive issues or attack the Presidency. (By contrast Moi's more vulnerable position at the apex of power, and his personal paranoia, inclined him to exert greater efforts to assure election of loyal MP's, undermining Kenya's grass-roots participation and tilting the system towards dictatorship.)

The tolerant attitude towards district level political outcomes could also only be tolerated so long as it did not result in the emergence of alternate national leadership in the Assembly, and the *de facto* one party system would not be challenged. (Kenya formally became a one-party state only in 1982 under Moi.) Any new political party (whether ethnic or ideological) that tried to register, even if electorally foredoomed within the splinterized Kenyan political context, was ruthlessly harassed for it threatened the pillars of the political system itself. So was any parliamentarian who strayed too far from the subservient parochial role assigned to him, especially if he mobilized a populist clientele, attacked the Presidency or addressed land-issues, the ultimate taboos.

This is not to suggest that debate on national issues never developed in the National Assembly. To the contrary, parliament saw many lively debates on sensitive matters such as executive excesses, unauthorized overspending, corruption, and Kariuki's murder. (There has also been much petty debate: e.g. whether the word "hell" may be used in parliamentary debates.) Question Time, when details can be prised from disdainful Ministers, and grievances can be aired, has been used effectively[68] since impressing upon the executive local constituent concerns "is the principal method by which MP's can hope to convert electoral promises into policy."[69] Unlike Malawi where parliamentary oratory has been stifling in its parochiality, Kenyan debates have been vigorous and at times—as after Kariuki's murder—threatening to the executive itself.

Still, the legislature is powerless compared to the executive, and especially so after the succession. Cabinet Ministers routinely ignore the Assembly, refuse to appear at hearings, and overspend their budgets. Infringements on executive prerogatives lead to the veto of bills originating in the legislature, even if identical ones are later submitted as Government motions. MP's occasionally reassert themselves via the creation of select committees, as in 1971 on unemployment, and again in 1975 after Kariuki's murder. But when deputies transgress too much from the bounds of the permissible, they are reminded of the reality of political power in Kenya through the Assembly's closure, detention without trial, and even liquidation as the example of Kariuki underscores.

The Liquidation of Kariuki

Since land is the fount of power in Kenya, land issues polarized KANU from inception, including in the 1966 split that led to the emergence of the KPU. The full range of the State's instruments of coercion have been used against any Kenyans who raise the populist banner, or try to use land issues to advance their career.

Josia Mwangi Kariuki was a leader of the Nyeri Kikuyu who had been detained for seven years by the British during the Mau Mau rebellion, to emerge as Kenyatta's private secretary in 1961, MP from Nyandarua since 1963, and briefly Assistant Minister of Tourism. A dashing personality in his Rolls Royce, a snappy dresser, well-known playboy, and owner of race-horses, Kariuki amassed wealth through various activities including gambling, a monopoly over the sale of school textbooks, and ivory poaching during his tenure in the Ministry of Tourism (while campaigning for the preservation of Kenya's dwindling wildlife) all with Kenyatta's blessing. But Kariuki developed higher ambitions, however, that he discovered non-Kiambu Kikuyu could not entertain: frustrated, he came to adopt populist postures, in the process moving closer to the position of the Luo opposition. Lashing out against corruption (though all knew he himself was no saint), he acquiring a patina of hero-worship among youth and labour. But in doing so he ignored the unwritten rules of the political game, and became a threat to Kiambu privilege, and the ageing Kenyatta himself.

Kariuki's vitriolic speeches hit home since they expressed mass perceptions of the abuses of power in Kenya: "a small but powerful group, a greedy self-seeking elite in the form of politicians, civil servants and businessmen, has steadily but very surely monopolized the fruits of independence to the exclusion of the majority of the people. We do not want a Kenya of 10 millionaires and 10 million beggars."[70] Since Kenyatta family members were the focal point of most lucrative deals (and much of the farmland around Nakuru, Kenya's granary, had been acquired by family members) Kariuki's sin was in "not only pointing to the vast lands that every peasant believes, correctly, the Royal Family has acquired," but also in "inviting his audience to remember that Mau Mau had sprung from the land issue. He even said it plainly: 'Unless something is done now, the land question will be answered by bloodshed.'"[71]

Immediately Kariuki's lavish parties stopped being attended by senior government officials, and Provincial Commissioners denied him permission to deliver speeches, including in his own constituency. (Though thus prevented from campaigning for the next elections, he nevertheless retained his seat with an enlarged majority.) Three of his official junkets abroad were cancelled; banks foreclosed his loans, and he was even hauled to court, underscoring "the problem facing younger independent politicians who appear to be running too hard in the Succession Stakes."[72] Kariuki realized his personal danger, belatedly noting the likelihood of his being killed because of his stands. Shortly before his liquidation he was compiling a list of corruption charges against specific individuals that he planned to present to parliament.

Whether or not Kariuki was involved, in February 1975 leaflets began to circulate about Kenyatta's wealth. The latter's farms in Rongai were burned, and some of the cattle was hamstrung. Three bombs exploded in Nairobi, the work of students, unemployed, or landless peasants (known as *maskini*, poor people) allegedly inspired by Kariuki's speeches. In the last incident 27 people were killed and 73 were wounded. A Maskini Liberation Organization claimed credit for the bombing and rumours abounded of blood-oathings in the hills around Nairobi. The next evening Kariuki left the Nairobi Hilton in the company of Benjamin Gethi (head of the paramilitary General Service Unit) never to be seen alive again. His body was found in the hills 12 miles outside Nairobi, but despite being a well-known personality his corpse lay "unidentified" in the morgue until his wife gained access via a ruse nine days later.

Kariuki's murder electrified Kenya, widened the Nyeri-Kiambu rift, and plunged the country into its most destabilizing crisis to date. Student riots and a march in downtown Nairobi was violently dispersed by the police. The university, hotbed of radical sentiments where Oginga Odinga and Kariuki were lionized, was closed down after unrest and pamphlets calling for a Revolution. Several schools were also closed, and even Parliament was adjourned. When the Assembly reconvened a 15-man Select Committee was set up against Kenyatta's express wishes to investigate Kariuki's murder. Headed by government critics such as Shikuku and Seroney, the assumption from outset was that the Government was implicated,[73] part of a wider plot to liquidate all those who stood for truth and democracy in Kenya: "We are being ruled by gangsters...are we being ruled by people or devils?"[74]

The same charges were repeated at Kariuki's emotional funeral at Gilgil. Eulogies claimed Kariuki had been murdered because he spoke out against a "new style of colonialism, and on behalf of the poor"; that "a mafia existed that liquidated leaders whom the establishment feared"; that "the finger of accusation...[pointed] at the president's own household."[75] A Presidential spokesman was prevented by the crowds from reading a message from Kenyatta. Internationally the fallout was also severe. The *Daily Telegraph* pointed out "in less than a week the Government of President Jomo Kenyatta has fallen from a position of absolute authority to one of being openly and fearlessly challenged by parliament, press and the people." The *Times* drew attention to the fact that "the deaths by assassins and misadventure of a succession of outspoken leaders are now linked in open discussion in a sinister political pattern, from the killing of the party organizer Da Gama Pinto, through the deaths of Tom Mboya, Ronald Ngala and Argwings-Kodhek, and others...All were men who, though loyal to Kenyatta, were ready to criticize the Kikuyu group which has ably but profitably monopolized in large measure the key positions in cabinet and administration."[76] And *The Sunday Times'* three articles on "Kenya at the Brink" linked Kenyatta with Kariuki's murder, and blamed Kenyatta family members (specifically Mama Ngina) of massive ivory poaching and the desertification of the country through the burning of forests for charcoal.[77]

The Parliamentary Select Committee's Report was a bombshell, noting "a massive cover-up operation" by the Special Police under Bernard Hinga, the CID under Nderi, the Police under Mungai, and the officer officially in charge of the murder investigation, concluding the Police knew who was responsible for Kariuki's murder, but were unwilling to arrest them, and that no progress was possible until the top Police/CID officers were replaced, and Benjamin Gethi was arrested either as the murderer or as an accomplice to Kariuki's murder. The Report also recommended attention be focused upon the possible personal culpability of the Mayor of Nakuru, General "China" (an ex-Mau Mau detainee now deputy director of National Youth Service and personal bodyguard of Mbiyu Koinange), and Koinange himself. Koinange's name was ultimately deleted from the Report at the demand of Kenyatta himself. An issue of the Sunday Times was even banned in Kenya for printing the allegation of Koinange's culpability in Kariuki's liquidation.[78] There was much foreign acclaim for the report: as one diplomat put it "This couldn't happen in any other country in Africa. No other country could afford to have its top police brass attacked in this way."[79]

Still, nothing came of the report since administration of Justice was under Kenyatta's control via his Attorney General Charles Njonjo. Sporadic bombs exploded in Nairobi and near Kenyatta's home in Mombasa; leaflets circulated calling for land redistribution; more of Kenyatta's cattle were maimed Mau Mau style, his Nakuru farm crops were burnt, and traditional dancers refused to dance in front of him, or sang songs against corruption and high consumer prices. In the July 1975 by-elections for Kariuki's seat, his loyal followers showed their last respects by refusing to participate in the election: only 7,671 of the 31,293 registered voters turned up.

Though the Assembly gave the executive its first defeat ever, it ultimately lost out. The *Weekly Review* pointed out that a "showdown between the President and Parliament today would be won by the President hands down"[80]; a bout of parliamentary repression followed the Assembly's hollow victory as Kenyatta reminded deputies that "the hawk was always in the sky ready to swoop on the chickens."[81] All those who had opposed Kenyatta paid for their sin in one way or another. Minister of Works Masinde Muliro and two Assistant Ministers were dismissed from office for voting against the Government. Mark Mwithaga, Vice Chairman of the Committee and MP from Nakuru had his October 1974 election victory nullified by the High Court, following which he was arrested over a marital dispute that had happened 19 months previously, and was sentenced to two years in prison. The most critical MP's, Martin Shikaku and Marie John Seroney (a Nandi backbencher), were arrested on 15 October 1975 as they left the Assembly, and the latter itself was adjourned for several months. Only when Seroney gave assurances to Vice President Moi that he would refrain from criticizing Kenyatta, was he released, to be elected deputy-Speaker of the reconvened Assembly. Other deputies saw their sources of patronage dry up as the regime cracked down on dissent. Later, in May 1977, another MP, George Anyona, was arrested inside Parliament, after announcing his intention to push for a committee to investigate corruption in the allocation of government grants. Throughout Kenyatta disclaimed he was ruling by force: "I am ruling because the *wananchi* [the people] want me." [82]

Presidential Authoritarianism

Notwithstanding some political space for local-level political contenders, power in Kenya has always been squarely lodged in the President's hands, and by extension in an inner circle of informal advisers, family members, cronies, selected political influentials, key cabinet ministers and ranking members of the bureaucracy. This is where consequential decisions are reached, to be passed down for implementation by the formal structures of government.

Until the recent multiparty pressures surfaced in Kenya, the Presidency was never contested: the route to that office was via the Vice-Presidency on the death of the incumbent. To become a Presidential candidate one had to be nominated by a party, impossible until the 1990's since Kenyatta had suppressed alternate parties (e.g. KPU) on technical grounds, while Moi passed the 1982 constitutional amendment creating a *de jure* one party system. And in the era of one-party rule the Vice-Presidency itself was a dangerous post to contest without presidential approval: not only did it require an internal KANU poll or election, rare in Kenya, but it pitches aspiring candidates against an entrenched incumbent with multiple sources of support, as efforts to dislodge Moi in 1976 revealed. Vice-Presidents, however, can easily be ousted by the President at will: Kenyatta kept Moi until his death, but Moi has had three Vice-Presidents since he assumed power.

Below the top two posts concentric rings of increasing influence exist, the innermost during the Kenyatta era being referred to as "The Family", reflecting the predominance of Kenyatta blood-relatives among them, but also the internal cohesion and stability of the ruling group. A similar inner ruling group exists under Moi (referred to in Nairobi as "the Gang") including the latter's family, personal and ethnic cohorts. Under Kenyatta the majority of influentials who played a role in decision-making were Kiambu Kikuyu from the Nairobi suburbs of Kiambu, Kiambaa, Gatundu and Limuru. The Kikuyu clans of Nyeri, Nyandaru, and especially Murang'a, were left at the fringes of power, with few exceptions frozen out of senior positions. The concept of "Kikuyu" control of Kenya was thus an oversimplification. Compared to other groups certainly the Kikuyu as a whole benefited most under Kenyatta. But it was specifically the Kiambu Kikuyu that established a stranglehold in the country, and in particular specific clans and families.

Kenyatta's immediate circle of confidantes was fairly small and stable, for he trusted few people. "His long years of exile, prison and anti-colonial clandestine activities have bred in him both a love for intrigue, and sensitive antennae to detect conspiracies."[83] At the core of the nucleus was his brother-in-law, Mbiyu Koinange, the abrasive Minister of State in the Presidential Office who controlled the powerful provincial administration under seven hand-picked Provincial Commissioners and networks of political informers; his favored cousin and personal physician, Dr. Njoroge Mungai, who filled an Assembly seat vacated for him by his sister, Mrs. Gechaga, and who served for some time as Minister of Foreign Affairs; and Charles Njonjo, Kenyatta's long-serving adviser and Attorney General, in some ways the *eminent grise* of the regime. All three were from Kiambu, and it was rare for Kenyatta to travel anywhere without most as part of his retinue.

The second concentric circle of "The Family," all-Kikuyu, and mostly from Kiambu, included Kenyatta's youngest (fourth) wife, Mama Ngina, a major economic power in her own right, associated in the scandals relating to the decimation for profit of Kenya's wildlife, and who controlled the portals of presidential patronage; colonial era politician Eliud Mathu, who served as the Comptroller of State House and Kenyatta's Private Secretary; and an array of loyal Kikuyu-Embu-Meru leaders who controlled the key cabinet ministries—James Gichuru, the Kiambu Defence Minister; Mwai Kibaki, the Nyeri Minister of Planning and Finance; Julius Gikonyo Kiano from Murang'a, Minister for Local Government; Jeremia Nyagah, the Embu Minister of Agriculture; and until he deserted the group, Jackson Angaine, political boss of Meru and Minister for Lands and Settlement.

Some of these were members of GEMA—the powerful Gikuyu, Embu and Meru Association—set up in 1971 as an economic vehicle for the enhancement of Kikuyu, Embu, and Meru interests, originally in land and farming, later through the mushrooming public GEMA Holdings Company in other domains. (The Kamba and Luo had similar organs protecting their ethnic interests, the New Akamba Union, and the Luo Union respectively.) GEMA, with Kenyatta as its patron, and Mbiyu Koinange as Trustee, supported parliamentary candidates, mobilized public opinion for the regime, raised funds for elections, and in general stood for the expansion of Kikuyu privilege. GEMA's Board was a Who's Who of the Kikuyu Establishment. Its political and economic clout was so great that Moi could not allow it to survive Kenyatta's death: it was soon prosecuted for infractions of corporate law that had been long-tolerated, and banned as an "ethnic" association, GEMA was forced to broaden its membership, thus losing its political thrust.

Kenyatta relatives were also found throughout Kenya's establishment; one sat on 87 public and private company boards. Among them one could note Kenyatta's eldest daughter Margaret Kenyatta, Mayoress of Nairobi; his son Peter Mugai Kenyatta, MP for Juja and Assistant Minister of Cooperative Development; nephew, Ngengi Mungai, chairman of MacKenzie (Kenya) Ltd. one of the country's biggest firms; and his son-in-law Udi Gecaga, chairman of Lonhro's East Africa operations. The latter two were multi-millionaires in their early thirties, but they lost their political usefulness, and high posts, with Kenyatta's death.

The outer ring of the Kenyatta circle was more balanced and included leaders of the three ethnic groups that originally allied themselves with Kenyatta: Moi, the Vice President and Minister of Home Affairs, controlling a segment of the Kalenjin (the others were chafing at Kikuyu land-encroachments in the Rift Valley Province); Ngei, the main Kamba political baron and Minister of Housing; Ngala, until his controversial 1972 death in a car "accident", the main Mijikenda leader, as Minister of Power and Communications. Other leading Kikuyu leaders were also in this secondary grouping—Duncan Ndegwa, the Nyeri Governor of the Central Bank; Bethuel Gecaga, the Murang'a Managing Director of British-American Tobacco Ltd., etc.

Only beneath these two inner groups came the key members of Kenyatta's cabinet. While the composition of the cabinet changed over time, membership was ethnically balanced and no major group was completely locked out of power since "tribal balance rather than ability was the first criterion."[84] The fact that the Kikuyu were *not* unduly over-represented at cabinet level (see Table 7) camouflaged the fact that below the "representative" cabinet Kikuyu staffed all key posts in the administration, and a disproportionate number of all salaried positions in many ministries.[85] Initially rationalized as but reflecting the drive of Kenya's most upwardly-mobile group and/or correcting colonial era ethnic imbalances, the result was that by the 1970's the majority of Provincial Commissioners, most senior department heads in the administration, heads of the security services and parastatals, and a large percentage of Kenya's officer corps came to be dominated by Kikuyu. Nellis calculated with respect to 174/5 key posts in Kenya

Table 15: Ethnic Composition of Kenyan Cabinets

Ethnicity	1963 N.	1963 %	1964 N.	1964 %	1966 N.	1966 %	1969 N.	1969 %	1974 N.	1974 %	1979 N.	1979 %
Kikuyu	6	35.3	6	31.6	7	30.4	7	31.8	7	31.8	8	29.6
Luo	4	23.5	4	21	3	13	2	9.1	2	9.1	3	11.1
Luhya	1	5.9	1	5.3	2	8.7	2	9.1	2	9.1	3	11.1
Kamba	1	5.9	1	5.3	2	8.7	2	9.1	2	9.1	3	11.1
Kalenjin	0	0	1	5.3	1	4.4	2	9.1	2	9.1	4	14.8
Others	5	29.4	5	26.3	9	39.1	7	31.8	7	31.8	7	25.9
Total	17		19		23		22		22		27	

Source: Vincent B. Khapaya, p. 23.

(including the Presidency, cabinet, permanent secretaries, Provincial Commissioners etc.) that already by 1972 the Kikuyu had dramatically improved their numerical presence compared to 1969 (See Table 8).

Table 16: Ethnic Composition of Leading Kenyan Government Positions

Ethnicity	% of Population	Positions in 1969 No.	%	Positions in 1972 No.	%
Kikuyu	20.1%	53	30.3	72	41.4
Kalenjin	10.8%	17	9.7	17	9.8
Luhya	13.2%	21	12.0	18	10.3
Luo	13.9%	19	10.8	15	8.6
Unknown		14		18	
Kamba	10.9%	24	13.7	8	4.6
Coast	5.4%	4	2.3	6	3.4
Taita	1.0%	2	1.1	5	2.9
Kisii	6.4%	6	3.4	6	3.4
Embu/Meru	7.0%	4	2.3	5	2.9
Somali	2.2%	1	0.5	3	1.7
Maasai	1.4%	4	2.3	1	0.6
Non-Africans		6		0	

John R. Nellis, "The Ethnic Composition of Leading Kenyan Government Positions," Research Report N.24, Uppsala, Scandinavian Institute of African Studies, 1974, p. 13, 14, 15.

Such ethnic imbalances triggered considerable debate in the 1970's. Martin Shikaku complained the Ministry of Agriculture had been "Kikuyuised" from top to bottom; as early as 1966 the posts of Permanent Secretary, Deputy Permanent Secretary, Under-Secretary, Director of Agriculture, and several others in the hierarchy were in Kikuyu hands. Rejecting this Kikuyu monopoly and the inevitable neglect of the Western Province he warned against "one tribe taking everything...We are 42 tribes in Kenya," and one day that one offender could be eaten up by the other forty-one,[86] a prophesy that came true under Moi.

Other MP's claimed the Ministry of Commerce and Industry had become a "Kikuyu Ministry," and that "today, when we look at the top jobs in the government, we find that most of the ministries...have been taken over by people from the Central Province...If one tribe alone can take over about 72% of the Kenya jobs, and they are less two million people, how can you expect 25 per cent of the jobs to go to more than eight million people who belong to other tribes?"[87] Apart from six of the 22 ministers (including the Foreign and Finance Ministers), Kikuyu (mostly from Kiambu) held 9 of 22 permanent secretaries in the civil service (the highest nonpolitical appointments); four of the seven powerful provincial Commissioners were also Kikuyu, as were the Attorney General, Commissioner of Police, Director of Intelligence, Controller of State House.

At the apex of these loyalty pyramids stood Kenyatta, who within a few years eschewed formal government and cabinet meetings and set up his headquarters at his Kiambu country home in Gatundu, twenty-five miles from Nairobi. Like ancient personal rulers Kenyatta rotated his residence between Gatundu, Nakuru, State House in Nairobi and his Presidential lodge at Mombasa, with his "Court" moving with him. The number of formal cabinet meetings declined to 6-8 per year as Kenyatta aged. Instead cabinet ministers commuted to wherever he was ensconced to secure his agreement on matters of policy, or to hear decisions already reached by him. There they were joined by streams of delegations from all parts of the country paying homage to the *Mzee*, contributing to his personal *harambee* projects while pleading special cases. Increasingly Kenyatta shunned Nairobi, and Nakuru for all practical purposes became the State capital, replete with guesthouses and traditional dancers for his visitors. As Kenyatta aged and a 2-3 hour work-day became the norm, the number of ministerial meetings declined even more, and governance even ground to a halt in the last years of the Kenyatta Presidency. All matters awaiting a decision, or his adjudication, were deferred, as Kenyatta, increasingly reluctant to make any decisions procrastinated, and Ministers and civil servants alike, always intimidated by him, dared not proceed on any course of action without his direct approval.

Kenyatta's personal rulership style was derived in part from the decision-making style of Kikuyu elders. Despite his Kikuyu base, Kiambu stranglehold, national stature, and awesome powers, Kenyatta remained throughout a juggler of interests, an ultimate arbiter, a dispenser of patronage, a Paramount Chief above petty issues, rather than an *initiator* of policy. Kenyatta set his personal stamp on Kenya's evolution, placing the country solidly on its capitalist, pro-Western course, but neither day to day policy nor bureaucratic detail was his *forte*. Consulting only his inner circle of confidantes and relatives on grand policy, Kenyatta then secured the consensus of other influentials to whatever decision had been reached, following which the relevant

Minister was summoned to receive his brief for implementation, usually in the form of enabling legislation or edicts. Kenyatta had no patience for routine matters, concentrated only on issues of broad policy or those of particular concern to him. Day to day administration was left to trusted lieutenants; yet he did not really delegate authority, since important matters had to be cleared through him, underscoring "the instrumental nature of the rest of the state apparatus"[88] in a system of personal rule.

In the absence of a disciplined party that could act as a Presidential control mechanism, and the fragmentation of many of the country's ethnic groups as well[89], Kenyatta built up two networks to serve that function. The first was the provincial bureaucracy—point of contact of the average Kenyan with the State—that became the most powerful regulator of all activity in the country. And the second was a patronage network that could reward as well as punish.

The bureaucracy became the prime bastion of Presidential power, with local political barons using their ethnic bases to negotiate the nature of their role in government in exchange for their regional support. At the center of the Kenyan bureaucracy stands the powerful provincial administration under its seven hand-picked Provincial Commissioners. Possessing dictatorial prerogatives unchecked by Parliament, the administration is the main tool of presidential authoritarianism to this day, under Moi as under Kenyatta. Through the Provincial Commissioners and their forty district commissioners and 150-180 divisional officers, Nairobi's tentacles spread over the periphery. Inheriting wide regulatory powers from colonial days, commissioners had their powers augmented after independence, so that anything transpiring in their geographical domains can legally be disallowed at their discretion. It is they who control the population in the district, its resources, development, and policy implementation of decisions taken in Nairobi. Commissioners may even ignore legislation passed by the National Assembly (depending upon instructions from the President's Office) though all Presidential directives are enforced as if they were law. Even informal Presidential wishes, that have no legal standing, or may be illegal, are accepted by Commissioners as "an instruction which remains confidential and which is carried out by the administration as though it were law."[90] An illustration is Kenyatta's unwritten instruction to the Coastal Province administration not to allow any land transfers to foreign nationals, though no such law exists on Kenya's statute books.

Commissioners chair security and intelligence committees, are responsible for law and order, command the police forces in their districts, and are heads of all aspects of civic administration, including the licensing and control of public meetings. They are empowered to prevent, at any pretext, MP's from meeting with their constituents, and permission to hold meetings are not granted to those in the Presidential "black list." No local authority has autonomous powers in Kenya, except Nairobi's during the Kenyatta era, and then only because Margaret, Kenyatta's headstrong and capable daughter was for some time the capital's Mayoress.

Accountable only to the Presidential Office the Provincial Commissioners fall under the aegis of a Minister of State in the Presidential Office. During Kenyatta's reign the occupant was Mbiyu Koinange, the President's *alter ego*, brother-in-law through his second wife, trusted crony of forty years standing, and an intimidating House of Mumbi arch-conservative. Ruthless, vindictive, opinionated and ambitious, Koinange represented Kikuyu hard-line traditionalists, and provided the "law and order" input in the Presidential ear that usually won the day. Directly implicated by the National Assembly in Kariuki's 1975 liquidation, Koinange is regarded in many circles to also be the "big man" who ordered Mboya's assassination in 1969. On Kenyatta's death some Kikuyu leaders supported a Koinange succession—despite his advanced age—desiring a strong Kikuyu dynasty that only he could provide. The 1978 succession conspiracy aimed at that; it has always been assumed that such a conspiracy could not have been hatched in the Presidential back-yard (Nakuru) without Koinange's knowledge or support.

However that may be, the Commissioners reported daily to Koinange. Four of the seven were Kikuyu (as were 50% of the DC's), and one was a relative of Koinange. Most served throughout Kenyatta's fifteen year tenure; with one exception all were retired on Moi's rise to power, as were most incumbent DC's. Moi's Commissioners were placed under a Maasai Assistant Minister in the Presidential Office as the entire ethnic basis in the administration and army was changed. Acting as agents of the executive in the countryside, the provincial administration counterbalances Kenya's fissiparous party, providing a "strong centralized hierarchical machine...the grid that held the country together."[91]

The second Presidential control network is a clientelist one based on patronage and turning a blind eye to corruption. Both Kenyatta's and Moi's administrations rested on a bedrock of patronage and corruption. Patronage takes the form of appointments to senior positions in the bloated civil service, parastatal sector, and marketing boards, that offer opportunities for self-enrichment. As Barkan reminds us "the civil service is less an instrument for the pursuit of public policy as...an avenue for promoting private ambitions and interests."[92]

Presidential patronage also includes contributions to district *harambee* projects, buttressing the status of incumbent lieutenants; it includes promoting influential ethnic leaders to Assistant Ministers (the function of which has never been spelled out, and the number of which is unlimited), allowing the creation of lower networks of patronage. It is not surprising that all efforts at reform in Kenya (e.g. the 1980 Waruhiu Report that argued a separation of personal from public activities in the civil service) have been unsuccessful. The "gross neglect of public duty and misuse of official positions,"[93] has been regarded by the executive as an unavoidable cost of a higher goal—political stability. Implementation of even more moderate recommendations in the Waruhiu Report meant dissolving the basic glue of the political system itself.

For most civil servants and MP's in Kenya hold at least one additional government post, and try concurrently to operate up to twenty commercial enterprises. Virtually any economic activity in downtown Nairobi in one way or another is linked to a political figure. As one observer put it "I know some civil servants, very senior and respected....who in addition to barber shops and shoe shine business also own tea kiosks in the streets...want to own farms...cultivate barley...own shares in factories...run factories...and to own shops...to trade in gems...all at the same time."[94] Though patronage filtered down to virtually every group and province, the lion's share has always gone to the Presidential ethnic group and/or province, and to his closest allies from other ethnicities. During the Kenyatta era this meant primarily the Kiambu Kikuyu. During the Moi Presidency, the Kalenjin were the net beneficiaries, though in light of Moi's isolation in the (Kikuyu) lion's den, and the smallness of his ethnic group, the flow of patronage to the Kikuyu did not dry up immediately, and considerable patronage began to flow (for the first time) to the Maasai and Abaluhya leaders, who became his staunchest allies.

As the supreme power-source and dispenser of patronage, nothing is beyond the President's ability, especially for proven allies by whose side he always stood. Examples abound from both the Moi presidency, notably the latter's retention at his side of key aides implicated in crass murder and gross embezzlement, and from the Kenyatta presidency. Here the best example was Kenyatta's standing to the end by the side of Moi, the Kalenjin who had joined forces with him in 1964, despite pressure from within his own family to jettison Moi, and assure a Kikuyu Presidential succession. (Certainly the 1976 attempt to block a Moi Presidency by changing the Constitution would have been successful had Kenyatta given it his support.) Kenyatta also immediately reinstated Ronald Ngala in 1970 when the latter was ousted by rebel rank and file members as district chairman of the always difficult to govern Mombasa KANU branch. And when Paul Ngei's political career seemed to come to an end with the Courts denying him his 1974 election victory due to fraud and intimidation, Kenyatta rammed through a retroactive Constitutional amendment allowing the President to pardon MP's guilty of electoral irregularities. The ex-Mau Mau leader, popular in his constituency, was the first beneficiary of the law, and once in the Assembly re-joined the cabinet as Minister of Local Government. (Ngei has constantly been in the headlines, but always immune from prosecution: notably when he was arrested for reckless driving; later for threatening to shoot a Nairobi businessman who refused to forgive him his debts, etc.)

That the Kikuyu network of privilege would be eclipsed if the presidency passed to non-Kikuyu hands, was obvious to all, explaining the nervousness of the Kikuyu establishment as the *Mzee's* health deteriorated, leading to the attempt to change the constitutional rules of succession in 1976, and the 1978 conspiracy on Kenyatta's death.

The Succession

By 1976 the succession struggle was in full swing. The contenders were Moi and former Foreign Minister and Kenyatta nephew Dr. Njoroge Mungai. Two undeclared contenders also existed: Mbiyu Koinange, not popular outside Kiambu, and Finance Minister Mwai Kibaki, a respected technocrat, but neither charismatic nor ambitious enough, and a Nyeri Kikuyu to boot. (He was to become Moi's first Vice President.)

At a KANU meeting in Nakuru on September 26th, twenty cabinet ministers, power brokers and MP's, including Minister of

Defence James Gichuru, Paul Ngei (Cooperatives), Njoroge Mungai, and GEMA leader Njenga Karume, backed a constitutional amendment by Jackson Angaine (Minister of Lands and Settlements) aimed at preventing the automatic assumption of interim powers by the Vice-President in the case of the President's death. Since strict provisions already existed in the Constitution to prevent abuses of power during the interim period, the intent of the caucus was to prevent Moi from consolidating his not inconsiderable powers during the interim 90-day period. Though the movement gained strength, and it was assumed that it could not have surfaced without the tacit consent of the *Mzee*, it was blocked by Moi, who had developed powerful support networks during his lengthy stint as Kenyatta's lieutenant. The Maasai Minister Stanley Oloitiptip (handsomely rewarded for his support) mobilized 98 MP's who called the amendment (that required passage by two-thirds vote of the 171-member Assembly) "unethical, immoral and bordering on criminality," proposed by "power-hungry self-seekers."[95] Moi's position became unassailable when the much-feared Attorney General Charles Njonjo ominously reminded all and sundry that "it is a criminal offence for any person to compass, imagine, devise or intend death or the deposition of the President...[or] express, utter or declare such compassings, imaginations, devices or intentions."[96] Njonjo's support for Moi was also handsomely rewarded by Moi though Njonjo—a Kiambu Kikuyu with many enemies and no popular base—had presidential aspirations to be manifest later.

With the constitutional battle lost, diehard Kiambu elements and Kenyatta relatives next tried to block the actual transfer of power via the Ngoroko plot[97] that aimed at assassinating Moi and his Kikuyu allies Kibaki and Njonjo. The latter, with his files on the wrongdoings of every public figure and with the CID behind him, was seen as Moi's prime prop. The plot was to be consummated by the elite 200-man Stock Theft Unit erected in 1977 in Nakuru, near the Presidential lodge. Outfitted with sophisticated firepower, trained by unsuspecting British instructors, the Unit was commanded by the Rift Valley Commissioner of Police Mungai, the same officer with whom Kariuki was last seen alive. (When the plot fizzled he fled to Sudan, returning only after being granted immunity on the grounds that it would not be in the national interest to prosecute him.)

The plot assumed Kenyatta would be in Nakuru which, being Kikuyu territory, could be sealed off until the assassinations took place and a cover story was issued. As it happened Kenyatta did not die in Nakuru, but far from the reach of the plotters at his Mombasa lodge, early in the morning of August 22nd 1978. The plot had, in any case, been penetrated by Njonjo, who had forewarned Moi. Details on it were kept secret, however, until after Moi's accession to power, when the Unit was disbanded and its personnel were dispersed among the General Service Units.

The Moi Presidency

The Transitional Years 1978-1982

It is difficult to appreciate today, when Presidential hegemony is under immense pressure from all directions, and the regime responds with despotic repression, the degree to which Moi's accession to power was popular in 1978. The constitutional change in leadership negated near-unanimous doomsday prognoses, and catapulted Kenya into the handful of African states to have successfully negotiated a succession crisis. More importantly, in a country where ethnicity was the prime riveting factor, a Kalenjin had peacefully replaced a Kikuyu as all-powerful Head of State.

Aware of the novelty of the succession Moi adroitly pledged "Nyayo"—continuity of policies, Nyayo meaning "in the footsteps" [of Kenyatta])—as attested by retention of Kikuyu over-representation in his cabinet and the appointment of Mwai Kibaki to the Vice Presidency. (Only after the 1983 elections did Kikuyu representation decline from 30% to 19%) But he also raised the prospect of change by attacking corruption for the first time ever, releasing all political prisoners (there were only 23, including Shikuku, Anyona, and Seroney), policies that elicited the first-ever pro-government demonstration in Kenya since independence. A reconciliation with the Luo East also appeared to be in the offing, and a popular 10% across the board pay-hike and abolition of primary school fees, were additional portenders of a new era.

Moi's first cabinet retained all of Kenyatta's appointees, even the 71-year old conniving Koinange, but a persistent drive to Kalenjinize the Kikuyu civil and military state control apparatus started virtually with the succession. Utilizing Njonjo and his files, an array of Kikuyu officers and senior officials were rapidly dislodged from the summit of the police, army and administration on charges of corruption.

Most of the Provincial Commissioners were retired or reassigned to parastatal posts since they simply could not be trusted of blindly supporting the new ethnic array of power. Police Commissioner Bernard Hinga, his deputy, and other suspect officers were forced to resign under threat of prosecution for corruption, although for a decade it was common knowledge that senior Police officers were linked with smuggling into Tanzania and Uganda. The head of the GSU (a Njonjo, hence also Moi, ally) Ben Githi, assumed Hinga's post. Five of the seven provincial assistant police chiefs were also replaced by Kalenjin or other loyalist officers. Moi's first military promotions/appointments saw two top officers retired and eight senior military officers, including the Kamba Lt. General Jack Mulinge, advance in rank. Some of the latter were promoted in order to cement their fealty, some merely to speed up their eventual retirement or the promotion beneath them of Kalenjin officers! By 1981 Moi felt strong enough to neutralize the powerful GEMA, as previously noted, that had tried to block his succession both in 1975 and 1978.

Early pledges that Kenya was now somehow different, and that the country would be free of political prisoners, was however, reneged upon; by 1986 Kenya was a major Amnesty International concern. Harassment of critics continued as in Kenyatta days. In 1980 former Mau Mau leader Waruru Kanja touched upon a political taboo when he raised in the Assembly the question of Mboya's murder. He was promptly dismissed as Assistant Minister, lost his Assembly seat, was found guilty of illegally possessing foreign exchange, and imprisoned for three years. (Every Kenyan has foreign exchange.) Other bothersome MP's were neutralized by lawsuits filed over their huge indebtedness (most normally would never repay such debts), since a bankruptcy verdict requires MP's to resign their seats.

That nothing had changed in Kenya's governance style was made evident by a graphic, and by now famous, speech that Moi delivered to parliamentarians in 1984. For fifteen long years assuming a self-effacing role in the shadow of the *Mzee*, tolerating snubs while clocking time, once his apprenticeship was over Moi demanded the same loyalty his former master had commanded from him and all others.[98]

I call on all Ministers, Assistant Ministers and every other person to sing like parrots in issues I have mentioned. During Kenyatta's period I persistently sang the Kenyatta tune until people said "this fellow has nothing to say except to sing for Kenyatta." I say "I didn't have ideas of my own. Who was I to have my own ideas? I was in Kenyatta's shoes and therefore I had to sing whatever Kenyatta wanted. If I had sung another song do you think Kenyatta would have left me alone?" Therefore you ought to sing the song I sing. If I put a full stop, you should also put a full stop. This is how this country will move forward. The day you become a big person, you will have the liberty to sing your own song and everybody else will sing it.

Yet the Tugen Daniel Toiritich arap (son of) Moi, was neither a founding father nor a charismatic figure such as Kenyatta, to whom others (even Odinga) deferred, but rather "a tough but somewhat unimaginative figure."[99] Moreover, the Kenya over which he assumed power in 1978 was not the Kenya of 1964. Gone were the plentiful sources of patronage decolonization, Africanization, and the boom years had allowed; the cost of existing sinecure posts, and inefficiency and corruption heavily weighed down the economy. Social tensions were simmering as Kenya finally started paying the price of fifteen years of government kleptocracy under Kenyatta. Times of austerity aggravated by bouts of drought coincided with the Moi presidency. Mass unemployment soared, biting into Kenya's large pool of university graduates and school leavers. Already in 1983 there were six million unemployed; seven million more joined their ranks in the next decade—"a time-bomb ticking at the heart of the country's economy."[100] Unchecked imports made Kenya's trade deficit unmanageable, mushrooming nearly tenfold in one year, from $43 million in 1977 to $389 million in 1978; and though a rebound occurred by 1989 it had soared to $1.4 billion, when the debt service ratio stood at 37%, more than triple that in Kenyatta years.

The honeymoon with Moi was therefore brief as it became clear a new Kenya was not in the making, but an ethnic restructuring of the old system of social, economic and political privilege. Kenyatta Family members were slowly dislodged from office. Koinange died a bitter man in 1981, totally humiliated when he failed to be re-elected in his own home constituency. Njoroge Mungai, Moi's 1975 rival in 1975, was left out of public life. Kenyatta son-in-law, Udi Gecaga, who was soon dismissed by Lonhro/Kenya because his Kenyatta family link was now a liability rather than an asset for the company; his replacement was none other than Moi's natural son, Mark arap Moi. And the avaricious Mama Ngina, began to be hassled by the Internal Revenue for huge tax arrears. Two of Kenyatta's children, however, were retained in senior posts: Peter Muigai Kenyatta, as Assistant Minister (though he was to die late in 1979), and Margaret Kenyatta who remained Ambassador.

The overture to the Luo via their leader, Oginga Odinga, came to nought, as Moi found both too threatening. Odinga was barred from contesting the 1978 KANU elections (the first in 12 years) due to his KPU involvement, and he was also not allowed to compete in the following year's legislative elections. (Odinga was, however, given a patronage sop in the form of the Chairmanship of the Kenya Cotton Board.) His final political shunting came in 1981, when a speech striving to justify his originally bolting KANU (hoping to re-enter the Assembly via a bye-election) backfired badly. For Odinga crudely disparaged Kenyatta's memory (by lumping him with the "landgrabbers" Odinga had tried to bloc), and Moi—under intense Kikuyu pressure—was forced to bar Odinga's candidacy, triggering the first of a series of student demonstrations to plague Moi's presidency until the 1982 Air Force mutiny.

By that year Moi's cabinet contained only six old faces, though it remained ethnically representative. There now existed *eighty* Ministers and Assistant Ministers, an expansion of 28 positions, attesting to Moi's greater utilization of patronage to stabilize his rule. At the core of the new power-hierarchy stood three Moi-Kikuyu—every one of whom was to fall by the wayside—Charles Njonjo in the Attorney General's office; Godfrey Gitahi Kariuki, Minister of State and *de facto* Chief of Staff in the Presidential Office; and Vice President and Finance Minister Mwai Kibaki. One Kalenjin, that surfaced at this time—Nicholas Biwott—was to become the regime's No. 2 man.

The Moi-Njonjo-Kibaki alliance seemed to confirm the truism that given the continued alienation of the Luo, the other numerical heavyweights in Kenya, the Kikuyu had to be retained near the core of the power-nexus. But this was not strictly true. Moi's ethnic alliance was very much based on *renegade* Kikuyu without much grass-roots support. Njonjo was from a discredited Kiambu lineage; and Moi's other Kikuyu allies were both from Nyeri, not Kiambu. And secondly, the twin traumas of the 1982 Air Force mutiny and Njonjo's unexpected bid for power, exacerbated Moi's ethnic paranoia, and accelerated his "Kalenjinization" of the civil and military power hierarchies in Kenya. By 1990 both the Luo and Kikuyu had been politically and economically marginalized, the new ethnic alliance in Nairobi being a novel Kalenjin-Maasai-Abaluhya one.

The Njonjo Affair

The ambitious sixty-year old Njonjo made his opening bid for the Presidency (via the Vice Presidency) by resigning his powerful post as Attorney General to seek elected office as an ordinary MP. Though "it has been traditional in Kenya's post-independence politics for contenders for high office to conceal their aspirations until the last moment," [101] Njonjo's motives were transparently clear. In terms of Kenya's constitution only elected deputies could join the cabinet and be eligible for the Vice-Presidency. Njonjo was also at the civil service retirement age, though at the peak of his ambitions.

Njonjo was easily "elected" in his home district, after bribing the incumbent to withdraw from the contest (with 160,000 shillings and a parastatal job), and after assuring that another potential candidate was detained by the Special Branch until after the deadline for filing papers. But Njonjo's move aroused intense unease in Nairobi, where he had always been feared, sometimes respected, but never admired. Son of the collaborationist Chief Josiah Njonjo, he had many enemies among KANU ex-Mau Mau. As Kenya's long-term Attorney General (to whose office the CID and Special Branch were attached) he had created numerous others, being personally "identified with the long invisible and merciless arm of the Kenyan regime...[becoming] almost synonymous with all the darker aspects of the Kenyan regime."[102] With his files bulging with documentation on the indiscretions of every single member of Kenya's establishment, he had a more than ample, and dangerous, war-chest for his drive to the pinnacle of power.

Moreover, though very well-regarded in expatriate and foreign circles, and a competent administrator, Njonjo was a social anachronism in Kenya. His elitist demeanor; his wealth and Euro-centric tastes; his ultra pro-Western, conservative world-view; his British wife, friends, contacts and Anglicized mannerisms (pin-striped suits were his favored attire) grated in the Kenyan context, certainly once he joined the plebeian oft-Swahili-speaking National Assembly. And

Njonjo's lack of true grass-roots support made him vulnerable outside the Attorney General's fortress. All the grievances against him, and the collaborationist House of Njonjo, resurfaced now he was a mere MP, with his only ally being Moi, beholden to him due to Njonjo's support in 1978, but wary of entering a private Kikuyu political feud.

Using the powerful Ministry of Home and Constitutional Affairs (to which he was appointed after the elections by Moi), as the position from which to oust Kibaki as Vice President, the ensuing Kibaki-Njonjo tug-of-war polarized the National Assembly, press, and much of society. The Nyeri Kikuyu were up-in-arms over the threat to their first-ever leader to attain high office (though Kibaki was not popular himself); the Kiambu Kikuyu, leaderless after Kenyatta's death refused to accept Njonjo's Kiambu credentials; the Kalenjin, relishing the fruits of Moi's rise to power, were aggravated by the early hint of a new Kikuyu supremacy, as were other ethnic groups coming into greater political prominence with Moi's succession. As Kibaki began to forge a Nyeri-Kiambu alliance against the "usurper" who was unacceptable to both, Njonjo's ambition began to threaten Moi's delicate balance of power, forcing him to move to demote, and then purge both. In so doing Moi disencumbered himself of a dangerous future rival who in unguarded moments had cast aspersions on Moi's intellect, and set a clear new precedent that the Vice Presidency did not automatically assure succession to the political throne.

The manner of Njonjo's demise has been assessed as "political statecraft of the highest order of cunning."[103] Since becoming Minister Njonjo had attracted an inordinate amount of criticism for the myriads of skeletons in his own cupboard: for his large farms; for sanctioning the cover-up of the Mboya murder when he controlled the CID; for travel (banned) to South Africa via Malawi; for being involved in the 1981 aborted mercenary invasion of the Seychelles; for (illegal), foreign exchange dealings; and for his expectations of special privileges at Nairobi airport. On May 8, 1983 Moi introduced a "traitor at the gates" theme in a speech in Kissi. While praising Kibaki, he claimed "foreign countries were grooming a certain person to take over the presidency of this country,"[104] though not naming Njonjo as the individual in question. The statement heightened tensions and speculation, elicited pledges of loyalty for Moi, and triggered a witch-hunt with broad hints at Njonjo, that undermined his position by innuendo, since everyone knew that he was the darling of the British establishment.

On June 30th Njonjo resigned from Parliament after being suspended from ministerial duties. His resignation was greeted in parliament with bouts of joy and applause, and a move "to adjourn to celebrate the resignation of the Honourable Njonjo."[105] A judicial committee set up to investigate the charges against him concluded its task after 110 days of hearings and testimony from 61 witnesses, proving several of the allegations against him; but "given that corruption and patronage are virtually endemic in Kenyan politics, most of the misdemeanors laid against Njonjo amounted to very small beer...and the graver accusations lack any basis of evidence or were, in fact, part of a covert Kenyan policy of the day."[106] A purge of Njonjoists led to the expulsion from KANU of three Ministers (including Stanley Oloitiptip) and four Assistant Ministers. (Oloitiptip died shortly later, a broken, destitute man.) Njonjo was pardoned by Moi in December 1984, to retire in obscurity.

Prior to the "Njonjo affair" came the 1982 Air Force mutiny. The fact the upheaval occurred, and the manner in which it was crushed, indelibly affected Moi's thinking. It also shattered the myth of Kenya's inherent stability, and aggravated the outflow of foreign capital. For in the upheaval most military units straddled the fence, rallying to Moi only when the revolt was evidently crushed, while students, civil servants, and policemen spilled onto the streets to prematurely celebrate Moi's overthrow.

Civil-Military Stability and the Kenyan Armed Forces

Despite Kenya's record of civil-military stability, its armed forces were never totally free from unrest. A month after independence a mutiny erupted, and Kenyatta's early presidency did not automatically assure subordination of the military to civilian hegemony. Still, the ethnic make-up of Kenya's officer corps, the staffing and promotion policies pursued, and a trade off of material rewards for loyalty, kept the armed forces relatively immune from interventionist temptations.

The better-trained and more sophisticated Kenyan regiments of the King's African Rifles—the core colonial armies in British East Africa—were the building blocs of the post-independence 2,500-man Kenyan Armed Forces. Africanization of the officer corps proceeded more slowly in Kenya than in Uganda and Tanganyika, even though more of the *effendi* (warrant officers, the highest rank an African could attain) in the KAR were of Kenyan origin—12 of the 17 appointed in 1957. Though most *effendi* became officers at independence, Africanization subsequently remained slow.

Ethnically, Kenya's army was not representative of society (see Table 17), but except for the Kamba and Luhya the skew was not serious, and, more importantly, ethnic strife was quite modest.[107] The Luo-Kikuyu tug-of-war was not replicated in the military, since most Luo in the army were in the technical services, especially Signals. There was a strong Kamba preponderance among officers, the result of historic out-migrations from Ukambani due to its poor soils. Being outside the Kikuyu-Luo rivalry, the large Kamba officer presence and the Kamba Chiefs of Staff (through 1982), insulated the armed forces from inter-ethnic antagonisms that might have erupted without such a neutral buffer. Later, Kenyatta's policy of Kikuyuizing the army acted to prevent the polarization of the army by ethnic appeals from alternate political contenders.

Table 17: Ethnic Composition of Military and Police, 1962

	Population	Police Posts	Officer Posts
Kikuyu	19.2 %	11.2 %	22.7 %
Luo	13.9	8.5	10.3
Luhya	12.9	16.5	0.4
Kamba	11.0	9.8	28.0
Kipsigis	4.0	7.6	2.8
Nandi	2.0	7.4	4.1

Source: Lee p. 109-110.

The 1964 mutiny

The first instance of civil-military strife in Kenya came on January 24, 1964 when the 11th battalion rebelled at bases near Nakuru and Nairobi, part of "pay-strikes" that also rocked Uganda and Tanganyika.[108] The Kenyan mutiny was less serious because Kenyatta had wide legitimacy; there were also more loyalist forces, fewer ethnic tensions, and British *in situ* troops could put down the mutiny even as reinforcements arrived from Aden. Finally, the manner in which the crisis was handled—in contrast to the case in Uganda and Tanganyika—assured its unequivocal resolution.

While Kenyatta redressed the pay anomalies noted by the mutineers, unlike as in Uganda was the army appeased; nor as in Tanganyika was it disbanded *en masse* and reconstituted as a "People's" Army. In Kenya legitimate grievances were corrected, but 170 mutineers were dismissed, 100 were court-martialed, and re-training commenced under British officers to assure 1964 did not repeat itself. What Kenyatta learned from the mutiny was that despite his popularity, coups could not be ruled out unless the armed forces were tightly controlled. And this control was to rest on two pillars: ethnic legitimacy and material self-interest.

Sources of Civil-Military Stability in Kenya

Despite two mutinies (1964; 1982), two conspiracies (1971; the 1978 Ngoroko affair), and two lesser plots, until 1990 the Kenyan army was effectively subordinate to civilian rule. The ease with which Nairobi nearly collapsed in 1964 to several hundred troops triggered the strengthening of the counter-insurgency GSU (of colonial origins)—"the regime's coercive arm against its internal enemies."[109] The GSU became a well-armed 2,000-man Kikuyu elite force, with airborne capability, commanded by hand-picked officers headed by Ben Githi. Using Mboya's murder as a pretext—though the assassin was a Kikuyu possibly connected to Mbiyu Koinange—the 1966 purge of the existing GSU left not a single Luo officer in the force, and few non-Kikuyu among the rank and file. Capable of defeating the the entire army by itself, during the tense days after Kariuki's murder, all armories were guarded by GSU units. After the Moi succession the force was completely Kalenjinized, and it was the "new" GSU, after some hesitation, that crushed the 1982 Air Force mutiny.

Kenyatta also initiated the recruitment of Kikuyu into the military's officer corps. As early as 1967 Kikuyu were co-equal to Kamba in the officer corps, though most were at junior levels. The commanders of the army's three battalions were of the main ethnicities—Kamba, Kikuyu and Kalenjin—though below them there was a large group of Kamba, and only further below a large number of junior Kikuyu officers. The ethnic matching of the military and political establishment was thus a slow process. In order not to aggravate intra-military tensions, promotions were routinized, and the Kamba entrenched in the senior and middle ranks were not skipped over. Military Intelligence, the Special Branch, and other spy-networks capable of ferreting out plots, civil and military, were bolstered and part-Kikuyized. Through normal attrition and promotion by the mid-1980's a near-total Kikuyu stranglehold over most command positions would have resulted. This did not take into account, of course, a Kalenjin succession, that initiated its own much more rapid ethnic recruitment policy, leading to a massive Kalenjin quasi-monopoly of the senior command as early as 1987/8, and a veritable ethnic vise by 1993.

The large police force was harnessed in the countryside as part of the administrative vise of Nairobi. The Mau Mau Emergency saw a doubling of the colonial force to 12,232 men in 1962. The bulk of this corps was retained after independence; but because of the police's lower educational levels and payscales, and its duties in riot control, tax enforcement, border patrol, and anti-smuggling, it became much detested, and succumbed to petty and grand corruption.

All key posts relating to security were during the Kenyatta presidency under Kikuyu/Kiambu hands. Koinange controlled the Provincial Commissioners and their local Police from the Presidential Office. James Gichuru (who stepped down as head of KANU in 1963 when Kenyatta was released from prison) was Kenyatta's long-serving Defence Minister. (Aged and inept, he was retained as such for some time by Moi, symbol of Nyayo.) Attorney General Charles Njonjo controlled the CID and Special Branch on behalf of Kenyatta (and during Moi's early years). So thorough was the symbiosis between the Kikuyu political and military elites under Kenyatta that "where personal ties between officers and civilian big men did not yet exist, they began to be created; during the seventies, the marrying of military officers into the families of the civilian elite became commonplace."[110]

Moreover, a British military link was retained; Kenya's armed forces were exposed to British training missions, seconded officers, joint exercises, and British forces have usually been physically present in Kenya, especially at times of political stress. Despite inroads by other external military influences (e.g. Israel and the U.S.) most Kenyan naval cadets routinely continue to go to the Royal Naval College, and army officer cadets attend Mons, Sandhurst and the Imperial War College, averting internal frictions multiple training programs have fomented in neighboring states. Association with Britain may have developed a greater sense of corporate continuity, but also the fact that there were usually resident/visiting British forces in the country deterred casual coupmanship attempts.

The country's armed forces were also not engaged in political duties, nor routinely called upon to prop up the government, insulating them somewhat from politicization, and the grievances of the *wananchi*. This because the regime possessed adequate alternate control mechanisms—the provincial administration, Police and the GSU—making it superfluous to call in the armed forces. Moreover, the shifta war with Somalia (in which *half* the army was involved), and the need for patrols along the border with Uganda during the Amin era, kept the army engaged in purely military tasks.

But the key to civil-military stability in Kenya was the overt, legal, and conscious integration of officers into the network of patronage and privilege, extending the civilian trade-off modality to the officers as well. Merely an ethnic matching of the civilian and military elites was not sufficient: a matching of the pecuniary interests of the two elites was the ultimate binding glue. As Goldsworthy has observed, the "growing ethnic solidarity at the top of the security apparatus certainly contributed to the strength of Kenyatta's control. But in addition, senior officers were being increasingly absorbed into the circles of privilege. Many were able to use their positions to serve their material interests—acquiring farms, commercial businesses and other forms of wealth—in very much the same manner of the politicians."[111]

Starting under Kenyatta, senior and middle-ranking military officers (and under Moi, increasingly junior ones as well) were encouraged to develop their personal enterprises, even empires, in transport, commerce, and especially in farming, all with generous loans, often defaulted on without prejudice, Kenya-style. An extension of the *de facto* right of public employees to engage in multiple private economic enterprises, military and police officers developed arrays of lucrative activities. One indication of the immense profitability of such activities was provided by the 1977 electoral campaign of a top police officer, whose entire costs (including *harambee* donations) were covered by the latter's "private" earnings while with the Police.[112]

Binding the self-interest of military barons to the survival of the political leadership is thus a basic underpinning of the trade-off modality of stability. It personally binds the commanding officers of the army to the civilian center, and *through them* ensures the fealty of the lower command.

Ethnic non-discrimination, and routinization of State- guaranteed benefits, further stabilizes the system. In a country with escalating unemployment, a career as an officer—with superior, permanent pay, fringe benefits, tenure, periodic courses overseas, prospects of upward mobility, potentials for petty graft and profit, and eligibility for State-guaranteed loans for farmland and other enterprises—is a sought-after option. In 1979 a low-keyed recruitment in Nairobi for 350 new posts in the army saw over 10,000 youths applying. Within this objective context few officers would jeopardize their positions by attempts at coupmanship; whatever additional pecuniary ambitions they might have developed can be satisfied by a completely legal, risk-free and highly lucrative "parallel" career while serving in the armed forces, which can sweep into oblivion any gripes they may have internalized.

The 1971 Conspiracy

Despite these policies several conspiracies came to light in Kenya. Early in 1971 thirteen individuals were arrested for an amateurish plot headed by a Lieutenant purged for his role in the 1964 mutiny, after which he had been jailed again for forgery. He then recruited a number of Luo, Kalenjin and Kamba fellow-discontents including a Kalenjin GSU officer dismissed for inefficiency (but claiming ethnic discrimination). Also involved were a Luo lecturer in Uganda, and a disgruntled Kamba former Assistant Minister dismissed when he drew attention to the resurgence of oathing forced upon Kamba including in the Army. The latter approached the Kamba Chief of Staff Brigadier J. M. Ndolo, and Kamba Chief Justice suggesting a military takeover. Ndolo procrastinated, unwilling to move against Kenyatta personally, but he did not arrest the plotters. Rather, it was Tanzania's President Nyerere, who was also approached, who alerted Kenyatta.

Neither Ndolo nor the Chief Justice were placed on trial, though they were forced to resign. Ndolo was replaced by the Kamba Major General Jack K. Mulinge, and retired on his military pension on a 9,416 acre farm near Machakos (bought at fire-sale prices with government loans), and together with income from other enterprises he continued his comfortable life. (Eight years later, another conspirator—the Rift Valley Commissioner and commander of the Stock Theft Unit, charged with attempting to block the Moi succession—was in similar manner amnestied "in the public interest" to return to pensionable retirement from Sudan.

Following the 1971 plot a large complement of Kikuyu recruits joined the officer corps where the Kamba hegemony was eroded. Colonel Dedan Gichuru and Lt. Colonel Kimaro (both Kikuyu) became the first Kenyan commanders of the Air Force and Navy, replacing British officers. The "Kamba" plot was seized upon as an opportune time to forcibly evict a number of Kamba farmers from the Highlands, and as in the aftermath of the 1964 mutiny, military salaries were raised and easier loans were authorized for officers wishing to set up private enterprises.

Transition from Kenyatta to Moi

Despite steady expansion, Kenya's armed forces remained much smaller than those of neighbouring Ethiopia (200,000), Somalia (120,000), Tanzania (60,000) or Uganda (60,000), and the force was largely non-mechanized. Only in 1978, faced by threats from Idi Amin's Uganda, increased border cattle-rustling, and Somali irredentism did Kenya expand her armed forces, and obtained also her first tanks and jets. (Somalia at the time had 250 tanks and 48 jets, while Tanzania possessed a large mechanized force.) In that year Kenya's armed forces numbered only 7,600 men (an army of 6,500, a navy of 340, and an Air Force of 760), with defence expenditures of $35 million, constituting 17% of the national budget, up from a previous low 3-5%. Expenditures on the military then zoomed from petty amounts to the second most onerous item in the budget, just below expenditures for education, and 30% higher than those for agriculture, forestry and fisheries.

The expansion of the military coincided with Moi's reign, allowing its more rapid Kalenjinization. The military first doubled to 14,000 men in 1980, with defence costs reaching $255.6 million in 1985. Later it zoomed up to 24,000. The military's expansion allowed Moi to mount recruitment drives among his ethnic kinsmen while affording scope for lateral promotions and various transfers to consolidate his ethnic grip on the army. Allocations of land and low-interest loans for the military also increased as Moi followed *Nyayo* in this respect as well.

Officers formerly bypassed at the patronage trough began to partake in the spoils of the game. Later, shaken by the 1982 Air Force mutiny, and by Jerry Rawling's coup and executions of corrupt politicians in Ghana, Moi began to spread patronage to the lower ranks as well, "keeping [them] well-cared for."[113] Soon "land grants in Kenya went to junior officers as well. Large areas around Nakuru and Ngong were handed out to keep the armed forces behind the government."[114] By 1987 it was estimated that nearly every officer from the rank of Major owned at least one *matate* (communal taxi), reaping hefty profits from their "military" careers.

The 1982 Air Force Coup

Early on August 1st, the Air Force in its entirety rebelled, to announce Moi's ouster. Celebrations erupted in Nairobi, with students, with foreknowledge of the coming coup, marching in town in solidarity with the putschists. Massive looting of Asian shops broke out with police participation, leaving downtown Nairobi a scarred and deserted area, with damages estimated at $200 million.

The conspiracy was mostly the work of NCO's, with the Air Cavalry spearheading a poorly-planned revolt, slated for the following week (when Moi was due to be overseas) but advanced to pre-empt another coup by a rival clique. (In actuality there were *three* concurrent plots to topple Moi.) Despite contingency plans for just such an eventuality, and the presence of several loyalist units near Nairobi, the revolt was only crushed at mid-day, with some three hundred deaths, military and civilian.[115]

Persistent questions remained for long about why the CID, Military Intelligence, Special Branch and other spy networks, normally very alert, had not uncovered and/or reported the plots. These doubts were exacerbated by revelations that the plots were commonly known in student circles at the University. For some time after the upheaval Moi appeared visibly shaken and off-balance, clearly unable to decide who in his entourage and cabinet was trustworthy.

Especially troubling was that it had been the modern, well-trained, elite Air Force, recently tripled at great cost to 2,000 men, that rebelled. Membership in the Force carried great prestige, good pay, professional training and conditions of service. Recruitment had been selective, with high minimal educational criteria. (Though the large number of university graduates in it suggested an entry source of civilian discontents.) But most disturbing was that though the army by and large remained loyalist, most commanders simply did not move to quell the revolt immediately. Many Kikuyu commanders reacted to the coup "by the book"—waiting for authorization to be received prior to moving against the insurgents, suggesting they were actually playing it safe by a "wait and see" ploy, not unwilling to see the regime collapse. For four hours no attempt was made by any officer or any unit, including the GSU, to quell the mutiny, officers in operational control of troops claiming later, at their trials, of a breakdown of communications and/or logistic problems.

With hindsight several factors had eroded the regime's legitimacy in the army, despite the liberal pork-barrel policies pursued. These included (a) a disillusionment with Moi's weak presidency, (b) Moi's aggressive self-enrichment—Rift Valley farms; transport, commercial, construction and franchise monopolies (fuel distribution, Firestone, food wholesaling, cinemas); Nairobi high-rise buildings etc.—worth $100 million and managed by two Asian advisors, (c) the excessive patronage given to Chief of Staff Mulinge, (d) intense dislike of the latter's deputy, the Kalenjin Army Commander Lt. General John Malan Sawe, slated to be the next Chief of Staff, (e) bread and butter gripes stemming from the decision not to construct new barracks, resulting in NCO's and junior officers living off-base without housing allowances, many in near-slum conditions, and (f) rejection by Luo and other elements in the Air Force of the continued banning from Kenyan politics of Oginga Odinga, who had recently been denied registration of a new party, the Kenya Socialist Alliance.

The rebellion was ultimately crushed by the GSU and regular army, but only after General Mahmud Mohamed, the deputy commander of the Army, unilaterally assumed command, authorized deployment of troops, and personally headed the counter-assault. For his initiative Mohamed, an ethnic Somali (normally likely to be viewed as unreliable) was given the task of creating a new Air Force, and was promoted Chief of Staff—a post he still retains. His brother, Hussein Maalim Mohamed, was brought into the cabinet, and other relatives were hooked into the Moi patronage network. The entire Air Force disbanded: 900 men were tried and sentenced to terms up to 25 years, 13 ringleaders—all Luo—received the death sentence and were executed.

A major shake-up in the security forces followed, with the top command being revamped. Officers commanding units that rebelled, who knew but did not report the plots, or who did not rally promptly to the regime, were imprisoned or cashiered. Kariuki, the Air Force commander, was imprisoned for four years as he apparently knew of the plots. He was replaced by another Kikuyu, Major General Wachira, though with a Kalenjin as deputy commander. The Ground Air Defence Unit, involved in its entirety and spearheading the putsch, was stricken off the Force's organizational chart, and its commander (a Lt. Colonel) was imprisoned for three years.

Although most of those arrested, and all those executed for their role in the upheaval were Luo (the authoritative *Weekly Review* called it "a largely Luo affair, with many of the active elements of the Air Force being motivated by tribalistic rather than ideological considerations,"[116] the majority of the *senior* officers that were arrested or dismissed after the upheaval were Kikuyu. The Kikuyu hold over the senior command since the Kenyatta era was greatly loosened, and a new ethnic predominance was clearly in the making.

The Kamba Chief of Staff was retained; for years he had not really been in control of the armed forces. Being more interested in his private affairs, Mulinge had been retained beyond retirement age because of Moi's indecision about a successor—heeding counsel of Military Intelligence and the Special Branch that promoting the Kalenjin General Sawe would trigger a military mutiny. In due course both Mulinge and Sawe were retired from the armed forces, the latter being first appointed to a State Board, later as High Commissioner to Canada. The Kamba Major General Joe Musomba, next in line for overall command of the armed forces, was also retired (and appointed Ambassador to Pakistan) since he was perceived to have political ambitions. The purge of the senior command left the succession clear for General Mohamed, who for all practical purposes had single-handedly saved Moi's throne, and as a minority Somali was incapable of constituting a threat or having ambitions.

The purges also allowed an equally non-threatening Samburu to assume command of the Army (flanked by a Kalenjin deputy), and a broad range of middle-ranking Kalenjin officers advanced another step up, many to deputy-command positions throughout the security forces. By 1985 the top six positions in the army were staffed by Kamba (3), Kalenjin (1), Samburu (1) and Somali (1) officers, but the Kalenjin were over-represented in the intermediate ranks, serving as deputy

Commander of the Army; deputy Air Force Commander; Staff College Commandant; Chief of Military Intelligence; Chief of Logistics, Director of CID, Commander of GSU; deputy Political Commissioner etc. Indeed *every important military base in Kenya now had a Kalenjin officer at least at deputy-commandant level*—in theory reducing prospects of future unpleasant surprises and/or lack of alacrity in supporting Nairobi against possible praetorian assaults. By 1990 many had moved to the top of their structures, with the Kalenjin in heavily disproportionate numbers in the command hierarchy; by 1995, the 28,000-man force, still under Chief of General Staff General Mohamed, was referred to in Nairobi as the "Presidential Army," an allusion to its overall Kalenjin composition.

The sweep of the armed forces was carried into the police and the para-military GSU, where a number of Kikuyu were arrested or dismissed. Ben Githi, for example, was summarily dismissed "in the public interest," though he was amnestied in June 1983. A Kamba replaced the Kikuyu Police Commissioner, and after an interim joint command by a Meru and European officer, the GSU came under a Kalenjin commander, with the new director of the CID also a Kalenjin. A shake-up in the Special Branch command resulted in three of the eight Provincial heads becoming Kalenjin, but its long-serving Kikuyu head, James Kanyotu, was retained (he saved Moi from several blunders) though he too was now flanked by a Kalenjin deputy.

A severe clampdown was imposed upon the University, that remained closed for rest of the year. (It had been shut down by the government 17 times since independence.) At the time of the rebellion thousands of students had streamed into downtown Nairobi to man roadblocks set up by the Air Force, urging a radical "revolution" and participating in the widescale looting. When the campus reopened an academic restructuring saw the elimination of the Department of Political Science, hotbed of Marxist sentiment and possibly also the source of the seditious *Pambana* and other revolutionary newsletters.[117]

Moi also acted to correct some of the substantive gripes that had triggered the rebellion. Despite Kenya's dire economic straits, urgent contracts were tendered for the construction of new barracks and several major pay hikes were announced to soothe urban and military tempers. The first of these, for the military establishment, came in November 1982, raising military salaries by between 15-30%.

Though these policies solidified Moi's grip over Kenya, the true lessons of the upheaval were not learned. Wedded to the "system," Moi reached the conclusion that as a Kalenjin succeeding a Kikuyu, a firmer hand was necessary on the reins of government, a more thorough ethnic matching of the control apparatus was needed, and greater munificence to the political and military barons was called for.

Yet the 1982 upheaval drew attention to the destabilization potential of (a) permanently keeping the Luo out of power, (b) of the cleavage between ostentatious life-styles of elites and the poverty of the masses, and (c) of the alienation of youth of all ethnic groups, facing little prospect of employment or advancement in a country groaning under the costs of government by patronage and corruption. Even as he tried to nail the door to future civil-military strife, societal pressures ignored for decades by power-wielders in Nairobi threatened to swamp the elite from other directions. A further military plot in mid-1985 indicated the road to civil-military peace remained replete with pot-holes. (In it a Kikuyu Major and 35 junior officers and NCO's at Gilgil barracks had methodically stolen arms in preparation for a scheduled June 1st assassination bid on Moi.) Increasingly, however, the real threat to the regime came from society at large, restless at Moi's heavy-handed grip.

1982-1990: Towards Dictatorship

As early as 1972 an observer had noted that "where Kenyatta can impose his will by being firm, his successor would either have to act in a more authoritarian manner or else be prepared to compromise more often than he has had to do." At the succession juncture another noted that Moi, "without the inhibiting hand of Kenyatta, could be ruthless with opponents."[118] It was maybe inevitable that the drab and uncharismatic Moi, facing fiscal pressures, social and economic de-mands, and challenges from all directions—to a degree Kenyatta's never faced—would move from rule resting largely on moral authority and/or legitimacy, to rule lodged primarily on force. Some 250,000 unemployed were annually entering the job market, constituting a swell of social discontent at a time when all the "soft options" pursued in *Mzee*'s days—land redistribution, civil service, and parastatal patron-age—were no longer available, being over-utilized. With the military revealing its own internal shaky reliability, Moi felt the need to tighten the reins of control to remain in power.

Even prior to the 1982 mutiny Moi had rammed through a Constitutional amendment transforming Kenya into a *de jure* one party state. The legislation was passed by the Assembly after only 45 minutes of debate on June 9, 1982, primarily aimed at blocking efforts by Oginga Odinga and George Anyona from registering a new party, the Kenya Socialist Alliance, the first such serious attempt since the KPU in the 1960's. At the same time a multifaceted drive was mounted to resuscitate KANU as a control mechanism—something Kenyatta neither needed, but the beleaguered Moi required. In June 1984 party membership was made obligatory of all civil servants. By mid-1985 party-membership reached 5 million, one stroke replenishing empty party coffers, while providing the regime with a strong whip. Since denial of membership, or expulsion from the party, was now linked to loss of civil service posts, this was a powerful tool for political quietism in the hands of the executive. So also was the erection of a party Disciplinary Committee with some teeth, that was aimed at exercising greater control over independent-minded Assembly deputies, who now could be hauled before the Committee for making comments, or voting in Parliament contrary to official policy. Though the Committee found it difficult to restrain political barons with significant grass-roots power, most of the assembly's former intermittent free-wheeling debates have been quelled.

A policy of granting priority to party members for jobs, contracts, licenses and tenders, and denying these benefits to individuals with records of political arrests, further restrained individuals by threatening their livelihood. (Previously individuals drummed out of KANU or detained for opposition, were barred from political life, but were not hampered in their economic activities.) A dramatic example of the implementation of this policy was seen when the acclaimed radical playwright Ngugi wa Thiong'o was released from detention, but not reappointed to his Chair of Literature at Nairobi University, and was forced into self-exile overseas.

Also, under Kenyatta though the Presidency was sacrosanct (to the degree that no-one could even be "president" of anything), press criticism of anyone below him was tolerated, even if with distaste. Moi's more threatened position led to a massive curtailment of basic press freedoms with criticism of Kenya equated to criticism of the Presidency, itself treasonable. The economic whip was also used to intimidate opposition elements and troublesome deputies who could suddenly find their trading licenses revoked, or their premises found as contravening some section of the (normally-ignored) construction code.

Moi also mounted efforts to sway local electoral contests, something Kenyatta only rarely did. Being throughout his career a regional, rather than national leader, Moi was forced to get involved at grassroots constituency level contests to create supportive personalist alliances of ethnic power-brokers—alliances that under Kenyatta had effortlessly coalesced. Presidential *harambee* funds flowed into districts electing the President's "men," whatever their ethnicities, especially when running against those regarded as "troublesome." Moreover whereas under Kenyatta *harambee* had usually been local communal affairs, only at times organized on a regional basis by important deputies, under Moi *harambee* became regional efforts, to which parliamentarians from all districts were supposed to donate funds, and in which the President via his own donations also acquired exposure, reflecting the more personalized style of rule in Kenya.

While the independent-minded Kenyan electorate was not totally bought off, and many of Moi's preferred candidates or incumbents were defeated, in a sufficient number of contests such efforts did pay off, resulting in a somewhat more docile Assembly. An expansion of the number of Assistant Ministers allowed Moi to claim that *every* one of Kenya's forty districts had at least one "representative" in the executive—attained at huge cost since now there were up to 54 Assistant Ministers on top of 24-27 full-fledged cabinet Ministers.

Moi's need to secure ethnic alliances ultimately led to the unpopular voting reforms of 1986 that were only withdrawn under pro-democracy pressures in December 1990. The reforms eliminated secret balloting by requiring voters to "queue up" in plain sight behind the candidate of their choice at primary (intra-party) elections, following which candidates securing 70% of the primary vote were entitled to run unopposed. The new voting rules were rationalized as being more authentically African, in that people should show their allegiances in public; and more democratic since powerful political barons that in the past determined who would be the local candidates were now by-passed. But the net effect was that only power brokers in opposition to Moi (especially in the Central Province) lost influence, since voters now had to identify themselves as opposing Presidential nominees opening themselves to possible negative repercussions.

Kenya's perennial gadflies, George Anyona and Martin Shikuku, for example, despite popularity in their districts, failed to be re-elected under the new electoral rules; and in the 1988 elections only 127 of 188 seats were contested, voter turnout plummeting, though as in previous elections many incumbents lost their seats.

Despite a more docile Assembly, a major negative side-effect of the reforms was that Moi's stress on building *personal* networks of ethnic proteges unglued the vibrant center-periphery interaction of Kenyatta days. Moi's greater use of executive prerogatives, enhanced KANU clout, and *harambee* funding shunted into political obscurity *de facto* ethnic barons with grassroots support, creating a class of local leaders disgruntled at being locked out of power, and an electorate dissatisfied with electoral outcomes, with destabilizing portents.

A reduction of the historic Kikuyu over-representation in the cabinet brought an infusion of ministers from hitherto peripheral groups, who benefited most under Moi. Yet though Moi's cabinet has been more meticulously balanced than Kenyatta's, Moi's kitchen cabinet, is, like Kenyatta's before him, far more important than the formal cabinet. Composed primarily of Tugen and Kalenjin, cronies and business managers, it is this group that has access to the Presidential ear and input in the decision-making process.

Moi has also greatly privatized Presidential power in his hands. Under Kenyatta many Permanent Secretaries wielded more power than their Ministers, the latter often appointed merely to balance the ethnic picture. Still, Kenyatta had a number of Ministers with significant powers. Moi by contrast, especially since 1982, has delegated extremely little authority to anyone, consulting only a handful of cronies, and has personally exercised follow-up and supervisory control over his minions. Moi, for example, hardly consulted any aides about the Kenya-US defence treaty under which naval rights were granted in exchange for military aid, and the treaty was not even formally reported to Parliament. The result of such decision-making style is even heavier bottlenecks than during the Kenyatta era, despite the fact that Moi puts in four times Kenyatta's office-hours.

By 1989 the accelerated drive to ethnically match the political and administrative hierarchies brought 32 of the 41 districts under Kalenjin District Commissioners, most reporting to Kalenjin Provincial Commissioners (in four cases in control of Kalenjin-headed local police forces), under overall command of John Keen, the veteran Maasai

Assistant Minister in charge of Internal Security in the Presidential Office. And despite a roughly balanced cabinet, nearly two-thirds (21 of 33) of the permanent secretaries in the various ministries were also Kalenjin, with the Kalenjin Head of the Civil Service, Joseph arap Letting, empowered to over-rule any ministerial action. A wide array of Kalenjin also staffed key positions in the economy, in many instances displacing Kikuyu incumbents. These include *inter alia* the Governor of the Central Bank; Minister of Cooperative Development; Commissioner of Cooperatives; Chairman of the Kenya Commercial Bank; Chairman of Kenya National Insurance; Director of Posts; Chairman of the Agricultural Finance Corporation; Chairman of the Agricultural Development Corporation; Director of Kenya Industrial Estates, Chairman of National Cereals and Produce Board; Director of the Kenya Broadcasting Corporation etc.

After the 1988 elections Moi also demoted Vice President Kibaki, and after another short-lived Kikuyu successor, the unwritten rule—that one of the two men at the helm of the nation must be a Kikuyu—fell by the wayside. Cynics even maintain Moi chose as Kibaki's successor a complete novice, Dr. Josephat Karanja, on purpose in order to more easily disencumber himself of Kikuyu Vice Presidents. With only a year's experience (as Assistant Minister), no grass-roots support (he had lost two elections before being elected in 1988), Karanja was easily ousted after an unanimous Assembly motion (initiated by Moi) on grounds of corruption, tribalism and arrogance. His replacement was the Professor of Mathematics George Saitoti, who is still in office today. He is a Maasai, one of the peripheral groups that would not normally figure in any position of importance in a Kikuyu or Luo cabinet. The portals to the Presidency are no longer in Kikuyu hands, further attesting to the fundamentally changed array of power, with peripheral groups (Kalenjin, Maasai, Abaluhyia) now ruling without the benefit of *either* of Kenya's most advanced groups, the Kikuyu or the Luo.

The Regime Unravels

Starting in 1986, Moi's administration came under incessant pressure to liberalize, and it reacted with major crackdowns on all sources of opposition. Hundreds of Kenyans were arrested for membership in the underground *Mwakenya* or Union of Nationalists for the Liberation of Kenya, the outgrowth of the December 12th Movement, that had been set up in 1982 by supporters of *Pambana* (armed struggle) when Kenya had been legislated a single-party state. Even reading *Mwakenya* literature now became a crime. Mostly composed of students and intellectuals ("the bearded men" according to Moi), roughly half were estimated to be Kikuyu, some of whom mounted oathing ceremonies. Though they mostly disseminated anti-Moi pamphlets (that even reached pigeonholes of all Assembly deputies), instances of sabotage followed, leading to armed police riding Kenyan trains for the first time since Mau Mau to prevent derailments or attacks.

The repression continued intermittently throughout 1987, when hundreds of additional *Mwakenya* elements were rounded up, and clampdowns were imposed on the freedom of the press. Private radio transmissions were prohibited throughout Kenya; reporters passing on "malicious lies" to overseas papers were harassed, even arrested; civil servants were required to secure prior permission before visiting foreign embassies; scholars were prohibited from releasing research findings to foreigners; and everyone was enjoined to report to the police any Westerners asking "suspicious" questions in the countryside. (An US political scientist polling Moi's popularity was shortly expelled from Kenya.)

In mid-1987 Amnesty International's 58 page report "Kenya: Torture, Political Detention and Unfair Trials" so incensed Moi that dailies referring to the report were censored, and *The Times* of July 22, 1987 hit news-stands with several pages torn out. So paranoid did Moi develop about negative press coverage that mere possession of papers critical of Kenya became *prima facia* evidence of treasonable intent. Bizarre rumours (e.g. a Klu Klux Klan plot to destabilize Kenya, supported by $100 million in Libyan funds) were given credence, leading to riots in Mombasa.

All the negative publicity Kenya attracted further eroded the country's plummeting image, slowed to a trickle incoming foreign capital, and for the first time brought strong pressure from abroad for liberalization. A livid Moi postponed a scheduled 1987 State Visit to Washington, and similar visits to Norway and Sweden were also postponed after massive foreign media criticism of his visit to these states. Moi's retaliation to these pressures and slights were typical: he haughtily rejected "interference" in Kenya's local affairs, ordered denial of visas to Scandinavian reporters, and redoubled efforts to control domestic groups spreading "lies" abroad.

The late-1980's thus saw new moves to crush, or subordinate, all remaining independent structures in Kenya under KANU's ambit. The thrust was especially against the judicial and the legal profession that appeared to be the main ones strongly standing up against Moi. But demands that the prestigious Law Society of Kenya and the legal profession (continuously at odds with both Kenyatta and Moi over executive excesses) accept KANU overlordship via a forced KANU affiliation and the licensing of lawyers, met strong resistance, gaining the regime additional notoriety abroad. Unlike Kenyatta, Moi had never lived in the West, nor had acquired a sense of the sensitivity of tinkering with the press or the judiciary. To him Kenya's aggressive legal profession, investigative reporters, and independent magistrates were simply an unacceptable anathema.

Starting in 1986 Kenyan judges began resigning over the erosion of *habeas corpus* and the politicization of their tenures. Hitherto appointed for life and immune from executive tinkering, a constitutional amendment in August 1988 changed their terms of service, allowing Moi to dismiss judges at will, whose life-tenure was terminated. The amendment came after earlier voiding of constitutional guarantees of the independence of Kenya's Attorney General and Auditor General, making both Presidential appointees. In June 1988 annual licenses for lawyers were introduced, in effect serving notice that lawyers would in the future be staking their professional livelihood on the line if they supported anti-regime causes. Moi rejected pleas the legal profession could not fulfil its mission if they were thus subject to intimidation as "absurd, ridiculous and obnoxious."[119]

The press clampdowns, elimination of a free judiciary and legal profession, were the clearest signs that authoritarian rule had given way to dictatorship in Kenya. And this at a time when the Berlin Wall was about to fall, the Cold War was over, Kenya's strategic value was much diminished, aid conditionalities were being imposed on countries with poor human records, and more astute African leaders were adjusting accordingly and surviving with their credentials intact. (See Chapter Five.) Kenya, far from being the former darling of the West was now one of Africa's sick men—a handful of states not only not seeing the handwriting on the wall, but actually backsliding into heavy-handed repression.

Late in 1989 a highly publicized incident symbolized the degree to which Moi was out of tune with reality. A prominent Nairobi lawyer, Paul Muite, travelled to the U.S. to accept the Robert F. Kennedy Human Rights Award on behalf of Oxford-trained Gibson Kamau Kuria, who had been denied a passport after nine months imprisonment and torture in 1987—for filing charges against the government for the torture of political detainees. (Mass violations of human rights continued routinely in Kenya: in July 1991 *Africa Watch* released a 329-page report listing some of the more blatant ones.) The immense press coverage given to the award in the US, and the profuse eulogies of Kuria, enraged Moi who earlier had threatened to jail without trial any Amnesty International official who set foot in Kenya. Muite himself was transformed into a martyr when on his return to Nairobi his own passport was revoked, rekindling the story in the global press.

In the meantime social and economic conditions in Kenya had greatly deteriorated and foreign aid was desperately needed. In 1990 unemployment stood at 2.5 million or 40% of the labor force, and crime and violence totally were out of control. Armed robberies took place in broad daylight in downtown Mombasa and Nairobi, and the (badly deteriorated) highway to Mombasa was the scene of banditry and mayhem. (Within a few years armed gangs would routinely invade foreign embassy buildings to rob all and sundry within them. Hooligans disrupted the televized Easter Marlboro Safari Race at Kisumu; game-poaching and banditry by heavily armed marauders (allegedly Somali) made all National Parks unsafe for tourists, many of whom were accosted. And the brutal murder of Julie Ward in the Maasai Mara Park, and the attempted police cover-up (including by the Police Commissioner), revealed the degree to which local game wardens and other State officials were involved in the lawlessness that was spreading throughout the country.

Kenya's 20,000-strong police had always been known, and criticized for excessive use of force, torture, killing of bystanders, and their routine whitewash of any allegation made against them. In 1989 on the average two innocent civilians were killed at the hands of the police every month, with an additional one "disappearing" while in police custody,[120] a figure that by 1995 was amended, by the Minister of Home Affairs himself, to *three deaths a day*! Though the Assistant Minister in charge of Internal Security, John Keen, spoke out against this, police abuses of power continued unabated. In an earlier (1981) incident a policeman arriving at the scene of a car collision in which

Commissioner Ben Gethi was injured and his daughter killed, summarily executed the driver of the second vehicle.

Corruption, always rife in Kenya, by 1990 had become pernicious. The civil service had doubled during Moi's first decade in power (1980-90) to 315,000, though some 34% of them were allegedly bogus employees, whose paychecks were pocketed by department heads and Ministers, at the cost to the State of $64 million per year. Every week details of additional scams and corruption surfaced. One involved Nairobi's announcement of the rejection of a US gift of 116,000 tons of maize (claimed to be of substandard quality) to be followed by the "purchase" at full price of an identical shipment from Thailand—a country that does not export maize. In another a French construction contract for a dam in the Northwest was so laced with government kickbacks that a major price-hike for Kenya's electricity was subsequently necessary. In yet another, prior to a State taxi company passing into receivership it sold eleven perfectly good Mercedes Benz cars to one official at $250-400 each. And audits revealed 40 percent of the 35 million pounds allocated for the hosting of the 1988 All Africa Games in Nairobi was either embezzled or misspent.

Celebrating Moi's 10th anniversary in power in 1988, an Italian marble monument was unveiled in Nairobi depicting Moi's hand grasping a white mace of office. The monument grossly offended the Kikuyu who saw in the *direction* the hand pointed—towards their sacred Mount Kenya—a symbol of Kalenjin overlordship. At the same time the distribution of free milk to pupils in schools had to be terminated when Kikuyu parents would not allow their children to drink it fearing the milk was laced with contraceptives to induce infertility—the penultimate Kalenjin plot to eliminate the Kikuyu as a people. And adding fuel to the fire was Moi's decision to support a Minister who had ordered a shop-owner to remove Kenyatta's portrait that was hanging on the wall alongside Moi's. Soon displaying Kenyatta's photographs was equated with subversion.

All the above underscore the incredible degree to which Kenya's inter-ethnic relations had decayed under Moi. Public life under Kenyatta was no panacea, and had its occasional violent side as has been noted, though the parameters of the permissible were known, and civil life not impinging directly upon the political domain was largely immune from the executive. Under Moi private gestures (commemorating Kenya's founding father) came to be viewed as subversive political manifestations, while Kikuyu could seriously suspect free milk distribution as intended genocide.

The much more highly charged political climate under Moi, and the mounting grievances, ethnic and systemic, against the regime, introduced a degree of instability in the country. That this did not translate in military coups or power-grabs is, of course, a function of the continuation of trade-off and pork-barrel policies that continued to buy the allegiances of those who counted most, and the massive ethnic transformation of the country's security forces, that by the 1990's were a veritable ethnic army. But the staggering costs to the country of such policies, the monumental milking of Kenya's resources by anyone in a position to do so, the mounting frustrations of those locked out of the system of privilege, and the huge grievances against the political system in general, may yet spill out in the form of a popular civic rebellion, especially if Moi runs, as he seems intent to, for another term of office in 1997, or if another Kalenjin (Biwott?) succeeds him. It is likely that in such contexts the Kalenjin units will continue propping the regime with very violent results: what is not clear is whether in such a regime will survive the external and internal repercussions.

Epilogue: Moi's End Game—
Stage-managing Democracy

Many other authoritarian leaders in Africa, aware they could not survive "democracy," resisted external pressures, some to this day, or stage-managed for the benefit of the West a democratic exercise. In Kenya the regime dug in its heels, and when it had its back against the wall, assured its triumphant "democratic" re-election. Nelson Mandela's gentle counsel on a visit to Nairobi, that oppression by black leaders was worse than apartheid, was rejected none-too gently as "totally inappropriate."

The first volley in the tug-of-war that was to usher multiparty-ism in Kenya came as the 1990 New Year pulpit speech of Presbyterian minister Njoya, who generalized from the lesson of Eastern Europe to Kenya's need for multipartyism. With many sources of opposition by now muzzled in Kenya, the clergy had emerged as Moi's main critics.

Njoya's call was vehemently denounced by KANU militants and cabinet ministers, but elicited support from other clergymen, including Bishops Muge and Okullu. The latter further suggested Presidents should be limited to two terms, while Muge, for long a gadfly in the side of the regime, expounded on the need to immediately root out corruption in Kenya.

In May 1990 two former Kikuyu MP's—the Murang'a Kenneth Matiba and Charles Rubia—called for the repeal of Moi's Constitutional amendment that had legislated unipartyism, and proposed a second party. Matiba was a wealthy businessman elected in 1988 by a landslide majority, subsequently to be ousted from KANU after he had publicly clashed with Moi over electoral rigging; Rubia was a very popular Nairobi politician on the regime's black list from Kenyatta days. Their challenge was doubly ominous since they initiated efforts to link up with Oginga Odinga, in a strategy to confront Moi with an unbeatable Kikuyu-Luo political alliance.

Others joined the groundswell of opposition to KANU, emboldened by the rollback of autocracy elsewhere on the continent, including environmentalist Professor Wangari Maathai, who convinced Western donors to withhold finance for the construction of Moi's cherished project—a 60-floor hotel, conference center, and KANU headquarters fronted by a larger-than-life statue of Moi, that would have been Africa's tallest building—but at the expense of decimating Nairobi's sole urban park. Over-reacting and digging his public-relations grave abroad, Moi by ordering her arrest, reminding her that "Kenyan tradition demanded that a woman not criticize a man," while referring to environmentalists as having "insects in their heads."[121]

Pressures for liberalization received a major boost when another in Kenya's political liquidations and police cover-ups took place at this sensitive juncture. The Luo Foreign Minister, Dr. Robert Ouko, was found dead on February 16, 1990, three miles from the farm he had left three days earlier never to be seen alive again. Beaten, then shot in the head, his corpse had also been partly burned in an effort to obliterate it: the police investigation that ensued concluded Ouko had committed suicide! The Luo technocrat had been loyal to the regime, and was a friend of Moi; with no grass-roots support (the Luo still regarded Odinga as their leader) he could not have had political ambitions, the main reason for liquidations to date.

The country's most massive and violent demonstrations since

1982 erupted at Ouko's funeral in Kisumu and in Nairobi, which were quelled by strong GSU contingents. Strong pressure from abroad (where Ouko, regarded as incorruptible, was greatly admired) forced a very reluctant Moi to invite Scotland Yard to review the evidence on Ouko's death. (The veteran Mau Mau leader and Minister Wararu Kanja compared Ouko's murder with Kariuki's when he lamented in Parliament "Is this the freedom we fought for? Did we fight for the freedom to eliminate one another?"[122] and was dismissed by Moi for his speech.) Just as with Julie Ward's murder (when Scotland Yard was also finally brought in), the 2,000-page report revealed a major police cover-up, and directly implicated several top Moi aides in Ouko's murder.

Despite Moi's pledge to do so, Scotland Yard's report was not published for six months. For those implicated in the murder were no less than the Minister of Energy Nicholas Biwott, Kenya's Head of Internal Security Hezekiah Oyugi (one of the few non-Kalenjin in Moi's innermost circle), and several other complete "untouchables" who "know the secrets of the Moi presidency, and could inflict serious damage if they were abandoned."[123] Ouko, it transpired, had clashed with Biwott (one of Kenya's richest men, with 200 million pounds in assets) over the gigantic corruption in the latter's Ministry that had triggered a World Bank ultimatum that no funds would be released to the Ministry so long as Biwott was at its head. Scotland Yard's report was finally released by the investigating officer. None of the individuals were reprimanded, let alone arrested. Oyugi was shifted to head General Motors/Kenya, while Biwott, Moi's closest confidante, former business manager, and Kenya's No. 2 man, was assigned to head the Ministry of Industry. (He remains at the pinnacle of power to this day, and is regarded as a likely successor to Moi.)

Further anger spread throughout Kenya when the Anglican Kalenjin Bishop, Kenya's youngest, Alexander Muge, was killed on August 14th, 1990 in an alleged collision with a truck on his way home from an out-of-town anti-Moi rally. Though possibly a victim of the notoriously high rate of road accidents in Kenya, Muge had been explicitly warned not to attend the rally, and most Kenyans assumed he too was murdered. His bishop-colleagues and the Anglican Council of Churches indeed concluded that "having due regards for the circumstances preceding his death, it would be imprudent to presume that our late brother died in an accident" since the Church's investigation revealed evidence "at variance with the police reports," suggesting foul play.[124] Anglican Bishop Okullu, delivering a sermon at Kisumu Cathedral, openly called on Moi to resign immediately.

It is against this explosive background that Matiba and Rubia mounted their pro-democracy challenge, aware that U.S. Congressional hearings and other foreign re-assessments of the regime would greatly constrain its reaction against them. A request for a permit to hold a mass meeting on multipartyism in Nairobi by their Foundation for the Restoration of Democracy (Ford) was, however, denied. The US Ambassador's public recommendation that dissenters be allowed to speak out evoked a banner headline "Shut Up Mr. Ambassador" in the government's *Kenya Times* daily on July 8th. In the absence of a permit Matiba and Rubia cancelled their meeting, and called on supporters not to come. They were nevertheless arrested with 17 others, the first of hundreds to follow.

Large crowds began marching in downtown Nairobi (and in the Kikuyu towns of Nakuru, Naivasho, Nyeri, Murang'a and Kiambu) with placards calling "Free Matiba" and chanting "Down with Moi." A three-day orgy of violence ensued, the most bloody since the 1982 military mutiny. The crowds were joined by supporters of the underground Mwakenya calling for armed insurrection, with Ngugi wa Thiong'o being named as Moi's replacement. Heavy units of the GSU dispelled the masses by first shooting in the air, later by shooting into the crowds. The death toll was not revealed, but was in the hundreds. The riots stiffened Moi's resolve not to give in to "hooligans and drug addicts" spurred by "the Scandinavian countries and the U.S" and a wave of 1,500 arrests soon commenced.[125]

Foreign retaliation to Kenya's turmoil was swift. The Scandinavian countries issued an ultimatum calling for multipartyism and the release of political detainees as a condition for any further aid, as did the EEC and the U.S., that also condemned suppression of dissent, and defended the U.S. Ambassador's grant of asylum to Gibson Kamau Kuria. The State Department issued travel warnings to Americans, threatening Kenya's prime foreign exchange earner, tourism. The International Bar Association became the first of several to cancel a world congress in Nairobi citing Kenya's human rights violations and instability. The regime joined battle by accusing the US and other governments of "mastermind[ing] and abett[ing]" opposition to KANU; the American Ambassador was specifically referred to as a "racist slave-owner with contempt for Africans."[126]

The tug-of-war between Moi and pro-democracy elements continued, with competitive elections equated with a return to ethnic politics that would lead Kenya to chaos from which it had been spared by the "national" KANU: "We are being asked to risk that which we have so painstakingly built in order to live up to some generalized universal prescriptions of political behaviour."[127] And in an attempt to split Kikuyu loyalties and deflect Murang'a's power bid, Moi appointed an old foe, Kiambu Njoroge Mungai to the cabinet.

Despite the universality of the democracy movement, the main leaders were initially Kikuyu. All the towns that experienced major disturbances in 1990 were Kikuyu. Since Moi all along saw his gravest threat coming from the Kikuyu, their leaders and interests were especially harassed, and in the process the Kikuyu became even more marginalized. Their main leaders were shunted aside; their representation in the cabinet went down below their demographic numbers, and few Kikuyu held any of the key Ministries. Budgetary allocations saw a shift of resources for road-building, industry, clinics and schools from the Central Province to other regions, notably Moi's own Rift Valley. A controversial new educational quota system also favored the less populated provinces, discriminating against the populous Central Province, further antagonizing education-prone Kikuyu. Kikuyu economic interests also suffered deeply. Though 80% of Kenya's coffee crop was grown in Kikuyuland, their lobby—the Kenya Coffee Growers Union—was deregistered, and Moi loyalists (especially Kalenjin, including a Presidential brother-in-law) were appointed to key posts in the marketing of coffee. The same occurred with respect to the tea industry in which 60% of tea-growers were Kikuyu.

To placate public opinion and project an image of reason, Moi sent Vice President Saitoti to explore possible structural reforms needed to quell the public malaise. Saitoti gathered so much evidence of basic antagonisms to the regime that his report was not published, though the Assembly debated some of its findings. In December 1990, however, Moi annulled the 1988 queueing electoral change in a belated bid to regain the support of district political barons, and to appease overseas critics. The gesture, for what it was worth, was wasted, since by then only open competitive elections were acceptable.

In February 1991 the sick, almost blind, indomitable 80-year old Oginga Odinga challenged the regime to arrest him by announcing his affiliation with Ford while launching a new party, defying existing legislation that he publicly declared was null and void since it was undemocratic. The fact that Odinga was not arrested (except briefly), was the best testimony of the immense pressures being brought upon Moi to liberalize, and by the end of 1991 the pressures finally paid off.

Warning of the dire consequences of the introduction of "ethnic politics" in Kenya, Moi amended the constitution in mid-December to allow multipartyism. Immediately a massive political re-alignment took place as numerous former KANU stalwarts deserted for the opposition, including KANU's Secretary General who joined Ford. Observers noted how "as more former Moi aides climb aboard, Ford will find it increasingly difficult to argue that its new members will bring new and honest government to Kenya."[128] Moreover, though in January 1992 Ford was able to mobilize hundreds of thousands of people in Kenya's first legal anti-government rally, within a week of its legalization the party was sharply divided as to who would lead it.

Both the Luhya Martin Shikuku and Luo Oginga Odinga claimed leadership. Shikuku soon dropped as frontrunner, to be replaced by the Kikuyu millionaire businessman Matiba and Paul Muite (of the Law Society of Kenya), with the 70-year old veteran MP and Ford Vice-Chairman Masinde Muliro trying to soothe the cleavages. By August Ford's unity was in complete tatters, and Muliro's death that month removed a neutral bridge between the two main camps. As Odinga's leadership was categorically unacceptable by the Kikuyu political barons, Ford split along historic Kikuyu-Luo lines. One group, known as Ford-Kenya, and largely Luo and Luhya emerged under Odinga's leadership, the other, largely Kikuyu emerged as Ford-Asili, under Matiba's leadership with Shikuku as his increasingly independently-minded deputy. Together with six additional parties that also emerged (notably a Democratic Party, under the Nyeri Kibaki's leadership), Moi's and KANU's electoral prospects suddenly were not as dim as had appeared earlier.

More ominously, a wave of ethnic killings (mostly by Kalenjin) spread throughout the Rift Valley Province, as if to vindicate Moi's dire warning that multipartyism would heighten ethnic strife. The overt involvement of the security forces (for over two years) in transporting Kalenjin warriors (armed with spears and arrows) to "ethnically cleanse" the Rift Valley localities taken over by the Kikuyu before and during the Kenyatta presidency, put to mock such claims and suggested instead that a "KANU Zone" was being solidified in the West.[129]

(By mid-1993 some 1,000 people had been killed in the Valley, and 120,000 had been displaced to refugee camps.)

In the run up to the December 1992 elections a large amount of money was printed by the government, a fact that helped the beleaguered Moi, and additional funds were printed after the elections, contributed to the heavy inflation in subsequent years. Though there was evidence of vote-rigging in the elections that were monitored by outside observers, ultimately it was really the disunity of the opposition that handed Moi his double-barrelled electoral victories. KANU captured 100 of the Assembly's 188 seats (plus 12 more the President is entitled to nominate), while in the Presidential contest Moi won with 36 percent of the vote. (Shortly later Odinga's death resulted in another split within Ford-Kenya, as Michael Kijana and one of Odinga's sons, Raila, tore the party apart.)

With Kenya having met basic Western demands for political liberalization, various aid programs recommenced, though only in spurts for now it was the massive corruption and ever-brazen embezzlement of funds to trigger ultimatums. In 1994 a World Bank investigator brought in for that purpose uncovered a scam in Kenya Post and Telecommunication that cost Kenya at least $100 million; the managing director who was dismissed at the insistence of the West, was merely shifted to head a Development Authority, with only slightly lesser opportunities for graft. As one source observed "No major cabinet member or civil servant has ever been prosecuted for fraud,"[130]

The "democratized" regime, moreover, rapidly fell into its old ways, and by mid-1993 there were again assaults against the freedom of the press, that by now was one of the continent's most harassed. Publications were banned, printing presses were publicly destroyed by the police, and editors and reporters were imprisoned for writing reports critical of the regime. In February 1996 a Press Bill was passed that once and for all muzzled unacceptable reporting.

As Kenya lurches towards its second "free" elections in 1997, Moi has few of the traditional props the trade-off modality offers, though his security forces have stood by him throughout. He is hemmed in by budgetary deficits, mass unemployment, intermittent freezes on foreign aid and foreign capital, little grass-roots support outside his own region and none from the ethnic barons he emasculated in the 1980's. He is by now also personally threatened by Ford pledges to place him on trial for political and economic misdeeds should Ford win the elections, and during the 1992 elections there were also threats of a bloody retribution against the Kalenjin should Moi have lost the elections. The country is sharply divided; the Luhya, once part of the Moi alliance have largely deserted Moi after the elimination of some of their key leaders in 1993, while on the coast an Islamic Party of Kenya has emerged among the Kiswahili.

A succession looms on the horizon, that is also clouded by some curious machinations by Moi. His intermittent talk about "majimbo" (federalism), together with the continuing Rift Valley ethnic cleansing, and a project to build an international airport at Eldoret, his home town, suggested an attempt to give the Kalenjin some protection should the aftermath of his presidency bring retribution. For both sick, and aged, at 70, Moi has at most one more term he could serve, if at all. His vice-president and technically heir-apparent, is the Maasai, Saitoti, both unpopular and without a powerful ethnic base. Just like a decade and a half previously when plots abounded to oust Moi before he could assume the Presidency, so are there currently manoeuvrings, notably by Nicholas Biwott.

In January 1995 Moi collapsed in a State function in Nakuru, following which he had a phlebitis operation. It is within this context that a new political formation emerged when Dr. Richard Leakey, the scientist and environmentalist, announced the formation of a new party, Safina (Noah's Ark), together with Paul Muite. Immediately vilified as a racist and colonialist, Leakey became the target of war-chanting Maasai, a "spontaneous" but organized physical assault in Nakuru in which the police did not intervene and indeed blamed Leakey for instigating the violence, and later of assassination threats. What scared the establishment was that Leakey's challenge might just work in politics-weary Kenya precisely because it was so novel, and in light of Leakey's immense prestige abroad, and reputation at home in succeeding in everything he commenced. Though technicalities were used not to register the party, Leakey's greatest enemy seem to have been an inability to convince either his partner, or the other parties whom he approached, to form a united front and concentrate on defeating Moi. Ultimately it may be this perennial Kenyan inability to join across ethnic boundaries that has proven its undoing.

Miller has noted that stability based on trade-off rests "on whether or not the elite can garner enough resources—money, jobs, contracts and the like—to keep Kenya's patronage system operating."[131]

Stability came to Kenya because of "the growth of an entrepreneurial and professional elite linking politicians, civil servants, businessmen, the military, large-scale farmers and professional people."[132] In 1977 Kibaki reiterated Kenya rejected "a policy of social justice at the expense of individual freedom," since the Constitution provided equality of opportunity but not of income.[133] Apart from Moi's dissipation of legitimacy via authoritarian policies, instability has been growing in Kenya precisely because the binding glue of individual free enterprise wheeling-dealing has been eroded by State patronage over- commitments starting towards the latter days of the Kenyatta Presidency and gathering greater momentum under Moi's. Today the regime cannot satisfy minimal societal needs; it has been unable to cater "to new needs, has shunted true change and new blood...and via the uneducated unemployed [has] become unstable."[134] *The Economist* noted in its November 1991 assessment "kleptocracy and tribalism have not served Kenya badly." It was excessive "greed" and the "extortionate" costs of patronage under Moi that helped erode his Presidency[135], by completely stunting wider societal development prospects and wider individual upward-mobility, and by drying up the very wells of patronage that ultimately sustained the regime. The following can be seen as summing up the main grievances against Moi: "Under Kenyatta everybody stole and everybody was encouraged to get big. Now people are afraid to get big, because if they do, the president might notice and take their businesses."[136]

NOTES

1. For just a sample of the voluminous early literature on Kenya see the 5981-item (plus addenda) bibliography by Ole Norgaard, *Kenya in the Social Sciences. An Annotated Bibliography 1967-1979*, Nairobi, Kenya Literature Bureau, 1980.

2. Norman N. Miller, *Kenya: The Quest for Prosperity*, Boulder, Co., Westview Press, 1984, p.1.

3. Godfrey Muriuki, "Background to Politics and Nationalism in Colonial Kenya," in Bethwell A. Ogot (ed.), *Politics and Nationalism in Colonial Africa*, Nairobi, East African Publishing House, 1972, p. 7.

4. Robert L. Tignor, *The Colonial Transformation of Kenya: The Kamba, Kikuyu and Maasai from 1900 to 1939*, Princeton, Princeton University Press, 1975, p.14. Or as Meisler put it, "wealth counts more than genealogy." Stanley Meisler, "Tribal politics harass Kenya," *Foreign Affairs*, vol. 49, 1970, pp. 111-121.

5. Kivuto Ndeti, *Elements of Akamba Life*, Nairobi, East African Publishing House, 1972, p. 189.

6. See John Lamphear, "The Kamba and the Northern Mrima Coast," in Richard Gray and David Birmingham (eds.), *Pre-Colonial Africa Trade*, London, Oxford University Press, 1970, pp. 75-101; J. Forbes Munro, *Colonial Rule and the Kamba: Social Change in the Kenya Highlands, 1889-1939*, Oxford, Clarendon Press, 1975.

7. Dirk Berg-Schlosser, *Tradition and Change in Kenya: A Comparative Analysis of Seven Major ethnic groups*, Paderborn (Germany), Ferdinand Schoningh, 1984, p. 148. See also J. E. G. Sutton, "The Kalenjin," in B. A. Ogot (ed.), *Kenya before 1900*, Nairobi, East African Publishing House, 1976.

8. S. S. Ole Sankan, *The Maasai*, Nairobi, East African Literature Bureau, 1971.

9. Bethwell A. Ogot, *The History of the Southern Luo*, Nairobi, East African Publishing House, 1967; H. O. Ayot, *A History of the Luo-Abasuba*, Nairobi, Kenya Literature Bureau, 1979.

10. J. Osogo, *A History of the Baluyia*, Nairobi, Oxford University Press, 1966; Gideon S. Were, *A History of the Abuluyia of Western Kenya, c.1500-1930*, Nairobi, East African Publishing House, 1967.

11. Berg-Schlosser, p. 104.

12. See the section on the Mijikenda in B. A. Ogot (ed.), *Kenya Before 1900*.

13. See F.S. Berg, "The Coast from the Portuguese Invasion to the Rise of the Zanzibar Sultanate," and Neville H. Chittick, "The Coast before the Arrival of the Portuguese," both in Bethwell A. Ogot (ed.), *Zamani: A Survey of East African History*, London, Longman, 1973, pp. 115-34 and pp. 98-114 respectively. See also A. I. Salim, *People of the Coast*, London, Evans Brothers, 1978.

14. See A. T. Matson, *Nandi Resistance to British Rule 1890-1906*, Nairobi, East African Publishing House, 1972. Groups collaborating with the British included the Maasai, some Kamba and some Luhya.

15. Colin Leys, *Underdevelopment in Kenya: The Political Economy of Neo-Colonialism, 1964-1971*, Berkeley, University of California Press, 1974, p. 29. The best study on the origins of the White Highlands remains M.P.K. Sorrenson, *The Origins of European Settlement in Kenya*, Nairobi, Oxford University Press, 1968. See also D. Kennedy, *Islands of White: Settler Society in Kenya and Southern Rhodesia 1890-1939*, Durham, Duke University Press, 1987.

16. For the general outlines of British colonialism see *inter alia* B. A. Ogot, "Kenya Under the British, 1895 to 1963," in B. A. Ogot (ed.), *Zamani. A Survey of East African History*; John Lonsdale and Bruce Berman, "Coping with the Contradictions: The Development of the Colonial State in Kenya 1895-1914," *Journal of African History*, vol 20, 1979, pp. 487-505; Richard D. Wolff, *The Economics of Colonialism: Britain and Kenya 1870-1930*, New Haven, Yale University Press, 1974; George Bennett, *Kenya. A Political History*, London, Oxford University Press, 1973; M. R. Dilley, *British Policy in Kenya Colony*, London, Cass, 1966, and Leys, *Underdevelopment in Kenya*.

17. See the tables in Morrison et al., *Black Africa*, p. 70, 79.

18. Philip M. Mbithi and Rasmus Rasmusson, *Self-Reliance in Kenya: The Case of Harambee*, Uppsala, Scandinavian Institute of African Studies, 1977, p. 14.

19. For very interesting data on Nandi ex-*askaris* suggestiing that a lesser acculturation role should be assigned to service in Britain's colonial forces see Lewis J. Greenstein, "The Impact of Military Service in World War I on Africans: the Nandi of Kenya," *Journal of Modern African Studies*, September 1978, pp. 495-507.

20. H. F.Morris, *The Indians in Uganda. Caste and Sect in a Plural Society*, London, Weidelfeld and Nicolson, 1968, p. 11.

21. The root of the words have never been satisfactorily explained. For its origins see F. Furedi, "The Initial Composition of the Mau Mau movement in the White Highlands," *Journal of Peasant Studies*, vol.1 N.4, 1973. See also chapter 6 of John Spencer, *KAU: The Kenya African Union*, KPI Ltd., London, 1985, that provides very useful background.

22. Carl G. Rosberg and Jack Nottingham, *The Myth of Mau Mau*, New York, Praeger, 1966, p. 44. The work is still one of the best on Mau Mau, and the first to recognise the movement as a *nationalist* one. See also especially David W. Throup, *Economic and Social Origins of Mau Mau, 1945-53*, London, James Currey, 1987, and "The Origins of Mau Mau," *African Affairs*, July 1985, pp. 309-433.

23. Kenya. *Legislative Council Debates*, December 20, 1948, column 508.

24. Herbert H. Werlin, *Governing an African City: A Study of Nairobi*, New York, Africana Publishing Co., p. 46.

25. George Bennett and Carl G Rosberg, *The Kenyatta Election: Kenya 1960-1961*, New York, Oxford University Press, p. 5.

26. John J. Okumo, "The Problem of Tribalism in Kenya," in Pierre Van den Berghe, *Race and Ethnicity in Africa*, Nairobi, East African Publishing House, 1975, p. 189.

27. Tom Mboya, *Freedom and After*, London, Andre Deutsch, 1963, p. 75.

28. Werlin, p. 76.

29. The two parties have been accurately described as "cartels composed of district organizations over which the national leadership had little influence." Joel D. Barkan and John J. Okumo, "'Semi-Competitive' Elections, Clientelism, and Political Recruitment in a No-Party State: The Kenyan Experience," in Guy Hermet et al., *Elections without Choice*, London, Macmillan, 1978, p. 94.

30. For biographical details on all Kenyan personalities see Bethwell A. Ogot, *Historical Dictionary of Kenya*, Metuchen, N. J., Scarecrow Press, 1986. For Odinga's autobiography see his *Not yet Uhuru*, London, 1967. For a masterful study of the evolution of the Kenya African Union see John Spencer's *KAU: The Kenya African Union*, London, KPI Ltd., 1985.

31. See David Goldsworthy, "Ethnicity and Leadership in Africa," *Journal of Modern African Studies*, vol. 20 N. 1, 1982, p. 114) as well as that author's *Tom Mboya. A Man Kenya wanted to Forget*, London, Heinemann, 1982.

32. For Kaggia's autobiography see his *Roots of Freedom 1921-1963*, Nairobi, 1975.

33. John W. Harbeson, "Land Reform and Politics in Kenya 1954-1970," *Journal of Modern African Studies*, August 1971, p. 245. See also his *Nation-building in Kenya: The Role of Land Reform*, Evanston, Northwestern University Press, 1973.

34. "Public Opinion Poll N. 4," Nairobi, The Market Research Co. of East Africa, 1961 p. 9.

35. Harold D. Nelson, *Kenya: A Country Study*, Washington, D. C., Government Printing Office, 1984, p. 38.

36. For details see George Bennett, "Kenya's Little General Election," *World Today*, August 1966. See also Cherry Gertzel, *The Politics of Independent Kenya 1963-8*, Nairobi, East African Publishing House, 1972, chapter 4; and Susanne D. Mueller, "Government and Opposition in Kenya, 1966-9," *Journal of Modern African Studies*, vol. 22 N. 3, 1984.

37. Mboya's Kikuyu assassin implicated people higher up in the government, and Goldsworthy (in his work *Tom Mboya*) traces the order to elements close to Kenyatta.

38. Michael F. Lofchie, "Kenya's Agricultural Success," *Current History*, May 1986, pp.221.

39. D. K. Fieldhouse, *Black Africa 1945-1980. Economic Decolonization and Arrested Development*, London, Allen Unwin, 1986, p. 163.

40. G. K. Ikiara and T. Killick "The performance of the Economy since Independence," in Tony Killick, (ed), *Papers on the Kenya Economy*, London, Heinemann, 1981 p. 17.

41. Donald Rothchild, "Hegemonial Exchange: An alternative model for managing conflict in Middle Africa," in Dennis Thompson and Dov

Ronen, *Ethnicity, Politics and Development*, Boulder, Co., Lynne Rienner, 1986, p. 6. Former Finance Minister Mwai Kibaki put it bluntly "Kenya will not pursue a policy of social justice at the expense of individual freedom," adding the classical argument that the Constitution provided equality of opportunity and not of income. *Nairobi Times*, December 4, 1977.

42. International Bank for Reconstruction and Development, *Kenya: Into the Second Decade*, Baltimore, The Johns Hopkins University Press, 1975, p. 5.

43. William J. House and Tony Killick "Inequality and Poverty in the Rural Economy" in Tony Killick, (ed), *Papers on the Kenya Economy*, p. 165. See also John Carlsen, *Economic and Social Transformation in Rural Kenya*, Uppsala, Scandinavian Institute of African Studies, 1980.

44. Hazelwood, *The Economy of Kenya*, Table 5.5. The majority of the Gross Domestic Product has remained foreign-controlled; in 1982 fully 62%, up from 59% in 1972 and 57% in 1967.

45. See Michael Bratton "Structural Transformation in Zimbabwe: Comparative Notes from the neo-colonization of Kenya," *Journal of Modern African Studies*, vol 15, N.4, 1977, p.597. There is controversy in the literature as to whether local capital has, or could ever have, supplanted external capital. In various ways Leys (*Underdevelopment in Kenya*), Langdon (*Multinational Corporations*) and Kaplinsky (Rafael Kaplinsky, "Capital Accumulation in the Periphery: Kenya," in M. Fransman (ed.), *Industry and Accumulation in Africa*, London, 1982, and R. Kaplinsky, "Capitalist Accumulation in the Periphery—the Kenyan case re-examined," *Review of African Political Economy*, vol. 17, 1980, pp. 83-113) have argued that local Kenyan capitalists cannot, and have not been able, to stand up to multinationals. Rather, Kenyans have used State backing to acquire lucrative but powerless senior positions with local subsidiaries of the multinationals, or have similarly served as titular front men for foreign interests progressively being squeezed out by the various indigenization restrictions.

46. IBRD, *Kenya*, p. 298; Fieldhouse, p. 166.

47. Njonjo, A. "The Kenyan Peasantry: A Reassessment," *Review of African Political Economy*, N. 20, April-June 1981, p. 39.

48. Fieldhouse, p. 171.

49. Hazlewood *The Economy of Kenya*, p. 175. Or as two other authors put it, "inequality has been built into the country's rural economy by the forces of nature," William J. House and Tony Killick, "Social Justice and Development Policy in Kenya's Rural Economy," in Dharam Ghai and Samir Radwan, *Agrarian Policies and Rural Poverty*, Geneva, ILO, p. 31.

50. R. Bates, *Markets and States in Tropical Africa*, Berkeley, University of California Press, 1981, p. 27.

51. The Waruhiu Report, 1980, p. 37

52. P. Anyang' Nyong'o, "State and Society in Kenya: The Disintegration of the Nationalist Coalitions and the Rise of Presidential Authoritarianism," *African Affairs*, April 1989. For some key studies of Kenya's politics see Cherry Gertzel, *The Politics of Independent Kenya 1963-1968*, Nairobi, East African Publishing House, 1972; Henry Bienen, *The Politics of Participation and Control*, Princeton, Princeton University Press, 1974; Joel D. Barkan and John J. Okumu (eds.), *Politics and Public Policy in Kenya and Tanzania*, New York, Praeger, 1979 and Norman N. Miller, *Kenya: The Quest for Prosperity*, Boulder, Co., Westview Press, 1984.

53. "Kenya: Watching the Wananchi," *Africa Confidential*, Oct 5, 1973, p.5.

54. *Ibid*.

55. Joel D. Barkan, "The Electoral Process and Peasant-State Relations in Kenya," in Fred Hayward (ed.), *Elections in Independent Africa*, pp. 213-15.

56. *Ibid*.

57. John J. Okumu, "Party and Party-State Relations," in Joel D. Barkan and John J. Okumo, (eds.), *Politics and Public Policy*, p. 59.

58. The rubric under which Kenyatta is placed by Robert H. Jackson and Carl G. Rosberg in their classic *Personal Rule in Black Africa*, Berkeley, University of California Press, 1982.

59. Donald Rothchild, "Hegemonial Exchange: An alternative model for managing conflict in Middle Africa," in Dennis Thompson and Dov Ronen, *Ethnicity, Politics and Development*, Boulder, Co., Lynne Rienner, 1986. p.80.

60. *Joe* (Nairobi), October 1974.

61. John Anderson, *The Struggle for School*, Nairobi, Longman's, 1976, p. 162.

62. *Afriscope* (Lagos), January 1975.

63. *Daily News* (Nairobi), November 8, 1979.

64. *Weekly Review* (Nairobi), 26 February 1982. Note that the issue of acquiring wealth in office is *not* at question, only the amount. For an excellent study of the National Assembly see Charles Hornsby, "The Social Structure of the National Assembly in Kenya, 1953-1983," *Journal of Modern African Studies*, vol. 27 N. 2, 1989.

65. Barkan in Hayward (ed.), p. 232. See also Joel D. Barkan, "Comment: Further Reassessment of 'Conventional Wisdom': Political Knowledge and Voting behaviour in rural Kenya," *American Political Science Review*, vol. 70 N. 2, 1976, pp. 452-55.

66. Philip M. Mbithi and Rasmus Rasmusson, *Self-Reliance in Kenya: The*

Case of Harambee, Uppsala, Scandinavian Institute of African Studies, 1977. p. 14. See also Barbara P. Thomas, "Development through *harambee*: Who wins and Who loses? Rural self-help projects in Kenya." World Development, vol. 15 N. 4, 1987, pp. 463-81.

67. Barkan in Hayward (ed.). pp. 230-231.

68. There were, for example, 1617 questions fielded at the front benches in 1964. (Gertzel, *The Politics of Independent Kenya*, p. 160.) In 1968 backbenchers asked 1477 questions (compared to 4 only in Zambia), and presented 35 substantive motions and one bill (vis 0 in Zambia.) Jay R. Hakes and John L. Helgerson, "Bargaining and Parliamentary Behaviour in Africa: A Comparative Study of Zambia and Kenya," in Allan Kornberg (ed.), *Legislatures in Comparative Perspective*, New York, David McKay, 1973, p. 350.

69. Raymond F. Hopkins, "The Kenyan Legislature: Political Functions and Citizen Perceptions," in G. R. Boynton and Chong Lim Kim (eds.), *Legislative Systems in Developing Countries*, Durham, Duke University Press, 1975, p. 216.

70. Cited in *Africa Research Bulletin*, Political Series, April 1975.

71. *The Sunday Times*, London, August 10, 1975.

72. Legum (ed.), *Africa Contemporary Record 1975-76*, p. B129.

73. See "Kenya: On the slippery Slope," *Africa Confidential*, March 21, 1975.

74. *Africa Confidential*, June 20, 1975.

75. *The Times*, March 17, 1975.

76. As Gertzel notes (*The Politics of Independent Kenya*, p. 67) "Kenyan politics has a tradition of violence." Kenya's first political murder was that of the lawyer and Specially Elected KANU deputy Pio Gama Pinto—a radical nationalist Indian who had been imprisoned by the British in 1954 for four years for actively supporting Mau Mau—who was assassinated in downtown Nairobi in February 1965, much like Tom Mboya's later liquidation in 1966. Though Njenga Njeroge was hanged for Mboya's murder, he claimed to have been commissioned to do so, complaining "Why pick on me? Why not the Big Man? We did what we were told." Colin Legum (ed.), *Africa Contemporary Record 1969-70*, p. B213.

77. *The Times*, March 17, 1975.

78. *Sunday Times* 7 August 1975.

79. *Financial Times*, June 5, 1975.

80. *Weekly Review* (Nairobi), October 27, 1974.

81. *The New York Times*, October 17, 1975.

82. Cited in Colin Legum (ed.), *Africa Contemporary Record 1975-76*, p. B220.

83. Colin Legum (ed.), *Africa Contemporary Record, 1973/4*, p. B226.

84. Colin Legum (ed.), *Africa Contemporary Record 1973/4*, p. B127.

85. See Donald Rothchild "Ethnic Inequalities in Kenya" *Journal of Modern African Studies*, vol. 7 N. 4, 1969, pp. 689-711.

86. Colin Legum (ed.), *Africa Contemporary Record 1975-76*, p. B172.

87. G. F. O. Oduya in the National Assembly debates; see Kenya. *House of Representatives Debates*, XIV, Sixth Session, 27 February 1968, col. 66.

88. Colin Leys, *Kenya*, p. 249.

89. The well-known Kiambu/Murang'a/Nyeri split among the Kikuyu is parallelled, for example, by the Maasai split into two ethnic blocks supportive of Stanley Oloitiptip and John Keen; the Paul Ngei and Mwendwe/Munyashya factions among the Kamba; the antagonistic Moi-Seroney split of Kalenjin loyalties etc.

90. "Kenya: Patterns of Power," *Africa Confidential*, September 6, 1974, p. 4.

91. Gertzel, *The Politics of Independent Kenya*, p. 28.

92. Joel D. Barkan, "Legislators, Elections, and Political Linkages," in Barkan and Okumu (eds.), *Politics and Public Policy*, p. 105.

93. Waruhiyu Report, p. 39. See also H. J. Nyamu, "The State of the Civil Service Today," Nairobi, Government Printer, 1974.

94. *Third World Record*, June 28, 1976, p. 3.

95. *Sunday Daily Nation*, October 9, 1976.

96. *Sunday Times*, October 7, 1976.

97. Njonjo revealed the plot to Parliament at the end of October. See *Weekly Review*, November 4, 1978, and Joseph Karimi and Phillip Ochieng, *The Kenyatta Succession*, Nairobi, 1980. See also Mordechai Tamarkin, "From Kenyatta to Moi: The anatomy of a peaceful transition of power," *Africa Today*, vol. 26, N. 3, 1979 and Vincent B. Khapoya, "The Politics of Succession in Africa: Kenya after Kenyatta," *Ibid*.

98. Cited in Legum (ed.), *Africa Contemporary Record 1984-5*, 1985, p. B262.

99. *Africa Confidential* November 27, 1970. Moi's philosophy is encapsulated in his *Kenya African Nationalism*, Nairobi, Heinemann, 1986. See also George I. Godia, *Understanding Nyayo*, Nairobi, Transafrica, 1984. An austere missionary-educated Tugen (the smallest of the Kalenjin groups), Moi was born to a poor farming family in the arid Baringo district of the Rift Valley

Province, becoming a schoolteacher and later headmaster. In 1955 he became one of Kenya's first eight MP's, and joined Kenyatta's government as Minister of Home Affairs, later, after Odinga's eclipse, as Vice President. For biographical details see Ogot, *Historical Dictionary of Kenya*.

100. Legum (ed.), *Africa Contemporary Record 1983-84*, 1984, p. B269.

101. Legum (ed.), *Africa Contemporary Record 1982-83*, 1982, p. B191.

102. Mordechai Tamarkin, "Recent Development in Kenyan Politics: The Fall of Charles Njonjo," *Journal of Contemporary African Affairs* (Pretoria), vol. 3 N. 1/2, October 1983-April 1984, p. 60, 68.

103. Legum (ed.), *Africa Contemporary Record 1984-5*, 1985, p. B261. See also "Kenya: The Emperor's Clothes,"

104. *Africa Research Bulletin*, Political Series, April 1982.

105. Kenya, *National Assembly Debates*, 30 June 1983, vol. 60, col. 2346-7.

106. "Kenya: The Emperor's Clothes," *Africa Confidential*, January 2, 1985, p.5.

107. "Kenyatta's Kenya," *Africa Confidential*, Nov. 27, 1970, p. 2.

108. Ali Mazrui and Donald Rothchild, "The Soldier and the State in East Africa: Some Theoretical Conclusions on the army mutinies of 1964," *Western Political Quarterly*, N. 2, 1971, pp. 82-96.

109. Tamarkin, "The Roots of Political Stability," p. 301.

110. Goldsworthy in Baynham, p. 108.

111. *Ibid.*

112. *Weekly Review*, March 7, 1977.

113. *Africa Confidential*, 15 October, 1981.

114. Tamarkin, "The Roots of Political Stability," p. 301.

115. For the Air Force revolt see "Kenya: How?" *Africa Confidential*, August 4, 1982; "A mercifully short Reign of Terror," *Weekly Review*, August 6, 1982, pp. 3-17; "Kenya: Post-mortem," *Africa Confidential* August 25, 1982. *Africa Research Bulletin*, Political Series, September 1982.

116. *Weekly Review*, December 31, 1982.

117. The *Weekly Review* noted in its October 22, 1982 issue that there had been a steady accretion of Marxist lecturers on campus, and that a major generational gap had developed between students and intellectuals and the wider public. *Pambana* (Wrestling) was the organ of the December 12th Movement, a well-written documentation of the various peccadilloes and misdemeanours of the establishment, mere possession of which in October 1982 carried a six year prison sentence.

118. Colin Legum (ed.), *Africa Contemporary Record 1971-72*, 1972, p. B126; and Financial Times, August 30, 1978, respectively.

119. "Kenya: Lawyers Lament," *Africa Confidential*, 26 January 1990, p. 4.

120. *Africa Newsfile*, March 1989.

121. *The New York Times*, February 11, 1989.

122. Todd Shields, "Lawyers vs. The Law," *Africa Report*, September 1990, p. 20.

123. "Kenya: Ouko's ghost," *Africa Confidential*, May 31, 1991, p. 5.

124. Shields, p.16.

125. *Ibid*.

126. *Africa Research Bulletin*, Political Series, November 1991.

127. *Africa Research Bulletin*, Political Series, August 1990.

128. *Africa Research Bulletin*, Political Series, December 1991.

129. See *Divide and Rule: State-Sponsored Ethnic violence in Kenya*, New York, Africa Watch, 1993.

130. "Kenya: A Difficult Courtship," *Africa Confidential*, October 8, 1993, p. 5.

131. Miller, *Kenya: The Quest for Prosperity*, p. 149.

132. Colin Legum (ed.), *Africa Contemporary Record 1972-73*, 1973, p. B150.

133. *Nairobi Times*, December 4, 1977.

134. Emmit B. Evans Jr.,"Sources of Socio-political instability in an African State: The case of Kenya's educated unemployed," *African Studies Review*, vol. 20 N. 1, April 1977, p. 52.

135. *The Economist*, November 30, 1991.

136. Michael Maren, "Kenya: Hear No Evil," *Africa Report*, November-December 1986, p. 70.

CHAPTER FIVE:

TOWARDS THE REDEMOCRATIZATION OF THE CONTINENT[*]

Possibly as unanticipated as the monumental changes that transpired in Eastern Europe was the sudden coalescence of a critical mass of pro-democracy pressures in Africa in the late 1980's. Demonstrations in favor of a new political order began to be heard in a continent where scholars have argued "it cannot be said that democracy has failed... because in most countries it has never been tried."[1] Bongo himself was to refer to these rumbles of discontent as "wind from the East that is shaking the coconut trees"[2]—an effort to belittle a movement soon to force him to share his own monopolistic political throne. Spawned by stifling political authoritarianism and economic decay, and triggered by the spectacle of the fall of titans in Bucharest and elsewhere, in 1990 a powerful backwash of demonstrations for a return to multi-party politics flooded Africa. By 1991 the backwash was a tidal wave, transforming the political map of the continent.

The events in Africa took many scholars by surprise, since most doubted Africa could move towards democracy. As late as the mid-1980's one argued that "by reason of their poverty or the violence of their politics" African states were "unlikely to move in a democratic direction"[3]; another adding that "to have expected democracy to flourish would have been historical blindness,"[4] since "outside the core [industrialized states] democracy is a rarity,"[5] support for Tilly's thesis "why Europe will not occur again"[6]—"with a few exceptions, the limits of democratic development in the world may well have been reached."[7]

Moreover, hitherto the signals emanating from the continent had been different. The administrative "softness"[8] of the African State, "excessively authoritarian to disguise the fact that it is inadequately authoritative"[9] seemed to argue the need for greater, not lesser, central authority, in order to contain fissiparous tendencies. Human rights violations were on the rise—especially in hitherto safe havens such as

---

*Previously published in *African Affairs*, January 1991.

Kenya—but the threat to democracy, even of the restrictive one-party variety, seemed to be from the direction of religious fundamentalism (in Sudan, Algeria, Nigeria) and from youth, intellectuals and unionists, pressing civilian and military regimes alike for the adoption of Afro-Marxism—the epitome of centralized authoritarian State political and economic power.[10]

Yet within the space of barely eighteen months fundamental political change took place throughout Africa. All the continent's People's Republics have renounced Marxism, moving to adopt a market economy. Gone are yesteryear's fire-eating advocates of command economies as entire public sectors are privatized. Instincts of self-preservation and differing degrees of sincerity, have driven both benign autocrats and some venal dictators to metamorphose into born-again democrats. Single-party rule—once hailed as Africa's contribution to political philosophy—has been rolled back across a swathe of Africa, giving way to competitive elections and multipartyism.

Whatever democratic advances have been attained in Africa to date have to be still seen as largely structural; they are certainly a strong breath of fresh air, but likely to end up in some countries as only cosmetic and/or temporary. The process has a long way to go in much of the continent. Some leaders (Malawi's Banda; Zaire's Mobutu) still resist it; others (including Kenya's Moi, and Gabon's Bongo) try to tame it in a variety of ways; and yet still others (Strasser in Sierra Leone, Rawlings in Ghana) seem to have attained nothing with it. As in Eastern Europe the new democratic hybrids must prove themselves viable, hardy and lasting; they must prove themselves significant, attesting a *real shift of power from autocratic personal rulers who in many instances still cling to the pinnacle of authority* to elites both representative of, and responsive to, society's various groups; and meaningful, in ushering greater civic and human rights, more political space, better and less wasteful styles of governance, with greater political accountability leading to real economic development.

However, whatever the ultimate verdict—that as with all social change, is likely to be mixed—the political *atmosphere* in Africa today is radically different: exhilarating, ebullient, optimistic. Former awe-inspiring leaders have without ceremony been cut down in size. Kenneth Kaunda, for example, was utterly humbled when his pre-independence party headquarters—a Lusaka political shrine—was gutted by rampaging pro-democracy crowds, at one stroke denying his historic relevance as father of the nation; Mathieu Kerekou shed tears of frustration when the National Conference he organized to liberalize Benin denied both the relevance of his seventeen years in office, and even rejected an interim leadership role for him.

Leaders bucking the democratic trend have faced demonstrations mobilizing crowds at times (Lusaka, 1990) as large as those in Leipzig. Those adept at stage-managing "popular" support (Eyadema in Togo) have seen decades of benevolent-leadership negated by spontaneous upheavals of mass hatred, sending them scurrying to the "safety" of a multiparty system. Already in one country—Mali—the first die-hard holdout, Moussa Traore, incapable of reading the writing on the wall was ousted "Roumanian-style," with a double-barrelled return to civilian rule and competitive politics. If at the time of the fall of the Berlin Wall (1989) thirty-eight of 45 sub-saharan African states were governed by civilian or military one-party systems of greater or lesser authoritarian hue, 18 months later a handful had actually travelled the whole road, *and over half* had committed themselves to competitive multiparty elections and major limitations on executive powers.

The Failure of the Monolithic Party-State in Africa

The prime rationale for constraining political choice—defended by African leaders to the day they were forced to concede multipartyism—is that competitive politics is an imported luxury neither needed nor affordable in developing countries, that can in any case devise other *equally democratic* structures (one-party democracy), more suitable to their unique circumstances.[11] A multiplicity of political parties merely mirrors, even politicizes, existing social cleavages (ethnic, clan, regional, religious) since these are the most easily mobilizable sources of political support and power in Africa, while countries actually need unity and rapid development rather than Western-style liberal democracy.

Sierra Leone's President Siaka Stevens referred to multipartyism as "a system of...institutionalized tribal and ethnic quinquennial warfare euphemistically known as elections [which] contributes an open invitation to anarchy and disunity,"[12] a view endorsed by Tanzania's Julius Nyerere to whom "where there is one party, and that party is identified with the nation as a whole, the foundations of democracy are firmer than they can ever be where you have two or more parties, each representing only a section of the community."[13] Zimbabwe's Mugabe even recommended the one-party system for America to an incredulous U.S. Congress during a recent State Visit. The idea of an "Opposition Party" as a check on arbitrary rule is summarily rejected, in Malawi even on quasi-theological grounds: "there is no Opposition in Heaven. God himself does not want opposition—that is why he chased Satan away. Why should Kamuzu [President Banda] have opposition?"[14] Legitimate programatic differences of opinion can be accommodated within the the single "national" party where all streams of opinion and societal groups are represented. And even if a developmental-oriented authoritarian system does ensued, the basis would be laid for a better-endowed future generation that could *then* partake of the current generation's forbidden fruits.

Later, the spread of Marxism in Africa, added other rationales in defence of (now vanguard) single-party rule. Afro-Marxism provided lofty and socially-satisfying nationalist goals capable of anchoring society's restless and destabilizing elements—students, urban youth, labour—binding them to military regimes intent on remaining in power. The nationalization of the "heights of the economy" that accompanied Afro-Marxism also tapped deep anti-colonial sentiments; though rationalized as the engine of the revolution that by siphoning middle-man profits would spin off new development projects, the State sector actually provided scope for patronage, societal loot, and stepping-stones to power. Constant "refuelling" deficitory State sectors, and disdain for "capitalist" cost-accounting principles were behind the *economic* collapse of what passed as the "Marxist" experiment in Africa,[15] just as only slightly less *etatist* policies elsewhere also "foundered on the weak capacity of public institutions...[and] far from promoting the private sector, the state often actively curbed private initiative."[16]

One need not rehash old debates on the actuarial possibilities of one-party democracy—which *can* be beguilingly appealing. Suffice it to note that the theory and practice of single party rule is an example of the myth-reality syndrome that plagues much of Africana. With only few exceptions correlations between *either* consensual governance or meaningful economic development and single party rule are empirically negated by three decades of Africa's statehood. Legum notes Africa aspires to democracy a much "as in any other part of the world," but "there is no convincing evidence to show that [single party states] achieved better results than the old or the extant multi-party states, either in developing a greater sense of national unity or in promoting economic development."[17]

The single party system has been the means to govern society relatively benevolently—by Julius Nyerere, Kenneth Kaunda and Felix Houphouet-Boigny in Tanzania, Zambia and Cote d'Ivoire respectively—more harshly but still responsibly—by Kamuzu Banda and Thomas Sankara in Malawi and Burkina Faso—to venally plunder it—as have Mobutu Seke Sese and Samuel Doe in Zaire and Liberia—or as a camouflage for personal or class tyranny—as under Jean-Bedel Bokassa, Mengistu Haile Mariam or Macias Nguema in the Central African Republic, Ethiopia and Equatorial Guinea. But nearly universally the single party system has "degenerated into a form of oligarchic patrimonialism that was even unknown in pre-colonial Africa."[18] Whether ruled by Prince, Autocrat, Prophet or Tyrant[19], relatively developed or not, unaccountable personal rule in institutionless voids, utilizing clientelism as the glue social cohorts to leaders, has helped pile up violations of human rights, stultifying national debts, and chronic systemic instability, contributing to "the overwhelming majority view...that Africa is a disaster,"[20] while Edem Kodjo suggests "there isn't one state in Africa that is independent and worthy of being called a state...they are not viable, and only assume sovereignty at the U.N."[21]

Supposed to represent "the organization and mobilization of all politically relevant sectors of the population for purposes of achieving a number of common objectives of development and national unity...[it] has failed with respect to the major objectives of democracy and development. In reality the party is everywhere a network through which ambitious individuals strive to maximize their access to state resources."[22] Julius Nyerere, the greatest champions of single party rule, acknowledged this at a time when there was hardly any opposition single party rule in Tanzania—when in January 1990 he stated that "Tanzanians should not be dogmatic and think that a single party is God's wish" especially one that "was not close to the people, stagnating, losing vitality, and therefore needing competition...to reinvigorate it."[23]

Instead of Africa's "contribution" to the art of governance, the hegemonic Party-State became an "autocratic patrimonial state...that whether in military or civilian guise, whether capitalist or socialist in official ideology, seems detached from the vital creative energies of the

African people and their societies."[24] It produced presidential authoritarianism[25] of varying degrees of repression, and *de facto* domination by whatever ethnic group "possesses" the Presidency; it has been instrumental in plundering the economy, directly or indirectly; it resulted in disdain for civic and human rights, and with few exceptions has paid minimal attention to agrarian/rural populations; and the guiding "party" has often been an atrophied non-entity (Zaire, C.A.R.), a control mechanism (Benin, Congo), a debating society (Malawi, Zambia), or a source of patronage for lesser influentials (Kenya, Gabon, Togo). Presidential family cliques and regional political barons—at times joined by by trusted soothsayers (Niger, Benin, Gabon, C.A.R., Zaire)—have often decided policies, options, priorities. It is not "just" that nowhere have the masses been the beneficiaries of alleged remedial benefits of single party rule; that rarely have "national" policies been truly espoused or societal benefits distributed equitably. Rather a small cabal of influentials have eroded all semblance of accountability, legitimacy, democracy and justice in much of Africa.

While globally absence of democracy has not necessarily resulted in economic decline (e.g. Japan, South Korea, Taiwan), "benevolent" authoritarian rule has *also* not been that frequently the recipe for economic development and nation-building (e.g. the Middle East and Latin America)—the bottom line of justifications for the single party state. In Africa, with extremely few exceptions, there has usually been *neither* democracy *nor* economic development or national unity; more often there has been *both* authoritarian government *and* economic pauperization and decline.

Even coups—the functional equivalent of elections, virtually the only way of "throwing the rascals out"—with time became highly *institutionalized, personalized, patrimonialized*, as military cliques and sub-cliques—often intervening less out of ultruistic motives than for a host of personalist reasons[26]— arrogated to themselves the function of dictating national goals and ideologies, rather than, as in earlier days, serving as "cleansing" brooms prior to a return to competitive politics. Not surprising by the late 1980's even Marxists—East Europe's rejection of Marxism has *not* produced a total ideological catharsis in Africa[27]— no longer subscribed to arguments in favour of single-party rule, and were more concerned with securing and expanding political space and human rights.

Fundamentally unaccountable, purchasing a measure of stability—in the absence of systemic legitimacy—via the social glue of patronage or external props, assuming ambitious statist economic policies that rest on myopic assessments of their capability to sustain the requisite costs, both civilian and military regimes have bankrupted themselves, mortgaging their futures to the demands of the day.

Factors behind the Democratic Upheavals in Africa

While the pro-democracy movement came of age in 1990, popular strivings for liberalization emerged from the day the one-party system locked out competitive elections and started impinging upon individual civic and human rights in the name of the "collective good." But in those early days of wine and roses, so to speak, nationalism, patriotism, civic idealism did carry some value as the coin of the realm. Democratic aspirations could temporarily be put aside, especially since competitive elections proved to be little more than ethnic tugs-of-war. Groups pressing for change—youth, unionists, intellectuals—were often more preoccupied with either gaining a greater share of the *status quo* pie, or proselytizing for alternate, more radical developmental roads—entailing similar restrictions on civic freedoms. Still, as Naomi Chazan put it "democratic pressures persist while authoritarian rule prevails,"[28] and these became irresistible forces in 1990.

It would be ethnocentric and too facile to assume the pro-democracy pressures in Africa were merely knee-jerk reactions to events in Eastern Europe.[29] It is true one can not exaggerate the psychological effect of pictures of the trial and execution of Ceusescu (well-known in Africa as the Soviet Union's surrogate), or of Bucharest's removal of statues of Lenin by a hangman's loop-winch around their neck, which African leaders tried to keep out of their State-controlled media. Africans could clearly see that their own country's "departures from democratic standards...closely parallel defects exposed in Eastern Europe."[30] The redemocratization of Latin America likewise added to the global critical mass of democracy, with the result, according to Bates, that "the world is experiencing a wave of democratization. Not since the mid-19th century have so many popular uprisings toppled rulers and filled the boulevards with crowds affirming freedom and self-governance."[31] The spillover-effect, that definitely crystallized and catalyzed pro-democracy demonstrations in Africa does not tell the whole story. The continent was already more than *ripe* for upheaval, and there were additional, internal and external factors that a played crucial role in leading the democratic pressures to successful fruition.

Internal Variables

Among the internal variables was the forementioned fact that Africa was at a political dead-end, morally and economically bankrupt, inherently unstable to the degree that "no state can count itself safe from a wind of change once it starts to blow."[32] The call for democracy was not "just" for a political birthright, but for a total revision of the fundamental charter of the State, underpinned by political liberalism and accountability. Over the years all ideological and developmental options had been tried—under one-party rule—and found wanting; all styles of governance—including tyranny—had been unsuccessful in controlling or binding masses to leaders in stable relationships[33], and Africa was also trapped in a free-fall to economic oblivion to boot.

In conference jargon "The Crisis of the African State" had become intertwined with the "African Debt Crisis" resulting in morally, politically and economically bankrupt entities. For parallel to the political sterility of the African one-party state, most economies were bankrupt. Latin America's national debts of $100 billion and more inures us to look down, say, at Togo's puny $1 billion debt. But debt repayment loads in Africa are much more onerous, even if in absolute terms the amounts are small and the continent's total debt is modest—$143 billion. For the latter figure is equal to the continent's entire annual GDP, 370% of total export earnings[34], and individual repayment ratios are in some instances stratospheric—1,500% for Sudan and Mozambique, 2,000% for Gambia, etc.

Nor are conditions getting better, as Structural Adjustment Programs and other IMF "fixes" attest to the temporal and limited nature of any improvement. One observer has noted "the prevailing view of the continent in the mainstream media is of unremitting gloom"; Africa's total GNP remains smaller than Belgium's that has less than 2% of its population, while "Africa's share of world trade is half of what it was a decade ago...private investment has virtually stopped...[and] at independence Ghana—a classic case—had a larger GNP than South Korea"—which thirty years later was a regional economic super-power while Ghana had become a basket-case.[35] Utterly marginalized, Africa is "not suffering from a temporary crisis…but from a lasting inability to make itself part of the world economy and to hold onto its share of the market there—let alone increase its share."[36] Despite an annual in-flow of $15 billion of aid, standards of life have declined since independence.[37] This has happened both in countries grossly mismanaged (Guinea, Chad, Equatorial Guinea) and in re-spected states such as Tanzania, where urban real wages fell by 65% and standards fell by 2.5% annually between 1969 and 1983. Today 16 countries have annual per capita incomes below $370 (the current threshold of absolute poverty); Mozambique ($100) and Ethiopia ($120) are at the bottom of the pile, but even Kenya is borderline at $370.

Africa scores at the bottom of every criteria of development. Average life expectancy is 50 years, and as low as 37; demographic growth is inordinately high; disease and famine ravage the continent. More distressingly, Africa is not just the poorest continent, but the only one *backsliding*, with its meagre advances eroded by high birth rates and economic mismanagement. The World Bank estimates that within 25 years (and some countries, as early as the year 2,000) the continent will need twice current amounts of foodstuffs, hospitals, schools and trained personnel, *merely to maintain existing standards.*[38]

The causes of this economic decline need not detain us; but one factor is the dissipation of fiscal resources on large, functionally redun-dant civil services. Already in 1981 the World Bank noted public employment had reached levels of 40-75% of total employment in seven African states; that in an additional twenty, expenditures had been growing at *twice the pace of economic growth*, and in others at even higher rates. By 1989 the picture was worse, with public employment—more determined by "patrimonial interests than economic efficiency"[39] —*eve-rywhere* consuming 60-80% of national budgets, and more than 50% of non-agricultural employment, compared to 36% in Asia, and 27% in Latin America. In many states, assuming a proper rural-urban distri-bution, a full work-day, and the elimination from the payroll of non-existent phantom-workers, existing civil services could be halved without prejudice to existing State services and activities.

Whether pursuing radical or market-economy developmental strategies, African states have grafted the worst traits of both, not pursuing cost-effectiveness nor harnessing State sectors to *productive* ends. The result has been fiscal paralyses, never-ending budgetary crises, financial constraints on development, mushrooming public debts, greater dependency relationships *vis-a-vis* external donors, and no scope for political manoeuvrability. Corrective measures—IMF structural adjustment programs and the like—aimed at reintroducing fiscal orthodoxy, supply-demand relationships, and/or caps on public expenditures, are viewed by many Africans (and radicals overseas) as conspiracies to recolonize Africa by imposing Western values.[40]

This moral, political and economic bankruptcy of much of Africa is set against a background of the continent's changed population, the third domestic variable of import. For by the late-1980's Africa's population was both larger and compositionally different from that of the 1960's, with the consequence that the continent's internal political dynamics are different today than at independence.

Intra-state variations notwithstanding, the population of most non-Equatorial countries was in 1990: (a) much *larger*, in some (e.g. Kenya) by as much as 300%[41]—hence with greater societal needs; (b) *more urban and de-traditionalized*, with urbanization levels in several (Gabon; C.A.R.) up by over 300%—reflecting heightened modern/urban expectations and needs leading (inevitably) to social frustrations; (c) *impatient and no longer reverent of political leaders*, since there are limits beyond which symbolic outputs can satisfy concrete demands; or charisma, ideology, repression can assure political quietism; (d) *with a vastly expanded percentage of educated youth*—a result of decades of educational advances leading to 95% scholarization levels in some (e.g. Gabon)—complicating prospects of employment and undermining legitimacy in a population (e) more aware of the democratic "option" abroad but denied at home; (f) *economically hurting* by inflation and recession, and the downward economic spiral (at best static conditions) and (g) *politically indignant* at authoritarian regimes with little legitimacy arrogantly intent on ruling forever, errors of omission or commission notwithstanding. As one Zimbabwe critic put it "You can't have economic problems and fail to blame those who are in charge."[42]

It is such a populace that revolted in 1991 after President Eyadema—stage-manager of many a "spontaneous" demonstration on his behalf—boasted to foreign reporters that Togolese did not desire the multipartyism sweeping neighbouring states, as attested by the absence in Lome of petitions to that effect. Demonstrations the likes of which had never been seen in Lome—even in the days when tens of thousands of Northerners were brought south to "implore" Eyadema to remain in office—soon broke out. In one clean swoop the Eyadema regime was sent scurrying for the safety of multipartyism.

Fourth and finally, of import also is the fact that in the thirty years since independence a host of sophisticated civic and ecological pressure groups have sprung up in Africa. Monitoring local violations for parent bodies overseas (e.g. Amnesty International), such groups were making life difficult for a host of African leaders. One of these was the increasingly beleaguered Daniel arap Moi, who was to discover the muscle of "environmentalist power" in Kenya. Foreign funds committed for the construction in Nairobi of Africa's highest tower-building—a "monument" to his reign—was withdrawn when vocal publicity drew attention to the fact the project entailed ruining one of the city's few public parks. And when Moi vent his fury at the person who had most thwarted his pet project, fuming that "Kenyan tradition demanded that a woman not criticize a man," he discovered that "women power" had reached Kenya as well.[43] Even Felix Houphouet-Boigny experienced unheard-of criticism of his own monument to posterity—the costly Yamoussoukro Basilica—with the Pope for long postponing its consecration, aware of mobs calling for the urban renewal of progressively seedier Abidjan instead. It is against such a background of internal legitimacy voids, and changed societal forces, that the external pressures, arising out of the changed international picture, can better be appreciated.

External Factors

The collapse of global Marxism created a unipolar world that at one stroke eliminated the Cold War. And with it disappeared any artificially-enhanced global value that Third World states had been able to extort from the former Cold War protagonists. *What literally transpired was a massive devaluation in the "worth" of Africa.* African states were transformed from Cold War pawns, into irrelevant international clutter. They are no longer sought-after "allies", since UN votes (mortgaged to one or another of the major powers) cannot go to the highest bidder in a world of no players.

It is no longer necessary to control, or deny to others, sources of mineral ores or geopolitically strategic localities. Even France—in the past jealously guarding former colonial reserves against external encroachments (primarily from the US!)—has relaxed her bear-hug, parallel to a disinvestment from Africa of private French capital. French investments have been in decline since 1980; from a net annual inflow of *circa* one billion dollars at the decade's beginning, to $53 million in 1985, and a net *outflow* of $824 million in 1988, part of the fact that as a whole Africa now receives foreign investments at the rate of only $200-300 million a year, one tenth of the amount estimated to be needed to sustain the continent's economies.[44] *Le Monde* has observed that risk capital, hurting by the continent's economic decline, and attracted by opportunities in Eastern Europe and the post-1992 EEC, were "only thinking of packing their bags and quitting Africa. Black Africa no longer interests economic circles. Deprived of means of blackmailing Paris, its leaders have a smaller and smaller margin for manoeuvre."[45]

African states financially or militarily dependent upon the Soviet Union began collapsing first, as their patron withdrew its support. With military "solutions" to multifaceted internal conflicts no longer feasible (e.g. civil strife in Angola, Mozambique, Ethiopia), such states undertook ideological somersaults, and conciliatory overtures to avert possible defeat. (Ethiopia was unable to do so, in light of Mengistu's iron mind-set, and the much more generalized nature of the conflict, including separatist movements, hence the continuing war until the May 1991 abandonment of Addis.) Other former Afro-Marxist states followed suit, some reluctantly (Congo), others driven by fiscal bankruptcy (Benin), but all under tumultuous pressure by societal allies of yesteryear disillusioned with the nakedness of their former ideological Emperor. For as the Chairman of the Zambian Congress of Trade Unions (ZCTU) put it, if the "originators of Socialism" have rejected it as inappropriate "who were African imitators" to become its main proponents![46]

But the rollback of Marxism was just the tip of the iceberg. Drastic falls in commodity producer prices completely eroded the viability of most African economies, placing a over a score of countries at the mercy of a by now thoroughly exasperated World Bank and IMF. Thus simultaneous with the increased domestic pressures for change, and the new global balance of power, came powerful international demands for "better governance" (an end to corruption), more democratization (civic and human rights), and ultimately, a free economy. Barber B. Conable Jr., President of the World Bank expressed this new mood well when he noted his "fear that many of Africa's leaders have been more concerned about retaining power than about the long-term development interests of their people."[47] The IMF head similarly noted his exasperation at the large amounts of foreign aid that change direction to become an outward "flood of capital and the buying of big apartments in nice European countries."[48]

The frustration of the international donor community received a powerful thrust from Paris. Fiscally sustaining one-third of the African states to the point of annually balancing the budgets of many, France had "not hesitated to make and unmake governments by direct military intervention...exercis[ing] the same sort of close and muscular influence over a host of African countries that the USSR used to wield in Eastern Europe."[49] In conjunction with the World Bank/IMF and the USA, all "explicitly demanding political change as a condition for further loans to Africa,"[50] French leverage in Africa attained the deepest and most immediate results.

Virtually from his succession to the Presidency, Francois Mitterand had been itching to disencumber himself of residual unconditional "Gaullist" obligations to a multitude of oppressive, kleptomaniac client-states, whose heavy-handed domestic policies (e.g. Chad, C.A.R., Gabon) and swollen multiple private Swiss banking accounts had increasingly tarnished France's reputation, and had drawn serious negative domestic political repercussions in Paris as well. The end of the Cold War and Africa's economic decline—that saw a massive erosion in the ongoing French economic presence in Africa, and in Africa's importance to France[51]— provided the backdrop for the sudden new pressures from Paris on its client-states. Early in 1990 a senior French official suggested in *Le Monde* that France should disengage from an Africa that had become the "conservatory of the ills of humanity," noting there was actually no debt crisis in French Africa since "the personal fortunes of Africa's elites outside the continent were greater than the debts of the countries in question"; in 1988, for example, the Bank of France had purchased $1.8 billion worth of CFAF banknotes fraudulently transeferred to Europe in "full suitcases and diplomatic bags."[52]

Progressively clearer messages conveyed France's new "line" to Francophone Africa: severe political conditionalities on aid, with higher levels of French budgetary and other subventions to countries introducing basic political reforms. More ominously, France renounced automatic future honouring of long-standing "mutual defence" treaties *under whose very loose interpretation* French force of arms had been committed to sustain regimes threatened by insurrection. In this domain too the French position was that such support, *if at all forthcoming*, would be determined by the country's human rights record, and whether it was moving towards democratic reforms.[53]

Several Francophone leaders did not get the message initially, since Paris had made similar noises before and it was the kind of rhetoric they had become accustomed to hear.[54] But the threat was made explicit at the June 1990 La Baule Francophonic summit meeting. The meeting ended with a declaration stressing "the need to associate the relevant population more closely with the construction of their political, social and economic future," towards which end extra aid would be forthcoming to countries moving fastest in that direction. Some blunt informal advise by President Mitterand to the effect that "the sooner you organize free elections, the better it will be for the youth of your countries who need to express themselves"[55] conveniently "leaked" out, adding to the budding pressures in Africa.

Two leaders, Felix Houphouet-Boigny and Omar Bongo, early on saw the handwriting on the wall and embarked on programs of liberalization; another, Mathieu Kerekou in totally insolvent Benin, was already being literally bulldozed to implement reform and withdraw from office. But Mitterand's tenor at La Baule was resented by some Africans who viewed it as arrogant neo-colonialism, especially in light of the penalties for non-compliance. A few adamantly rejected France's right to prescribe for them political reform, and many discounted France's resolve—some to subsequently discover their feet of clay in the absence of France's stabilizing military help.

Such was specifically the case of Hissene Habre. The latter viewed himself immune to threats from Paris, since he was a proven bulwark against Libyan designs on Chad that in the past had evoked knee-jerk reactions in Paris. Despite Chad's economic irrelevance, French troops had on several occasions been airlifted to Ndjamena, some to die for the country's defence.[56] Habre scoffed at French conditionalities at La Baule. His unwillingness to relax Ndjamena's heavy-handed rule over the South, and to move towards national reconciliation, sealed his fate. French troops *in situ* in Chad did not budge from their bases as Habre's estranged Chief of Staff, Idriss Deby, swept in from the Sudanese border with several hundred soldiers to defeat and chase Habre into exile. Libya's complicity in the insurgency (cause for French *and* US military support for Ndjamena in the past) was judged of little import. And as if to attest to the fact that he understood France's new line, once installed in Ndjamena Deby de-emphasized the Libyan "connection," and pledged a prompt return to civilian rule and multiparty elections, the first since 1961. Other Francophone leaders, hitherto also holding out against populist demonstrations and pressures, began giving in, and the re-democratization bandwagon entered into high gear.

Paradoxically at the outset French pressures for political reforms were quite modest. Certainly Paris did not counsel, expect, or even countenance what was soon to become the norm of re-democratization—convening populist National Conferences (*a la* France's 18th Century Estates General) of all the country's social, ethnic, economic, regional, religious and occupational groups, leading to formal Constitutional revisions, and eventually full-fledged multiparty elections. Originally *minimalist* changes were demanded: "the catchwords [were] 'governance' and 'democratization' rather than 'democracy' or 'multipartyism.'" This meant "less corruption, more financial accountability, better human rights observance and freer judiciaries and media, rather than completely open multiparty systems, for which most Africanists think Africa is not yet suited or equipped."[57]

Certainly when the first Francophone country to re-democratize—Marxist Benin[58], brought to its knees by striking civil servants not paid for a year—French counsel (given also to Guinea) was *against competitive multiparty elections*. A single-party system (mass, not vanguard), offering constituency-level choice of a multiplicity of candidates all running under the same party label (a la pre-1990 Cote d'Ivoire) was France's advice. Apart from the fact that the democratic flood-gates could not be closed in maverick Cotonou, *France's suggested model of Ivoirien "democracy" was at that very moment being rejected by demonstrators in Abidjan herself,* who were calling for complete freedom of political association, multipartyism and prompt open elections. Only in mid-1990 did French Premier Michel Rocard see the futility of recommending midway houses, and multiparty democracy became the target.

If change came first to Francophone Africa due to pressures from France and the World Bank, and to Marxist Africa as the result of the disappearance of their ideological model, other states while "studiously avoiding comparisons" slowly reached the inescapable conclusion that "the parallels between what has transpired in Eastern Europe and the mounting pressures for change on the continent are becoming increasingly difficult to ignore,"[59] yielding to increasingly vehemently expressed demands for a return to square one: the multipartyism of the immediate pre- and post-independence eras.

A few leaders continued to hold out complaining they could not implement Structural Adjustment Plans (invariably including dismantling deficitory parastatals, reducing civil service employment levels and staple foodstuff subsidies) without authoritarian policies. These arguments had been sustained by numerous scholars who perceived in the "praetorian" nature of Third World societies the necessity for "developmental dictators."[60] Such arguments were categorically undermined by recent hard-nosed World Bank and IMF re-assessments of the long-term value and utility of the SAP's themselves *in the absence of political "pre-conditions."* For even where solid growth has resulted (criticism in radical circles notwithstanding, there have been striking successes) *sustained growth* has rarely ensued. This rethinking of fundamentals led to the path-breaking conclusions of the recent World Bank assessment of Africa's prospects of sustainable growth—an assessment that is now the "Red Book" of all democrats! For the gloves are now off, and the World Bank's position is unequivocally that Africa has no chance of attaining meaningful economic growth and development unless it *first* moves squarely into modalities of governance that include political accountability, participatory politics and a free market-economy.

Specifically, "history suggests that political legitimacy and consensus are a precondition for sustainable development... Underlying the litany of Africa's problems is a crisis of governance."[61] And if radical African intellectuals reject the neo-colonial bondage implicit and explicit in many tenets of IMF and World Bank policy, some are at least agreed that there is "a definite correlation between the lack of democracy in African politics and the deterioration in socio-economic conditions."[62] If only out of pragmatic considerations "increasingly forces of the left have come to accept liberal democratic platforms and alliances as a means of securing the survival of popular democratic organizations and to expand the 'democratic space.'"[63] Nigerian Claude Ake, for example, "the problems of persistence of underdevelopment is related to lack of democracy in Africa...democracy is not just a consummatory value but also an instrumentalist one."[64]

Democracy, valuable in its own right, is also valuable because it provides *a politically enabling atmosphere for development to proceed.* The World Bank Report posits a *causal relationship* between democracy and sustained growth, claiming it is no mere chance that Botswana and Mauritius,

Africa's top economic performers, are the only ones with multiparty systems on the continent. Other scholars note that states with high growth rates not fuelled by mineral and/or petroleum wealth—Kenya, Cote d'Ivoire and Malawi—also share one feature of the democratic cluster of values: they manifest greater levels of political accountability, *even if only incrementally so*, than other one-party states with depressed growth scores.[65]

In 1991 the US Agency for International Development *explicitly* endorsed past implicit assumptions, that "there is growing evidence that open societies that value individual rights, respect the rule of the law, and have open and accountable governments provide better opportunities for sustained economic development than do closed systems which stifle individual initiative." And in March American foreign aid guidelines were clearly spelled out in Congress: "foreign aid to individual countries will take into account their progress towards establishing democracy...democracy will be placed on an equal footing with progress towards economic reforms and the establishment of a market-oriented economy, two key factors which have already been used as criteria for allocating US foreign aid."[66]

This view is consonant with linkages postulated by some scholars correlating political democracy, a free-market economy and economic development. Charles Lindblom put it most eloquently when he noted that *"only within market-oriented systems does political democracy arise*. Not all market-oriented systems are democratic, but every democratic system is also a market-oriented system. Apparently, for reasons that are not wholly understood, political democracy has been unable to exist except when coupled with the market. An extraordinary proposition, it has so far held without exception."[67]

That "the newly articulated demand by senior US and Western officials that the level of democratization within Africa will soon condition the amount of assistance allocated to it"[68] was more sincere than previous rhetoric allegedly guiding US policy with respect to Human Rights violations, was best attested by Kenya's experience. Very much the darling of the West despite escalating abuses of human rights, growing restrictions on political space, and curtailment of the press and judiciary autonomy, by 1991 Kenya was virtually cut off from most foreign aid programs, forcing an extremely reluctant and unpopular Moi to concede in 1992 what he hated most—competitive elections. Though he actually succeeded to win a new Presidential mandate for himself and a plurality of the parliamentary seats for his KANU party by a combination of playing on inter-ethnic fears, intimidation, and vote-rigging, Kenya will never be the same again. Nor will Gabon ever be the same though Bongo remains firmly in power, having astutely outmanoeuvred his opposition, granted them political legitimacy, trounced them electorally, and dragneted them into an expanded personalized patronage sysem not unlike the one in force under the single-party era.

Systemic legitimacy has become the name of the game. This is in essence what changed in 1990. For purposes of understanding the sources of stable civil-military relations and stable civilian rule in Africa in the post Cold War era, neither the Trade Off nor the External Guarantor modality *in and of itself suffice any more*. Indeed the External Modality has been renounced (in theory at least) by France that in the past sustained most client-states, while the Trade Off Modality, even in some of the better endowed states has increasingly shown it is unequal to the task of satisfying large numbers of civil and military needs. The modalities *still have* validity for purposes of stabilizing civilian rule, as the Gabonese and Kenyan examples illustrate from the case studies, but only in conjunction with a healthy measure of the third modality—systemic legitimacy. Where the two are not intertwined—as increasingly in Kenya—both political and civil-military instability creep in.

The Redemocratization Process

It is still too early to pass a firm verdict on the value of what has been attained to date in Africa, and its long-term significance. With all the "democratization" going on in Africa, in reality only a handful of countries (among them Benin, Cote d'Ivoire, Gabon) have actually *completed* the implementation of structural re-organization, political reform, civilianization (in the case of military regimes), and grass-roots (and external) demand for competitive legislative and presidential elections. Many more have only very recently, and reluctantly, commenced their multi-party democratic rule experiences under clouds of suspicion of electoral fraud, vote-rigging and autocratic intentions (e.g. Kenya, Cameroun, Ghana.) And a significant number (e.g. Zaire, Malawi, C.A.R.) still resist—despite extreme external and internal pressures—a rollback of uniparty, military or autocratic rule, fighting rear-guard battles and haggling with pro-democracy movements.

Zambia is a good example of a "hold-out" regime that lost everything by misreading the new rules of the game. Kaunda, not the most astute African Head of State, but neither the most autocratic or venal, for long argued the irrelevance to Africa of the developing events in Eastern Europe, since "the circumstances which made us rally behind the one-party system have not changed...our situation today is in no way similar to the one in Europe."[69] Kaunda's conception of Zambian-style democracy was so rosy-tinted that he even suggested Eastern Europe should emulate Africa since "what we have been doing ever since our hard-won independence Eastern Europe and the Soviet Union are starting to do only now."[70] Vacillating under diametric pressures, Kaunda finally gave in to demands for multipartyism but tried to mark time, thus digging his political grave. He set up a constitutional revision committee, to be followed by a plebiscite on the new constitution, a process that could have dragged on for years. Violent riots in Zambia's urban centers served to "convince" Kaunda that the slow cumbersome process was not really necessary; but the footdragging demolished what little residual support he might have had throughout the country, while allowing the opposition the time to organize for an open electoral campaign that kaunda could not, and indeed did not win.

While pressures for re-democratization have inter-acted with each state's unique internal dynamics to produce somewhat different outcomes, several common patterns stand out, and several likely developments in the near future can be projected.

First, it is crystal clear that the pro-democracy pressures are continent-wide, and are not likely to spare any state except those few (Botswana, Mauritius, Namibia, Gambia, Senegal) with meaningful competitive multiparty systems and significant civic and human rights freedoms. Moreover, since few countries possess reservoirs of popular legitimacy, and most are in socio-economic quagmires, there is a fair chance of a "spillover" of the pro-democracy turmoil into some *de facto* multiparty countries (e.g. Egypt, Morocco, Senegal) to merge with festering problems that have less to do with democratization (though certainly democracy can be shored up) and more with fundamental economic and religious re-arrays of power. (Abdou Diouf's overtures to Senegal's parliamentary Opposition, is an example of a country providing "extra" democracy to avoid inviting the turmoil of neigh-bouring non-democratic countries.)

Secondly, the more African autocracies resembled in their fea-tures the discredited regimes in Eastern Europe, the greater the chal-lenge from below for total change, and a purge of the past: witness the total eclipse of the Afro-Marxist state. For as Anglin notes "most of the departures from democratic standards...closely parallel defects exposed in Eastern Europe...The supremacy of the party over the government, the vanguard party concept, politicisation of the public service and security services, monopoly of party power in perpetuity, subordina-tion of mass organisations (such as trade unions, women's and youth groups), the media, etc. to party control, the cult of personality, abuses of power including corruption, permanent states of emergency."[71]

Thirdly, *military* rulers have fared poorly in the democratization sweepstakes, and are likely to continue doing so in the future. Some (e.g. Chad's Hissene Habre) completely underestimated France's re-solve in disengaging from oppressive and corrupt client-states; others (e.g. Mali's Moussa Traore and Benin's Mathieu Kerekou) totally mis-judged the venom and speed with which urban populations would turn on them; and yet others (e.g. Ethiopia's Mengistu Mariam) simply could not accept the humiliation of withdrawal from power. Kerekou right to the end could not comprehend the "ungratefulness" of Beni-nois—whom he ruled under an iron fist for seventeen years—who rejected his leadership in either a new "above politics" Presidential capacity, or even as Chairman of the national Conference he convened to decide the nature of the reforms to be initiated. Other army will likely vacate office in similar manner through military defeat, mass upheavals that split the loyalty of the officer corps, or consequent to electoral defeats by the democratic forces they were forced to unleash under pressure from below. Though some may tarry, or try to stir up ethnic problems in desparate efforts to retain power (e.g. Eyadema in Togo), their efforts are clearly foredoomed.

Fourthly, despite the continental dimension of democratiza-tion, *some* countries may bypassed until the forces of change spend themselves. This may occur because the modern urban sector is too small or weak to threaten the establishment; because the country is isolated at the social periphery of the continent (Equatorial Guinea?); or because the forces of repression have too much to lose by relaxing their grip over the reigns of power (Burundi, Sudan?), external pressures notwithstanding. The fact that several countries that fall into these categories have nevertheless relaxed their monopoly of power (Sao Tome e Principe), or have shown signs of flexibility where none was expected (Mauritania), may prove that the pressures are too irresistible. Still a few states might manage to hold out *until the first wave of failures of the "new democracies" start cropping up, when the "not by democracy alone" argument is likely to score some points*; that juncture may provide a respite from international pressures for autocratic holdouts.

Fifthly, the image of the political impregnability of Africa's civilian founding-fathers, and of the invincibility of long-ruling iron generals, has been completely eroded by the spectacle of "people-power" (cum French and IMF-clout), a fact that may well have major long-run repercussions for political generations to come. Direct mass action has unseated several political autocrats, and will undoubtedly overthrow others. The lesson has sunk deep: there can be little doubt that mass direct action can be expected in the future to be turned against *benign* but, for whatever reason, unpopular leaders with equally deadly success.

Finally, the few *civilian* leaders who early grasped the significance of the changed global rules of the game, promptly came to terms with them, liberalized their administrations and created new political space, have usually been able to survive the trauma, with enhanced legitimacy and a greater mandate to enact draconian policies called for by their ailing economies. Since the pro-democracy pressures are not spreading at the same pace in every country, this means other African leaders can avoid political eclipse if they compromise early. Telling is the manner in which both Bongo and Houphouet-Boigny retained political primacy even upon relaxing their grip on the political reigns, assuring their continuity in office with enhanced status and prestige they did not possess, whereas even twelve months previously their political futures were gravely in doubt.

Adjusting to the inevitability of the changed reality, properly assessing societal pressures for change and reacting accordingly, has allowed African leaders—even hitherto relatively unpopular ones—to grasp the democracy tiger by the tail and tame it. They have been able to seize the initiative and project the image of *leading* (rather than bending to) the movement for reform, in the attending societal euphoria distancing themselves somewhat from the worst abuses of their own *ancien regimes*. But far more importantly, such African leaders have been able to pre-empt more threatening popular demands they would have faced at later junctures had they not compromised. By their flexibility when political opposition groups are still timid, disorganized, or self-exiled, and political reform still but a hope, such African leaders were able to dictate the pace of reform and its all-important ground-rules, avoiding excessive executive-shackling national-conference pressures while maintaining the centrality of their role in any political outcome. The usual outcome has been a bicephalous executive, with incumbents partly withdrawing to the sanctity of an above-politics Presidency, relinquishing day-to day government to a "clean" technocratic Premier accountable (or not) to more powerful multiparty National Assemblies.

The two early quasi-voluntary democratic metamorphoses in French Africa (Cote d'Ivoire and Gabon) are significant for what they illustrate. Master-tactician Houphouet-Boigny, faced by near-daily street riots for liberalization (fuelled by economic stress) completely outmanoeuvred the pro-democracy movement by promptly legalizing all political parties, and acceding to their fullest demands—open Presidential and legislative elections—rushing the democratic transformation before opposition leaders could expand or redefine their demands, sharpen their tactics, or properly organize for electoral contests that last saw opposition parties thirty years ago. Indeed, representatives of the 26 political formations that were legalized were called into Houphouet-Boigny's office and peremptorily advised of the forthcoming elections. When some requested a delay (so they could get organized) this was rejected on the grounds of *their own* recent demonstrations for instant national elections. Election funds were allocated to all parties so they could not claim being in a disadvantage (some parties took the funds and withdrew from the elections!), and the outcome was never in doubt.[72]

Houphouet-Boigny's tactic resulted in elections under his own (PDCI) party's supervision, with a PDCI quasi-monopoly of the media, and oiled in the proper direction by PDCI largess. All this is not to play down the significance of the political reforms in Abidjan, or the opening up of new political space in Cote d'Ivoire; nor does it diminish from the magnitude of Houphouet-Boigny's and the PDCI's subsequent stunning electoral victories though some have pointed at instances of vote-rigging and other irregularities. The outcome of the the three-tiered elections were not really in doubt with no opposition party capable of fielding even half a full complement of candidates, while the main presidential challenger (Laurent Gbagbo, who got 18.3% of the vote) simply not geared to run a national race.[73] Houphouet-Boigny's early flexibility not only revived from the doldrums his own relevance to Cote d'Ivoire, saved from oblivion a ruling party grown complacent in office, but also prevented a much more fundamental restructuring of the Cote d'Ivoire State.

In Gabon a similar democratic metamorphosis took place when the beleaguered Bongo showed astuteness in giving in to pressures for a convention-brokered re-array of power. By playing upon everyone's fear of the northern Fang bogeyman (prime beneficiaries of democratization), Bongo presided over the economic decentralizing of a State now no longer his private preserve, assuring his own region—rich in mineral wealth, but demographically weak—a measure of future autonomy. Bongo's prompt capitulation to popular pressures removed the Presidency and his own tenure in it, from the fray, while gaining some acclaim for ushering in the return of competitive elections to Gabon. Had he tarried, relied, as in the past, on French military assistance (in light Gabon's immense mineral wealth), or tried to suppress mounting unrest with his ethnic-mercenary Guard[74] Bongo, with no viable ethnic constituency, would no doubt have been overwhelmed by the pro-democracy movement, and relegated to oblivion. Indeed, shortly later massive anti-government riots erupted in Port Gentil after the death of an opposition leader. Though French troops were ferried over from Libreville to protect and evacuate French nationals, Bongo was pointedly reminded that "he would receive no military help in maintaining law and order," since while France "would remain actively involved in the continent [it] wished to stay out of the continent's internal affairs."[75]

For some leaders, especially military, temporizing, hoping the movement will dissipate itself, may be the only viable option, since they have no chance of surviving in an open political system. This is most clearly Mobutu's case. Platitudes about commitment to democracy or liberalization in Zaire are precisely that—plattitudes—and they are rejected outright by political groups that above all else wish his own ouster. In like manner Mbosogo has responded with intimidation to pro-democracy tracts in Equatorial Guinea, since possibly the first act of a free legislature would be to order his own arrest for State brutalities since 1975.

The Significance, and Constraints, of the Redemocratization of Africa

Assuming the process of democratization continues to its logical conclusion in much of the continent, what is its significance, and what are its prospects of survival in the future? What will have been attained—and, given continued external conditionalities, can to some extent be sustained—is Africa's political rebirth. Indeed, it is a sort of return to square one—decolonization, though from *domestic* politically hegemonic groups—but, given the severe aid conditionalities that can be expected, this "second independence" may well be a virtual *recolonization* by global donor agents, very much in the saddle in a unipolar world with only one source of capital, greatly in demand.

Countries completing the process of redemocratization will have hammered out—most via Constituent National Conferences—a new democratic charter for the African State. This dispensation to govern provides political space for all groups, more modes of political participation and representation than the narrow one of the past, accountability of executives, strengthened legislatures, commitment to a liberal market-economy (in ex-Marxist states), and, everywhere, espect for civic and human rights, and a free judiciary and press. The democratization of Africa is of monumental import, but it also carries negative repercussions. The "not by democracy alone" argument is *not* without validity, and few economic pay-offs are in the offing for most states since in *substance* nothing has changed with political democratization, and little is likely to in the near term.

A massive debt write-off could turn the economic clock to square one, constituting a New Deal for Africa, but is doubtful. Hence economic benefits are minimal, because any developmental thrusts flowing from politically-enabling atmospheres—itself, as noted, an academically contentious question—will only accrue in the distant future—while African states are in economic collapse *now*. Most African states have few economic potentials of *any* significance (many, literally nothing) that could attract foreign risk capital—which is why entrepreneurs did not flock into them in the past, *irrespective* of ideology or level of democracy! And to rely on local capital to fuel development is to foredoom many to perpetual marginality.

Moreover, current conditionalities do not dangle the prospect of much *increased* aid, but rather continuation of existing levels. African states now have to run faster (i.e. be democratic) just to remain in the same place (secure existing levels of aid), that is one tenth of their minimal requirements. No "peace dividend" is in the offing as a result of the end of the Cold War, certainly not for Africa—though Marshall Plans have been mooted for Eastern Europe. Constant economic fiascoes, and the inability of any African state to pull itself up by its own bootstraps, has produced donor fatigue, visible even with respect to humanitarian aid where Kurds are preferred over thrice salvaged Ethiopians. As Former American Assistant Secretary of State Chester Crocker noted "most secretaries of state have just wanted to keep African issues off their desks...The idea of putting big money into African economic development remains anathema."[76]

But democratization has opened political floodgates swamping countries with *scores* of political parties, most narrow ethnic and personal power-machines, and thousands of power-aspirants. In Benin, a country of four million, legislative elections saw fully 1,800 candidates of twenty-six political parties (an Albanian-oriented Communist Party, the main ideological one), seeking election for the drastically reduced (from Marxist-days) 64-deputy National Assembly. And fourteen individuals (some "fantasy candidates") [77], presented themselves for the Presidential election. Ethnic voting, political intimidation, vote-trading, political wheeling-dealing spilled into national life as if a lengthy one-party interregnum never took place.

Next door a typically-Nigerian lengthy military transition to civilian rule winds up with the flaws of the yet-to-follow civilian regime clearly visible. Indeed, to Uwazurike current preparations for civilian rule resemble in their ethnic overtones the run-up to the doomed "democratic" civilian Second Republic. These "endless rivalries and negative developmental consequences of inter-party violence help explain the general aversion to multi-party systems across much of Africa."[78] Bouts of "political cleansing" by several military regimes have not affected Nigeria's penchant for "virtually the worst forms of unstable democracy: most parties were narrowly based, tied to some 'great and unassailable' leader who tended to stamp the organization not with any grand ideological vision but his personal biases. Besides, each was ethnically based, mass-mobilizing and confrontational in orientation."[79] The picture is repeated across the breadth of Africa, reaching its nadir in Zaire where nine-six parties have requested registration to date. And even in small Gabon, eleven parties, most ethnic-regional, have appeared, mirroring *exactly* society's fracture lines. In Kenya Kikuyu-Luo antagonisms ran to deap to allow a coalition against the man both groups hated most of all, Daniel arap Moi!

Moreover, not everywhere has political democracy resulted in more *social* space; in Algeria the FIS's stunning victory immediately brought *constrains* on social and cultural modes of expression as Muslim fundamentalist power emerged with the opening up of the country via competitive elections. His disillusionment with "democracy" was summed up by one voter when he noted "I've always wanted democracy for Algeria, but I expected a modernist party to take power, not a party of the Middle Ages."[80] In a dozen other states restrictive fundamentalism is coming into the political centerstage as a result of the democratization of the continent.

Apart from the religious plane of polarization, the voting modality visible in whatever free elections have been held in Africa has been along predictable ethnic lines, underscoring the continued relevance of sub-nationalism three decades into statehood. Houphouet-Boigny's presidential protagonist in Cote d'Ivoire, Laurent Gbagbo, made inroads among youth and urban populations tired with thirty years of PDCI rule; but in the countryside Gbagbo was supported primarily by his own Bete, with a scattering of anti-Baoule (the President's ethnicity) voting in districts bypassed by the now-over Ivoirien "economic miracle." In Benin there was an even more exact parallelism between ethnic affiliation and voting during the 1990-91 elections: *percentage-wise* the vote in most districts was *nearly identical to that of 1970, which itself was exactly that of a decade earlier.* Politicized ethnic sentiment remains the most meaningful force in Africa's syncretic, marginal, non-nation states, implying that politics in the "new democracies" will constantly reflect this tug-of-war with all its deleterious and divisive negative effects.

The destabilizing potentials of ethnic politics combined with persevering economic decay, against backgrounds of psychologically heightened expectations attending democratization, can produce explosive results. Multiparty elections may transform "expressions of principle to discussions of rules"[81], but greater moderation and give and take is entailed in this, which conditions of scarcity and zero-sum mentalities prevent. As Jackson and Rosberg remind us "in many countries the problem of establishing democracy is secondary to the problem of establishing order, stability and civility...[since] in more than a few countries this basic foundation is still lacking."[82] Put concretely with respect to Zambia, democracy and Kaunda's ouster will not solve a single problem: indeed, "in the short run, things are likely to get worse."[83]

The collapse of authoritarian rule produces widespread feelings that "the future is open, and that ideals and decisions count as much as interests and structures."[84] But the concrete experience of other regions in "transition" from authoritarian rule suggests that countries not backsliding have *not* experienced a significant degree of economic advances; the inevitable disjunction between aspiration and concrete attainments, and concomitant disillusionments, are likely to be high in Africa.

Some scholars see in Africa's social pluralism *the* justification for democracy, a consummatory value in its own right quite apart from any linkage to economic development: "if there is social pluralism, that is in fact an argument for a democratic form of governance,"[85] which *will* work out in Africa since it provides specific solutions to concrete political problems in the most satisfying manner for most groups.[86] But others focus on the *instrumental* value of democracy, and challenge Lindblom's correlating political democracy and economic development, and the World Bank's equation of less State intervention in the economy with better governance, maintaining that within the context of weak states only a "burcaucratic-authoritarian state" can contain fissiparous tensions *and* lead to a free-market economy.[87] And born-again radicals find they can jettison Lenin while clinging to Marx, arguing *inter alia* that "Africa cannot have 'bourgeois' democracy so long as there is no proper bourgeoisie."[88]

At the same time, even French observers question the wisdom of imposing conditionalities linking aid to *Western-style liberal democracy*, which *mutatis mutandi* includes a multipartyism they feel Africa is simply not ready for.[89] This school of thought—gaining ground in many circles—posits that more surgically precise or specifically-targeted is-sue-specific conditionalities might have been better, though the end result might have been a more visible recolonization of the continent. Conditionalities could have been linked, for example, to strict respect for civic and human rights; to the principle of executive accountability, legislative responsibility, freedom of the press and the judiciary; they could specify cut off of funds unless bloated civil services are trimmed,

deficitory State sectors privatized, strict fiscal accounting of development funds delivered. (There are precedents, such as the American
customs-monitoring presence in Monrovia in the mid-1980's.)

Regarding France's budgetary subventions to former colonies
(*intended* to assist weak states meet civil service payrolls) it has even been
suggested direct payment (by individual checks!) from Paris to civil
servants—in order to avoid the common phenomena of a 10-20% ratio
of non-existent "phantom-workers," and the osmosis of foreign funds
to Africa's politico-bureaucracy Swiss banking accounts[90]. Such variations on political conditionalities would leave intact chastened, ex-
ternally-circumscribed semi-authoritarian regimes (thinned to weed
out the more obnoxious dictators), deemed necessary to keep a lid on
societal frustrations and implement what are at the very least highly
unpopular and destabilizing policies.

Such disconcerting ideas are emerging as euphoria fades in
official circles, and the realization sinks that despite redemocratization
"democratic" leaders are facing exactly the same destabilizing demonstrations their non-democratic brethren (often themselves!) used to
face. Both Benin's and Gabon's always volatile student populations
have been aggrieved at their decrepit campuses, residences, late payment of grants, food services; the recent momentous changes in these
states not-withstanding, students have rioted against the current
democratic regimes in office just as they have been doing against
authoritarian regimes—with identical concrete results! Ndjamena's
relief from Hissene Habre's brute terror and Idriss Deby's pledge of
democracy and elections did not prevent massive urban strikes two
weeks into his administration when he proposed a "war effort tax" to
assist in the reconstruction of the country. And conversely, there is
considerably *more* repression in Moi's post-"democratic" Kenya, than
when the country was a de-jure single party system!

The dilemma comes into sharp focus if we examine Africa's
showcase of the "new" democracies—Cote d'Ivoire. Never authoritarian
like its neighbours, Houphouet-Boigny institutionalized all the reforms asked by France and domestic Opposition, and then convincingly proved via competitive elections that he was still nationally
popular. But the *political* reforms changed nothing in the economic or
fiscal domains. No new capital is flowing into Cote d'Ivoire. Indeed,
the outflow of capital and expatriates in Francophone Africa is at its
severest in Abidjan that may have lost over half of its original 60,000-

odd French residents since 1988. Virtually insolvent despite its highly competent Premier Alassane Ouattara and austerity policies (e.g. a cabinet cut from a 29-40-member complement to 19), by mid-1991 Cote d'Ivoire was considering defaulting on its sizeable national debt. For notwithstanding Abidjan's new "democracy," none of the country's social and economic parameters have changed an iota. Though "kicked upstairs" according to the Constitution, Houphouet-Boigny still calls the shots whenever he sees fit, at times without the knowledge of his own Premier. He recently personally arranged the sale of the national electricity company to a French firm (at no profit to Abidjan) and paid from State funds the $20 million funeral costs (!) of an old crony.[91] Normal belt-tightening exercises are simply incapable of ameliorating the country's fiscal crisis; and Ouattara has been unwilling to initiate more traumatic cuts that would be politically suicidal requiring as they do "strong (authoritative) governments to sack public officials or increase consumer food prices without incurring equivalent off-setting expenditure on the military or on repairing riot damage."[92]

Such cuts would involve sharply slashing the country's 130,000-strong civil service (whose upper echelons have already been pruned)[93], rolling back salaries and fringe benefits (the highest in Africa, and even higher than in Spain and Portugal) of the country's 45,000 teachers, fully privatizing the country's remaining parastatals, further trimming cocoa and coffee producer prices, whose current depressed levels have already resulted in lower production levels and drops in farmers' income of up to 75%. Such austerity policies would lead to explosive disenchantment with the PDCI in rural areas, and massive unrest in the cities—similar to those in 1988-89 that gave birth to the pro-democracy movement—but now *without the former era's "immutable"[94] French militarily guarantees for the civilian order in Abidjan.*

More importantly for purposes of illustration, the net effect of all these "unthinkable cuts," *even if affectuated* would in absolute terms be petty compared to the country's interest payments on the public debt. In 1991 these were equivalent to 100% of Cote d'Ivoire's anticipated State revenues. The fiscal shortfall (over $1 billion) needing coverage if the administration was not to close down, would barely be touched by the economies, and there are no other ones to be adopted short of literally shutting down the State! Nor would the sell-off of the country's 79 parastatals generate much revenue since there are no takers:

"private business has been leaving the country for years and there is a pattern of net disinvestment."[95]

These are some of the "constraints" on democracy in Africa, within a very *mechanistic* conception of democracy. But democracy is not just a political system with certain trappings, but a system sustained by a set of cultural values, a democratic ethos. These are not necessarily missing in Africa, but are ingrained, when found, at *subnational levels*. And even then societal scarcity and acute pressures produce inevitable zero-sum mentalities and modalities of interaction which by definition are non-democratic. With a history of authoritarian colonial and post-independence rule, in a context of continued scarcity and ethnic strife, democratic values and commitments are difficult to sustain, and the ethos is difficult to spread.

Larry Diamond notes that "it is unrealistic to think that such countries can suddenly reverse course and institutionalize stable democratic government simply by changing leaders, constitutions and/or public mentalities. If progress is made toward developing democratic government, it is likely to be gradual, messy, fitful and slow, with many imperfections along the way."[96] Some countries—the more important ones, or those with greatest value to the world—are likely, with continued neo-colonial bondages and external aid keeping them in line, to surmount the "obstacles" posed by democracy, developing relatively stable multiparty systems. But it hard to escape the conclusion that many other African states, in the absence of constant munificent benefactors (and when the global fervour with "democracy" possibly goes out of vogue?) will be seen as a bad bet and let loose to drift their own way, backsliding into political strife, social chaos, single-party and military rule.

NOTES

1. Robert H. Jackson and Carl G. Rosberg, "Democracy in Tropical Africa," *Journal of International Affairs*, Winter 1985, p. 293. See also Larry Diamond, Juan J. Linz and Seymour M. Lipset (eds.), *Democracy in Developing Countries*, Boulder, Co., Lynne Rienner, 1988, vol. 2.

2. *West Africa*, April 9, 1990.

3. Samuel Huntington, "Will More Countries become democratic?" *Political Science Quarterly*, vol. 99 N.2, Summer 1984, p. 214.

4. P. Chabal, *Political Domination in Africa: Reflections on the Limits of Power*, Cambridge, Cambridge University Press, 1986, p. 5.

5. Daniel Chirot, *Social Change in the Twentieth Century*, New York, 1977, p. 22.

6. Charles Tilly (ed.) *The Formation of National States in Western Europe*, Princeton, Princeton University Press, 1975, p. 81.

7. Huntington, "Will More countries become Democratic?" p. 218.

8. "The state is simultaneously strong in the sense that the state sector comprises a large proportion of the national economy, weak in the sense that the political leadership lacks legitimacy (i.e a capacity to command obedience) among its citizens, strong in the sense that the public sector bureaucracy is the only cohesive and organized group in national politics, and weak in the sense that certain regional groups are disaffected and secessionist because excluded from this bureaucracy." M. Moore, "Interpreting Africa's crisis—political science versus political economy," *IDS Bulletin*, vol. 18 N. 4, 1987, p. 8. See also Robert H. Jackson and Carl G. Rosberg, "Why Africa's Weak States Persist: The Empirical and Juridical in Statehood," in Atul Kohli (ed.), *State and Development in the Third World*, Princeton, Princeton University Press, 1986.

9. Ali A. Mazrui, "Political Engineering in Africa," *International Social Science Journal*, vol. 25 N. 2, 1983, p. 293.

10. Samuel Decalo, "The Morphology of Radical Military Rule in Africa," in *Journal of Communist Studies*, September 1985.

11. See Martin Kilson, "Authoritarian and Single-party tendencies in African Politics" *World Politics*, vol. 25 N. 2, January 1963.

12. *West Africa*, 26 April 1982.

13. Julius K. Nyerere, *Freedom and Unity*, Dar-es-Salaam, Oxford University Press, 1966, p. 196.

14. *Malawi News* (Blantyre), December 20, 1964.

15. See Samuel Decalo, "Ideological Rhetoric and Scientific Socialism in Benin and Congo/Brazzaville," in Carl G. Rosberg and Thomas Callaghy (eds.), *Socialism in sub-Saharan Africa*, Berkeley, Institute of International Studies, University of California, 1979. See also Crawford Young's seminal work, *Ideology and Development in Africa*, New Haven, Conn., Yale University Press, 1982.

16. World Bank, *Subsaharan Africa: From Crisis to Sustainable Growth*, Washington, DC., 1990, p. 34.

17. Colin Legum, "Africa's Search for nationhood and Stability," *Journal of Contemporary African Studies*, October 1985, p. 35.

18. P. Chudi Uwazurike, "Confronting Potential Breakdown in Africa: the Nigerian Re-Democratization Process in Critical Perspective," *Journal of Modern African Studies*, vol. 28 N. 1, 1990, p. 67.

19. Robert H. Jackson and Carl G. Rosberg, *Personal Rule in Black Africa: Prince, Autocrat, Prophet, Tyrant*, Berkeley, University of California Press, 1982.

20. Colin Legum, *"Africa's Search for nationhood and Stability,"* p. 21.

21. Edem Kodjo, *Et Demain l'Afrique*, Paris, Stock, 1985, p. 7.

22. Nzongola-Ntalaja, "The African Crisis: The Way Out," *African Studies Review*, vol. 32 N. 1, 1989, pp. 121-2.

23. *The New York Times*, January 27, 1990.

24. Cited in "Needed: More Glasnost," *West Africa*, 13 November 1989.

25. From Peter Anyang' Nyong'o, "State and Society in Kenya: The Disintegration of the Nationalist Coalitions and the Rise of Presidential Authoritarianism," *African Affairs*, April 1989.

26. For illustrations see Samuel Decalo, *Coups and Army Rule in Africa: Motivations and Constraints*, 2nd ed., New Haven, Conn., Yale University Press, 1990, chapter 1.

27. See for example Walter O. Oyugi et al (eds.), *Democratic Theory and Practice in Africa*, London, John Currey, 1988.

28. Naomi Chazan in Diamond, Linz and Lipset (eds.), *Democracy in Developing Countries*, p. 119.

29. *The Financial Times*, July 10, 1990.

30. Douglas G. Anglin, "Southern African Responses to Eastern European Developments," *Journal of Modern African Studies*, vol. 28 N. 3, 1990, p. 448.

31. Robert H. Bates, "Socio-Economic Bases of Democratization in Africa; Some Reflections," in *African Governance in the 1990's*, Atlanta, Carter Presidential Center, 1990, p. 29.

32. "Africa: Winds of Change," *Africa Confidential*, March 9, 1990, p. 1.

33. Samuel Decalo, *Psychoses of Power. African Personal Dictatorships*, Boulder, Co., Westview Press, 1989.

34. *Africa Research Bulletin*, Economic Series, August 1990; December 1990.

35. "USA/Africa: Policy? What Policy," *Africa Confidential*, 11 January 1991, p. 2.

36. Jeune Afrique as cited in *Africa Research Bulletin*, Economic Series, April 1990.

37. Nzongola-Ntalaja notes how "after nearly 30 years of internationally-supported development programs in Africa, there is little evidence to suggest that standard of living of ordinary Africans has improved." See his "The African Crisis: The Way Out," *African Studies Review*, vol. 32 N. 1, 1989, p. 118.

38. World Bank, *Annual Report, 1990*, Washington, 1991.

39. Trevor W. Parfitt and Stephen P. Riley, *The African Debt Crisis*, London, Routledge, 1989, pp. 33-4.

40. See for example the papers in Bade Onimode (ed.), *The IMF, the World Bank and the African Debt*, 2 vol., London, Zed Press, 1989.

41. For reasons that need not detain us, countries in Equatorial Africa (e.g. Zaire, Central African Republic, Gabon) have extremely depressed population growth rates—e.g. 0.9% in Gabon, versus 3.9% in Kenya at the opposite extremity, and a mean of 3.4%.

42. Cited in Colleen Lowe Morna "Pluralism: A Luxury No More," *Africa Report*, November 1990, p. 34.

43. *The New York Times*, February 11, 1989.

44. *Le Monde*, February 28, March 31, 1990. But more ominous is the visible global psychological disengagement from Africa, and decline in interest in all things Africana—social, economic, political or humanitarian.

45. Cited in *Africa Research Bulletin*, Economics Series, June 1990.

46. *The Times of Zambia* (Lusaka), 31 December 1990.

47. *Africa Research Bulletin*, Political Series, May 1990.

48. "Africa: Winds of Change," *Africa Confidential*, March 9, 1990, p. 1.

49. "Africa: The roots of Reform," *Africa Confidential*, 27 July 1990, p. 3.

50. For some recent literature on France's role in Africa see *inter alia* John Chipman, *French Military Policy and Africa's Security*, London, 1985, as well as his *French Power in Africa*, London, Basil Blackwell, 1989; Paul Chaigneau, *La Politique Militaire de la France en Afrique*, Paris, CHEAM, 1984; George E. Moose, "French Military Policy in Africa," in William J. Foltz and Henry S. Bienen (eds.), *Arms and the African: Military Influences on Africa's International Relations*, New Haven, Yale University Press, 1985, and Francis T. McNamara, *France in Africa*, Washington, National Defense University, 1989.

51. "La Cooperation avec l'Afrique: perspectives pour les enterprises francaises," *Afrique Contemporaine*, N. 149, 1989.

52. Quoted in Kaye Whiteman, "The Gallic Paradox," *Africa Report,* January-February 1991, p. 19.

53. For France's "old" interpretation of its military obligations see Samuel Decalo, "Modalities of Civil-Military Stability in Africa," *Journal of Modern African Studies,* March 1990.

54. See Jean-Francois Bayart, *L'Etat en Afrique: la politique du Ventre,* Paris, Fayard, 1989.

55. See *Africa Research Bulletin,* Political Series, July 1990.

56. See Samuel Decalo, "Regionalism, Political Decay and Civil Strife in Chad," *Journal of Modern African Studies,* vol. 18 N. 1, 1980; M.P. Kelley, *A State in Disarray: Condition of Chad's Survival,* Boulder, Co., Westview Press, 1986; and V. Thompson and R. Adloff, *Conflict in Chad,* London, Hurst, 1981.

57. "USA/Africa: Policy? What Policy," p.3.

58. In many ways Benin has been a pace-setter for Francophone Africa. For background see "Benin," in Decalo, *Coups and Army Rule in Africa,* and Vivian Lowery Derryck, "The Velvet Revolution," *Africa Report,* January-February 1991.

59. Colleen Lowe Morna "Pluralism: A Luxury No More," *Africa Report,* November 1990, p. 33.

60. For some of the literature see especially Samuel Huntington, *Political Order in Changing Societies,* New Haven, Yale University Press, 1968; Guillermo O'Donell, *Modernization and Bureaucratic Authoritarianism,* Berkeley, University of California Press, 1973, and his "Reflections on Patterns of Change in the Bureaucratic-Authoritarian State," *Latin American Research Review,* vol. 13 N. 1, 1978.

61. World Bank, *Sub-Saharan Africa: from Crisis to Sustainable Growth,* Washington DC, The World Bank, 1989, p. 34.

62. Peter Anyang Nyong'o, "Political Instability and Prospects for Democracy in Africa," *Africa Development,* vol. 13 N. 1, p. 72.

63. Bjorn Beckman, "Whose Democracy? Bourgeois versus Popular Democracy," *Review of African Political Economy,* N. 45/6, 1989, p. 84.

64. Claude Ake, "The Case for Democracy," in *African Governance in the 1990's,* Atlanta, Carter Presidential Center, 1990, p. 2.

65. Peter Anyang Nyong'o, "Democracy and Political Instability: A Rejoinder," in *African Governance in the 1990's,* Atlanta, Carter Presidential Center, 1990, p. 5.

66. James Butty, "The Democracy Carrot," *West Africa,* 22 April 1991.

67. Charles E. Lindblom, *Politics and Markets,* New York, Basic Books, 1977, p. 116. Emphasis in the original.

68. Salim Lone "Challenging Conditionality," *Africa Report*, November 1990, p. 32.

69. *Zambia Daily Mail* (Lusaka), 9 March 1990.

70. *Zambia Daily Mail* (Lusaka), 15 March 1990.

71. Anglin, "Southern African Responses to Eastern European Developments," p. 448

72. "Cote d'Ivoire: Hard Work brings results," *Africa Confidential*, 23 November 1990.

73. See Gerald Bourke, "A New Broom," *Africa Report*, January-February 1991.

74. See the Gabon chapter.

75. *The Guardian Daily*, May 26, 1990.

76. "USA/Africa: Policy? What Policy," p 1.

77. A term coined by *L'Aube Nouvelle* (Cotonou) with respect to candidates in the 1968 army-sponsored Presidential elections. Cited in *West Africa*, April 27, 1968.

78. P. Chudi Uwazurike, "Confronting Potential Breakdown: the Nigerian Re-democratization Process in Critical Perspective," *Journal of Modern African Studies*, vol. 28 N. 1, 1990, p. 55, 66.

79. *Ibid*, p. 66.

80. Cited in *Africa Research Bulletin*, Political Series, July 1990.

81. Guillermo O'Donnell & Philippe Schmitter, "Tentative Conclusions about Uncertain Democracies," in their *Transitions from Authoritarian Rule: Prospects for Democracy*, Baltimore, Johns Hopkins University Press, 1986, vol. 4, p. 58-59. See also Dankwart Rustow, "Transitions to Democracy: Towards a Dynamic Model," *Comparative Politics*, April 1970.

82. Jackson and Rosberg, "Democracy in Tropical Africa," p. 305.

83. "Africa: Democracy gathers momentum," *Baltimore Sun*, July 22, 1990.

84. Guillermo O'Donnell, Philippe C. Schmitter and Laurence Whitehead (eds.), *Transitions from Authoritarian Rule*, 4 vols., Baltimore, Johns Hopkins University Press, 1986, vol. 4, p. 19.

85. Claude Ake, "The Case for Democracy," in *African Governance in the 1990's*, Atlanta, Carter Presidential Center, 1990, p. 4.

86. Larry Diamond, Juan J. Linz and Seymour Martin Lipset (eds.), *Democracy in Developing Countries*, vol. 2 Africa, Westview Press, Boulder, Co., 1988. See also Larry Diamond, "Beyond Authoritarianism and Totalitari-

anism: strategies for democratization," *The Washington Quarterly,* Winter 1989.

87. Guillermo O'Donnell, "Reflections on the Patterns of Change in the Bureaucratic-Authoritarian State," *Latin American Research Review,* vol. 13 N. 1, 1978.

88. Bjorn Beckman, "Whose Democracy? Bourgeois versus Popular Democracy," *Review of African Political Economy,* N. 45/46, 1989.

89. *Le Monde,* June 23, 1990.

90. Trevor W. Parfitt and Stephen P. Riley, *The African Debt Crisis,* London, Routledge, 1989.

91. "Cote d'Ivoire: Unrest Ahead," *Africa Confidential,* 19 April 1991, p. 3.

92. M. Moore, "Interpreting Africa's crisis—political science versus political economy," *IDS Bulletin,* vol. 18 N. 4, 1987, p. 9.

93. Most African civil services could be slashed by at least 35-50% without commensurate decline in services, assuming residual workers were not bunched up in urban centers as they tend to be.

94. Interview with a senior French diplomat, Abidjan, 12 July 1988.

95. "Cote d'Ivoire: Unrest Ahead," *Africa Confidential,* 19 April 1991, p. 3. See also Colleen Lowe Morna, "Enticing Investment," *Africa Report,* January-February 1991, p. 42.

96. Larry Diamond, "Beyond Autocracy: Prospects for Democracy in Africa," in *Beyond Autocracy in Africa,* Atlanta, The Carter Center of Emory University, 1989, p. 24.

BIBLIOGRAPHY

Adedeji, Adebayo. "Foreign Debt and Prospects for Growth in Africa during the 1980's." *Journal of Modern African Studies*, vol. 23 no. 1, 1985.

Africa Confidential (fortnightly).

"Africa: The roots of Reform," *Africa Confidential*, 27 July 1990.

Africa Research Bulletin. (monthly), Economic Series; Political Series.

"Africa: Winds of Change," *Africa Confidential*, March 9, 1990.

Ake, Claude, "The Case for Democracy," in *African Governance in the 1990's*, Atlanta, Carter Presidential Center, 1990.

Alexandre, Pierre. "Proto-histoire Beti-Bulu-Fang," *Cahiers d'Etudes Africaines*, No. 7, vol. 2, 1962.

———. and Jacques Binet, *Le Groupe dit Pahouin*, Paris, Presses Universitaires, 1958.

Ambouroue-Avaro, Joseph, *Un Peuple Gabonaise à l'aube de la colonisation: le Bas Ogowe au xixe siecle*, Paris, Karthala, 1981;

Ammi-Oz, Moshe. "L'Evolution de la place et du role des forces publiques Africaines." *Le Mois en Afrique*, March 1977.

Amnesty International, "Unfair Trial and other Amnesty International concerns in the Republic of Gabon." London, Amnesty International, 1984.

Anglin, Douglas G. "Southern African Responses to Eastern European Developments," *Journal of Modern African Studies*, vol. 28 N. 3, 1990.

Anyang' Nyong'o, P. "Democracy and Political Instability: A Rejoinder," in *African Governance in the 1990's*, Atlanta, Carter Presidential Center, 1990.

———. "Political Instability and Prospects for Democracy in Africa," *Africa Development*, vol. 13 N. 1.

———. "State and Society in Kenya: The Disintegration of the Nationalist Coalitions and the Rise of Presidential Authoritarianism," *African Affairs*, April 1989.

Ayot, H. O. *A History of the Luo-Abasuba*, Nairobi, Kenya Literature Bureau, 1979.

Balandier, Georges. *Sociologie actuelle de l'Afrique Noire*, Paris, Presses Universitaires de France, 1963.

Barkan, Joel D. "Comment: Further Reassessment of 'Conventional Wisdom': Political Knowledge and Voting behaviour in rural Kenya," *American Political Science Review*, vol. 70 N. 2, 1976.

———. "The Electoral Process and Peasant-State Relations in Kenya," in Fred Hayward (ed.), *Elections in Independent Africa*, New York, Macmillan, 1978.

Barkan, Joel D. and John J. Okumo, "'Semi-Competitive' Elections, Clientelism, and Political Recruitment in a No-Party State: The Kenyan Experience," in Guy Hermet et al., *Elections without Choice*, London, Macmillan, 1978.

———, and ———. (eds.), *Politics and Public Policy in Kenya and Tanzania*, New York, Praeger, 1979.

Barnes, James F. *Gabon Beyond the Colonial Legacy*, Boulder, Co., Westview Press, 1992.

Barrows, Walter L. "Changing Military Capabilities in Black Africa." in William J. Foltz and Henry S. Bienen, *Arms for the African*. New Haven, Yale University Press, 1985.

Bates, Robert. *Markets and States in Tropical Africa: The Political Basis of Agricultural Policies*. University of California Press, Berkeley, 1981.

———. "Socio-Economic Bases of Democratization in Africa; Some Reflections," in *African Governance in the 1990's*, Atlanta, Carter Presidential Center, 1990.

Bayart, Jean-François, *L'Etat en Afrique: la politique du Ventre*, Paris, Fayard, 1989.

Beckman, Bjorn, "Whose Democracy? Bourgeois versus Popular Democracy," *Review of African Political Economy*, N. 45/6, 1989.

Bennett, George, *Kenya. A Political History*, London, Oxford University Press, 1973.

———. "Kenya's Little General Election," *World Today*, August 1966.

———. and Carl G. Rosberg, *The Kenyatta Election: Kenya 1960-1961*, New York, Oxford University Press, 1972.

Berg, F. S. "The Coast from the Portuguese Invasion to the Rise of the Zanzibar Sultanate," in Bethwell A. Ogot (ed.), *Zamani: A Survey of East African History*, London, Longman, 1973.

Berg-Schlosser, Dirk, *Tradition and Change in Kenya: A Comparative Analysis of Seven Major ethnic groups*, Paderborn, Ferdinand Schoningh, 1984.

Bienen, Henry S. *Armies and Parties in Africa*. New York, Africana, 1978.

———. *The Politics of Participation and Control*, Princeton, Princeton University Press, 1974.

————. and Nicolas van de Walle. "Time and Power in Africa." *American Political Science Review*, March 1989.

Boeder, Robert B. "Prospects for Political Stability in Malawi." in Calvin Woodward (ed.), *On the Razor's Edge: Prospects for Political Stability in Southern Africa*. Pretoria, Africa Institute of South Africa, 1986.

————. *Silent Majority: A History of the Lomwe in Malawi*. Pretoria, Africa Institute of South Africa, 1984.

————."We won't die for Fourpence", *Journal of Modern African Studies*, January 1977.

Bon, Daniel and Karen Mingst, "French Intervention in Africa: Dependency or Decolonization." *Africa Today*, vol. 27 no. 2, 1980.

Bourke, Gerald, "A New Broom," *Africa Report*, January-February 1991.

Bratton, Michael, "Structural Transformation in Zimbabwe: Comparative Notes from the neo-colonization of Kenya," *Journal of Modern African Studies*, vol. 15, N. 4, 1977.

Brunschwig, H. "Expeditions punitives au Gabon 1875-1877," *Cahiers d'Etudes Africaines*, vol. 2 No. 7, 1962;

Bucher, Henry H. "Mpongwe Origins: Historiographical Perspectives," *History in Africa*, vol. 2, 1975.

Butty, James, "The Democracy Carrot," *West Africa*, 22 April 1991.

Cabrol, Claude and Raoul Lehaurd, *La Civilisation des peuples Bateke*, Lyon, Multipress, 1976.

Carlsen, John, *Economic and Social Transformation in Rural Kenya*, Uppsala, Scandinavian Institute of African Studies, 1980.

Chabal, Patrick (ed.). *Political Domination in Africa. Reflections on the Limits of Power.* Cambridge, Cambridge University Press, 1986.

Chaigneau, Pascal. *La Politique Militaire de la France en Afrique*. Paris, CHEAM, 1984.

Chamberlain, C. "The Migration of the Fang into Central Gabon," *International Journal of African Studies*, vol. 11 No. 3, 1978.

Chanock, Martin L. "Ambiguities in the Malawian Political Tradition," *African Affairs*, vol. 74, 1975.

————. *Law, Custom and Social Order: The Colonial Experience in Malawi and Zambia*, Cambridge, Cambridge University Press, 1985.

Chilivumbo, A. "Malawi's Lively Art Form," *Africa Report*, October 1971.

Chipman, John. *French Military Policy and African Security* London: The International Institute for Strategic Studies, 1985.

————. *French Power in Africa*, London, Basil Blackwell, 1989.

Chirot, Daniel, *Social Change in the Twentieth Century*, New York, 1977.

Chittick, Neville H. "The Coast before the Arrival of the Portuguese," in Bethwell A. Ogot (ed.), *Zamani: A Survey of East African History*, London, Longman, 1973.

Chiume, M. W. Kanyama *Kwacha. An Autobiography*, Nairobi, East African Publishing House, 1975.

Christiansen, Robert E. "Financing Malawi's Development Strategy," in *Malawi: An Alternate Pattern of Development*, Edinburgh, Edinburgh University Press, Centre for African Studies, 1985.

————."The Pattern of Internal Migration in Response to Structural Change in the Economy of Malawi 1966-1977," *Development and Change*, vol. 15, 1984.

Chudi Uwazurike, P. "Confronting Potential Breakdown: the Nigerian Re-democratization Process in Critical Perspective," *Journal of Modern African Studies*, vol. 28 N. 1, 1990.

Clausewitz, Carl von. *On War*. London, Routledge and Kegan Paul, 1966.

Clayton, Anthony. "Foreign Intervention in Africa." in S. Baynham (ed.). *Military Power and Politics in Black Africa*. London, Croom Helm, 1986.

Cohen, William B. *Rulers of Empire*, Hoover, Stanford University Press, 1971.

Conac, Gerard. "Le Presidentialisme en Afrique Noire. Unite et Diversite. Essai de Typologie." in *L'Evolution Recente de Pouvoir en Afrique Noire*. Bordeaux, Centre d'Etudes d'Afrique Noire, 1977.

"La Cooperation avec l'Afrique: perspectives pour les enterprises françaises," *Afrique Contemporaine*, N. 149, 1989.

Coquery-Vidrovitch, Catherine *Le Congo au temps des grandes compagnies concessionaires 1898-1930*, Paris, Mouton, 1972.

"Cote d'Ivoire: Hard Work brings results," *Africa Confidential*, 23 November 1990.

"Cote d'Ivoire: Unrest Ahead," *Africa Confidential*, 19 April 1991.

Cox, T. S. *Civil-Military Relations in Sierra Leone*. Cambridge, Harvard University Press, 1976.

Crocker, Chester. "France's Changing Military Interests." *Africa Report*, June 1968.

Curtis, Michael (ed.), *Israel and the Third World*, New Brunswick, N.J., Transaction Press, 1976.

Darlington, Charles F. and Alice B. *African Betrayal*, New York, David McKay, 1968.

Decalo, Samuel. *Coups and Military Rule in Africa: Motivations and Constraints.* New Haven, Yale University Press, 1990.

———. "Ideological Rhetoric and Scientific Socialism in Benin and Congo/Brazzaville," in Carl G. Rosberg and Thomas Callaghy (eds.), *Socialism in sub-Saharan Africa,* Berkeley, Institute of International Studies, University of California, 1979.

———. *Malawi.* Santa Barbara, Clio Press, 1995.

———. "Modalities of Civil-Military Stability in Africa," *Journal of Modern African Studies,* December 1990.

———. "The Morphology of Radical Military Rule in Africa." *Journal of Communist Studies,* January 1987.

———. *Psychoses of Power: African Personalist Dictatorships.* Boulder, Co., Westview Press, 1989.

———. "Regionalism, Political Decay and Civil Strife in Chad." *Journal of Modern African Studies,* July 1980.

De Gaulle, Charles *Memoires d'espoir; le renouveau, 1958-1962,* Paris, Plon, 1970.

Decraene, Philippe. "Gabon," in his *L'Afrique Centrale,* Paris, CHEAM, 1989.

Deschamps, Hubert, *Quinze Ans de Gabon: Les debuts de l'etablissement francais, 1839-1853,* Paris, Maisonneuve & Larose, 1965;

———. *Traditions orales et archives au Gabon,* Paris, Berger-Levrault, 1962.

Diamond, Larry, "Beyond Authoritarianism and Totalitarianism: strategies for democratization," *The Washington Quarterly,* Winter 1989.

———. "Beyond Autocracy: Prospects for Democracy in Africa," in *Beyond Autocracy in Africa,* Atlanta, The Carter Center of Emory University, 1989.

———., Juan J. Linz and Seymour M. Lipset (eds.), *Democracy in Developing Countries,* Boulder, Co., Lynne Rienner, 1988.

Dilley, M. R. *British Policy in Kenya Colony,* London, Cass, 1966.

Divide and Rule: State-Sponsored Ethnic violence in Kenya, New York, Africa Watch, 1993.

Doorn, Jacques van. "Political Change and the Control of the Military." in J. van Doorn (ed.). *Military Profession and Military Regimes.* The Hague, Mouton, 1969.

Duhamel, Olivier. "Le Parti Democratique Gabonais," *Le Mois en Afrique,* May 1976.

Dunn, John. "The Politics of Representation and Good Government in post-colonial Africa." in Patrick Chabal (ed.). *Political Domination in*

Africa: Reflections on the Limits of Power, Cambridge, Cambridge University Press, 1986.

Economist Intelligence Unit. "Mozambique and Malawi. Country Report." 1994.

Effort Gabonais (Libreville), daily.

Enloe, Cynthia H. "The Military Uses of Ethnicity." *Millenium*, vol. 4 no. 3, 1975.

Evans Jr., Emmit B. "Sources of Socio-political instability in an African State: The case of Kenya's educated unemployed," *African Studies Review*, vol. 20 N. 1, April 1977.

Fernandez, James W. "The Affirmation of Things Past: Alar Ayong and Bwiti as Movements of Protest in Central and Northern Gabon," in Rotberg and Mazrui (eds.), *Protest and Power in Black Africa*, New York, Oxford University Press, 1970.

———. "Christian Acculturation and Fang Witchcraft," *Cahiers d'Etudes Africaines*, vol. 2 No. 2, 1961.

Fieldhouse, D. K. *Black Africa 1945-1980. Economic Decolonization and Arrested Development*, London, Allen Unwin, 1986.

Finer, Samuel. *The Man on Horseback: The Role of the Military in African Politics*. London, Pall Mall, 1962.

———. "The Morphology of Military Regimes." in Roman Kolkowicz and Andrzej Korbonski (eds.). *Soldiers, Peasants and Bureaucrats*. London, George Allen & Unwin, 1982.

Foltz, William J. and Henry S. Bienen (eds.), *Arms and the African: Military Influences on Africa's International Relations*, New Haven, Yale University Press, 1985.

"La Force d'Intervention et le Remaniement du Dispositif Français en Afrique Noire et à Madagascar." *Fréres d'Armes*, April 1963.

Forster, Peter G. "Culture, Nationalism and the Invention of Tradition in Malawi," *Journal of Modern African Studies*, vol. 32 no. 3, 1994.

Fuglestad, Finn. "The 1974 Coup d'etat in Niger: Towards an Explanation." *Journal of Modern African Studies*, vol. 13 no. 3, 1975.

Furedi, F. "The Initial Composition of the Mau Mau movement in the White Highlands," *Journal of Peasant Studies*, vol.1 N. 4, 1973.

Gabon. *Conference nationale*. Libreville, Service Documentation de l'Union, 2 vol. 1991.

"Gabon," in International Monetary Fund, *Surveys of African Economies*, Washington, I. M. F., 1974.

Gabon Aujourd'hui (Libreville), daily.

"Gabon: Putsch or Coup d'etat," *Africa Report*, March 1964.

Gann, L. H. "Malawi, Zambia and Zimbabwe," in Peter Duigan and Robert H. Jackson (eds), *Politics and Government in African States 1960-1985*, Stanford, Hoover Institution Press, 1986.

Gardinier, David E. *Historical Dictionary of Gabon*, Metuchen, N.J., Scarecrow Press, 1981.

Gaulme, François. *Le Gabon et son ombre*, Paris, Karthala, 1988.

———. *Le Pays de Cama: Un ancien etat cotier du Gabon et ses origines*, Paris, Karthala, 1981.

Gautier, Jean M. *Etude historique sur les Mpongoues et tribus avoisinantes*, Montpellier, Lafitte, 1950.

Gertzel, Cherry, *The Politics of Independent Kenya 1963-8*, Nairobi, East African Publishing House, 1972.

Ghai, Dharam and Samir Radwan, "Growth and Inequality: Rural Development in Malawi 1964-78", in their *Agrarian Policies and Rural Poverty in Malawi*, Geneva, ILO, 1983.

Gide, Andre *Voyage au Congo*, Paris, Gallimard, 1927.

Godia, George I. *Understanding Nyayo*, Nairobi, Transafrica, 1984.

Golan, Tamar. "A Certain Mystery: How Can France do Everything that it does in Africa—and get away with it?" *African Affairs*, January 1981.

Goldsworthy, David. "Armies and Politics in Civilian Regimes." in Simon Baynham, *Military Power and Politics in Black Africa*. London, Croom Helm, 1986.

———. "Civilian Control of the Military in Black Africa." *African Affairs*, January 1981.

———. "Ethnicity and Leadership in Africa," *Journal of Modern African Studies*, vol. 20 N. 1, 1982.

———. "On the Structural Explanation of African Military Interventions." *Journal of Modern African Studies*, vol. 24 no. 1, 1986.

———. *Tom Mboya. A Man Kenya wanted to Forget*, London, Heinemann, 1982.

Gollnhoffer O. and R. Sillans, "Phenomenologie de possession chez les Mitsogho," *Anthropos*, vol. 74 No. 5-6, 1979.

Greenstein, Lewis J., "The Impact of Military Service in World War I on Africans: the Nandi of Kenya," *Journal of Modern African Studies*, September 1978.

Guillemin, Jacques. "L'Importance des bases dans la politique militaire de la France en Afrique Noire francophone et á Madagascar." *Revue Française d'Etudes Politiques Africaines*, August-September 1981.

———. "L'Intervention exterieure dans la politique militaire de la France en Afrique Noire francophone et a Madagascar." *Revue Francaise d'Etudes Politiques Africaines*, June-July 1981.

Guiringaud, Louis de. "La Politique africaine de la France." *Politique Etrangere*, June 1982.

Gutteridge, William. "Undoing Coups in Africa." *Third World Quarterly*, January 1985.

Hakes, Jay R. and John L. Helgerson, "Bargaining and Parliamentary Behaviour in Africa: A Comparative Study of Zambia and Kenya," in Allan Kornberg (ed.), *Legislatures in Comparative Perspective*, New York, David McKay, 1973.

Harbeson, John W. "Land Reform and Politics in Kenya 1954-1970," *Journal of Modern African Studies*, August 1971.

Harbeson, John. (ed.). *The Military in African Politics*, New York, Praeger, 1987.

———. *Nation-building in Kenya: The Role of Land Reform*, Evanston, Northwestern University Press, 1973.

Hodder-Williams, Richard. "Dr. Banda's Malawi." *Journal of Commonwealth and Comparative Politics*, March 1974.

———. "Malawi's Decade Under Banda," *Round Table*, No. 249-52, 1973.

———. "'Support' in Eastern Africa: Some Observations from Malawi," in Timothy M.Shaw and Kenneth A. Heard, *The Politics of Africa: Dependence and Development*, London, Longman's, 1979.

Hopkins, Raymond F. "The Kenyan Legislature: Political Functions and Citizen Perceptions," in G. R. Boynton and Chong Lim Kim (eds.), *Legislative Systems in Developing Countries*, Durham, Duke University Press, 1975.

Hornsby, Charles, "The Social Structure of the National Assembly in Kenya, 1953-1983," *Journal of Modern African Studies*, vol. 27 N. 2, 1989.

House, William J., and Tony Killick, "Social Justice and Development Policy in Kenya's Rural Economy," in Dharam Ghai and Samir Radwan, *Agrarian Policies and Rural Poverty*, Geneva, ILO, 1984.

Hughes, Arnold and Roy May. "The Politics of Succession in Black Africa." *Third World Quarterly*, January 1988.

Huntington, Samuel. "Civilian Control of the Military: A Theoretical Statement." in Heinz Eulau, Samuel J. Eldersveld and Morris

Janowitz (eds.). *Political Behavior: A Reader in Theory and Research*, Glecoe, The Free Press, 1956.

————. *Political Order in Changing Societies*, New Haven, Yale University Press, 1968.

————. "Will More Countries become democratic?" *Political Science Quarterly*, vol. 99 N.2, Summer 1984.

Ikiara, G. K. and Tony Killick "The performance of the Economy since Independence," in Tony Killick, (ed), *Papers on the Kenya Economy*, London, Heinemann, 1981.

Institute for Strategic Studies. *The Military Balance 1983/4*. London, ISS, 1984.

International Bank for Reconstruction and Development, *Kenya: Into the Second Decade*, Baltimore, The Johns Hopkins University Press, 1975.

Jack, J. W. Daybreak in Livingstonia, Edinburgh, 1901, Jackman, Robert "The Predictability of Coups d'Etat. A Model with African Data." *American Political Science Review*, vol. 72 no. 4, 1978, September 1978.

Jackson, Robert H. "The Marginality of African States." in G. M. Carter and P. O'Meara. *African Independence; The First 25 Years*. Bloomington, Indiana University Press, 1986.

————. and Carl Rosberg, "Democracy in Tropical Africa," *Journal of International Affairs*, Winter 1985.

————. *Personal Rule in Black Africa. Prince, Autocrat, Prophet, Tyrant*, Berkeley, University of California Press, 1982.

————. "Why Africa's Weak States Persist." in A. Kohli (ed) *The State and Development in the Third World*. Princeton, Princeton University Press, 1986.

Jeannel, C. "La sterilite en Republique Gabonaise," Offenberg Press Service Company, Geneva, 1962.

Johnson, Thomas H., Robert O. Slater and Pat McGowan. "Explaining African Military Coups d'Etat, 1960-1982." *American Political Science Review*, vol. 78 no. 3, September 1984.

Kaggia, Bildad. *Roots of Freedom 1921-1963*, Nairobi, 1975.

Kamara, Mamadi. "Franceville: Activites et role dans l'organisation de de son arriere-pays," *Cahiers d'Outre-Mer*, vol. 36 N.143, 1983.

Kaplinsky, Rafael, "Capital Accumulation in the Periphery: Kenya," in M. Fransman (ed.), *Industry and Accumulation in Africa*, London, 1982.

————. "Capitalist Accumulation in the Periphery—the Kenyan case re-examined," *Review of African Political Economy*, vol. 17, 1980.

Karimi, Joseph and Philip Ochieng. *The Kenyatta Succession*. Nairobi, Transafrica, 1980.

Kelley, M. P. *A State in Disarray: Condition of Chad's Survival*, Boulder, Co., Westview Press, 1986.

Kennedy, D., *Islands of White: Settler Society in Kenya and Southern Rhodesia 1890-1939*, Durham, Duke University Press, 1987.

Kenya. *House of Representatives Debates*. Nairobi.

Kenya. *Legislative Council Debates*.

Kenya, *National Assembly Debates*, Nairobi.

Kenya. *The Waruhiu Report*, 1980.

"Kenya: A Difficult Courtship," *Africa Confidential*, October 8, 1993.

"Kenya: The Emperor's Clothes," *Africa Confidential*, January 2, 1985.

"Kenya: How?" *Africa Confidential*, August 4, 1982;

"Kenya: Lawyers Lament," *Africa Confidential*, 26 January 1990.

"Kenya: On the slippery Slope," *Africa Confidential*, March 21, 1975.

"Kenya: Ouko's ghost," *Africa Confidential*, May 31, 1991.

"Kenya: Patterns of Power," *Africa Confidential*, September 6, 1974.

"Kenya: Post-mortem," *Africa Confidential* August 25, 1982.

"Kenya: Watching the Wananchi," *Africa Confidential*, Oct 5, 1973.

"Kenyatta's Kenya," *Africa Confidential*, Nov. 27, 1970.

Khapoya, Vincent B. "The Politics of Succession in Africa: Kenya after Kenyatta," *Africa Today*, vol. 26, N. 3, 1979.

Kilson, Martin, "Authoritarian and Single-party tendencies in African Politics" *World Politics*, vol. 25 N. 2, January 1963.

Kodjo, Edem, *Et Demain l'Afrique*, Paris, Stock, 1985.

Kydd, Jonathan G. "Malawi: Making Effective Use of Aid Resources," *Aid Bulletin*, vol. 17, No. 2, 1986.

————. and Robert E. Christiansen, "Structural Change in Malawi since Independence. Consequences of a Development strategy based on large-scale agriculture," *World Development*, vol. 10, May 1982.

Lamphear, John "The Kamba and the Northern Mrima Coast," in Richard Gray and David Birmingham (eds.), *Pre-Colonial Africa Trade*, London, Oxford University Press, 1970.

Legum, Colin (ed.), *Africa Contemporary Record*, New York, Africana Publishing, 1969-1989.

———. "Africa's Search for nationhood and Stability." *Journal of Contemporary African Studies*, October 1985.

———. "Why Tanganyika accepted a Chinese Mission." *Africa Report*, vol. 9 no. 9, October 1964.

———. et. al. *Africa in the 1980's*. New York, McGraw Hill, 1984.

Le Monde (daily).

Lele, Uma. "African experiences with Rural Development," International Bank for Reconstruction and Development, Staff Working Paper No. 195, Washington, DC., 1975.

Lerat, S. "Le manganese du Gabon," *Cahiers d'Outre Mer*, October-December 1966.

Leys, Colin, *Underdevelopment in Kenya: The Political Economy of Neo-Colonialism, 1964-1971*, Berkeley, University of California Press, 1974.

Liebenow, Gus. "The Military Factor in African Politics: A Twentyfive Years perspective." in G. Carter and P. O'Meara (eds.). *African Independence: The First 25 Years*. Bloomington, Indiana University Press, 1986.

Linden, Ian. "Chewa Initiation Rites and Nyau Societies: The Use of Religious Institutions in Local Politics at Mua," in Terence O. Ranger and John Weller (eds), *Themes in the Christian History of Central Africa*, Berkeley, University of California Press, 1974.

Lindblom, Charles E. *Politics and Markets*, New York, Basic Books, 1977.

Lofchie, Michael F., "Kenya's Agricultural Success," *Current History*, May 1986.

Lone, Salim, "Challenging Conditionality," *Africa Report*, November 1990.

Lonsdale, John and Bruce Berman, "Coping with the Contradictions: The Development of the Colonial State in Kenya 1895-1914," *Journal of African History*, vol 20, 1979.

Lowery Derryck, Vivian, "The Velvet Revolution," *Africa Report*, January-February 1991.

Luckham, Robin. "A Comparative Typology of Civil-Military Relations." *Government and Opposition*, vol. 6 no. 1, 1971.

———. "French Militarism in Africa." *Review of African Political Economy*, vol. 24, May-Aug. 1982.

McCracken, John. *Politics and Christianity in Malawi 1875-190: The Impact of the Livingstonia Mission in the Northern Province*, Cambridge, Cambridge University Press, 1977.

————. "Underdevelopment in Malawi: The Missionary Contribution," *African Affairs*, April 1977.

McGowan, Patrick and Johnson, Thomas S. "African Military Coups d'Etat." *Journal of Modern African Studies*, vol. 22 no. 4, 1984.

Mafuka, K. Nyamayara. *Missions and Politics in Malawi*, Kingston (Ont.), The Limestone Press, 1977.

Malawi. *Legislative Assembly Debates*.

Malawi. *Proceedings of the Legislative Council*.

Malawi Congress Party, "The Constitution of the MCP," Limbe, Malawi Press, 1965.

Malawi News (daily).

Maren, Michael, "Kenya: Hear No Evil," *Africa Report*, November-December 1986.

Martin, Guy. "The Historical, Economic, and Political Bases of France's African Policy." *Journal of Modern African Studies*, vol. 23 no. 2, 1985.

————. "Uranium: A Case Study in Franco-African Relations," *Journal of Modern African Studies*, vol. 27 No. 4, 1989.

Martin, Phyllis M. *The External Trade of the Loango Coast*, Oxford, Oxford University Press, 1972.

Mary, Andre. *La Naissance á lenvers: essai sur le rituel du Bwiti Fang au Gabon*, Paris, Harmattan, 1983.

Matson, A. T. *Nandi Resistance to British Rule 1890-1906*, Nairobi, East African Publishing House, 1972.

Mazrui, Ali A. "Political Engineering in Africa," *International Social Science Journal*, vol. 25 N. 2, 1983

————. and Donald Rothchild, "The Soldier and the State in East Africa: Some Theoretical Conclusions on the army mutinies of 1964," *Western Political Quarterly*, n. 2, 1971.

Mbithi, Philip M. and Rasmus Rasmusson, *Self-Reliance in Kenya: The Case of Harambee*, Uppsala, Scandinavian Institute of African Studies, 1977.

M'Bokolo, Elikia. "Le Gabon precolonial," *Cahiers d'Etudes Africaines*, vol. 17, 1977.

————. *Noirs et Blancs en Afrique Equatoriale: les societes cotiers et la penetration français 1820-1877*, Paris, Harmattan, 1977.

————. "La Resistance des Mpongwe du Gabon a la creation du comptoir francais (1843-1845)," *Afrika Zamani*, December 1978.

———. "Le Roi Denis," in Charles-Andre Julien (ed.), *Les Africains*, vol. 6, Paris, Jeune Afrique, 1977.

———. *Le Roi Denis: La premiere tentative de modernisation du Gabon*, Dakar, Nouvelles Editions Africaines, 1976;

Mboya, Tom, *Freedom and After*, London, Andre Deutsch, 1963.

Me Engouang, Fidele Mengue. "Reflexions sur les regimes fiscaux priviligies du code des investissements au Gabon," *Le Mois en Afrique*, June-July 1985.

Meisler, Stanley "Tribal politics harass Kenya," *Foreign Affairs*, vol. 49, 1970.

"A mercifully short Reign of Terror," *Weekly Review*, August 6, 1982.

Metegue N'nah, Nicolas. *Economies et societes au Gabon dans la premiere moitie du XIXe siecle*, Paris, Harmattan, 1979.

———. *L'Implantation Coloniale au Gabon. Resistance d'un Peuple*, Paris, Harmattan, 1981.

Miller, Norman N. *Kenya: The Quest for Prosperity*, Boulder, Co., Westview Press, 1984.

Miller, N. N. *Malawi: Central African Paradox*, Hanover, 1978.

Mkandawire, Mulomboji. "Markets, Peasants and Agrarian Change in the Post-Independence Malawi," *Journal of Contemporary African Studies*, vol. 4 No. 1/2. April 1985.

Mlia, Ngoleka. "The Role of Capital Cities in regional and national Development in Malawi," Zomba, National Archives of Malawi, 1983.

Moi, Daniel arap. *Kenya African Nationalism*, Nairobi, Heinemann, 1986.

Le Monde (Paris), daily.

Moore, M. "Interpreting Africa's crisis —political science versus political economy," *IDS Bulletin*, vol. 18 N. 4, 1987.

Moose, George E. "French Military Policy." in William J. Foltz and Henry S. Bienen, (eds.). *Arms for the African*. New Haven, Yale University Press, 1985.

———. "French Military Policy in Africa," in Francis T. McNamara, *France in Africa*, Washington, National Defense University, 1989.

Morna, Colleen Lowe, "Enticing Investment," *Africa Report*, January-February 1991.

———. "Pluralism: A Luxury No More," *Africa Report*, November 1990.

Morris, H. F. *The Indians in Uganda. Caste and Sect in a Plural Society*, London, Weidelfeld and Nicolson, 1968.

Morrison, Donald G. et al. *Black Africa: A Comparative Handbook*. New York, The Free Press, 1972.

Morton, Kathryn. *Aid and Dependence. British Aid to Malawi*. London, Croom Helm, 1975.

Mtewa, Mekki. *Malawi Democratic Theory and Public Policy*, Cambridge, Mass., Schenkman Books, 1986.

Mueller, Susanne D. "Government and Opposition in Kenya, 1966-9," *Journal of Modern African Studies*, vol. 22 N. 3, 1984.

Muller, Edward N. and Mitchell A. Seligson, "Inequality and Insurgency. *American Political Science Review*, vol. 81 no. 2, June 1987.

Munro, J. Forbes, *Colonial Rule and the Kamba: Social Change in the Kenya Highlands, 1889-1939*, Oxford, Clarendon Press, 1975.

Muriuki, Godfrey "Background to Politics and Nationalism in Colonial Kenya," in Bethwell A. Ogot (ed.), *Politics and Nationalism in Colonial Africa*, Nairobi, East African Publishing House, 1972.

Murray, J. "Succession Prospects in Kenya," *Africa Report*, November 1968.

Nairobi Times (Nairobi), daily.

Ndeti, Kivuto, *Elements of Akamba Life*, Nairobi, East African Publishing House, 1972.

Ndoume Nze, Maurice. *Elections legislatives gabonaises*. Paris, Harmattan, 1991.

Nelson, Harold D. *Area Handbook for Malawi*, Washington, Government Printing Office, 1976.

———. *Kenya: A Country Study*, Washington, D.C., Government Printing Office, 1984.

The New York Times (New York), daily.

Ngayap, F. P. *Cameroun: Qui Governe?* Paris, Harmattan, 1983.

Nguema, M. "Legende traditionnelle Fang," Libreville archives, mimeo.

Njonjo, A. "The Kenyan Peasantry: A Reassessment," *Review of African Political Economy*, N. 20, April-June 1981.

Nkrumah, Kwamah. "Politics is not for Soldiers." Accra, Government Publishing Company, 1962.

Nordlinger, Eric A. *Soldiers in Politics: Military Coups and Government*. Englewood Cliffs, Prentice Hall, 1977.

Norgaard, Ole. *Kenya in the Social Sciences. An Annotated Bibliography 1967-1979*, Nairobi, Kenya Literature Bureau, 1980.

Nyamu, H. J., "The State of the Civil Service Today," Nairobi, Government Printer, 1974.

Nyerere, Julius K. *Freedom and Unity*, Dar-es-Salaam, Oxford University Press, 1966.

Nzongola-Ntalaja, "The African Crisis: The Way Out," *African Studies Review*, vol. 32 N. 1, 1989.

Odetola, T. O. *Military Regimes and Development*. London, George Allen & Unwin, 1982.

Odinga, Oginga, *Not yet Uhuru*, London, Deutsch, 1967.

O'Donell, Guillermo, *Modernization and Bureaucratic Authoritarianism*, Berkeley, University of California Press, 1973.

——. "Reflections on Patterns of Change in the Bureaucratic-Authoritarian State," *Latin American Research Review*, vol. 13 N. 1, 1978.

——. and Philippe Schmitter, *Transitions from Authoritarian Rule: Prospects for Democracy*, Baltimore, Johns Hopkins University Press, 1986, 4 vol.

Ogot, Bethwell A. *Historical Dictionary of Kenya*, Metuchen, N. J., Scarecrow Press, 1986.

——. *The History of the Southern Luo*, Nairobi, East African Publishing House, 1967.

——. "Kenya Under the British, 1895 to 1963," in ——. (ed.), *Zamani. A Survey of East Africa*, London, Longman, 1973.

Okumu, John J. "Party and Party-State Relations," in Joel D. Barkan and John J. Okumo, (eds.), *Politics and Public Policy in Kenya and Tanzania*, New York, Praeger, 1979.

——. "The Problem of Tribalism in Kenya," in Pierre Van den Berghe, *Race and Ethnicity in Africa*, Nairobi, East African Publishing House, 1975.

Ole Sankan, S. S. *The Maasai*, Nairobi, East African Literature Bureau, 1971.

Omer-Cooper, J. D. *The Zulu Aftermath*, London, Longman, 1966.

Onimode, Bade (ed.), *The IMF, the World Bank and the African Debt*, 2 vol., London, Zed Press, 1989.

Ossa, Albert Ondo. "Le Paradoxe du Gabon: un pays riche, mais sous-developpé," Ph.D. thesis, University of Nancy, 1984.

Osogo, J. *A History of the Baluyia*, Nairobi, Oxford University Press, 1966.

Ottaway, David and Marina. *Afrocommunism*. New York, Africana Publishing House, 1981.

Oyugi, Walter O. et al (eds.), *Democratic Theory and Practice in Africa*, London, John Currey, 1988.

Pachai, Bridglal. *Malawi: The History of the Nation*, London, Longman, 1973.

Pachter, Elise Forbes. "Contra-Coup: Civilian Control of the Military in Guinea, Tanzania and Mozambique." *Journal of Modern African Studies*, vol. 20 no. 4, 1982.

Parfitt, Trevor W.and Stephen P. Riley, *The African Debt Crisis*, London, Routledge, 1989.

Pattersen, K. David. *The Northern Gabon Coast to 1875*, Oxford, Clarendon Press, 1975.

———. "The Vanishing Mpongwe: European Contact and Demographic change in the Gabon River," *Journal of African History*, vol. 16 No. 2, 1975.

Peane, Pierre. *Affaires Africaines*. Paris, Fayard, 1982.

Perlmutter, Amos. "Civil-Military in Socialist Authoritarian and Praetorian States: Prospects and Retrospects." in Roman Kolkowicz and Andrzej Korbonski (eds.). *Soldiers, Peasants and Bureaucrats*. London, George Allen & Unwin, 1982.

Phiri, D. D. *From Nguni to Ngoni*, Limbe, Popular Publications, 1982,

Pike, John G. *Malawi: A Political and Economic History*, London, Pall Mall Press, 1968.

"The Post-Sobhuza Power Struggle." *Africa Report*, Jan.-Feb. 1984.

Pourtier, Roland. *Le Gabon*, 2 vol., Paris, Harmattan, 1989.

Pryor, Andrew. *Malawi and Madagascar*, Washington DC., The World Bank, 1990.

"Public Opinion Poll N. 4," Nairobi, The Market Research Co. of East Africa, 1961.

Raponda-Walker, Andre and Roger Sillans, *Rites et Croyances des Peuples de Gabon*, Paris, Presence Africaine, 1962.

Ravenhill, John. "Comparing Regime Performance in Africa: The Limitations of Cross-National Aggregate Analysis." *Journal of Modern African Studies*, vol. 18 no. 1, March 1980.

Reed, Michael C. "Gabon: A Neo-colonial Enclave of Enduring French Interest," *Journal of Modern African Studies*, vol. 25 No. 2, June 1987.

Report of the Nyasaland Commission of Enquiry (Devlin Report), London, HMSO, July 1959.

Rey, Pierre Phillipe *Colonialisme, neo-colonialisme, et transition au capitalisme. Exemple de la "Comilog" au Congo-Brazzaville*, Paris, Maspero, 1971.

Richardson III, Henry J. "Administration in the Malawi Government and its relationship to Social Change," in E. P. Morgan (ed) *The Administration of Change in Africa*, New York, Dunellen, 1974.

———. "Malawi between Black and White," *Africa Report*, February 1970.

Ronen, Dov (ed.). *Democracy and Pluralism in Africa*. Boulder, Co., Lynne Rienner, 1986.

Rosberg, Carl G. and Jack Nottingham, *The Myth of Mau Mau*, New York, Praeger, 1966.

Ross, A. C. "The Political Role of the Witchfinder in Southern Malawi during the Crisis of October 1964-May 1965," in *Witchcraft and Healing*, Edinburgh, Centre for African Studies, 1969.

———. "White Africa's Black Ally," *New Left Review*, No. 45, September/October 1967.

Rothchild, Donald, "Ethnic Inequalities in Kenya" *Journal of Modern African Studies*, vol. 7 N. 4, 1969.

———. "Hegemonial Exchange: An Alternative Model for Managing Conflict in Middle Africa," in Dennis Thompson and Dov Ronen, *Ethnicity, Politics and Development*, Boulder, Co., Lynne Rienner, 1986.

Rustow, Dankwart, "Transitions to Democracy: Towards a Dynamic Model," *Comparative Politics*, April 1970.

Salim, A. I. *People of the Coast*, London, Evans Brothers, 1978.

Sandbrook, Richard. *The Politics of Africa's Economic Stagnation*. Cambridge, Cambridge University Press, 1985.

Schuster, George. *Private Work and Public Causes: A Personal Record*, Cambridge, 1979.

Segal, Edwin S. "Projections of Internal Migration in Malawi: Implications for Development," *Journal of Modern African Studies*, vol. 23, No. 2, 1985.

Shepperson, George "The Jumbe of Kota Kota and some aspects of the history of Islam in British Central Africa," in I. M. Lewis (ed), *Islam in Tropical Africa*, London, 1966.

———. and Thomas Price, *The Independent African*, Edinburgh, 1958.

Shields, Todd, "Lawyers vs. The Law," *Africa Report*, September 1990.

Short, Philip. *Banda*, London, Routledge and Kegan Paul, 1974.

Sutton, J. E. G. "The Kalenjin," in B. A. Ogot (ed.), *Kenya before 1900*, Nairobi, East African Publishing House, 1976.

Sorrenson, M. P. K. *The Origins of European Settlement in Kenya*, Nairobi, Oxford University Press, 1968.

Spencer, John *KAU: The Kenya African Union*, London, KPI Ltd., 1985.

Tamarkin, Mordechai. "From Kenyatta to Moi: The anatomy of a peaceful transition of power," *Africa Today*, vol. 26, N. 3, 1979.

———. "Kenya: The End of an Illusion." *Race and Class*, Winter 1983.

———. "Recent Developments in Kenyan Politics: The Fall of Charles Njonjo," *Journal of Contemporary African Affairs* (Pretoria), vol. 3 N. 1/2, October 1983-April 1984.

———. "The Roots of Political Stability in Kenya." *African Affairs*, vol. 77 no. 308, July 1978.

Thomas, Barbara P. "Development through harambee: Who wins and Who loses? Rural self-help projects in Kenya." *World Development*, vol. 15 N. 4, 1987.

Thomas, Simon. "Economic Developments in Malawi since Independence", *Journal of Southern African Studies*, vol. 2, No. 1, 1974.

Thompson, Virginia and Richard Adloff, *Conflict in Chad*, London, Hurst, 1981.

Throup, David W. *Economic and Social Origins of Mau Mau, 1945-53*, London, James Currey, 1987.

———. "The Origins of Mau Mau," *African Affairs*, July 1985.

Tignor, Robert L. *The Colonial Transformation of Kenya: The Kamba, Kikuyu and Maasai from 1900 to 1939*, Princeton, Princeton University Press, 1975.

Tilly, Charles (ed.) *The Formation of National States in Western Europe*, Princeton, Princeton University Press, 1975.

The Times (London).

Tordoff, William. *Government and Politics in Africa*. London, Macmillan, 1984.

"USA/Africa: Policy? What Policy," *Africa Confidential*, 11 January 1991.

Vail, Leroy "The State and the Creation of Colonial Malawi's Agricultural Economy" in Robert I. Rotberg (ed.), *Imperialism, Colonialism and Hunger: East and Central Africa*, Lexington, Mass., Lexington Books, 1983.

Van Breugel, J. W. M."The Religious Significance of the Nyao among the Chewa of Malawi," *Cultures et Developpement*, vol. 17, No.3, 1985.

Viaud, Pierre and Jacques de Lestapis. *Afrique: Les souverainetes en Armes*. Paris, Fondation pour les études de defense nationale, 1987.

Wauthier, Claude. "Opposition in Disarray," *West Africa*, 31 August 1992.

Weekly Review (Nairobi), weekly.

Were, Gideon S. *A History of the Abuluyia of Western Kenya, c.1500-1930*, Nairobi, East African Publishing House, 1967.

Weinstein, Brian. *Gabon: Nation-building on the Ogooue*, Camridge, Mass., MIT Press, 1966.

―――. "Leon Mba: The Ideology of Dependence," *Geneve-Afrique*, vol. 6 No. 1, 1967.

Welch Jr., Claude E. (ed.). *Civilian Control of the Military: Theory and Cases from Developing Countries*. Albany, State University of New York Press, 1976.

―――. and Arthur K. Smith. *Military Role and Rule*. Duxbury Press, 1974.

Werlin, Herbert H. *Governing an African City: A Study of Nairobi*, New York, Africana Publishing Co., 1978.

West Africa (London), weekly.

Whiteman, Kaye, "The Gallic Paradox," *Africa Report*, January-February 1991.

Wilking, Staffan. *Military Coups in sub-Saharan Africa*. Uppsala, Scandinavian Institute of African Studies, 1983.

Williams, David. *Malawi: The Politics of Despair*, Ithaca, Cornell University Press, 1978.

Wolff, Richard D. *The Economics of Colonialism: Britain and Kenya 1870-1930*, New Haven, Yale University Press, 1974.

Wood, A. W. "Training Malawi's Youth: the work of the Malawi Young Pioneers," *Community Development Journal*, No. 5, 1970.

World Bank, *Annual Report, 1990*, Washington, 1991. Trevor W.

―――. *Subsaharan Africa: From Crisis to Sustainable Growth*, Washington, DC., 1990.

Young, Crawford, *Ideology and Development in Africa*, New Haven, Conn., Yale University Press, 1982.

Zambia Daily Mail (Lusaka), daily.

Zolberg, Aristide. "Military Intervention in the New States of Africa." in Henry S. Bienen (ed.), *The Military Intervenes*. New York: Russell Sage Foundation, 1968.

INDEX

A NOTE ON THE AUTHOR

Samuel Decalo is a naturalized Israeli, who majored in Political Science at the University of Ottawa, Canada, and obtained his MA and PhD from the University of Pennsylvania.

A specialist on African and Middle East affairs, Professor Decalo has been affiliated with several universities on three continents. In the US he taught, among others, at the University of Rhode Island, the Graduate Faculty of the New School for Social Research, Emory University, and most recently, at the University of Florida. He also been affiliated with the University of the West Indies (Trinidad), the University of Botswana, and the University of Natal, in South Africa, heading departments of Political Science, and/or of African Studies, for over twelve years.

Professor Decalo is the author of fifteen books, some of which are staple reference works, and nearly one hundred professional articles. A globally acknowledged expert on Francophone Africa and civil-military relations, he has conducted research in most African states on many occasions. His best-known book is the path-breaking *Coups and Army Rule in Africa* (Yale University Press, 1976; revised/expanded edition, 1990) that became a staple textbook in over four hundred universities worldwide. Another of his books, *Psychoses of Power: African Personal Dictatorships* (Westview Press, 1989) acclaimed by Library Journal as an "Outstanding Book of 1989," won a coveted university book prize for academic excellence.

Professor Decalo is currently finishing his most recent works *Not by Democracy Alone* and *Is Africa Different?* The former challenges current assumptions that the winds of democratization on the continent are likely to lead to much permanent change in Africa; the latter pessimistically compares Africa's developmental givens with the currently much-touted Southeast Asia's "model" approach.